THE CAMBRIDGE COMPANION TO
E. M. FORSTER

This new collection of essays, each one by a recognised expert, both brings Forster studies up to date and provides lively and innovative readings of every aspect of his wide-ranging career. It includes substantial chapters dedicated to his two major novels, *Howards End* and *A Passage to India*, and further chapters focus on *A Room With a View* and *Maurice*. Forster's connections with the values of Bloomsbury and the lure of Greece and Italy in his work are assessed, as is his vexed relationship with Modernism. Other essays investigate his role as a literary critic, the status of his work within the genres of the novel and the short story, his treatment of sexuality, and his attitude to and representation of women. This is the most comprehensive study of Forster's work to be published for many years, providing an invaluable source of comment on, and insight into, his writings.

DAVID BRADSHAW is Reader in English Literature at Oxford University and Hawthornden Fellow at Worcester College, Oxford. Among other volumes, he has edited *The Hidden Huxley*, *Decline and Fall*, *The Good Soldier*, *Brave New World*, *Women in Love*, *Mrs Dalloway*, *To the Lighthouse*, *A Concise Companion to Modernism* and, with Kevin J. H. Dettmar, *A Companion to Modernist Literature and Culture*. He is a Fellow of the English Association and the post-Romantic period Editor of the *Review of English Studies*.

THE CAMBRIDGE
COMPANION TO
E. M. FORSTER

EDITED BY
DAVID BRADSHAW

CAMBRIDGE
UNIVERSITY PRESS

73954879

CAMBRIDGE UNIVERSITY PRESS
Cambridge, New York, Melbourne, Madrid, Cape Town, Singapore, São Paulo

Cambridge University Press
The Edinburgh Building, Cambridge CB2 8RU, UK

Published in the United States of America by Cambridge University Press, New York

www.cambridge.org
Information on this title: www.cambridge.org/9780521542524

© Cambridge University Press 2007

First published 2007

Printed in the United Kingdom at the University Press, Cambridge

A catalogue record for this publication is available from the British Library

ISBN 978-0-521-83475-9 hardback
ISBN 978-0-521-54252-4 paperback

CONTENTS

CONTENTS

CONTRIBUTORS

ANN ARDIS is Associate Dean of Arts and Humanities and Professor of English at the University of Delaware. She is the author of *Modernism and Cultural Conflict, 1880–1922* (Cambridge University Press, 2002) and *New Women, New Novels: Feminism and Early Modernism* (Rutgers University Press, 1990). With Leslie Lewis, she has edited *Women's Experience of Modernity, 1875–1945* (Johns Hopkins University Press, 2002); with Bonnie Kime Scott, she has edited *Virginia Woolf: Turning the Centuries* (Pace University Press, 2000).

HOWARD J. BOOTH is Lecturer in English Literature at the University of Manchester. He has co-edited *Modernism and Empire* with Nigel Rigby (Manchester University Press, 2000) and is the author of many articles on nineteenth- and twentieth-century literature and culture.

DAVID BRADSHAW is Reader in English Literature at Oxford University and Hawthornden Fellow at Worcester College, Oxford. Among other volumes, he has edited *The Hidden Huxley, Decline and Fall, The Good Soldier, Brave New World, Women in Love, Mrs Dalloway, To the Lighthouse, A Concise Companion to Modernism* (Blackwell, 2003) and, with Kevin J. H. Dettmar, *A Companion to Modernist Literature and Culture* (Blackwell, 2006). He is a Fellow of the English Association and the post-Romantic period Editor of the *Review of English Studies*.

PETER CHILDS is Professor of Modern English Literature at the University of Gloucestershire. He has published widely on twentieth-century literature and on E. M. Forster, Ian McEwan, and Paul Scott in particular. His books include *Modernism* (Routledge, 2000), *Post-Colonial Theory and English Literature* (Edinburgh University Press, 1999), and *A Sourcebook on 'A Passage to India'* (Routledge, 2002). He is currently preparing a monograph on the subject of modernism and the postcolonial.

GARY DAY is a Principal Lecturer in English at de Montfort University, where he teaches drama, the eighteenth century, and modernism. He is the author of *Re-Reading Leavis: Culture and Literary Criticism* (Macmillan, 1996) and *Class*

(2001). He is writing a monograph on the history of literary criticism and is a columnist for the *Times Higher Education Supplement*.

JANE GOLDMAN lectures in English and American literature at the University of Dundee and is a General Editor of the Cambridge University Press Edition of the Writings of Virginia Woolf. Her recent publications include *Modernism, 1910–1945: Image to Apocalypse* (Palgrave, 2004) and *The Cambridge Introduction to Virginia Woolf* (Cambridge University Press, 2006). She is editing Woolf's *To the Lighthouse* for Cambridge, and writing a book called *Virginia Woolf and the Signifying Dog*.

DOMINIC HEAD is Professor of Modern English Literature at the University of Nottingham. He is the author of *The Modernist Short Story* (Cambridge University Press, 1992), *Nadine Gordimer* (Cambridge University Press, 1994), *J. M. Coetzee* (Cambridge University Press, 1997) and *The Cambridge Introduction to Modern British Fiction, 1950–2000* (Cambridge University Press, 2002). Most recently, he has edited the third edition of *The Cambridge Guide to Literature in English* (Cambridge University Press, 2006). A book on Ian McEwan is forthcoming from Manchester University Press.

JUDITH SCHERER HERZ is Professor of English at Concordia University in Montreal. She is the author of *The Short Narratives of E. M. Forster* (Macmillan, 1987) and *A Passage to India: Nation and Narration* (Twayne, 1993), as well as articles on, among others, Forster, Leonard Woolf, Milton, and Donne, including an essay in *The Cambridge Companion to John Donne*. She has been President of the John Donne Society and of the Association of Canadian College and University Teachers of English (ACUTE).

MARCIA LANDY is Distinguished Service Professor of English and Film Studies at the University of Pittsburgh. Her publications include *Fascism in Film: The Italian Commercial Cinema, 1930–1943* (Princeton University Press, 1986); *British Genres: Cinema and Society 1930–1960* (Princeton University Press, 1991); *Imitations of Life: A Reader on Film and Television Melodrama* (Wayne State University Press, 1991); *Film, Politics, and Gramsci* (University of Minnesota Press, 1994); *Queen Christina* (with Amy Villarejo) (BFI, 1995); *Cinematic Uses of the Past* (University of Minnesota Press, 1996); *The Folklore of Consensus: Theatricality in Italian Cinema, 1930–1945* (State University of New York Press, 1998); *Italian Film* (Cambridge University Press, 2000); *The Historical Film* (Athlone, 2001): *History and Memory in Media* (Rutgers University Press, 2001); *Stars: The Film Reader* (with Lucy Fischer) (Routledge, 2003); and *Monty Python's Flying Circus* (Wayne State University Press, 2005).

CHRISTOPHER LANE, Professor of English at Northwestern University, is the author of *The Ruling Passion* (Duke University Press, 1995), *The Burdens of*

Intimacy (University of Chicago Press, 1999), and *Hatred and Civility: The Antisocial Life in Victorian England* (Columbia University Press, 2004, 2006). He is also the editor of *The Psychoanalysis of Race* (Columbia University Press, 1998) and a co-editor of *Homosexuality and Psychoanalysis* (University of Chicago Press, 2001), and is currently completing a book on early modernism and secular transfiguration.

ELIZABETH LANGLAND specialises in Victorian literature, feminist and gender theory, cultural studies, and theory of the novel. She is the author or editor of eight books and numerous articles, among them *Telling Tales: Gender and Narrative Form in Victorian Literature and Culture* (Ohio State University Press, 2002) and *Nobody's Angels: Middle-Class Women and Domestic Ideology in Victorian Culture* (Cornell University Press, 1995). She joined the faculty of Purchase College in August 2004 as Professor of Literature and Cultural Studies and Provost and Vice President for Academic Affairs. She was previously Professor of English at the University of California, Davis.

DAVID MEDALIE is a Professor in the Department of English at the University of Pretoria. His research interests lie chiefly in the areas of Modernism and South African literature. In 2002, his book on E. M. Forster, *E. M. Forster's Modernism*, was published by Palgrave. His other publications include a collection of short stories, *The Shooting of the Christmas Cows*. His debut novel, *The Shadow Follows*, was published in 2006.

PETER MOREY is Reader in English Literature at the University of East London. He is the author of *Fictions of India: Narrative and Power* (Edinburgh University Press, 2000), *Rohinton Mistry* (Manchester University Press, 2004), and co-editor (with Alex Tickell) of *Alternative Indias: Writing, Nation and Communalism* (Rodopi, 2006). He has also published numerous essays and articles on colonial and postcolonial literature, especially pertaining to India.

PAUL PEPPIS is Associate Professor of English Literature and Culture at the University of Oregon. He is the author of *Literature, Politics, and the English Avant-Garde* (Cambridge University Press, 2000) and has published articles on a range of twentieth-century authors, including Ford Madox Ford, Wyndham Lewis, Mina Loy, and Gertrude Stein. He is currently at work on a book entitled, *Sciences of Modernism: Sexology, Psychology, and Anthropology*.

MAX SAUNDERS is Professor of English at King's College, London University, where he teaches modern English, European, and American literature. He is the author of *Ford Madox Ford: A Dual Life*, 2 vols. (Oxford University Press, 1996), the editor of Ford's *Selected Poems*, *War Prose*, and (with Richard Stang) *Critical Essays* (Carcanet, 1997, 1999, 2002), and has published essays on many other Modernist authors, and on Life-writing and Impressionism.

RANDALL STEVENSON is Professor of Twentieth-Century Literature in the University of Edinburgh. His publications include *The British Novel since the Thirties* (Batsford, 1986), *Modernist Fiction* (Prentice Hall, 1998), *Oxford English Literary History* vol. XII: *1960–2000 – The Last of England?* (Oxford University Press, 2004), and *The Edinburgh Companion to Twentieth-Century Literatures in English*, edited with Brian McHale (Edinburgh University Press, 2006). He is General Editor of the *Edinburgh History of Twentieth-Century Literature in Britain* series, to be published by Edinburgh University Press.

1879   Edward Morgan Forster born at 6, Melcombe Place, Dorset Square, London NW1 on 1 January, the only child of Edward Morgan Llewellyn Forster, an architect, and Alice Clara 'Lily', née Whichelo.

1880   Father dies of tuberculosis on 30 October.

1883   Two years of temporary lodgings and house-hunting come to an end when he moves with his mother to 'Rooksnest', the original for the eponymous Howards End, just outside Stevenage, Hertfordshire.

1887   Beginning of his formal education under a local schoolmaster. Bequeathed the large sum of £8,000 in trust by Marianne Thornton, his paternal great-aunt, who dies on 5 November.

1890   Enters Kent House, a preparatory school in Eastbourne, Sussex, where he will stay until 1893. Maurice Hall's prep school in *Maurice* is also situated in a south coast 'watering-place' near the downs.

1893   Mother moves from 'Rooksnest' to Tonbridge in Kent when her lease on the cottage is not renewed. Forster attends Tonbridge School as a day-boy, where he is bullied and generally unhappy, until 1897. Herbert Pembroke vilifies the day-boys of Sawston School (based on Tonbridge) in *The Longest Journey* and one boy is mercilessly bullied.

1897   Enters King's College, Cambridge, where he will remain until 1901 and where he first reads classics and then history.

1898   He and his mother move from Tonbridge to 10, Earl's Road, Tunbridge Wells, also in Kent. Back at King's, he begins to form a friendship with Goldsworthy Lowes Dickinson, one of the most important relationships of his life.

1900   Takes Second in the Classical Tripos, Part 1. He remains at King's for a further year studying history.

1901   Elected in February to the 'Apostles', an exclusive University society which primarily concerned itself with philosophical and moral questions. His friendships with Leonard Woolf, Lytton Strachey,

J. M. Keynes, and others are forged through it. His first paper is entitled 'Are Crocodiles the Best of Animals?'. He takes a second in the Historical Tripos, Part II. In October he embarks on a year-long tour of Italy with his mother. Many incidents and people from this trip find their way into *Where Angels Fear to Tread*, *A Room with a View*, and his short fiction such as 'The Story of a Panic' and 'The Eternal Moment'.

1902   Soon after returning to England he begins giving a weekly Latin class at the Working Men's College, Great Ormond Street, Bloomsbury, London.

1903   Visits Italy, Greece, and Turkey in the spring and early summer. Gives his first series of Cambridge University extension (extramural) lectures in the autumn and works intermittently on what would become *A Room with a View*. His first published story, 'Albergo Empedocle', appears in December.

1904   Works on, and by the end of the year almost finishes, *Where Angels Fear to Tread*. Moves with his mother to a suburban villa called Harham on Monument Green, Weybridge, Surrey. This will remain their home until 1924.

1905   Spends six months (March to August) in Pomerania, Germany, working as a private tutor. First novel, *Where Angels Fear to Tread*, is published on 5 October to much praise.

1907   *The Longest Journey* published on 16 April. Good press reviews but adverse criticism from the likes of Lytton Strachey. His friendship with a young Indian student, Syed Ross Masood, whom he met in 1906 and who is now an undergraduate at Oxford, begins to intensify.

1908   Commences occasional work as a University of London extramural lecturer in January and continues to lecture at the Working Men's College. *Howards End* begins to take shape from around June. Visits Italy again. Third novel, *A Room with a View*, is published on 14 October, once again to laudatory reviews but to less than buoyant sales. Begins reading the Koran with difficulty and falls more deeply in love with Masood.

1910   *Howards End* published on 18 October in London (and three months later in New York). His most successful novel to date, both critically and commercially, it is reprinted four times before the end of the year. Tells Masood he loves him in December.

1911   *The Celestial Omnibus*, his first collection of short stories, published in the spring. Begins to write stories with explicitly homoerotic themes in the summer, a number of them collected

posthumously in *The Life to Come and Other Stories* (1972).
Vacations in Italy with Masood. Begins work on what was
eventually published as '*Arctic Summer*: Fragment of an Unfinished
Novel' in 1963 and more fully as *Arctic Summer and Other Fiction*
(1980). In October, gives last extension lectures until 1922.

1912   Departs in October, with Goldsworthy Lowes Dickinson, for his
first visit to India. Travels widely and will remain there until April
1913. Becomes friendly with the Maharaja of Dewas State Senior.
These experiences later find their way into *A Passage to India*
(1924) and *The Hill of Devi* (1953).

1913   Growing sense of creative drought only intensifies on his return
from India, even though he makes good progress with *A Passage to
India* in the immediate aftermath of his trip to the subcontinent. In
September he meets the openly homosexual and intensely
progressive Edward Carpenter for the first time and this inspires
him to begin work on *Maurice*. By the end of the year, *A Passage to
India* has been set aside.

1914   *Maurice* substantially completed by July but not published until
1971. Renewed and deepening anxiety about the failure of his
creative energies and his role in life. The outbreak of the First World
War in August only exacerbates these feelings. Works in National
Gallery (London) until 1915 as a cataloguer.

1915   Begins working for the Red Cross's Wounded and Missing Bureau
in Alexandria, Egypt, in November. He continues in this position
until 1918.

1917   Appointed the Red Cross's Head Searcher in Egypt.

1919   Leaves Alexandria in January. Begins reviewing for the *Daily News*,
Daily Herald, *Athenaeum*, and other papers and journals in March.

1920   Appointed literary editor of the *Daily Herald* at the beginning of the
year but soon gives it up.

1921   Returns to India in March to take up the position of private
secretary to the Maharaja of Dewas, remaining there until January
1922. Sees a good deal of Masood during this sojourn in India.

1922   Recommences writing *A Passage to India*. Completes 'The Life to
Come', but does not attempt to publish this explicitly homosexual
story. *Alexandria: A History and a Guide* published in Alexandria
in December.

1923   *Pharos and Pharillon: A Novelist's Sketchbook of Alexandria
through the Ages* published on 15 May in London and 30 July in
New York.

1924   His last novel, *A Passage to India*, published on 4 June to
       unanimous critical acclaim. Friendships with T. E. Lawrence
       ('Lawrence of Arabia'), Thomas Hardy, and J. R. Ackerley
       developing.

1925   Moves with his mother to West Hackhurst, Abinger Hammer, near
       Dorking, Surrey, in January. Also rents a flat in London. Begins his
       Commonplace Book (published in 1985) in October.

1926   Begins his affair with a London policeman, Harry Daley.

1927   Delivers Clark Lectures at Cambridge University from January to
       March, published on 20 October as *Aspects of the Novel*.

1928   Second collection of short stories, *The Eternal Moment*, published
       on 27 March in London and 19 April in New York.

1929   He is fifty on 1 January. At end of June leaves for three-month tour
       of southern Africa.

1930   26, Brunswick Square becomes his London base until 1939. Begins
       his lifelong relationship with Bob Buckingham, another London
       policeman.

1932   Goldsworthy Lowes Dickinson dies on 3 August. Bob Buckingham
       gets married to May Hockey on 31 August with Forster as witness.
       Is now broadcasting regularly on BBC radio as well as continuing to
       review frequently for journals such as the *Listener*.

1934   Becomes first President of the National Council for Civil Liberties,
       forerunner of the modern day Liberty organisation, in March. His
       homage to his friend, *Goldsworthy Lowes Dickinson*, published on
       19 April in London and 7 June in New York.

1935   T. E. Lawrence killed in a motorcycle accident in May. Addresses
       International Writers' Congress in Paris in June.

1936   First volume of essays, *Abinger Harvest*, published on 19 March in
       London and 30 April in New York.

1938   Publication of the first critical book on his work, Rose Macaulay's
       The Writings of E. M. Forster.

1939   Moves from Brunswick Square to 9, Arlington Park Mansions in
       Chiswick, London.

1940   Broadcasts anti-Nazi talks on BBC. Continues to broadcast
       regularly for the BBC and to write for a range of publications
       throughout the Second World War.

1945   Mother dies on 11 March aged ninety. Broadcasting career
       continues. Visits India for the third and final time during last three
       months of this year.

1946 Elected to an Honorary Fellowship of King's College, Cambridge, in January and takes rooms there for the remainder of his life in November, while retaining his flat in Chiswick.

1947 Leaves for a tour of the USA on 14 April and remains there until July. *The Collected Tales of E. M. Forster* published on 10 July in New York and the following year in London.

1949 Returns to USA in May to lecture accompanied by Bob Buckingham. Is offered a knighthood but declines.

1951 *Two Cheers for Democracy* published on 1 November. Première of *Billy Budd*, the opera by Benjamin Britten for which he writes the libretto with Eric Crozier, on 1 December.

1953 Made a Companion of Honour. *The Hill of Devi and Other Indian Writings* published in October.

1954 Seventy-five on 1 January. Still reviewing widely and frequently.

1956 *Marianne Thornton, 1797–1887: A Domestic Biography* published in May.

1969 Ninety on 1 January. Awarded the Order of Merit.

1970 Dies in Coventry on 7 June at the home of Bob and May Buckingham. As a humanist, his ashes are scattered on a nearby rose garden.

1971 *Maurice* published on 7 October. *Albergo Empedocle and Other Writings* appears in the same month.

1972 *The Life to Come and Other Stories* published.

1980 *Arctic Summer and Other Fiction* published.

1999 *The Prince's Tale and Other Uncollected Writings* published.

ABBREVIATIONS

AE   *Albergo Empedocle and Other Writings*, ed. George H. Thomson (New York: Liveright, 1971)

AH   *Abinger Harvest and England's Pleasant Land*, ed. Elizabeth Heine, vol. 10 of The Abinger Edition of E. M. Forster (London: André Deutsch, 1996)

AN   *Aspects of the Novel and Related Writings*, ed. Oliver Stallybrass, vol. 12 of The Abinger Edition of E. M. Forster (London: Edward Arnold, 1974)

AS   *Arctic Summer and Other Fiction*, eds. Elizabeth Heine and Oliver Stallybrass, vol. 9 of The Abinger Edition of E. M. Forster (London: Edward Arnold, 1980)

GLD   *Goldsworthy Lowes Dickinson and Related Writings*, ed. Oliver Stallybrass, vol. 13 of The Abinger Edition of E. M. Forster (London: Edward Arnold, 1973)

HD   *The Hill of Devi and Other Indian Writings*, ed. Elizabeth Heine, vol. 14 of The Abinger Edition of E. M. Forster (London: Edward Arnold, 1983)

HE   *Howards End*, ed. Oliver Stallybrass, vol. 4 of The Abinger Edition of E. M. Forster (London: Edward Arnold, 1973)

LC   *The Life to Come and Other Stories*, ed. Oliver Stallybrass, vol. 8 of The Abinger Edition of E. M. Forster (London: Edward Arnold, 1972)

LJ   *The Longest Journey*, ed. Elizabeth Heine, vol. 2 of The Abinger Edition of E. M. Forster (London: Edward Arnold, 1984)

M   *Maurice*, ed. Philip Gardner, vol. 5 of The Abinger Edition of E. M. Forster (London: André Deutsch, 1999)

MS   *The Machine Stops and Other Stories*, ed. Rod Mengham, vol. 7 of The Abinger Edition of E. M. Forster (London: André Deutsch, 1997)

MT   *Marianne Thornton*, ed. Evelyne Hanquart-Turner, vol. 15 of The Abinger Edition of E. M. Forster (London: André Deutsch, 2000)

PI   *A Passage to India*, ed. Oliver Stallybrass, vol. 6 of The Abinger Edition of E. M. Forster (London: Edward Arnold, 1978)

PT   *The Prince's Tale and Other Uncollected Writings*, ed. P. N. Furbank, vol. 17 of The Abinger Edition of E. M. Forster (London: André Deutsch, 1998)

RV   *A Room with a View*, ed. Oliver Stallybrass, vol. 3 of The Abinger Edition of E. M. Forster (London: Edward Arnold, 1977)

TCD   *Two Cheers for Democracy*, ed. Oliver Stallybrass, vol. 11 of The Abinger Edition of E. M. Forster (London: Edward Arnold, 1972)

WAFT   *Where Angels Fear to Tread*, ed. Oliver Stallybrass, vol. 1 of The Abinger Edition of E. M. Forster (London: Edward Arnold, 1975)

INTRODUCTION

DAVID BRADSHAW

E. M. Forster's career as a novelist was spectacularly lopsided. Born in 1879, he published his first four novels in quick succession (*Where Angels Fear to Tread* (1905), *The Longest Journey* (1907), *A Room with a View* (1908) *and Howards End* (1910)), had largely finished what would eventually appear as *Maurice* by 1914, and published his most famous and ambitious novel, *A Passage to India*, ten years later (though it is worth mentioning that he started writing it in the wake of his 1912–13 visit to India and struggled to bring it to completion). Then, in the mid-1920s, with the plaudits of both reviewers and the wider reading public ringing in his ears, buoyant sales in both the United Kingdom and the United States, and two prestigious prizes for *Passage* on his mantelshelf, Forster the novelist shut up shop. His last is the only one of his six novels to be entirely set abroad and at the time it seemed to signal Forster's departure for new fictional horizons, yet in reality it marked his journey's end. He was only halfway through his life (he died in 1970) but he would never again be tempted to repeat *Passage*'s extravagant success. 'I cant [*sic*] believe there will be anoth[er] novel', he told a correspondent around this time. 'The legs of my camera could not stand the strain.'[1]

However, while Forster the novelist retired prematurely, the professional man of letters remained as busy as ever, and in the long, anxious build-up to the Second World War (and the decades that followed it), he established an international reputation, through his essays, reviews, lectures, and broadcasts, as one of the most prominent, authoritative, and engaging public intellectuals of his day, an aspect of his career examined in depth by David Medalie in Chapter 2 of this volume. By the late 1920s, Forster had also become well known as a literary critic and, in *Aspects of the Novel* (1927), he produced what Nicholas Royle has called 'a very powerful book whose originality tends to be overlooked at the present time . . . arguably the most important twentieth-century critical study of English fiction: no book has been more widely read or more influential in its account of "writers and their work"'.[2] The position of *Aspects* in Forster's oeuvre is one of the foci of Gary Day's essay (Chapter 14).

Forster continued to write literary criticism throughout his life, but in the 1930s and 1940s (as well as broadcasting regularly for the BBC) he became increasingly active in the National Council for Civil Liberties, forerunner of the modern day Liberty organisation, ending up as the NCCL's first president. At the same time, in books such as *Goldsworthy Lowes Dickinson* (1934) and *Marianne Thornton* (1956), he turned his hand to biography. Over the years, there has been a tendency to either downplay or ignore the later Forster and to dismiss the post-1924 period as a kind of threadbare coda to his brief but glittering career as a novelist. But, as the essays by Max Saunders, David Medalie, and Gary Day all argue in their different ways, the writings of the post-*Passage* Forster have much to offer and should not be set aside or disregarded so readily. As Saunders puts it, 'while it is true that [Forster] was never to recapture the incandescence of his Edwardian novels, his biographical writing is extraordinarily good; and his shift towards life-writing has its own significances, not least for the understanding of his own biography'.

The reasons why Forster dried up as a novelist are touched on by a number of contributors to this book, but there can be little doubt that being homosexual at a time when homosexuality was not just a crime, but, in the precarious aftermath of the Oscar Wilde trials of 1895, an offence that brought with it a disproportionate level of opprobrium, was undoubtedly a factor: the law, in effect, discouraged Forster from writing about the desires and experiences that were closest to his heart. Of course, we now know that he continued to write short stories after the publication of *A Passage to India*, often explicitly homosexual in content, but he neither wished to publish them nor deceived himself that their publication would have gone unnoticed by the authorities. (Some of these posthumously published stories are discussed by Dominic Head and Christopher Lane in their essays.) The publication of *The Life to Come and Other Stories* in 1972 marked a key moment in the gradual emergence of 'queer Forster' in the years immediately following his death, primarily through the publication of *Maurice* in 1971, but also by way of the many volumes of the Abinger Edition of his works, which has placed a wide range of his previously unpublished writings in the public domain. Finally, towards the end of the 1970s, P. N. Furbank's magisterial authorised biography, *E. M. Forster: A Life* (1977–8), enabled us to approach and appreciate the man behind the novelist for the first time and, in turn, this greater intimacy with Forster helped to further stimulate the posthumous revival of interest in his work which was then in full swing. The subsequent appearance of Forster's *Selected Letters* (1983, 1985) and his

Commonplace Book (1985) provided yet further insights into both Forster the man and Forster the writer.

Once Forster's life-long need to veil his sexuality had become a matter of public record, it was too tempting for some commentators to resist locating the source of his alleged narrowness and tepidity as a novelist, and his running out of steam in that role, in his matriarchal upbringing. Many other critics, however, have set out to scotch the kind of simplistic reading of Forster's work that posits a straightforward and inevitable link between his aborted career as a novelist and his covert inner being. For it is now abundantly clear to most open-minded readers that Forster the writer exceeds and transcends the sum of his parts and his comparatively elevated place in the annals of twentieth-century literature is increasingly assured. Indeed, with each new addition to the critical idiom – Englishness, queer studies, postcolonialism, for example – Forster's relevance is reconsidered and enhanced. The essays by Paul Peppis, Christopher Lane, and Peter Morey all engage with recent appropriations of Forster, and, like every other contributor to the collection, they seek to promote a more rounded and sophisticated appreciation of Forster's fictional and non-fictional prose and to see him neither as icon nor stooge, but a writer with whom it is well worth spending time.

Having stressed the importance of looking beyond Forster's private life as well as bearing it in mind, Forster's sexuality plainly helped determine the shape of his career, and perhaps another reason he gave up writing novels is that he felt not just that his realist 'camera' had already taken more than enough images of a (heterosexual) world from which he felt excluded, but also that it had tended to take the same or a similar photograph time and again. It is noticeable, for instance, that his novels tend not only to recycle characters – Harriet Herriton and Charlotte Bartlett, for example, or Cecil Vyse and Tibby Schlegel, or the first Mrs Wilcox and Mrs Moore – but that characters from one novel have a knack of popping up in another, reinforcing the criticism that is sometimes levelled at Forster that his fictional world is overly restricted. Is the 'Miss Herriton' mentioned in the 'Sawston' section of *The Longest Journey* (Chapter 16), for example, none other than Miss Harriet Herriton of Sawston (*Where Angels Fear to Tread*)? Is the 'Miss Quested' who plays the piano at the Schlegels' lunch party in Chapter 9 of *Howards End* the same person as *A Passage to India*'s Hampstead-based Adela Quested? And is the 'wretched, weedy' Mr Vyse, whom Tibby and Margaret Schlegel discuss in Chapter 13 of *Howards End*, the non-tennis playing and fervently aesthetic Cecil Vyse of *A Room with a View*?

All of Forster's novels are structured around contrasts, and when Caroline Abbott and Lilia Herriton set off for Italy from a fog-bound Charing Cross at the beginning of *Where Angels Fear to Tread*, they also entrain for his idiosyncratic sphere of antitheses: North versus South; suburbia versus the country; the country versus the city; the medieval versus the modern; prohibition versus liberation; propriety versus mischief; emotions versus conventions; the orthodox versus the pagan; the everyday versus the exceptional; the real versus the fantastic; pretence versus honesty; prose versus passion, common sense versus imagination; death versus life. Yet although they depend on these contraries, his fiction is not restricted by them. And while it may suit some readers to continue pigeonholing Forster as an old-maidish chronicler of Edwardian England's endless summer, a kind of tame and trousered Jane Austen, the Edwardian period was far from tranquil and neither are Forster's novels. The more we read them, the more we feel their fissures and fractures and sense all manner of ideological and sexual pressures at work between their covers. In the deftly chosen words of one recent critic, Forster's novels are 'not only . . . queer . . . but also . . . in certain respects, queerer than queer', texts that emphasise 'the cryptic, furtive and singular' and that accommodate 'subterranean feelings and strange subtexts . . . the discontinuous and the unpredictable'.[3] So although he is always compared with her, and she was clearly his greatest influence, Forster's novels differ markedly from Austen's in a number of ways and not least in their tendency to admit sudden violence and death, such as the death of Lilia Herriton and the subsequent killing of her baby in *Where Angels Fear to Tread*; the unexpected death of Gerald Dawes in a sporting accident and the almost ritualistic killing of Rickie Elliot by a train in *The Longest Journey*; the stabbing of a Florentine man in *A Room with a View*; the deaths of Mrs Wilcox and Leonard Bast in *Howards End*; the abrupt murders that irrupt into stories such as 'The Life to Come' and 'The Other Boat' and whatever it is that happens, if anything happens at all, in the Marabar Caves. An early (1903) draft of *A Room with a View* indicates that Forster even thought of concluding that novel not with George Emerson and Lucy Honeychurch embracing in Italy but with George 'killed . . . at once' by a falling tree while out cycling near Summer Street.[4] Forster called *A Room with a View* his 'nicest' novel, but there is a lot more to it than niceness, as Judith Scherer Herz discovers in her essay in this volume. Three other contributions (by Howard Booth, Peter Childs, and me) are devoted to arguably his other best-known and/or most important texts, *Maurice*, *A Passage to India*, and *Howards End*, while Ann Ardis situates *Where Angels Fear to Tread* and *Room* in the important contexts of Edwardian Hellenism and the appeal of Italy as a long-standing cultural mecca.

Although Forster tends to be celebrated for his emphasis on the need for connection between different races, classes, sexes, and sides of the individual self, and although all of his novels are delivered by reassuringly wise-sounding narrators with a seemingly sage and solid grasp of human nature, a number of the contributors to this collection see his work as marked by ambivalence and uncertainty; even, in the case of my own essay, by prejudice. All those participating in the volume were invited to contribute to it on the strength of their reputations as scholars and critics, not for their willingness or ability to sing from the same song-sheet. Paul Peppis's account of Forster and Englishness, for instance, draws conclusions that are difficult to square with my own reading of *Howards End* but which, of course, are all the more welcome because they are different. The only judge of these essays that counts will be the reader, not the editor. No attempt has been made to massage away conflicts of opinion, and the fact that Forster may be read divergently is taken as a sign, critically speaking, of his finally coming of age. I conclude my reading of *Howards End*, for example, with the proposal that Forster's fourth novel 'spotlights not the sturdiness of [his] liberal values, but their relative frailty. Patently a novel of contrasts, *Howards End* is no less fundamentally a novel of contradictions.' But whether I'm correct or not is not for me to say. And far from indicating any dissatisfaction with the novel or hostility towards Forster on my part, my angle on *Howards End* is, I hope, symptomatic of a new recognition that his novels, though clearly not complex in the manner, say, of Joyce's, are more than sufficiently complicated and substantial enough to encompass a wide range of interpretation. In *A Passage to India*, for example, it could be that Forster's unease with the place is far more intriguing and obtrusive than the sympathy we know he had for the sub-continent and its peoples.

In contrast with later appraisals of Forster's novels, Virginia Woolf thought she knew exactly where to position him. 'But, to make a clearance before I begin,' she wrote in 'Character in Fiction' (1924), 'I will suggest that we range Edwardians and Georgians into two camps; Mr Wells, Mr Bennett, and Mr Galsworthy I will call the Edwardians; Mr Forster, Mr Lawrence, Mr Strachey, Mr Joyce, and Mr Eliot I will call the Georgians.'[5] Woolf, in other words, saw Forster as part of the post-Edwardian avant-garde, and while shoehorning him into the canon of high modernism alongside Eliot and Joyce now seems more than a touch audacious, his various affinities with the writings of Lawrence, Strachey, and Woolf are obvious enough. Elizabeth Langland looks at Forster's relationship with his novelist contemporaries in depth, while Randall Stevenson and David Medalie analyse Forster's problematic relationship with modernist writing. Of course in recent years a great many people have come to know Forster's novels through film adaptations and this phenomenon is the subject of Marcia Landy's essay. Indeed, with so much of Forster on film, his novels are almost certainly more widely known than those of his more distinguished modernist contemporaries, such as Joyce. Ironically, Forster prohibited the filming of his work during his lifetime and, as Gary Day reminds us, he regarded 'the movie-public' of the 1920s as 'the modern descendants of cave men'.

Despite his comment on cinema fans, Forster remains synonymous with certain values and virtues: tolerance, compassion, freedom, liberal humanism. Yet the writer who emerges from these freshly commissioned essays is also prone to straying away from the qualities he is meant to exemplify. Just as he is more of a modernist, perhaps, than we have been inclined to acknowledge, he is less enlightened about race and class than he might seem on first acquaintance. But these observations are not intended to be pejorative: as Max Saunders says, Forster was in many ways 'the chronicler of precisely the things he felt most ambivalent about: suburbia; intellectualism; modernism; liberalism; sexuality; imperialism; Englishness'. And women. For as Jane Goldman explains at the beginning of her innovative essay, 'the status and relevance of the word "woman" in Forster's writing' is puzzlingly elusive, and that is why her essay sets out to consider 'Forster's representations of women and, more broadly, the changing understanding of what such representation might involve'.

Forster has always had legions of admirers, but he has also tended to attract the odd high-profile detractor. '[He] never gets any further than warming the teapot', a disgruntled Katherine Mansfield noted on browsing through *Howards End* some time after first reading it. 'He's a rare fine hand at that. Feel this teapot. Is it not beautifully warm? Yes, but there ain't going to be no tea.'[6] More recently, the novelist Julian Barnes told readers of the *Sunday Times* (30 August 1998) that reading '[m]ost of E. M. Forster' was 'like drinking skimmed milk',[7] while V. S. Naipaul has been notoriously contemptuous of both Forster's sexuality and *A Passage to India*, which, in 2001, he dismissed as 'utter rubbish'.[8] True, none of Forster's novels carries the epic clout of *Ulysses* (1922) or *To the Lighthouse* (1927), but Barnes' comment suggests he has sipped Forster through lips too pursed to appreciate him and Naipaul's curt assessment only defines itself.

Forster was no Woolf, no Joyce, but his novels will keep critics, academics, and general readers contentedly occupied, if not for hundreds of years, as Joyce once quipped of *Ulysses*, then certainly for the foreseeable future. But the Forster that will be read and is addressed in this volume is both a more interesting and a more conflicted writer than of old. As David Medalie puts it at the conclusion of his contribution: 'Perhaps there has been too much of the comforting Forster and too little of the discomforting one. Veneration has made him too tame and the time is now ripe to revere him less but to listen to him all the more intently.'

David Bradshaw

Notes

1. Quoted in J. H. Stape, *An E. M. Forster Chronology* (Basingstoke and London: Macmillan, 1993), p. 87.
2. Nicholas Royle, *E. M. Forster* (Plymouth: Northcote House in association with the British Council, 1999), p. 2.
3. Royle, *E. M. Forster*, p. 6.
4. E. M. Forster, *The Lucy Novels: Early Sketches for 'A Room with a View'*, ed. Oliver Stallybrass, vol. 3a of The Abinger Edition of E. M. Forster (London: Edward Arnold, 1977), p. 130.
5. Virginia Woolf, 'Character in Fiction', rep. in *The Essays of Virginia Woolf*, ed. Andrew McNeillie, vol. III (London: Hogarth Press, 1988), pp. 420–38. Quote from p. 421.
6. *The Katherine Mansfield Notebooks*, ed., Margaret Scott, vol. II (Canterbury and Wellington, New Zealand: Lincoln University Press and Daphne Brasell Associates, 1997), p. 93.
7. Cited at: www.geocities.com/SoHo/Atrium/9231/litra/BIBLIOFL.HTM.
8. 'Interview: Farrukh Dhondy Talks to V. S. Naipaul', *Literary Review*, 278 (August 2001), 28–36. Quote from p. 33.

I

MAX SAUNDERS

Forster's life and life-writing

When *A Passage to India* was published in 1924, Forster feared – rightly – that it would be his last novel. He was only forty-five, in good health, and, as it turned out, still had half his life ahead of him, during most of which he remained an active man of letters. The central question for his literary biography, then, is why he stopped writing novels so early in his career. He didn't stop writing. But his subsequent work takes other forms: stories, essays, reviews, broadcasts, lectures. The only works of length, apart from essay collections, that he published after the 1920s were his three biographical books, yet he thought all this writing less significant than his novels, and continually worried that his creativity had dried up. But while it is true that he was never to recapture the incandescence of his Edwardian novels, his biographical writing is extraordinarily good; and his shift towards life-writing has its own significances, not least for the understanding of his own biography.

After he had finished his last book, in 1955, Forster asked Leonard Woolf what he might write next. Woolf, whose thoughts were perhaps already turning toward the five-volume autobiography that would prove his *magnum opus*, advised Forster to write his autobiography. But, as P. N. Furbank explains, it was advice Forster felt he couldn't take: 'He thought he might be able to handle isolated incidents but he did not understand his own life sufficiently to describe it as a whole.'[1] This striking – and entirely characteristic – self-deprecation was perhaps a smokescreen, obscuring what Forster understood perfectly: that a homosexual life could not be described fully in print in the 1950s; perhaps even that the criminalisation of homosexuality had necessitated his living his life in a fragmentary way. It was only after Forster's death in 1970 that this aspect of his life could be addressed openly and comprehensively in Furbank's excellent two-part biography of 1977–8. Like anyone writing about Forster's life, I am greatly indebted to Furbank.

Forster had given the famous epigraph 'Only connect' to his last published novel before the First World War, *Howards End* (1910), and in 1915 he had told his friend Forrest Reid in a letter: 'My defence at any Last

Judgement would be "I was trying to connect up and use all the fragments I was born with"' (quoted Furbank II, p. 14). This might suggest he should have taken Leonard Woolf's advice. Yet from another point of view, handling isolated incidents from his life is exactly what his writing had always done. And if Forster didn't write his own life story, his novels, like all novels, certainly have an autobiographical dimension. Furbank describes the plots of his novels, where they involve children, as like 'miraculous "nativity-stories" about himself' (Furbank II, p. 131). This is especially striking in his second, and favourite, novel, *The Longest Journey*, which draws on both his unhappiness at Tonbridge School, and his sense of the potential for happiness offered by aesthetic Cambridge.[2] Furbank, as critical biographers must, argues for deeper correspondences between the life and work, especially between *The Longest Journey* and Forster's meeting of a young lame shepherd at Figsbury Rings. They conversed, the boy offered Forster a smoke of his pipe, and he impressed Forster as one of the most remarkable people he had ever met. Furbank calls the meeting a 'momentous encounter with the spirit of place' (Furbank I, p. 116). Certainly, that movement from a charged human encounter to a visionary experience of landscape – whether Italy (in *A Room with a View*), England again (in *Howards End*), or India – was to prove a key motif in his novels. But it is, of course, an encounter with more than the spirit of place. Freud said a cigar was sometimes only a cigar, but the pipe in this episode is more like Magritte's, which is not a pipe, or not only one. It is a token of an intense intimacy which sparks across several abysses: across the taboo on homosexuality; the gulf between classes; and the gap between adequacy and inadequacy. Furbank shrewdly connects the shepherd's physical handicap with Forster's homosexuality, suggesting that part of the effect of the meeting was to show Forster how what made him feel inadequate might be 'courageously overcome'.[3] He gave Rickie Elliot (his alter ego in *The Longest Journey*) the shepherd's limp, thus presenting himself as a modern Oedipus confronting the riddle of his own life.

In the 1920s Forster joined the Bloomsbury 'Memoir Club', in which members read candid autobiographical papers (Furbank II, p. 66). One of Forster's contemplates how such moments can provide the inspiration for a novel:

> The original experience – of the kind called human, but really fatuous and shallow – is of no importance and may take any form. Soon it goes, and the continual births and deaths of such are part of the disillusionment and livingness of this our mortal state. We do constantly invest strangers and strange objects with a glamour they cannot return. But now and then, before the experience dies it turns a key and bequeaths us with something which philosophically may

be also a glamour but which actually is tough. From this a book may spring. From the book, with the violence and persistency that only art possesses, a stream of emotion may beat back against and into the world.

(quoted Furbank I, p. 119)

Before the First World War, Forster invested two other glamorous young men with a love they could not return: his two closest friends at Cambridge, H. O. Meredith – to whom he dedicated *A Room with a View* – and Syed Ross Masood – to whom he dedicated *A Passage to India*. It was not until he went to Alexandria, where he spent the war working for the Red Cross, that he had his first consummated sexual experiences; first with a soldier on a beach, fleetingly, then a sustained relationship with a tram conductor, Mohammed el Adl. (His attraction to people in uniform was to continue after the war, in his longest but more ambiguous intimacy with the police-man Bob Buckingham, and his wife May, a nurse. See Furbank II, pp. 35, 166–8.)

The genesis of something as complex as a novel is bound to be intricately over-determined, and Forster's biographers can be no surer than Forster of why he was no longer inspired to write them after *A Passage to India* (which was anyway begun before the war, after his first visit there in 1912–13, then abandoned till he returned from his second visit in 1921). However, when one considers the autobiographical dimensions of his other novels possible interpretations arise.

In *A Room with a View* (1908: his third published novel, but probably con-ceived first, and drafted from 1903), there is perhaps a touch of self-mockery in the portrayal of Cecil Vyse, the aesthete who thinks he should marry Lucy Honeychurch, and doesn't yet realise he is more strongly attracted to men. In his essay 'Notes on the English Character' (1926), Forster diagnosed 'the difficulties of Englishmen abroad' as stemming from the curious institution of the public school, which sends forth its products 'with well-developed bodies, fairly developed minds, and undeveloped hearts' (*AH*, pp. 4–5). The difficulties caused by an undeveloped heart when confronted by otherness, and the need for a sentimental education, is the subject of all his novels, and their chief claim to liberalism. Cecil and Lucy are both examples. But Lucy is something of a divided character. Her social self has all the limitations of the middle classes that middle-class Forster found both fascinating and repellent. ('Middle class people smell', he wrote in a letter of 1917, quoted in Furbank II, p. 41.) But she is also (like Forster) a gifted pianist who seems when playing to touch another stratum of existence. In this respect she has more in common with passionate, depressive, George Emerson. And Forster's deepest identification in the novel seems itself divided, between

Lucy and George. Forster's extensive travels in Italy with his mother during 1901–2 figure both as George's with his father, and Lucy's with her older cousin Charlotte.

A psychobiographical reading might see George as embodying Forster's developed heart and visionary apprehension of nature and sexuality. In a disturbing moment that causes Lucy to faint and George to rescue her, she sees an encounter between two men in the Piazza Signoria which leads to one stabbing the other. If Lucy's dreamlike state begins to unlock her feelings towards George, it also suggests that same-sex entanglements can be deadly in a world which only countenances the gratification of heterosexual desire. George is very much the kind of young man Forster invested with glamour: in touch with feelings and nature; intelligent but unaffected; and from the working class. Forster worried that his writing might suffer from his inexperience of the world of labour, but the only job he took besides war-work and being a Maharajah's companion was to give lectures at the Working Men's College in Bloomsbury (Furbank I, pp. 138, 147). His Cambridge, on the other hand, was predominantly upper-middle class and the aesthetic circle he moved in there, influenced by the philosopher George Moore, made a cult of friendship, especially between men (see Furbank I, p. 166 and Furbank II, p. 295). But in Forster's experience, as homosocial intimacy turned into homosexual desire, the all-important friendships were jeopardised. By 1910 he appears to have reconciled himself to celibacy: 'However gross my desires, I find I shall never satisfy them for the fear of annoying others', he wrote, adding, perhaps to cheer himself up: 'I am glad to come across this much good in me' (Furbank I, p. 183). Yet the fiction contemplates a somewhat different story. By aligning himself with Lucy, he can imagine being kissed by George. In *Howards End*, too, it is with the central female character, Margaret Schlegel, that Forster most identifies. With its publication, Forster was recognised as one of the leading novelists of his generation. He had found a successful formula for writing of heterosexual personal relations in ways which encoded a homosexuality impossible to express more directly so soon after the trial of Oscar Wilde. Why then did he nevertheless feel blocked?

Furbank properly considers various answers. First, that Forster was basically a one-situation novelist, who had exhausted the potential of the situation of the middle-class English heart having its horizons broadened. That is certainly the fundamental story of the first four novels (as it is of the English *Bildungsroman* in general). Yet not only is it also the basis of *Maurice* and *A Passage to India* – showing that Forster hadn't exhausted its potential – but those books themselves broaden the horizons of the British novel, offering new emphases on sexuality and race. Second, Furbank presents Forster as an example of the type identified by Freud as 'Those Wrecked by Success' (Furbank I, p. 191; Furbank II, p. 131). There's truth here too. In 1911 Forster was already anticipating 'the inevitable decline of my literary reputation' (Furbank I, p. 197); and even began to imagine his personal decline too, in the form of a nervous breakdown. Artists (like any public figures) may be anxious about being able to repeat their successes. Yet, again, this does not explain why instead of suffering from 'second book syndrome' Forster had written four superb novels, each better than the last.

It might be countered that this was because effectively all four had been gestating simultaneously; that the inspiration for all of them preceded his success. But there are two problems with this argument. Furbank says Forster 'began to fear sterility as a writer' in 1910; but, as he observes earlier, Forster had already begun to anticipate wreckage and deterioration even before the publication of his first novel, *Where Angels Fear to Tread* (Furbank I, pp. 192, 121). 'My life is now straightening into something rather sad & dull to be sure, & I want to set it & me down, as I see us now', he wrote, in his customary New Year's Eve self-analysis at the end of 1904: 'Nothing more great will come out of me' (quoted Furbank, I, p. 121). He appears to have had an elegiac tone about himself from the start; a feeling that his life was all over before it had begun. True, he was thinking of his 'two discoveries' – the loss of religious faith around 1900 and realisation of his homosexuality in 1902. True, too, that he had already drafted his first three novels. It may, then, be the excitement of creative success that he felt was wrecking him. But it is perhaps more likely that the expectation of failure began even earlier, in the family assumption that he was 'delicate' – itself an understandable response to his father's premature death in his early thirties. On 1 January 1911 Forster had turned thirty-two. In the middle of that month his maternal grandmother died: an event he felt wrecked the life of his mother, Lily, and darkened her character and their relationship. Lily Forster, with whom he was still then living, appeared to have an infantilising effect on him. (Furbank writes of the 'love-affair' that sprang up between them when Forster was a child (Furbank I, p. 21).) This was particularly evident when they were travelling in Italy, and she complained of his absent-mindedness, saying 'I never saw anybody so incapable' (Furbank I, p. 84). Shortly afterwards, Forster slipped down the *pensione* stairs and sprained an ankle, then fell again on the steps of St Peter's, and broke his arm. After that, his mother had to wash and dress him. Lucy Honeychurch falls twice in *A Room with a View*, and each time finds herself in George's arms. When Forster fell in Italy he was less fortunate, as he later came to realize. By the end of 1911, His New Year laments were becoming increasingly Beckettian:

'I seem through at last, & others begin to suspect it. Idleness, depressing conditions, need for a fresh view of all life before I begin writing each time, paralyse me' (Furbank 1, p. 204).

The other problem with the idea of Forster being 'wrecked by success' is shown by the two ways in which he was able, at least in part, to overcome his writing block. First, he decided to travel to India from 1912–13; not only to visit Masood, but to venture beyond European societies. He travelled with a group of Cambridge friends, including his mentor, Goldsworthy Lowes Dickinson. India was an enriching experience in many ways for Forster. He was introduced to the charismatic Maharajah of the engagingly surreal state of Dewas Senior (one half of an already small rajput principality divided by a family feud). Forster and the Maharajah were charmed by each other, and Forster returned after the war to act as the Maharajah's private secretary. On each visit he wrote a series of acute and amusing letters back to his friends and family, which were later to form the core of *The Hill of Devi* (1953). He also began writing a novel on Indian themes on his return; but soon he began to despair that he had been unable to escape his blockage: 'I am dried up. Not in my emotions, but in their expression. I cannot write at all' (Furbank 1, p. 249).

What happened next was to prove more decisive. Late in 1913 Forster was in Harrogate with his mother, who was taking a cure for rheumatism. He decided to visit Dickinson's friend Edward Carpenter, the radical sage who advocated the 'simple life', and pioneer sexologist, urging tolerance and understanding of homosexuality. When, in 1960, in his 'Terminal Note' to *Maurice*, Forster recalled these visits, he said that in his 'loneliness' he approached Carpenter 'as one approaches a saviour':

> It must have been on my second or third visit to the shrine that the spark was kindled and he and his comrade George Merrill combined to make a profound impression on me and to touch a creative spring. George Merrill also touched my backside – gently and just above the buttocks. I believe he touched most people's. The sensation was unusual and I still remember it, as I remember the position of a long vanished tooth. It was as much psychological as physical. It seemed to go straight through the small of my back into my ideas, without involving my thoughts. If it really did this, it would have acted in strict accordance with Carpenter's yogified mysticism, and would prove that at that precise moment I had conceived.

What he had conceived was the novel about homosexuality, *Maurice*. He began it immediately, feeling that at last his inspiration had returned, and that the writing of it would unleash future novels.

And *Maurice*, while judged one of his slighter achievements, was later to inaugurate a revival in his reputation – as well as one of several influential films of his novels. Just when Marxist criticism thought it had demolished Forster's liberal politics, *Maurice* revealed him to be a more radical investigator of sexual politics than he had been thought. (Similarly, subsequent critical waves of postcolonial criticism, studies of Englishness and of masculinities, have brought out more ambiguous and complex aspects of Forster's fiction.)

However, the novel turned out to be another *cul de sac*. He had previously been writing erotic stories which he kept private; and he had known all along that *Maurice* would be unpublishable 'until my death or England's' (Furbank I, p. 259). He had hoped it would free him to write further novels, but it hadn't. At first glance this sounds like the familiar problem of feeling he was finished as a writer. Yet his life was different after *Maurice*, in ways that may have made his attitude to writing different. On a personal level, the war enabled him to live out his homosexuality; and arguably the visit to Carpenter and the writing of *Maurice* had made this possible. He certainly felt transformed, initiated, by his affair with Mohammed. 'My luck has been amazing', he wrote. 'It isn't happiness, it's rather – offensive phrase – that I first feel a grown up man.'[4]

The force with which Carpenter and his lover inspired Forster suggests that his creative block had had another cause, though one which Furbank also considers: namely, that as a homosexual he got bored writing about marriage and heterosexual relations (Furbank II, p. 132). If this was true before 1913, it can only have become truer later. Having expressed his desires more directly in fiction and in life, it would have seemed false now to conceal them. This in turn suggests a further possible explanation. It may have been precisely his repression of his own sexuality that made him most creative. The novels, that is, might be seen as a form of sublimation: a transformation of what couldn't be expressed more directly. His gradual de-repression from 1913 and through the war may thus have dismantled the very structure that had inspired his novels. The writing of *Maurice*, rather than releasing future creativity, may have short-circuited it. And his feeling of blockage after it, rather than being a continuation of his old anxieties, may instead have been a new state of mind.

Forster's developing sense of his sexuality wasn't the only factor, however. He felt the First World War had destroyed his faith in humanity, and his hope that connections could be made, redemption and vision achieved. Like many of the postwar 'lost generation', he felt that the war had undermined the very civilisation it claimed to preserve. Such disillusion led many writers to turn away from liberal democracy towards totalitarianism (Yeats, Pound, Lewis) or anti-industrial utopianism (Lawrence, Ford); Forster somehow retained his public-spiritedness: 'Decent work rather presents itself as an alternative.'[5]

Fearing that his middle age would be a matter of 'Always working, never creating', he decided to write to the Maharajah of Dewas Senior to ask if he could go and work for him, again hoping that India would restore his creativity (Furbank II, p. 54). His return enabled him to return to his Indian novel. But the triumphant success of *A Passage to India* left him feeling once more that he had finished his last novel. As in Eliot's *The Waste Land*, the turn towards India may have seemed like an escape from the devastation of Europe, yet the insidious negativity encountered in the Marabar Caves, whatever else it is, suggests in its 'Boum' an echo of the war that fell between Forster's two visits to India. Certainly, by the 1920s he had become more ambivalent about humanity. '[P]ersonal relationships', he said, '. . . still seem to me the most real things on the surface of the earth, but I have acquired a feeling that people must go away from each other (spiritually) every now and then, and improve themselves if the relationship is to develop or even endure. *A Passage to India* describes such a going away' (quoted in Furbank II, p. 124). But the private writings – his letters and the *Commonplace Book* he began after *A Passage to India* – tell a different, more cynical story, of unredeemable rather than merely undeveloped hearts:

> I think that most Indians, like most English people, are shits, and I am not interested whether they sympathize with one another or not. Not interested as an artist; of course the journalistic side of me still gets roused over these questions.[6]

It was this 'journalistic side' that was to predominate in the second half of his career: broadcasts, reviews, essays, biographies, travel books.

As Forster became more of a journalist and a public figure he felt increasingly alienated from his creativity. In a brilliant essay 'Anonymity: An Enquiry', published the year after *A Passage to India*, he argues 'that all literature tends towards a condition of anonymity, and that, so far as words are creative, a signature merely distracts us from their true significance' (*TCD*, p. 81). The essay continues a little further on:

> Just as words have two functions – information and creation – so each human mind has two personalities, one on the surface, one deeper down. The upper personality has a name. It is called S. T. Coleridge, or William Shakespeare, or Mrs Humphry Ward. It is conscious and alert, it does things like dining out, answering letters, etc., and it differs vividly and amusingly from other personalities. The lower personality is a very queer affair. In many ways it is a perfect fool, but without it there is no literature . . . It has something in common with all other deeper personalities, and the mystic will assert that the

common quality is God, and that here, in the obscure recesses of our being, we near the gates of the Divine . . . What is so wonderful about great literature is that it transforms the man who reads it towards the condition of the man who wrote, and brings to birth in us also the creative impulse.   (*TCD*, pp. 82–3)

There had always been a mystical tendency in his fiction: a pagan alternative to the Christianity he eschewed, which connects the world of Pan and dryads with the world of tea-parties and tourism; the spirit of place with money and society; the unconscious and the conscious. Indeed, it became his signature trick of style to yoke the physical and metaphysical together in a phrase: telegrams and anger; making the inner life pay; and so on.

He was increasingly drawn towards those writing autobiographically, but also lyrically or mystically. He had read Proust on his return from India, then T. E. Lawrence's *Seven Pillars of Wisdom*; and both inspired him to complete *A Passage to India* (Furbank II, pp. 107, 119). The advice he had found most inspiring had been his friend Hilton Young's, that 'the path to creation is to be found not by looking about one, but by peering into the lumber room of one's mind' (Furbank II, p. 65). This was what modernist 'stream of consciousness' techniques were already attempting. But, as Virginia Woolf saw, Forster's self-contemplation sought something more transcendental. When she heard of his return to India in 1921, she wrote: 'He will become a mystic, sit by the roadside and forget Europe' (quoted Furbank II, p. 67). Well, he returned to live in England; but having written about Egypt and India, perhaps there was a sense in which Europe ceased to stir his creative imagination.

Forster was invited by Trinity College, Cambridge, to give the 1927 Clark Lectures. These were published as *Aspects of the Novel* later that year and represent a phase of intense scrutiny of the novel form, and of his attitude to modernism. The lectures were not intended as his farewell to novel writing. Mary Lago argues that Forster 'twice abandoned the novel form'.[7] But, as we have seen, it was more a matter of his still wanting to write novels, yet feeling that the form had abandoned him. As Furbank suggests, 'A different kind of difficulty was that he had come to feel bored with orthodox fictional form' (Furbank II, p. 106). This weariness comes out in the famous remark in *Aspects of the Novel*, in which Forster imagines a 'sort of drooping regretful voice' saying: 'Yes – oh dear yes – the novel tells a story . . . and I wish that it was not so, that it could be something different – melody, or perception of the truth, not this low atavistic form' (*AN*, p. 17).

As a public personality, Forster remained committed to the public world of time and place. He had been active in PEN since the 1920s and in 1934 the National Council for Civil Liberties invited him to be its first president (Furbank II, p. 186). Yet privately, just as he felt twice unable to continue as a novelist, so he lost faith in civilisation for a second time during the 1930s. When he wrote a despairing letter to Dickinson, he copied it into his *Commonplace Book*, noting that he did so because 'it is now only in letters I write what I feel: not in literature any more, and I seldom say it, because I keep trying to be amusing':

> I am well and personally happy, though personal happiness has little meaning in these tragic days . . . But what a civilisation! All one's goods are private and depend on one's meeting the right people. As soon as one looks into the general world, which one's emotions should enrich and be enriched by, there is nothing but negation & destruction.[8]

Such sentiments entail a loss of faith in the general world of literature and its general reader. Yet Forster spoke at the International Congress of Writers in Paris in 1935, telling Virginia Woolf: 'We do represent the last utterances of the civilized.'[9] If that note of doom roused him to public utterance, it seemed fatally to undermine any creative work: 'the collapse of civilisation seems to eat up from below into any thing I do', he wrote in the *Commonplace Book*.[10]

In 1924, Forster's aunt Laura had died, and left him her house at Abinger in West Hackhurst, Surrey. When the Second World War broke out, Forster remained based there, saying he was preparing himself for 'comforting my mother through bottling fruit and Armageddon' (Furbank II, p. 234). In the face of even more widespread 'negation & destruction', and his despair at the 'general world', he might have been expected to retreat into a private, spiritual one. Yet, impressively, he continued his public work, becoming increasingly active as a broadcaster on the BBC, especially in programmes for India. This isn't to say that he took the popular, or propagandist line. On the contrary, like many in our own era of negation and terror, he felt it necessary to protect civil liberties against the totalitarianising forces of wartime. In the celebrated essay 'What I Believe' he wrote bravely (it was 1939): 'if I had to choose between betraying my country and betraying my friend I hope I should have the guts to betray my country' (*TCD*, p. 66).

Though the Second World War made the public journalistic self more active, it confirmed the novelist's end. With the death of his mother in 1945 he was further devastated. 'I cannot speak to others of my worst trouble, which is that I have got tired of people and personal relationships', he said in 1948 (Furbank II, p. 282). For someone tired of people he certainly continued to make a lot of new friends, especially amongst the queer artistic community, such as William Plomer, W. H. Auden, Christopher Isherwood, Benjamin Britten, and Peter Pears. He continued writing for the *Listener*, edited by one of his closest friends of these years, J. R. Ackerley. He was now treated as a grand old man of literature, and accepted invitations to travel in India and the USA. Again, he had hoped his impressions would inspire him, but now he felt they were too fragmentary. In 1946 he had been given an Honorary Fellowship at his beloved King's College, Cambridge. (When the College heard he had been forced to leave West Hackhurst after his lease expired, it invited him to live in King's, which he did for the rest of his life.) His last major public activity was to appear as a witness in the notorious *Lady Chatterley* trial in 1960 (Furbank II, pp. 311–12). But though his own life had become more public, he remained true to his preoccupation with the individual: 'He seems to me a divine achievement and I mistrust any view which belittles him' – by which he meant the totalitarianisms of both right and left, which he felt bearing upon the individual and his creativity (*TCD*, p. 55). This concern for individuality, and how it survives within the public figure, is at the core of the last books he was to write.

Many of his essays take the form of appreciations of individual writers which have significant biographical emphases; autobiographical too, since some were about his own friends. *Abinger Harvest* (1936), for example, includes pieces on Roger Fry, Forrest Reid, T. E. Lawrence, T. S. Eliot, and Virginia Woolf. The volume took its title from the village whose pageant it includes. But in a 'Prefatory Note' Forster explains: '[R]elatives of mine have been connected with Abinger, a village in Surrey, for nearly sixty years, and I have known the place all my life myself'; so '*Abinger Harvest* suggested itself as possible for the whole collection' (*AH*, p. xxi). If the volume is the harvest of the spirit of place, it is also a form of family history, as well as a form of autobiography: a portrait of Forster's home-counties roots, and of his role as public man of letters.

He had been invited to prepare a large edition of the letters of T. E. Lawrence. Though Lawrence's brother did not want a biography written, Forster's conception of the project was essentially biographical: following Desmond MacCarthy's advice, he aimed to provide a commentary on each section, 'the whole to lead gradually to a final grand character-portrait and estimate of Lawrence' (Furbank II, p. 208). Forster became worried that the letters would be attacked as libellous, and that he would be held responsible. Eventually he resigned from the editorship, and, according to Furbank, was too 'discouraged and thwarted' to attempt another book 'for fifteen or more years' (Furbank II, p. 211). This is a little exaggerated. As we have seen, it was because he already felt thwarted that he was contemplating such work instead of novel writing. The intervention of the Second World War cannot have helped. Forster didn't stop writing essays, though, and the second volume of these, *Two Cheers for Democracy* (1951), which includes his responses to the war (under the heading 'The Second Darkness') also gathers a number of biographical essays on Gerald Heard, Ronald Kidd,

George Orwell, Edward Carpenter, Woolf again, Reid again, Eliot again, Auden, and Masood.

Life-writing was now all he felt he could produce on a larger scale. His last three monographs were all biographical. Yet rather than seeing this turn as a personal defeat, it should be seen in the wider context of the reinvention of life-writing that was centred in Bloomsbury: what Virginia Woolf called 'The New Biography';[11] and which included not only the ironic character sketch assassinations of Lytton Strachey, but also the experiments by writers like Harold Nicolson, and, of course, Woolf herself, fusing biography and fiction into strange new forms, like *Orlando*, or *Flush*, her biography of Elizabeth Barrett Browning's spaniel. Forster's late works are his version of the New Biography.

Goldsworthy Lowes Dickinson

Goldsworthy Lowes Dickinson (1934), is a memoir of the political scientist and humanist who taught at Cambridge and the London School of Economics. He was best known for three books: *The Greek View of Life* (1896); *Letters from John Chinaman* (1901), expressing concerns about imperialist Britain seen from the outside at the time of the Boer War; and *The International Anarchy* (1926), which expresses his despair at the world political system, or lack of it, that made the First World War possible, and seemed already to be threatening another. Dickinson's main public activity after the war, besides this massive book, was in being one of the prime movers in getting the League of Nations (forerunner of the United Nations) established. He was not only an astoundingly cultivated and open-minded man, but passionately committed to the cause of peace; nobly so, since (like Forster) he didn't relish involvement in public affairs.

Dickinson was some sixteen years older than Forster. They met in 1898 when Forster was an undergraduate at King's College, Cambridge, where Dickinson was a don. Forster didn't get to know him well for more than another decade. Though he was never himself taught by Dickinson, his friends had been, and he had joined Dickinson's discussion society:

> The papers I forget, with the exception of one on Sex, read by George Barger (now Professor of Chemistry at Edinburgh). Sex was not mentioned at Cambridge in those days – that is to say, not in the small circle I knew – and there were some high anticipations about Barger's paper, and some care on Dickinson's part to ensure that only serious-minded youths should attend. The paper was statistical, the discussion stilted, the evening interminable, yet I recall it as an example of his sensitiveness and tact; he knew just how large a stone it is wise to drop into the pond. (*GLD*, p. 85)

Forster is equally tactful about Dickinson's own sexual chemistry. Though his memoir is closely based on Dickinson's own 'Recollections', which were then unpublished, he encrypted Dickinson's homosexuality almost entirely, letting the knowing glimpse it in the occasional oblique remark: 'Although he was never drawn to women in the passionate sense, all his deepest emotions being towards men, his life would have been empty and comfortless without them' (*GLD*, p. 47). Some of the remarks he quotes about women suggest that Dickinson, like Forster himself, could actually be misogynistic. But such passages also make it clear why he was such a role model for Cambridge and Bloomsbury homosexuals or bisexuals. After Dickinson died in 1932, his surviving sisters (who contributed to the Schlegel sisters in *Howards End*) asked Forster to write the memoir. It gave him the chance not only to pay a handsome tribute to his friend, but to demonstrate how such friendships were at the core of the civilisation that Cambridge represented for him – 'King's stands for personal relationships',[12] he wrote – just when the twentieth century seemed destined to negate such civilisation.

Like all Forster's books of life-writing, *Goldsworthy Lowes Dickinson* is not just a memoir, but also a meditation on the nature of memoir: on what it can and should do, and what it cannot; and on why we write them. His Epilogue explicitly addresses the question of biography, via a fantasy about Mephistopheles – which picks up Goldsworthy's admiration for Goethe and opera, as well as his exercises in writing dialogues:

> Mephistopheles, who should inhabit a cranny in every biography, puts his head out at this point, and asks me to set all personal feelings aside and state objectively why a memoir of Goldsworthy Lowes Dickinson need be written. If I say 'Because I want to', the answer is 'Who are you?' If I say 'My friend was beloved, affectionate, unselfish, intelligent, witty, charming, inspiring', the devil will reply, 'Yes, but that is neither here nor there, or rather it was there but it is no longer here.' (*GLD*, p. 199)

Forster concedes that the devil has points. Dickinson's life lacked adventure or hardship or excitement. He was not a great writer. Of his work for the League of Nations the best Forster could say in 1934 was that time will tell: with Hitler and Mussolini in power, he knew the League couldn't guarantee world peace. As a thinker he accepts Dickinson's own self-deprecating valuation that 'he ranks as a Cambridge philosopher below either McTaggart, Moore or Bertrand Russell, and takes no place in the philosophic hierarchy of the past' (*GLD*, p. 200). 'The case of Mephistopheles would appear to be watertight', he sums up: 'and a biography of my friend and master uncalled for' (*GLD*, p. 200). But then Forster rounds on the Devil for mistaking a man for merely 'the sum of his qualities':

it is to the qualities named at the beginning of this epilogue, the 'beloved, affectionate, unselfish, intelligent, witty, charming' which were so easily brushed aside, that I return for his overthrow. These qualities in Goldie were fused into such an unusual creature that no one whom one has met with in the flesh or in history the least resembles it, and no words exist in which to define it. He was an indescribably rare being, he was rare without being enigmatic, he was rare in the only direction which seems to be infinite: the direction of the Chorus Mysticus. He did not merely increase our experience: he left us more alert for what has not yet been experienced and more hopeful about other men because he had lived. And a biography of him, if it succeeded, would resemble him; it would achieve the unattainable, express the inexpressible, turn the passing into the everlasting. Have I done that? *Das Unbeschreibliche hier ist's getan?* No. And perhaps it only could be done through music. But that is what has lured me on.

(GLD, p. 201)

Virginia Woolf in her biography of Roger Fry (1940) – a contemporary and in many ways comparable work – records Fry's reaction to Forster's *A Passage to India*:

I think it's a marvelous texture – really beautiful writing. But Oh lord I wish he weren't a mystic, or that he would keep his mysticism out of his books . . . I'm certain that the only meanings that are worth anything in a work of art are those that the artist himself knows nothing about. The moment he tries to explain *his* ideas and *his* emotions he misses the great thing.[13]

It is a classic statement of modernism's ideal of impersonality. But is the line between Forsterian mysticism and modernist epiphany so easy to draw? Forster certainly doesn't keep mysticism out of these memoirs. He is writing about the Cambridge of the turn of the century, pervaded by an idealism that is itself mystical. In one of the best passages in the book Forster quotes from Dickinson's 'Recollections' describing his friend the philosopher Jack McTaggart:

McTaggart . . . was, from the philosophic point of view, quite uninterested in the concrete, for he did not believe that philosophy could handle it, except – important exception – at one point. He held then, and I suppose does still, that in the relation of love we come into the closest contact we can attain with Reality; that Reality is an eternally perfect harmony of pure spirits united by Love. This idea is the key to McTaggart's philosophy, and the real thing that drove him to pursue it. The rest has been a continuous and (I suppose) vain effort to prove it by logic.

(GLD, pp. 59–60)

It is a brilliant and chastening example of what Nietzsche meant when he said that all philosophy was a species of unconscious autobiography. McTaggart has an illogical conviction about what Love is, and that drives his whole philosophical project, without his being able to see its flaw. Under McTaggart's spell, Dickinson too aimed at what he calls McTaggart's heaven, of the 'company of pure spirits related to one another by perfect love'. But he came to see what was wrong with that heaven: 'I . . . cannot understand how I thought that this personal passion in transitory individuals could be the key to the universe', Dickinson comments rather plaintively (*GLD*, p. 63). Forster quotes this just after an account of Dickinson's intense friendship with a man called Ferdinand Schiller, who 'was to occupy the supreme position in Dickinson's life' (*GLD*, p. 62):

> Devoted to Schiller, but constantly parted from him, and doubtful whether his devotion was returned, Dickinson suffered for many years from a sense of frustration which the sensitive will understand. (*GLD*, p. 63)

Part of Forster's own characteristic sensitivity here is in not claiming that unrequited love, or love you're not sure is requited, is exclusively the preserve of homosexual lovers; and also in not being so crude as to assert that Dickinson's idealism was a sublimated homoeroticism. But there is surely a suggestion that such frustration was as determining for Dickinson as McTaggart's idealism was for him. That certainly seems to be the drift of Forster's preface, where he argues that Dickinson cannot quite be trusted to speak for himself:

> To what extent can a man be trusted to review his own past? Something must always be discounted, and in Dickinson's case we must discount a thin veil of melancholy which interposed between him and the paper as soon as he sat down to type. He was aware of this and tried to neutralise it, and it is, I think, his only defect as an autobiographer . . . except for the tendency to write it down as rather sadder than he felt it to have been – his record may be accepted. (*GLD*, p. xxi)

This perhaps anticipates another diabolical objection – why write a biography when you could have published (even in abridged form) Dickinson's autobiography? – the answer to which is that the two modes move in different ways. As he says of the portrait of McTaggart:

> Note Dickinson's method of depicting character: he begins from within, and then proceeds to the oddities which make up the visible man. Method of the dialogue-writer rather than of the novelist, who hopes, by recording the surface, to indicate the forces beneath it. (*GLD*, p. 59)

The 'method of the dialogue-writer' is also the method of the philosopher – especially the follower of Plato. Forster's biographical writing takes the novelist's approach rather than the metaphysician's; though he too seeks to connect the inner lives of his subjects with their public and historical selves.

As an example of Dickinson's autobiographical melancholia, one could take a letter he wrote to an Indian correspondent in 1931, the year before his death:

> When I was a young man I became much absorbed first in Plato, and then Plotinus. I am one of the few Englishmen who have studied Plotinus from cover to cover, though that was years ago. I thought then that there must be some way of reaching ultimate truth (or perhaps I should say ultimate experience) by some short cut. I suppose the principal thing that happened to me, in the course of my life, was the disappearance of this idea. (*GLD*, p. 190)

Here he reads his own life, as he reads McTaggart's, as unlockable by a single key: an idea. The idea is the same: transcendence through love. But whereas McTaggart's story is the refusal to let go of the idea, despite its unamenability to proof, Dickinson's story is the disappearance of that idea, that hope. It is an extraordinary autobiographical moment: to claim, as perhaps only a philosopher could, that the main event in your life was the disappearance of an idea. It is an extraordinary moment of refracted autobiography when Forster quotes it: not only because he shared Dickinson's disillusion about personal relations leading either to truth or to civilization; but because the principal thing in his own life had become the disappearance of an idea – the idea of himself as a novelist. Worrying about that gave Forster his own melancholy, which perhaps in turn contributed to his reluctance to write his autobiography. He was unflinchingly scathing in his annual autobiographical accounts; but the story of creative decline may have simply been too depressing to tell at length. Yet such passages from his lives of others are rich with such thoughts about, and examples of, life-writing, and with wondering how it relates to novel writing.

The Hill of Devi

The Hill of Devi (1953) is the shortest of the three biographical books, and also the most read – not only for the context it provides for *A Passage to India*, but for its insight into aristocratic Hindu life under the Raj both before and after the First World War. It was republished by Penguin in the 1960s and 1980s (in the Penguin Travel Library) on the waves of Western interest in things Eastern. It consists of edited versions of the letters Forster wrote home from India, framed with a narrative about the Maharajah and his family.

It is remarkable for its depth of sympathy with Indians, though Forster has no illusions about the Maharajah's failings, and writes humorously about his self-destructive inefficiency and inability to manage people. It includes a hilarious section about how Forster received an 'Official Insult' from the

Agent to the Governor General of Central India. He was passed over during a reception ceremony, so as to suggest both that the Government didn't recognise the Maharajah's right to have Europeans working under him, and also that by assuming Indian dress Forster had lost his European status. He was bemused, though the Maharajah was angry on his behalf, which improved Forster's status. However, as the book ends, it becomes clear that it is a serious and passionate resistance to precisely that imperialist contempt, when it recurred in the official response to the Maharajah's death:

> *The Times* of London duly carried an obituary notice of him. It is a model of ungenerosity and prim indignation and I read it with rage. The rage has subsided, for after all what else could *The Times* carry? Here was an Indian Ruler who had not been a success, who had maladministered his State and got into debt and given the Government of India trouble, who had not even been frank when invited by British officials to be so. 'He came of an ancient and renowned dynasty, and in the early years of his rule gave some promise of doing well, but an ungovernable temper and self-indulgence led to serious deterioration.' The progress of the deterioration is traced; his marriage and its failure, the departure of the Kolhapur Princess, his feud with her house, his troubles with his son are all described, not from his point of view, but the point of view of his enemies; his appeal to Ramsay MacDonald and his penitential fasts are sneered at. There is not one hint that he was lovable and brilliant and witty and charming, and (more exasperating still) not one hint that he was complex. He will go down to history as a failure. That is the sort of thing that does go down to history. (*HD*, pp. 112–13)

Forster wants to turn the official life-writing inside out, as did Virginia Woolf in her reaction against the patriarchal and judgemental forms of life-writing associated with her father's *Dictionary of National Biography*. But again, Forster's aesthetics are mystical rather than psychological. The Maharajah, he says, was 'never simple, never ordinary, never deaf to the promptings which most of us scarcely hear' (*HD*, p. 113). *The Hill of Devi* too ends on a rather mystical invocation of music:

> One of the puzzling things about the dead is that it is impossible to think of them evenly. They all go out of sight and are forgotten, they all go into silence, yet we cannot help assigning some of them a tune. Most of those whom I have known leave no sound behind them, I cannot evoke them though I would like to. He has the rare quality of evoking himself, and I do not believe that he is here doing it for the last time. (*HD*, p. 113)

Perhaps the key word in that passage, still scandalised by all *The Times* missed out, is 'lovable'. For one thing all three books have in common, is that they are labours of love; books about people Forster loved, or has come to love, each in very different ways. Though intense, Forster's friendship with the Maharajah was not a sexual one. But it was his supportive attitude towards Forster's accident-prone affairs (which are excluded from the book) that brought them closer together, and made him feel the Maharajah was saintly.

They are also, as biographies characteristically are, all books of the dead; about death; about carrying on after the death of people you have loved. Biography is frequently criticised for offering false consolation; for being in denial of death, and asserting the meaning and value of an individual life for an age that has begun to doubt both. The biographical attempt to bring some-one back to life from the dead might seem an act of bad faith. But if Forster's life-writings have their nostalgia, they also have no illusions about the possi-bility of putting back the clock. They are elegiac, but it is a necessary part of elegy to recognise that you have to let the dead go in order to carry on living.

Marianne Thornton

'We have to carry on differently' (*TCD*, p. 161). Forster wrote these words towards the end of an essay on 'Gibbon and his Autobiography', acknowl-edging that the biographer must recognise the pastness of the past. One could no longer live or write like Gibbon. The year was 1942, when Britain itself was in jeopardy of passing into history. Forster's last book, *Marianne Thornton* (1956), is very much concerned with a vanished way of life. Its subject was Forster's great aunt, who had been born (just three years after Gibbon's death) at the end of the eighteenth century, and died, aged ninety, towards the end of the nineteenth. It was, though, the death of Forster's mother in 1945 that spurred him to write it. As he cleared out the house at West Hackhurst, he started reading his mother's hoard of family letters and papers. It took him a decade to write the book. It was a necessary therapy for a death that left him as devastated as Lily had been when her mother died. 'I partly died when my mother did', he told Christopher Isherwood.[14] Besides being an elegy for the nineteenth-century ways of life that two world wars had helped consign to oblivion, then, the book is also an (oblique) elegy for his mother; and for himself.

In many ways it is an old-fashioned family memoir, and risks appearing a tedious act of piety, charting a fairly uneventful life. Marianne lived with her brother until middle age; never married or had children, though she took in her orphaned nephew and niece, and later befriended Forster's mother. But, as in his other biographical books, he turns the form inside out, to produce something much more intriguingly personal, on three main counts. First, it is a belated and curiously metaphysical love-story. He calls his aunt:

'one who was herself affectionate and gay, and who loved her father and mother, her brothers and sisters, her nephews and nieces, and, finally, at the end of her long life, her great-nephew, namely myself' (*MT*, pp. 15–16). In a characteristically Forsterian touch, this love takes the form of money. She left him a legacy of £8,000 which paid for his education. Thus 'she and no one else made my career as a writer possible, and her love, in a most tangible sense, followed me beyond the grave' (*MT*, p. 289). The family name for her, 'Aunt Monie', thus begins to seem bizarrely appropriate. It is only fair, then, that he owes her a book. It is not only that the act of writing reciprocates her love, but that the kind of writer she enabled him to become is one who can create love out of his material. He was only eight when he heard of her death; he had scarcely known her then:

> I had not really loved Aunt Monie – she was too old, and the masses of presents she had given me had not found their way to my tiny heart. I cried because crying was easy and because my mother might like it, and because the subject was death.

But as his imagination plays over the family papers, and he begins to realise her and her life, his love for her takes form:

> Of later years I have loved Aunt Monie better – best of all now when I have been trying to trace the unfoldings of her good life.   (*MT*, p. 287)

Second, it offers rich insights into his fiction. Where *Goldsworthy Lowes Dickinson* provides the background for novels like *The Longest Journey* and *Maurice*, or *The Hill of Devi* does for *A Passage to India*, *Marianne Thornton* sheds most light on *Howards End*. The moral earnestness of the Thorntons and their circle goes into the Schlegels; whereas their success in banking, and obtuseness to poetry or metaphysics, inform the prosperous Wilcoxes in that novel. The book explains that the model for Howards End was his and his mother's home in Hertfordshire: Rooksnest, in Stevenage (*MT*, p. 269). Yet *Marianne Thornton* tells a different story: the story of another house, the Thorntons', Battersea Rise.

> To them it was a perfect playground and in after years a sacred shrine. It satisfied in them that longing for a particular place, a home, which is common amongst our upper and middle classes, and some of them transmitted that longing to their descendants, who have lived on into an age where it cannot be gratified.   (*MT*, p. 16)

Forster juxtaposes the idea of 'domestic biography' to public biography – the lives of public figures, such as Henry Thornton's great friends, the members of the so-called 'Clapham Sect', including William Wilberforce and Hannah More; the Macaulays and (Virginia Woolf's parents) the Stephens. But it is not just the biography of a private life; of a family, really; but also the biography of a house, a *domus*, Battersea Rise. Just as the house in *Howards End* acquires a mystical or spiritual quality, and presides over the book, so does Battersea Rise. That's what Forster means by saying the family regarded it as a sacred shrine.

Marianne spends most of her life in Battersea Rise, living with her brother, also called Henry Thornton after his father. He becomes a successful banker too. He marries and has two daughters. Then his wife dies young. Her sister moves in to help with the children. And Henry then decides he wants to marry her next. But she is his 'deceased wife's sister', and such a marriage was illegal in Britain (until 1907). This episode provides most of the high drama of the book. It causes a rift in the evangelical and highly moral family. Most of the others oppose him vigorously. He reacts like a man obsessed. He seems to have inherited all the reforming zeal of the Clapham sect, but directed towards a purpose that would have horrified them. He marries abroad, and has to spend much of his time out of the country as a result. So he abandons Battersea Rise, and Marianne and her sisters have to leave. When he and his second wife eventually come back to it, the rift is so bad that most of the family will not visit. Only Marianne does, because she has been the most diplomatic, and it is characteristic of Forster's liberalism that he admires his great aunt's ability to take the liberal line when all around her were intransigent.

Marianne was fifty-five when she'd left the house, and moved to the east side of Clapham Common. In 1881 – nearly thirty years later – Henry Thornton Jr died. And again the question arose of what to do with the house. He had left it to his daughters by his first wife, but Forster says they couldn't afford to live in it, so decided to let it to his widow. This only perpetuated the rift. 'Marianne was unreasonably upset', says Forster (who had himself been upset when told his lease on West Hackhurst would not be renewed): 'She cherished the illusion that at the death of her brother the sacred house would be released from its bondage and return to the true succession' (*MT*, pp. 263–4). Thus far it may seem a story of possessiveness, squabbles, and grudges. But it prepares us for a strange moment near Marianne's end:

A week before she died she wrote an extraordinary letter to Emily Thornton. She asked for some milk. No biographer could have foretold such a request, no novelist before Proust could have invented it. After thirty-five years' alienation she asks for some milk.   (*MT*, p. 287)

The letter and Emily's reply have not survived, but the next pair of letters have, and are courteous attempts to rebuild bridges. Whoever copied out the letters has annotated them, asking whether there isn't something 'regal' in Marianne's holding out the olive branch, but then wonders if this doesn't mean she's accepting responsibility for the estrangement.

> The latter explanation is the likelier of the two. But it is more probable still that Marianne was writing not to a person but to a place. The milk was a sacrament. She knew she was dying and before it happened she wished to be in physical touch with Battersea Rise. (*MT*, p. 288)

This, too, is a metaphysical touch, in which the spirits of places and persons interfuse; and feeling for property acquires a spiritual dimension.

Third, *Marianne Thornton* can be read as Forster's inverted autobiography. It's not just that it recounts the family heritage he sees as contributing to his own character – the Thornton wealth; their class position; their liberal social conscience; the elderly ladies that surrounded him in childhood – it's also that the book ends with his beginning: his birth and earliest years. In short, it shows Forster exploring his own life in relation to the lives of others.

So, in a sense, he *did* take Leonard Woolf's advice and wrote a *form* of *oblique* autobiography. And – perhaps – it was precisely because they gave so much of his own life; perhaps it was because taken together they do constitute a kind of composite autobiography – that they *were* his last books. This leads us towards a conclusion, which is that there are at least three main aspects these books share, and which connect them with his other writing. First, they are all formally inventive works, which explore and expand the forms of life-writing. This formal self-consciousness gives them an affinity with modernism. Even if we would not want quite to call them modernist, they're certainly instances of what Virginia Woolf termed 'The New Biography'. Forster's engagement in life-writing might, in the era of New Criticism, have seemed to be what distanced him from full modernist impersonality. But under postmodern eyes, it is perhaps, rather, an example of a modernist investment in life-writing that we are only now beginning to gauge. 'The New Biography', after all, seems increasingly central to the modernist project.[15] Thus an understanding of his life-writing may be what is necessary to clarify his ambiguous relation to modernism.

This formal self-consciousness is partly a matter of what might be called a 'metabiographical' commentary woven into the narratives, commenting on what life-writing does or should do; what letters do or should do; how much the biographer should know, and so on. It is also a matter of opening up the form: either by opening up conventional forms – the memoir, the family memoir etc., to become the biography of a house; an exploration of cultural differences; a dialogue with the devil; or by blending biography and autobiography (as Edmund Gosse had done before him in *Father and Son*, say); or blending auto/biography and letters. Forster's biographical books are also his literary autobiography not just in the sense that they represent aspects of someone – himself – who happened to be an author; but also in the senses that need to be true of all good literary autobiography: they illuminate why he wrote his other books as he did; and they illuminate the kind of life which is a writer's.

Second, all three books oppose the ethos of the English Middle Classes. Biography, which is often criticised as being a bourgeois form – a bastion of liberal individualism – may seem an odd vehicle for such opposition. Forster would, of course, have welcomed both accusations of liberalism and individualism. But his life-writing (like his fiction) also gestures beyond the parameters of bourgeois lives. His subjects are all socially motivated people. But he uses biography to interrogate the values of society: to provide what might be called a personal explanation of the social world. Though none of his subjects was working-class, and all three had some wealth and position, yet none was typically bourgeois. They could all be seen as marginal, not quite of the worlds in which they move: the philosophical don; the ineffectual ruler; the unhoused maiden great-aunt. Forster's procedure here is perhaps the obverse of his friend Lytton Strachey's in *Eminent Victorians*. Instead of debunking iconic figures, he is celebrating the non-eminent, the tangential; writing what Woolf called the 'Lives of the Obscure'.[16] Marginality and hybridity indeed seem constitutive for Forster, who appears as the chronicler of precisely the things he felt most ambivalent about: suburbia, intellectualism, modernism, liberalism, sexuality, imperialism, Englishness. Each book shows life thwarted by desires that disturb conventional society: desires for truth and personal relationships; for illicit sexualities; or for mysticism.

For, third, as we have seen, all three subjects are thwarted mystics: Dickinson in metaphysics; the Maharajah in religion; Marianne in good works and preservation of the family. And all three books, as they enact a metaphysical engagement with the dead, find their own form of mysticism: a mystical attitude to both character and death, and to what remains of the dead for the living. Their mystical endings might seem susceptible of a Marxist demystification, as being the last gasp of bourgeois individualism, asserting a transcendental uniqueness of the individual as a way of denying any social explanations. But as we have seen, Forster does want social explanations, and does give them in his novels as well as his biographies. It's just that he also wants there to be something else, something more than the sum of the circumstances.

Forster's sensibility may aspire toward the mystical, then, but he is no more confident of reaching absolute truth or experience or knowledge that way than was Dickinson; nor that we can reach transcendence through love, whether of God, or each other. But his life-writing *practice* expresses a hope that *people* can be known through love. Because they are complex, such knowledge will vary from person to person, and be partial, and be autobiographical. Or at least, as a novelist he knows that being in love makes people feel they are in touch with reality, in harmony with the universe.

Such a gesture seeks to unite biography and autobiography too, then; to transform the biographer towards the condition of his subject and bring to birth in him the creative impulse. That is to say, Forster's life-writings are not just autobiographies of the E. M. Forster who joined university debating societies, visited India, or inherited a legacy, the man who people found timid, modest, charming, amusing. They are autobiographies of that deeper personality that loved, and whose loves stirred him to create.

Notes

1. P. N. Furbank, *E. M. Forster: A Life* (2 vols., London: Secker and Warburg, 1977, 1978), vol. II, p. 301. Hereafter referred to as either 'Furbank I' or 'Furbank II' with citations incorporated into the main body of the text.
2. Mary Lago, *E. M. Forster: A Literary Life* (Basingstoke and London: Macmillan, 1995), p. 34.
3. Furbank I, p. 119. Most sexologists before Freud and Havelock Ellis saw homosexuality as not merely a physical but also a social and moral abnormality. Rickie's half-brother Stephen Wonham's illegitimacy could thus be seen as complementing Rickie's disability, so that together they possess all the stigmata of deviance.
4. Furbank II, pp. 36, 40. See also Lago, *E. M. Forster*, p. 89.
5. Letter to Malcolm Darling, 18 July 1928; quoted Lago, *E. M. Forster*, p. 97.
6. Forster to Masood, 27 Sept. 1922, quoted Furbank II, p. 106.
7. Lago, *E. M. Forster*, p. xi.
8. Letter to Dickinson, 26 Feb. 1932: *Commonplace Book*, ed. Philip Gardner (London: Scolar Press, 1985), p. 92.
9. Furbank II, pp. 192–4. Letter to Woolf, 6 June 1935: quoted Furbank II, p. 193.
10. *Commonplace Book*, p. 101.
11. Woolf, 'The New Biography' (1927), *Essays of Virginia Woolf*, ed. Andrew McNeillie, vol. IV (London: Hogarth Press, 1994), pp. 473–80.
12. Forster to Malcolm Darling, 15 September 1924: *Selected Letters of E. M. Forster*, ed. Mary Lago and P. N. Furbank, vol. II (London: Collins, 1985), pp. 63–4.
13. Woolf, *Roger Fry: A Biography*, ed. Diane F. Gillespie (1940; Oxford: Blackwell for the Shakespeare Head Press, 1995), p. 194.

14. Letter to Isherwood, 26 August 1945: quoted Furbank II, p. 259.
15. See for example Laura Marcus, 'The Newness of the "New Biography"', in *Mapping Lives: The Uses of Biography*, ed. Peter France (Oxford: Oxford University Press, 2002), pp. 193–218. And Max Saunders, 'Biography and Autobiography', in *The Cambridge History of Twentieth-Century English Literature*, ed. Laura Marcus and Peter Nicholls (Cambridge University Press, 2004), pp. 286–303.
16. 'The Lives of the Obscure', in *The Essays of Virginia Woolf*, ed. Andrew McNeillie, vol. IV (London: Hogarth Press, 1994), pp. 118–45.

2

DAVID MEDALIE

Bloomsbury and other values

Reputation

'I am so saturated in the writing . . . of E. M. Forster that I find it hard to look on either the works or the author behind them objectively.'[1]

'the effect of knowing Forster was that he became a kind of supplementary conscience tacked on to my own.'[2]

Comments such as these suggest how, for some of Forster's admirers, his popularity and the widespread view of him as an avuncular, yet morally provocative 'grand old man of letters'[3] have made it almost impossible for them to respond dispassionately to his work and, indeed, to separate the man from his writing. One of the main reasons for this, for the fact that Forster's status as a maker of literature is so closely intertwined with his broader cultural currency, is that his work has been seen as a repository of *value*. It is not a coincidence that the rather old-fashioned word 'sage' has often been used to describe him: he was 'the great liberal sage of the interwar and postwar periods'.[4] For his admirers, he embodied qualities that seemed especially desirable to those who had been through one or even two world wars: a firmly secular wisdom, anti-collectivist, rational, wry, stoical and wistful, saddened (but not overwhelmed) by the inevitability of compromise and the failure of ideals, not lacking in conviction, but refusing to be chauvinist.

A good example of the cluster of associated virtues which customarily attach themselves to Forster and his work may be found in a tribute by Malcolm Bradbury which was written in the 1960s, towards the end of Forster's life:

There are major writers whose work seems to us important as a contribution to the distinctive powers and dimensions of art; there are others whose work represents almost a personal appeal to value, and who therefore live – for certain of their readers, at least – with a singular force. There have not been many English novelists of our own time who have established with us the second function, but E. M. Forster is certainly one of them. He has served as an embodiment of the virtues he writes about; he has shown us their function and their destiny; he has left, for other writers and other men, a workable inheritance.[5]

This encapsulates the kind of thinking which has built and supported Forster's reputation. Most telling of all is the claim that his significance cannot be limited to the 'distinctive powers and dimensions of art': such categories will suffice where other 'major writers' are concerned, but are too narrow to accommodate one 'whose work represents almost a personal appeal to value'. Other writers, it seems, provide art; Forster provides *value*. Also revealing is the familiar inclination to merge the man and his work: he has 'served as an embodiment of the virtues he writes about'. Another common notion expressed in this tribute is the idea that Forster's readers are more than mere readers: they are heirs to whom a 'workable inheritance' has been bequeathed. A reader who is also an heir is one who is likely to feel a keen sense of obligation towards the writer who has provided the largesse. Such a reader will find it difficult to respond disinterestedly to the source of the benefaction, to set indebtedness aside, to disentangle the work from the associated ethical imperatives which it is seen to bear with it.

There is no need, of course, to begrudge Forster his admirers or his admirers the Forster they have construed. Where it becomes a problem, however, is when the reputation stands between the reader and the work, resulting in misreadings and missed readings, mistaken emphases and lost opportunities to value the work for what it *really* provides, rather than what it is desirable to impute to it. Forster criticism abounds in examples of all of these. The determination to see him as the secular sage, keeping his head and resolutely espousing reason, clarity, individuality, and liberal-humanism when all about him others were losing theirs and becoming fanatical, right-wing, muddled, and obscurantist, has come at a cost. It has, for example, prevented a full recognition of the extent to which a great deal of Forster's work offers a vigorous critique of contemporary liberalism and humanism; of the beleaguered status of liberals and humanists (and their dismaying inefficacy) in much of his fiction; of the importance of his preoccupation with the 'unseen'; of the elegiac elements in his writing and their significance; and – perhaps the most striking oversight of all – of the modernist elements in his later fiction. This is not to suggest that Forster's work does not engage with the question of value or offer values. The modernists were preoccupied with the problem of morality and the intricacy (sometimes the impossibility) of moral choices, but their stance was not amoral. If one looks past the dutiful gratitude of reader-heirs, then one is left with the crucial question: what values *does* his work offer?

In seeking an answer, it is necessary, from the outset, to distinguish between the fiction and the non-fiction. Forster's work in both areas is so well known that there has been a tendency to move between the two, using the one to shed light upon the other, as though this were entirely unproblematic. However, the fiction belongs, in the main, to an earlier period and engages with a different set of contexts: Forster produced no major work of fiction after 1924, when *A Passage to India* was published, whereas his best-known essays were written in the 1930s and 1940s. The fact that fiction and criticism employ different modes of writing should also be considered. The claim that the writing of fiction is an entirely different activity from the writing of criticism may be disputed; what is revealing, however, is that Forster believed strongly that it was – and his views have bearing upon the value that he attached to the two kinds of writing for which he became so well known, and the stance that he assumed in relation to his work as a critic.

In his essay 'The *Raison d'Être* of Criticism', he discusses chiefly the kind of criticism that appraises works of art rather than social criticism; nevertheless, the distinction he makes between what he calls 'creation' and 'criticism' has a wider significance. He considers whether there may be 'spiritual parity' (*TCD*, p. 110) between these two activities and concludes that the 'critical state . . . is grotesquely remote from the state responsible for the works it affects to expound' (*TCD*, p. 112). The essay reveals that Forster has what is essentially a Romantic idea of the process of creation; the work of art emerges from the subconscious, must be allowed to retain the mystery which lies at its heart – even to its creator – and is sorely damaged if the process of explication is too harsh or intrusive. It is 'a Sphinx who dies as soon as her riddles are answered' (*TCD*, p. 114). It does not engage in the same kind of way with the sphere of 'worldly knowledge' (*TCD*, p. 111) as do other kinds of discourse. For Forster, that is the source of its superiority; criticism of any kind will therefore always be a lesser, an inferior activity.

This accounts, in part, for the distinctly Forsterian mixture of conviction and misgiving, boldness and hesitation, which characterises the criticism. On the one hand, this blend of assertion and diffidence proceeds, as the discussion which follows will indicate, from a perception that the values that are being upheld are beleaguered, even anachronistic, yet indispensable if the malefactions of history are to be withstood; on the other, it is related to Forster's suspicion of the very activity that he is engaged in as a critic. In *Aspects of the Novel*, he laments the fact that '[m]an cannot be at the same time impressive and truthful'.[6] Whatever else this cryptic comment means, it does, presumably, provide an intimation of his suspicion of demagoguery and complacent language. The author of *Aspects of the Novel*, one of the most influential works of literary criticism of the twentieth century, and of some of the most cogent social criticism of the early and mid-century, was deeply sceptical of, if not antipathetic to, his own practice as a critic. Beneath the often strikingly declamatory tone of the non-fiction lies the hesitancy of the agnostic, participating reluctantly in the forms, the ceremony of criticism, yet filled with doubt as to the value of the rite and deeply suspicious of the act of faith towards which it is intended to lead.

Bloomsbury

The Bloomsbury Group was a set of intellectuals and artists, admired by some for being disciples of beauty, love, and friendship, derided by others who saw its members as elitist aesthetes, making a religion of artiness and their own convoluted relationships. They were 'worshipped by some and abominated by others'.[7] Whether one esteems them for exemplifying a refreshingly emancipated, un-Victorian commitment to interpersonal relationships, or criticises them for withdrawing from the world of wider obligations into the small cosiness of a coterie, the fact remains that friendship was central to their creed. It was friendship, rather than a single dogma to which everyone ascribed, that united the members of the group. Their conception of themselves and their activities was energetically polemical: they presented themselves as at war with Victorianism and stultifying conventionality, as daringly modern and iconoclastic.

The group had its beginnings in Cambridge at the turn of the century. Several of the male members of what later became the Bloomsbury Group belonged to a secret society at Cambridge University known as the Cambridge Apostles or the 'Conversazione Society' (Forster was elected in 1901). The Apostles debated questions of religion, morality, ethical conduct, and art in an atmosphere marked by candour and freedom from intellectual constraints. Several years later, some of the Apostles, but now with the important addition of two influential women, Virginia Woolf and her sister Vanessa Bell, formed what has come to be known as the Bloomsbury Group.

The Apostles discussed ideas drawn from turn-of the-century philosophy and, in particular, the work of the Cambridge philosopher G. E. Moore, who 'was unquestionably the most important philosopher and Apostle for the Group'.[8] Decades later, in an address entitled 'How I Lost My Faith', Forster referred to the influence of Moore, saying that he 'did not receive Moore's influence direct' and that he 'never read *Principia Ethica*' (*PT*, p. 313); but he also emphasised the extent to which Moore's ideas were central to the intellectual milieu in which he moved and the part they played in his intellectual awakening at Cambridge.

Moore's *Principia Ethica* (1903) is a work of moral philosophy, which seeks to identify and define the Good, which, for Moore, is constituted by the pursuits and states of consciousness which are most likely to enrich the life of the individual. One of the chief concerns, therefore, of *Principia Ethica* is the question of value. In his attempt to separate what is worthwhile from that which is not, Moore is concerned with what he calls judgements of 'intrinsic value', which are characterised by the fact that they 'are always true'.[9] His quest, as this definition of 'intrinsic value' suggests, is for the Good as expressed in absolute terms; the criterion for 'intrinsic value' is that things must be good even when existing 'in absolute isolation'.[10]

The Good, as Moore sees it, arises from and is defined by two phenomena, neither of which proceeds from the dictates of conventional morality, and both of which are firmly secular, this-earthly, and non-Idealist: 'By far the most valuable things, which we know or can imagine, are certain states of consciousness, which may be roughly described as the pleasures of human intercourse and the enjoyment of beautiful objects'.[11] The claims which he makes on behalf of these 'valuable things' are considerable, for he sees them as forming 'the rational ultimate end of human action and the sole criterion of social progress'.[12] Seen in this light, the 'pleasures of human intercourse' and 'the enjoyment of beautiful objects' are enlarged in significance to the point where they are far more than those pleasures which enrich the individual life and give it meaning: the social fabric itself is subordinated to their attainment.

Forster was associated with Bloomsbury, but he was not a central figure: according to David Garnett, 'Morgan Forster was on the periphery rather than at the heart of this circle'.[13] Joseph Bristow uses words like 'marginality' and 'ambivalence'[14] to describe Forster's place within the Cambridge Apostles and Bloomsbury and his attitude towards both groupings. This peripheral or ambivalent relationship is reflected in his work too. The values enunciated in his fiction and criticism have frequently been regarded as deriving to a great extent from the influence of Bloomsbury and his writings have been read as an uncomplicated elaboration of what the Group as a whole espoused. The situation is, however, a great deal more complex than this interpretation suggests. For a start, there are great differences within the Bloomsbury Group itself and it is problematic to generalise in this way. Art and what came to be known as 'personal relations' certainly did preoccupy the members of the Group, Forster included, but more often, in his case, as a starting-point than as a destination. In addition, his relationship with Bloomsbury was not clear-cut and his work, the fiction in particular, is much more profitably read as an exploration, even a critique, of Bloomsbury values than as an exposition of them.

It was not only Moore who linked art and appropriate conduct: Goldsworthy Lowes Dickinson, who influenced Forster greatly, also stressed the importance of this connection. In *The Greek View of Life*, he wrote that '[t]he key to the art of the Greeks, as well as to their ethics, is the identification of the beautiful and the good'.[15] Ancient Greece may have been conducive to such a happy identification; it was more than apparent to Forster that the twentieth century was not. His unremitting preoccupation with 'connection' arises from a keen sense – shared by other modernist writers – that the conditions of modernity provoke fragmentation and the absence of social cohesion. It is against this background, intensified by a perception that 'connection' is less likely than ever to prevail, that he investigates the value of art and 'personal relations'.

There can be no doubt that Forster believed fervently in the value of art, but his was always a qualified enthusiasm, as the tendentiously titled essay 'Art for Art's Sake' demonstrates: while affirming the importance of art, he subverts the most fervent and confident expression of its superiority as suggested by the Aestheticist creed which the title recalls. He does so by rejecting the kind of attitude which esteems art for its disassociation from the everyday world: '[m]any things, besides art, matter . . . Man lives, and ought to live, in a complex world, full of conflicting claims, and if we simplified them down into the aesthetic he would be sterilized' (*TCD*, p. 87). Similarly, he never ceased to stress the value and importance of 'personal relations', but here too he was deeply suspicious of overarching claims, warning, in 'A Note on the Way', that, particularly in times of crisis, '[a]rt is not enough, any more than love is enough' (*AH*, p. 70).

It is significant that few of the ambitions fuelled by the 'personal relations' ethos are fulfilled in Forster's fiction: the relationships between Lucy and George in *A Room with a View*, Maurice and Alec in *Maurice*, and Aziz and Mrs Moore in *A Passage to India* are among the few exceptions. For the most part, however, these desires are thwarted (*Where Angels Fear to Tread*, *The Longest Journey*, *Howards End*, and *A Passage to India* all contain examples of this) and, especially in the latter two novels, the quest itself is shown to have catastrophic repercussions for some of the characters. The difficulties arise always when the pursuit fails to take account of the 'complex world, full of conflicting claims' which, Forster suggests, the triumphantly circular logic of a creed such as 'Art for Art's Sake' fails to accommodate. That is why good intentions are so frequently shown to have negative consequences in his fiction: the implication is that it is not sufficient for these benevolent impulses to be worthwhile in themselves, they need also to be mediated in relation to contingency. This is what lies behind the satirical treatment of

Adela Quested in *A Passage to India*. She is clearly identified as a product of a Bloomsbury-type world – as a Bloomsbury ideologue, in fact – and seeks, in an environment which is conspicuously resistant to her designs, to implement her Bloomsbury values. The rebuff that she receives is a dramatisation of the perception that it is profoundly dangerous to attempt to transpose values without a careful consideration of the contexts in which they are to be applied.

What this suggests is that the most significant difference between Forster's position and Moore's is that Forster contextualises the quest for the Good by presenting it always in relation to the imperfections of society and a world which is drifting ever further from the ideal conditions Dickinson discerns in ancient Greece. He does not consider them, as Moore insisted one should, in absolute or deracinated terms. It is telling that, when Forster speaks of the role Moore's ideas played in his intellectual and spiritual transformation at Cambridge, he refers to 'the general spirit of questioning that is associated with the name of G. E. Moore' (*PT*, p. 313); for him, Moore's significance lies in the questions that he asks or provokes, rather than the answers he provides; and it is as part of an enquiry into the nature of value, not as a set of solutions, that the Moorean doctrines make their appearance in his writings.

Belief

One of the most tenacious aspects of Forster's popularity has been the widespread perception of him as a doughty spokesman for and zealous custodian of the liberal tradition: 'the hero of liberal values in liberalism's dark time'.[16] When 'the menace to freedom' (*TCD*, p. 9) which he warned of in the 1930s became all too plain, he was revered as one who sought, as he put it in 'What I Believe', to 'keep open a few breathing-holes for the human spirit' (*TCD*, p. 69). This reputation rests, to a great extent, on the essays in which, confronted by the rise and increasing threat of Nazism, and, later, the possibility that Germany and its allies could win the war, he rose to the defence of everything which a totalitarian state would inevitably seek to extinguish. He became a latter-day prophet, warning, admonishing, and prophesying.

However, Forster's most substantial inquiry into the values of liberalism and humanism took place much earlier. It is in his novels and short stories, written years before he began to respond with such prescient urgency to the dangers emanating from the Continent, that he explores most fully what he perceives as the potentialities and shortcomings of early twentieth-century liberalism and humanism. In *Howards End*, in particular, he considers their efficacy within the often deleterious conditions of modernity. Unlike many of his critics, Forster does not present liberalism and humanism in universalist or transhistorical terms; instead, he considers their value in relation to specific socio-historical conditions.

Howards End (1910) is a late-Edwardian response to what came to be known as the New Liberalism. This was a sustained attempt on the part of a number of Liberal ideologues and strategists (including L. T. Hobhouse and J. A. Hobson) to address the waning fortunes of contemporary political liberalism. One of the ways in which they sought to reinvigorate Liberal policy was by placing greater emphasis on the social aspects of identity and on social responsibility; arising from this was the concept of an organic society, which was central to the New Liberal ideology. In *Howards End*, Forster scrutinises the promise of an organic society (which is, of course, also a form of 'connection'). He does so by considering the pragmatic value of the New Liberal agenda within a society which he represents as increasingly fragmented and divisive.

The investigation of humanism in the novel includes an enquiry into the value and efficacy of Culture. The Arnoldian echoes in *Howards End* recall Matthew Arnold's belief that Culture could be an elevating and democratising social force. In response to this, the novel considers whether Culture, particularly when it is handed down from the past to the present, does indeed further connection and bring people together, or whether it entrenches social disparities and privilege, acting thus as an exclusionary force; whether, in other words, Culture is the solution or part of the crisis.[17]

Two decades later, the crisis was of a very different sort. As early as 1934, in 'A Note on the Way', Forster made it clear that what loomed was 'perhaps the roughest time that has ever been', in which nothing less than 'the collapse of all civilization' was a very real possibility (*AH*, p. 69). In seeking the appropriate weapons to withstand this cataclysm, he returned to the values he had been preoccupied with during the Edwardian period, the years of the Great War and the 1920s. These included liberal-humanism, but the status of political liberalism, the hopes of the New Liberalism and such ambitions as the 'organic society' were not now his chief concern. The situation in the 1930s had simplified itself into a stark contrast between, on the one hand, the appeal of a liberal society, loosely conceived, and, on the other, the threat of the most illiberal kind of society: a totalitarian state.

Forster returned, also, in these essays to 'personal relations' and art, but now changed circumstances made it easier for them to become much more wide-ranging in their application and political possibilities:

the rise of totalitarianisms in Europe brought a new kind of challenge. The cultivation of personal relationships, which could sometimes seem to be a form of weakness in the face of large political threats, was then found to nurture, in someone who took it as seriously as [Forster] did, a core of individual resistance, coupled with a welcome resilience of critical intelligence.[18]

The growing crisis in Europe brought the values that Bloomsbury had embraced to the fore in Forster's writing in a way that had never been possible for him during the Group's heyday. He had been a Bloomsbury agnostic when the religion of Bloomsbury had been so seductive; now, ironically, changed circumstances turned him into its most fervent polemicist, even if it was not always apparent that what he was espousing were values associated with the set whom it had been so tempting to deride as arty and inconsequential.

The Nazi danger made the liberty of individuals and the liberty of groups, even nations, become intertwined in a way that would have been unthinkable in Forster's Edwardian writings. David Garnett, describing the way in which Forster absorbed at Cambridge the philosophical ideas which were afterwards taken up by the Bloomsbury Group, explains that '[a]rtists, in which term I include imaginative writers, reflect a climate of opinion rather than devote themselves to ethical propaganda'.[19] This distinction may be usefully applied to the different ways in which, in different contexts, Forster makes use of liberal-humanist and Bloomsbury values: in his fiction, particularly the later novels, they function as the equivalent of a 'climate of opinion', a set of beliefs which have gained in certain quarters a moral currency, but which Forster interrogates in relation to the exigencies of specific social and political problems – class divisions, for instance, in *Howards End* and imperialism in *A Passage to India*. However, in the essays and broadcasts which deal with the rise of Nazism and the threat it poses, his attitude towards them resembles much more closely what Garnett calls 'ethical propaganda'. Many of the subtleties of the debate about liberalism and humanism in the early twentieth century and of the Bloomsbury ethos were lost, for when the enemy's designs are explicit and crass, the niceties of a complex set of values tend to fall away.

One of the recurring questions in Forster's fiction, most notably in *Howards End* and *A Passage to India*, is whether love, especially as expressed in the 'personal relations' doctrine, may be converted into a socially dynamic force. In these essays, even though Forster memorably grants democracy a mere two cheers in 'What I Believe' because '[o]nly Love the Beloved Republic deserves [three]' (*TCD*, p. 67), he makes what is for him an unprecedentedly strenuous effort to associate love with progressive social systems and to consider what love may offer within the context of social and political discourse:

> Man has another wish, besides the wish to be free, and that is the wish to love, and perhaps something may be born from the union of the two . . . Love, after a dreadful period of inflation, is perhaps coming back to its proper level and may steady civilization; up-to-date social workers believe in it . . . The desire to devote oneself to another person or persons seems to be as innate as the desire for personal liberty. If the two desires could combine, the menace to freedom from within, the fundamental menace, might disappear, and the political evils now filling all the foreground of our lives would be deprived of the poison which nourishes them. (*TCD*, pp. 10–11)

This excerpt from 'The Menace to Freedom', published in 1935, is revealing in a number of ways. For a start, it has little difficulty in accomplishing what Forster's fiction (and, indeed, modernist literature more generally) found so difficult: it moves smoothly between, on the one hand, claims about individuals and interpersonal relationships and, on the other, the wider socio-political environment – in particular, the looming crisis which Forster calls 'the political evils now filling all the foreground of our lives'. It also establishes a connection which is fundamental in Forster's best-known essays about society, politics, and civil liberty: the link between freedom and love, 'the wish to be free' and 'the wish to love', between 'the desire for personal liberty' and the 'desire to devote oneself to another person or persons'. The one, Forster suggests repeatedly, is not possible without the other. In his essay 'Tolerance', he cautions that 'love in public affairs does not work' (*TCD*, p. 44) and in 'What I Believe' he laments the fact that 'no device has been found by which . . . private decencies can be transmitted to public affairs' (*TCD*, p. 71). Nonetheless, the advent of a crisis of vast proportions makes it easier for him than it was before to elevate 'personal relations' and 'love' (albeit inconsistently and not without qualms) to a position where social freedom itself is predicated upon them; and, inversely and perhaps more controversially, to suggest that all socio-political questions and solutions be recast in terms of love, the individual and relations between individuals.

It is in this light that Forster's best-known essay should be read. Published in 1939, the year that war broke out, 'What I Believe' is widely regarded as one of the most famous essays of the twentieth century. It has been admired by many as a bold denunciation of totalitarianism, a courageous defence of reason, civilisation, secular morality, and the individual. It has also provoked great controversy, especially Forster's much-quoted claim that 'I hate the idea of causes, and if I had to choose between betraying my country and betraying my friend, I hope I should have the guts to betray my country' (*TCD*, p. 66).

This assertion has been deprecated as subversive, unpatriotic, and disloyal, and as an extreme, even fanatical expression of the cult of 'personal relations' and the determination always to place the individual first, no matter what the cost to the group.

The interpretation which does the greatest justice to 'What I Believe' lies somewhere between the reading which merely esteems its boldness and the one which focuses only on what it deems a deplorable disloyalty. It is important to look at the essay as a whole, for it is easy to isolate certain sentences and phrases and, in taking them out of context, to find justification for either response: this is partly what has given Forster's comment about the choice between betraying his country and betraying his friend its notoriety. Forster was certainly not unpatriotic, but he despised anything that smacked of jingoism. The only approach to patriotism which he could accept was the one he believed was exemplified by George Orwell: '[a]ll nations are odious but some are less odious than others, and by this stony, unlovely path [Orwell] reaches patriotism. To some of us, this seems the cleanest way to reach it' (*TCD*, p. 60). Here, as in other instances, the implication is that ideological preferences should never be too glibly maintained: avowal and disavowal should be yoked together and values such as patriotism should be reached only by a 'stony, unlovely path'.

The best clue as to how 'What I Believe' should be read lies in its tone. The voice that we hear in the essay, despite the declamatory stance which the title seems to promise, is not one of secure conviction. There are assertions made within the course of the argument which are self-assured, emphatic, even triumphant; but the general tone is subdued and the essay seems constantly in retreat from its own promise of boldness. Kenneth Graham has described Forster as 'intrinsically, from first to last, an ironist',[20] and it is the use of irony (and self-irony) in 'What I Believe' which has often been overlooked. So, too, is the fact that paradox is one of the chief rhetorical devices used in this essay: the very first sentence – 'I do not believe in Belief' (*TCD*, p. 65) – is, after all, an ostentatiously paradoxical statement. A paradox has an instability at its heart. Its use implies that the views and beliefs put forward, no matter how fervently they are propounded, are always in danger of collapsing in on themselves, of concealing slyly a disarming contradiction.

The hesitating or withdrawing tone also has an ideological motivation, related to a quality which Forster returns to frequently in these essays and which he believes to be the sine qua non of a civilised society: tolerance. Goethe, he says in one of his anti-Nazi broadcasts, is the 'arch-enemy' of the Nazis, for 'Goethe believed in toleration' (*TCD*, p. 37). Even his campaign against censorship is expressed in terms of tolerance and intolerance:

in 'Mr D. H. Lawrence and Lord Brentford', published in 1930, he concludes his condemnation of 'suppression' and his plea for a more enlightened censorship policy by urging his readers to listen to 'the dull drone of tolerance, tolerance, tolerance'. Tolerance is 'the principle which causes society the minimum of damage, because it admits that the people who constitute society are different' (*PT*, p. 98). In the essay entitled 'Tolerance', written during the war, Forster associates lack of tolerance with uncompromising pronouncements: 'I have lost all faith in positive militant ideals; they can so seldom be carried out without thousands of human beings getting maimed or imprisoned. Phrases like "I will purge this nation", "I will clean up this city", terrify and disgust me' (*TCD*, p. 45). From this perspective, the avoidance or subversion of declamatory speech and the tendency to treat even one's dearest beliefs with a measure of irony become a way of advancing an ideological position that is not ironclad, that makes a space for dialogue and dissent.

The tone of 'What I Believe' has another implication: the hesitations do not signify that the values being espoused have no merit in themselves, but they do suggest Forster's awareness that he does not speak from a position of strength or centrality. His is the voice of someone who is only too aware of his own peripheral status. In many of the essays, he intimates that the values he holds dear are anachronistic or in danger of becoming so – one example is his much-quoted comment in 'The Challenge of Our Time' that he belongs to 'the fag-end of Victorian liberalism' (*TCD*, p. 54). This comes through in 'What I Believe', too, where Forster suggests that the difficulty he experiences in making the values he holds dear prevail lies in part in the recognition that the modern world is inimical to them and that, consequently, they are likely to be seen as quaint and outmoded. After the assertive tone of the title, excerpts such as the following seem bathetic:

> And one can, at all events, show one's little light here, one's own poor little trembling flame, with the knowledge that it is not the only light that is shining in the darkness, and not the only one which the darkness does not comprehend. Personal relations are despised today. They are regarded as bourgeois luxuries, as products of a time of fair weather which is now past, and we are urged to get rid of them, and to dedicate ourselves to some movement or cause instead.
>
> (*TCD*, p. 66)

It is clear from this that Forster sees the 'personal relations' creed, central to his own values and those of Bloomsbury, as painfully beleaguered. Fascism, which was then growing so alarmingly in Europe, is merely the worst and most blatant expression of contempt for individualism and 'personal relations', but the intolerance is more widespread and often more insidious. As is so often the case in these essays, Forster is here the spokesman for a system of belief which has not lost its intrinsic worth, but which is hampered by its failure to prevail as an instrument of social change. The controversial sentences in which Forster expresses a preference for betraying his country rather than his friend come immediately after this. In this context they read less like the exultant voice of a 'personal relations' fundamentalist than as the lament of an elegist, a defiant yet rueful exponent of a 'despised' creed. The very choice that they enunciate, after the hope that 'personal relations' could be a mechanism for social transformation, is stark, polarising, and implacable. These are words of failure, not of triumph. They speak more of despair than of an overweening Bloomsbury sensibility. In such distressing times, however, despair may be the most appropriate response. In 'The Long Run', a review of Christopher Caudwell's *Studies in a Dying Culture*, Forster contends that 'there is nothing disgraceful in despair. In 1938–9 the more despair a man can take on board without sinking the more completely is he alive' (*PT*, p. 295).

The values that one advances from the midst of such despair may be endowed with an authority that no blithe confidence could hope to emulate. 'Tolerance, good temper and sympathy' are thus, paradoxically, empowered when they seem most enfeebled and in danger of being stamped out – when their action 'is no stronger than a flower, battered beneath a military jackboot' (*TCD*, p. 65). The shared threat makes the ideologies which resist it more tolerant of each other's shortcomings: '[t]he above are the reflections of an individualist and a liberal who has found liberalism crumbling beneath him and at first felt ashamed. Then, looking around, he decided there was no special reason for shame, since other people, whatever they felt, were equally insecure' (*TCD*, pp. 72–3). Monolithic systems such as totalitarianism diminish through force the value of dissenting creeds, but the danger of annihilation also makes one cherish all the more what is under threat:

> So this is what I feel about force and violence. It is, alas! the ultimate reality on this earth, but it does not always get to the front. Some people call its absences 'decadence'; I call them 'civilization' and find in such interludes the chief justification for the human experiment. (*TCD*, p. 68)

It is characteristic that Forster relegates civilisation to 'interludes' occurring between the remorseless onrush of 'force and violence'. His conception of history and its unfolding is essentially a gloomy one: he lacks the optimism which he discerns in H. G. Wells, of whom he writes, in a review of Wells's *The Outline of History*, that 'his heart is Victorian, with a quite Tennysonian trust in the To-be. To him evolution is progress' (*PT*, p. 61). The review was published in 1920, and already Forster had little faith in this teleological conception of history. In the years that followed, his despair deepened.

In contrast to the view attributed to Wells, Forster offers the following conception of history: '[m]en want to alter this planet, yet also believe that it is not worth altering and that behind it is something unalterable, and their perfect historian will be he who enters with equal sympathy into these contradictory desires' (*PT*, p. 62). History, in other words, is to be understood in terms of contradiction and dialectic. It cannot be made compatible with the shapes which people wish to impose upon it. Affirmation and negation, promise and withdrawal – which feature so prominently in Forster's fiction – are present, too, in his understanding of how we inhabit history, of how it acts upon us and of the opportunities which we have for intervening in its unfolding. His famous proclamations and equally famous ironies, his activism and his cynicism, should be interpreted within the context of this conception and of his dystopian view of the present, which abounds in 'dangers whose outcome we cannot foresee' (*TCD*, p. 52).

The notion that civilisation may exist only in the 'interludes' between force and violence conveys once more the extent to which Forster places himself and the values he represents on the edge or in the interstices of history. From that position he is able to see matters differently and, frequently, more clearly. He may not have been the kind of sage that some wished him to be, but his essays are nevertheless filled with examples of his prescience. In 'Jew–Consciousness', for instance, he deprecates the rise in anti-Semitism and concludes with a warning that those who share his alarm must 'dig in [their] heels, and prevent silliness from sliding into insanity' (*TCD*, p. 14). The essay was published in 1939.

If, as suggested earlier, the values imputed to Forster have more to do with what generations of readers have wanted or needed him to be, rather than what he is, then what values should one associate with him? They are those of someone for whom a mixture of assertion and bathos, conviction and irony best expressed the 'contradictory desires' (*PT*, p. 62) of modernity. Forster demonstrates the cogency of the peripheral vision, of the circumspect and multivalent word in a time of demagoguery. He speaks as one who – to use his own description of a sentence by the Alexandrian writer C. P. Cavafy – 'stands at an angle to the universe'.[21] Stephen Spender described him as 'one of the most comforting of modern writers, and at the same time one of the most uncomfortable'.[22] Perhaps there has been too much of the comforting Forster and too little of the discomforting one. Veneration has made him too tame and the time is now ripe to revere him less but to listen to him all the more intently.

Notes

1. Elizabeth Bowen, 'A Passage to E. M. Forster' in *Aspects of E. M. Forster*, ed. Oliver Stallybrass (London: Edward Arnold, 1969), pp. 1–12. Quote from p. 12.
2. Stephen Spender quoted in Nicola Beauman, *Morgan: A Biography of E. M. Forster* (London: Hodder and Stoughton, 1993), p. 363.
3. P. N. Furbank, *E. M. Forster: A Life* (2 vols., Oxford: Oxford University Press, 1979), vol. II, p. 288.
4. Christopher Gillie, *A Preface to Forster* (Harlow: Longman, 1983), p. 38.
5. Malcolm Bradbury, 'Two Passages to India: Forster as Victorian and Modern', in *Aspects of E. M. Forster*, ed. Oliver Stallybrass, pp. 123–42. Quote from p. 123.
6. E. M. Forster, *Aspects of the Novel*, ed. Oliver Stallybrass (Harmondsworth: Penguin, 1976), p. 133.
7. David Garnett, 'Forster and Bloomsbury', in *Aspects of E. M. Forster*, ed. Stallybrass, pp. 29–35. Quote from p. 30.
8. S. P. Rosenbaum, *Victorian Bloomsbury: The Early Literary History of the Bloomsbury Group*, vol. I (Basingstoke and London: Macmillan, 1987), p. 214.
9. G. E. Moore, *Principia Ethica* (London: Cambridge University Press, 1929), p. 166.
10. Ibid., p. 187.
11. Ibid., p. 188.
12. Ibid., p. 189.
13. Garnett, 'Forster and Bloomsbury', pp. 31–2.
14. Joseph Bristow, '*Fratrum Societati*: Forster's Apostolic Dedications', in *Queer Forster*, ed. Robert K. Martin and George Piggford (Chicago and London: University of Chicago Press, 1997), pp. 113–36. Quotes from pp. 116 and 117 respectively.
15. Goldsworthy Lowes Dickinson, *The Greek View of Life* (London: Methuen, 1904), p. 226.
16. Samuel Hynes, *The Auden Generation: Literature and Politics in England in the 1930s* (London: Pimlico, 1992), p. 303.
17. For a detailed discussion of Forster's liberalism and humanism, see David Medalie, *E. M. Forster's Modernism* (Basingstoke and New York: Palgrave, 2002), pp. 1–62.
18. John Beer, 'Introduction: The Elusive Forster', in *E. M. Forster: A Human Exploration: Centenary Essays*, ed. G. K. Das and John Beer (London and Basingstoke: Macmillan, 1979), pp. 1–10. Quote from p. 5.
19. Garnett, 'Forster and Bloomsbury', p. 30.
20. Kenneth Graham, *Indirections of the Novel: James, Conrad, and Forster* (Cambridge: Cambridge University Press, 1988), p. 10.
21. E. M. Forster, *Pharos and Pharillon* (London: Hogarth Press, 1961), p. 92.
22. Stephen Spender, *World Within World: The Autobiography of Stephen Spender* (London: Hamish Hamilton, 1951), p. 167.

3

PAUL PEPPIS

Forster and England

It is an opportune moment to consider Forster and England: the past few years have witnessed the publication of an important body of work in history, literary criticism, and cultural studies on Englishness during the late Victorian, Edwardian, and Georgian periods, when Forster came of age as an author.[1] Drawing on this work, a number of critics read *Howards End* as a 'condition of England' novel, a fictional expression of popular anxieties about rising poverty, imperial decline, and race degeneration.[2] Such analysts contend that *Howards End*, insistently focused on personal relations, also carries social and political implications. They interpret the novel as a national allegory in which interactions between various English types analyse England's unhealthy condition and project a better future. Other critics read *A Passage to India* as a dissenting imperial allegory, which assails the ills of Anglo-India and allegorises the impossibility of friendship between English and Indians under empire.[3] I argue similarly that most of Forster's literary works can be understood as national allegories that diagnose an ailing nation and offer literary cures for the malaise they anatomise. Thus while he frequently writes against Edwardian England, Forster is also something of a literary patriot.

Forster's national allegories function in two ways: as parables of Englishness enlivened and as fantasies of England reconciled. Some offer women and men suffering from the pathologies of middle-class Englishness a passage to nature, passion, and freedom. In *Where Angels Fear to Tread* (1905), *A Room with a View* (1908), and *A Passage to India* (1924), Forster's English abroad are confronted with individuals and events that shock them. His bravest and most sensitive characters react by embracing difference, discovering love, passion, and the hope of enduring happiness; his more timorous and close-minded characters fail or refuse to accept the lessons life offers them. These national allegories function parabolically: Forster dares English readers to learn from his characters' experiences, to refuse suburban repression and hypocrisy, and to embrace life and nature. Other Forster fictions prescribe cures more fantastic. The early short stories, first published between 1903–12 and collected in *The Celestial Omnibus* (1911) and *The Eternal Moment* (1928), present Forster's critique of Englishness through mythology and fantasy: a visit from Pan enlivens an English boy abroad ('The Story of a Panic' (1904)); a faun converts an English curate to paganism ('The Curate's Friend' (1907)); an Irish girl pursued by her domineering English husband disappears, dryad-like, into the trees ('The Other Kingdom' (1909)). Forster's novels generally refuse fantasy for realism. But a number of them (especially and not coincidentally those set entirely in England – *The Longest Journey* (1907), *Howards End* (1910), and *Maurice* (written 1913–14)) – conclude, often against significant odds and realist expectations, with the formation in idealised English places of unconventional but redemptive English families. These new national families redress England's maladies by connecting – in love, marriage, blood – different national types: suburbanites and farmers, intellectuals and clerks, gentlemen and gamekeepers. Offered as paradigms for a renewed England, Forster's cross-bred families embody the hope of a nation converted from urban 'progress' and capitalism, from suburban intolerance and repression, to rural decency, freedom, and truth. But because these novels are overwhelmingly realist in technique, their endings strike some as unconvincing, as if the deep-seated differences Forster so realistically elaborates between national types miraculously can be overcome through love or bridged by the comingling of different bloodlines. Yet even as his English novels conclude by affirming these pastoral idylls as social-political ideals, Forster questions them, acknowledging their fantastical status, authorising his most sceptical readers' doubts. This literary paradox exposes a political ambivalence that Forster's writings on England and the English never fully resolve.

That the plots of the English novels function therapeutically and their endings turn mythic and ambivalent focuses another paradox in Forster's treatment of England and Englishness that clarifies his literary liberalism – a topic of long-standing concern for critics – and its relations to British liberalism between 1906 and 1914.[4] On the one hand, the novels critique suburbia and the city, modernisation, and models of Englishness that authorise empire, confirming Forster's investments in an older, more individualistic and libertarian liberalism, rather than the statist and imperialist 'New Liberalism' of the British Government after 1906. On the other, Forster's English fictions idealise 'traditional' Englishness and locate the essence of England in the rural south, strategies compatible, as analysts of Englishness demonstrate, with a broader period project to relocate the essential English place, rehabilitate Englishness for the competitive realities of a new century, and to re-legitimate imperialism.

This paradox clarifies why Forester's narratives, keenly critical of Edwardian society, were easily adapted to the interests of Thatcherite England when filmed in the 1980s and early 1990s, becoming part of England's culture industry and cultural mythology. Unsurprisingly, England under Thatcher and Major (and America under Reagan and Bush père), responded powerfully to the films' idealisation of upper-class Englishness, an idealisation that domesticates the more critical and dissident aspects of Forster's vision. Analysis of Forster's literary treatments of England is therefore doubly productive: it illuminates his radicalism and the susceptibility of his England to political domestication and commercial co-optation. For Forster's potent critiques of suburban modernity and sincere celebrations of rural England also served key interests of the Edwardian urban and imperial establishment. The ideological process the films epitomise was initiated by the novels: the commodification of an idealised vision of a neo-feudal, rural England as the heart and soul of the nation, authorising Britain's rulers and the system of capitalist modernity they represent. Despite Forster's complicity with early-century efforts to reconstruct Englishness and relocate an authentic England, however, his national allegories imagine a nation notably illegitimate and unconventional. Forster's renderings of England position him alongside those who greeted the new century with concern, turning from the realities of urban modernity towards a mythic rural Englishness. But they also confirm him as one of the Edwardian period's greatest critics and analysts of England and Englishness.

The condition of Englishness

In Forster's works, England and its ailing condition are first approached through Englishwomen and men travelling abroad. As his early short stories and first novel render English tourists encountering people and places markedly different from their own, Forster begins articulating his characteristic critique of suburban, middle-class Englishness. These fictions analyse the repressed, close-minded, and timid English psyche. The typical plot portrays a conventional English person who encounters an unconventional male other, usually foreign or lower class, and is thereby transformed and enlivened, enabled to overcome to some extent the pathologies of Englishness and more fully accept passion, vitality, and difference.[5]

Forster's first published novel, *Where Angels Fear to Tread*, exemplifies the process. The opening chapters narrate recently widowed Lilia Herriton's attempt to escape from the repressive and close-minded society of suburban Sawston, epitomised by her in-laws. Forster makes readers sympathise with Lilia's rebellion even as he emphasises her naïveté, self-involvement, and arrogance. So while the novel mocks the prejudices, snobbery, and rigidity of the Sawston society she rejects, it exposes Lilia's errors and failings and renders the society of Monteriano, Italy, where she weds, as far from ideal. Eventually, Lilia realises that her Italian husband, the lively and passionate Gino Carella, is no prince charming, but a penniless and philandering dentist's son, and that Italy is not a dreamland of freedom and romance, but a nation as constraining as the one she fled. Lilia's pitiful fate – her suffering under Italy's repressive gender conventions and eventual death in childbirth – casts a sceptical light on the effort to escape Englishness, playing on popular English anxieties about intercourse with foreigners.

But if the first half of *Where Angels Fear to Tread* works as a parable about the dangers of an overly naïve attempt to escape nationality, the later chapters insist that encounters with otherness can be transfiguring, particularly if unplanned or violent. Forster emphasises the most terrible costs suburban Englishness exacts through the novel's tragic climax. Lilia's sister-in-law, Harriet Herriton, perhaps Forster's cruellest and most hilarious caricature of suburban Englishness, kidnaps Lilia's and Gino's son; later, in a carriage crash, the baby is killed. Forster's rendering of Harriet as an English harridan presents his critique of English normality at its most harsh: although she bears primary culpability for the death, she denies any guilt, returning quickly to her 'old self' (*WAFT*, p. 143). Some suburban Englanders are immune to any type of shock treatment, but Harriet's more sensitive and artistic brother, Philip, reacts differently, clarifying Forster's sense that violent contact with difference can shake some suburbanites out of complacency. Philip's education advances through a series of jolting events: Lilia's death; the kidnapping; the carriage accident that kills the infant and breaks Philip's arm; the climactic struggle between Philip and Gino (in which Caroline Abbott saves both men from further tragedy); and, finally, Miss Abbott's revelation that she loves not Philip (as he hopes), but Gino. Cumulatively, these shocks 'transfigure' Philip's perceptions of the novel's tragic events, Caroline, and himself, revealing their beauty and wonder (*WAFT*, p. 147). In rewarding Philip, Forster invites readers to consider him a better, healthier Englishman, touched by life and love. Philip's transfiguration refigures popular constructions of Englishness, which idealised conventional masculinity and identified the English with the masculine.[6] By promoting Philip, sensitive, artistic, imaginative, as an ideal Englishman, Forster resists the Englishness that idealises masculine insensitivity and aggression. This new paradigm of English manhood emphasises the dissenting aspects of Forster's allegories of Englishness.

Philip's transfiguration also has important implications for Forster's Edwardian readers. Like his English characters, Forster's English readers need to be shocked out of the complacencies and rigidities of (national) character. This awareness explains a recurrent motif in Forster's work that troubles critics: the unexpected occurrence of violence and death. Forster uses these tools of melodrama and unexpectedly shifts generic gears, swerving between comedy, romance, and tragedy, to maximise the likelihood of transforming readers. Ideally, such formal shocks will shake them into a more humble and humane Englishness. *Where Angels Fear to Tread* thus presents a therapeutic parable about the condition of Englishness, diagnosing a malady of nationality and offering its most responsive characters and readers possible cures: encounters – sometimes shocking – with difference.

The condition of England

Forster's diagnosis of modern Englishness also prepares readers for his analysis of modern England. His works anatomise a declining, unhealthy nation undergoing unprecedented historical transformation as rural life slips away under the relentless advance of modern 'civilisation', with its suburbs, motorcars, and apartment blocks. Suburbia and the city are literally taking over England's green and pleasant land, spreading repression, hypocrisy, and intolerance. These national vices lead Forster's Englishwomen and men away from the essence of their nation: the beauties and truths of nature, still alive, but under siege, in the downlands of the rural south. The 'undeveloped heart' of bourgeois Englishness is thus 'largely responsible' not only for 'the difficulties of Englishmen abroad', as Forster's 'Notes on the English Character' (1926) contends, but also for the difficulties of Englishmen at home (*AH*, p. 5). Just as *A Passage to India* condemns the middle-class arrogance and insensitivity fuelling British imperialism, Forster's English novels render suburbia and the city as alien colonies, conquering England's rural soul. This vision of internal colonisation by the forces of bourgeois modernity elaborates Forster's anti-imperialism: in his English novels, the heart of darkness lies not in Africa or India, but at home, where a battle is being fought between old England – the country, feudal social organisation, traditional values – and new England – suburbia, urbanism, empire.

Forster's second published and most autobiographical novel, *The Longest Journey*, exemplifies his anatomy of modern England and clarifies its conservative and mythologising ambitions. The first of Forster's novels set entirely in England, *The Longest Journey* maps the nation's ailing condition through three exemplary locales: Cambridge, a cloistered and fraternal community of homosocial privilege, near to nature and sympathetic to elite unconventionality; Sawston, Forster's quintessential English suburb of intolerance, selfishness, and cruelty, epitomised by the Machiavellian workings of

Sawston School; and Wiltshire, Forster's first extended portrayal of England's rural south, a place of natural beauty, mythic history, and human decency. (London appears only briefly, as the dark 'heart of the modern world' (*LJ*, p. 246), anticipating Forster's damning representation in *Howards End*.)

The Longest Journey at first seems a modern *Bildungsroman*, like Joyce's *A Portrait of the Artist as a Young Man* or Lawrence's *Sons and Lovers*, that records the journey of its protagonist, the Forster-like, Rickie Elliot, as he travels from the safety and happiness of Cambridge, through the degradation and misery of Sawston, to reconciliation and rehabilitation in Wiltshire. Typifying a tendency in Forster's English novels to naturalise character to place, Rickie's education is affected in each location by its quintessential inhabitant(s): in Cambridge, the brilliant but unconventional philosophy student, Stewart Ansell, son of a Jewish draper; in Sawston, the aggressively conventional schoolmaster Herbert Pembroke and his domineering sister Agnes (whom Rickie will misguidedly wed after the untimely death of her fiancé, the athletic bully Gerald Dawes); and, in Wiltshire, the coarse but vital natural philosopher Stephen Wonham, love child of an affair between Rickie's suburban mother and the Wiltshire farmer Robert. Forster leads readers to expect that Rickie will complete his education by reconciling with his illegitimate half-brother and embracing rural life and the Wiltshire countryside. But Forster unexpectedly derails the *Bildungsroman*: after Rickie resignedly drags the drunken Stephen off the tracks one night, he is run down by an oncoming train (a typical Forsterian symbol of modernity's inhumanity and violence).

Critics concentrate on Rickie's personal journey, especially his bloody fate, interpreting the novel finally as a sado-masochistic, mock-*Bildungsroman* which punishes its Forster-like protagonist for his failings.[7] Less attention is paid to how *The Longest Journey* works as a condition-of-England novel like *Howards End*, a national allegory of conflict, reconciliation, and regeneration. *The Longest Journey* diagnoses a national sickness in modern England, epitomised by the pathologies of Sawston and the Pembrokes – intolerance, selfishness, hypocrisy – and proposes as a cure a return to the values of brotherhood, honest labour, and natural morality that characterise the yeoman culture of Wiltshire. These ideals distinguish Wiltshire's native inhabitants: Mrs Elliot's lover Farmer Robert; their illegitimate son Stephen; and, in the final chapter, Stephen's wife and young daughter. Enabled by Stephen's realisation of familial responsibilities in response to Rickie's death – in this context a kind of national sacrifice – this new English family heals an ailing nation by reconciling class and regional differences (a pattern *Howards End* will repeat), embodying the hope for a better future that Stephen intuits in the novel's closing pages: 'Though he could not phrase it, he believed that he guided the future of our race, and that, century after century, his thoughts and his passions would triumph in England' (*LJ*, p. 289). Stephen's fantastic self-projection as guide of 'our' future suggests that Forster's allegories should be understood as national myths that interrogate and arraign the middle-class suburban status quo, daring readers to embrace their ideals of ruralism, brotherhood, and reconciliation.

In his 1927 Clark Lectures, Forster famously dismissed George Meredith for making 'the home counties pos[e] as the universe' (*AN*, p. 63), casting himself as the less provincial, more cosmopolitan writer. But the mythical ending of *The Longest Journey* confirms that Forster's works participate in the period idealisation of the rural south. Although Forster's narratives demonstrate that the Home Counties do not constitute the universe – his universe also includes London, its suburbs, Italy, Greece, Egypt, and India – they nonetheless locate an authentic England and an ideal Englishness there. Forster's England overtly criticises the relentless spread of urban modernity. But within the broader context of Edwardian society and politics, Forster's idealisation of rural life and the countryside serves certain interests of the modern British state, especially its effort to justify imperial expansion by 'stretching the short, tight skin of the nation over the gigantic body of the empire'.[8]

Fantasies of national reconciliation

If Forster's English novels narrate the passing of rural England in the face of relentless suburbanisation and urbanisation, they also resist that process, as *The Longest Journey* suggests, through plots that construct an ideal England by connecting disparate English types and literary modes and genres: comedy and tragedy, romance and satire, and, especially, realism and fantasy. A consideration of fantasy in Forster's fiction clarifies the importance of this formal hybridity for the allegorical project of the English novels. Narratives of Forster's career typically begin with a consideration of his short stories and the place of fantasy in his *oeuvre*.[9] In these accounts, the stories play two roles: as prototypes for the later work, which anticipate the themes, characters, and methods of the novels; as offspring of Forster's juvenile flirtation with an antiquated literary mode the novels thankfully outgrow. Forster's early forays into fantasy continue to resonate, as we've seen, in his later works. But fantasy is neither incidental to the novels, nor an aesthetic cul-de-sac they leave behind. Forster's conjunction of realism and fantasy is essential to his allegorical project, especially its diagnosis and treatment of an ailing nation and nationality.

Forster's first published short story, 'Albergo Empedocle' (1903), thematises the problem of fantasy and protests the modern tendency to psychologise and pathologise it. Foster's protagonist, Cantabrigian Harold, on a prenuptial trip to Greece with his soon-to-be in-laws, the Peaslakes (Forster's earliest satirical take on the English family), awakens from a cat nap aside his fiancée, Mildred, to the realisation that he lived a previous life as an ancient Greek, who '"loved very differently"' (*LC*, p. 25). Initially drawn to Harold's story, Mildred embraces it as proof of love's transcendent power. But when she asserts that she too has lived before and is '"remembering"', Harold calmly but firmly discounts her claim (*LC*, p. 26). Overwhelmed by the unspoken implications of this pagan past, Mildred recoils. Like her respectable father Sir Edwin, who will tolerate '"no queerness in a son-in-law!"' (*LC*, p. 19), she rejects Harold and his fantasy, pathologising her fiancé and reinterpreting his story as the hallucination of a mad man. From a conventional English perspective, as reductive and small-minded as the name Peaslake implies, Harold's conviction that his fantasy is real convicts him of mental illness.

Modern life, like modern realism, accepts neither what it dismisses as the delusional experiences of Harold nor the vindication of fantasy that concludes 'Albergo Empedocle'. Contemplating Harold's institutionalisation, Forster's narrator, Harold's best friend Tommy, rises to the defence. Consistent with his assertion on the opening page that Harold is 'the man I love most in the world' (*LC*, p. 10), Tommy asserts defiantly:

> I firmly believe that he has been a Greek – nay, that he is a Greek, drawn by recollection back into his previous life . . . And if I could look at the matter dispassionately – which I cannot – I should only rejoice at what has happened. For the greater has replaced the less, and he is living the life he knew to be greater than the life he lived with us. And I also believe that if things had happened otherwise he might be living that greater life among us.
>
> (*LC*, p. 35)

Given the homoerotic implications of Tommy's love for Harold and Forster's later decision not to republish the story until after his death, these words can be read as a passionate – though repressed – plea for tolerance of homosexuality. More importantly for us, Tommy not only believes Harold, but also entertains his own fantasy, which illuminates the genre's significance in Forster's work more generally. In Tommy's dream, 'if things had happened otherwise', the life Harold lives in his mind, would come alive 'among us'. This fantasy of a 'greater life' of neo-pagan, homosocial friendship alive in the modern world has critical force, despite its opposition to 'reality' and realism, because the story's arraignment of the Peaslakes and the middle-class close-mindedness they epitomise is so persuasive. Forster challenges readers to understand Harold and Tommy's fantasies neither as the delusions of defective characters nor as deviations of a defective narrative, but as aesthetic provocations toward a new consciousness.

In the Clark Lectures, Forster ruminates revealingly on the limits and powers of fantasy:

> The general tone of novels is so literal that when the fantastic is introduced it produces a special effect; some readers are thrilled, others choked off; it demands an additional adjustment because of the oddness of its method or subject-matter – like a side-show in an exhibition where you pay sixpence as well as the original entrance fee. Some readers pay with delight, it is only for the side-shows that they entered the exhibition, and it is only to them I can address myself now. Others refuse with indignation, and these have our sincere regards, for to dislike the fantastic in literature is not to dislike literature. It does not even imply poverty of imagination, only a disinclination to meet certain demands that are made on it.
>
> (AN, pp. 75–6)

This passage is important in part because it explains why readers have trouble with the English novels' closing turns to pastoral fantasy. In the passage's parlance, such readers are unwilling to make the additional adjustment, pay the further price, and attend to the fantastic 'side-show'. But the rigour of the novels' critique of the condition of England and Englishness suggests that Forster believes more is at stake in the modern resistance to fantasy than a matter of literary taste. Forsterian fantasy may appear a 'side-show' to readers who prefer realism's verisimilitude and social-political critique, but it nonetheless indicates and indicts, as Tommy's protest implies, the heart of an ailing nation.

Forster's English novels dare readers to pay the price and assent to their fantasies of national reconciliation not only because they offer imaginary refuge from the realities of modern life, but also because they expose England's unhealthy condition and prompt English readers to more natural, tolerant, and passionate lives. *Howards End* provides Forster's most elaborate fantasy of national reconciliation. The novel ends with the inheritance of the mythic English house, Howards End, symbol of England's rural heart, by Margaret Schlegel and her nephew, the illegitimate child of Helen Schlegel and Leonard Bast. This new English family connects English class factions, conjuring a new nation, more mongrelised and unconventional than the modernising and repressive England the novel diagnoses. This imagined nation, which unites rich and poor, prose and passion, finds its peace and promise in the places and traditions of rural England and serves as a paradigm for a rehabilitated, neo-feudal Englishness.

Given *Howards End*'s mythologising and, for some, reactionary conclusion, the novel has understandably provoked the most sustained and critical discussion of Forster's England. Less attention has been paid to how the Schlegel sisters' German lineage impacts the novel's handling of England and Englishness. Obeying a hereditarian logic, Forster imbues the Schlegel sisters with an imaginative idealism identified as 'German' and derived from their expatriate father. Mr Schlegel appears in the text as a romantic idealist German incompatible with the militaristic, materialist, and expansionist Germany of Edwardian popular literature.[10] Thus, despite their Aunt Juley's approving claim that she regards her nieces as 'English to the backbone' (*HE*, p. 5), the Schlegel sisters are 'to the backbone' neither English nor German.

In light of the novel's pastoral-idealist conclusion, Forster's rendering of the Schlegel sisters as Anglo-German hybrids evokes a common Edwardian concern about the fitness of the English 'race' and illuminates *Howards End*'s treatment for an ailing nation. Forster's fictive therapy entails not only the intermingling of different English types and bloodlines, as in *The Longest Journey*, but also the mixing of English and German bloods. Motivated by similar concerns about England's condition during the 1860s, Matthew Arnold, in works like *Culture and Anarchy* (1869) and 'The Literary Influence of Academies' (1875), had urged the unimaginative and provincial English to look to the Greeks and French. But Forster's implication that England's ills can be cured in part through infusions of German blood is more racialist than Arnold's cultural internationalism, and, in the increasingly anti-German atmosphere of prewar England, more provocative politically. The literalising logic that underwrites Forster's new English families – in which the reconciliation of factions of English society requires the mingling of their bloodlines – shows Forster partaking of Edwardian hereditarianism, but in unconventional ways. Early-century racialists defensively idealised the pure-blood Englishman, exposing concerns that foreign blood might weaken or overwhelm Englishness.[11] In contrast, Forster idealises mixed-blood Englishness and foreign intermixture, making them integral parts of his fictional treatment for the nation's disease. Evoking the biologistic and racialist terms of Edwardian science, Forster literalises Arnold's ideal of cultural internationalism, as if to make his ideal of national reconciliation more solid, substantive, real.

Just as *The Longest Journey* and *Howards End* find closure in fictional families that connect disparate national types, classes, and bloods, embodying Forster's fantasy of national reconciliation and rejuvenation, they connect disparate literary genres – realism and fantasy, comedy and tragedy, satire and romance – to embody that ideal formally. This formal hybridity, especially the fusion of realism and fantasy, is critical to Forster's allegorical project. The English novels' tendency to migrate from realism to pastoral fantasy, which troubles some readers as an aesthetic and political failing, a deviation from 'truth' and political analysis, demonstrates Forster's convictions that fantasy can function as an instrument of cultural critique, and, most important, that the mingling of literary genres enacts aesthetically the political ideal of national reconciliation. Understanding Forster's generic fusion and its mythic ambitions not as aesthetic faults, but as formal strategies essential to his allegorical treatment of England and Englishness clarifies the stakes of his particular, peculiar style and its relations to canonical modernism. For Forster's English novels anticipate the modernist generic hybridity and 'mythic method' that achieve their most elaborate and spectacular realisation in Eliot's *The Waste Land* and Joyce's *Ulysses*.

Querying national allegory

If *The Longest Journey* and *Howards End* are animated by a desire to realise a fantasy of national reconciliation, Forster's next English novel, the posthumously published, homosexual romance, *Maurice*, interrogates that imagined England with its fantasy of class-crossing gay love, a fantasy that finally requires the social excommunication of Forster's two lovers, Maurice Hall and Alec Scudder. Like *The Longest Journey* and *Howards End*, *Maurice* concludes with the formation of a new English family, unconventional and illegitimate, connecting different English types, social positions, and national locations. The novel's penultimate chapter binds the bourgeois suburbanite Hall to the gamekeeper Scudder in a union of lasting love. Forster's 'Terminal Note' (1960) calls this 'happy ending' (M, p. 215) imperative because it realizes in fiction the homosexual union Edwardian laws and mores made impossible. Forster's fantasy of gay love provides Hall and Scudder a home together in England's 'greenwood', 'for the ever and ever that fiction allows' (M, pp. 219, 216). But *Maurice* is crucial in our context not only because it sustains Forster's idealisation of rural England and elaborates his critique of English masculinity. It also interrogates the fantasies of national reconciliation his English novels render, emphasising the doubts and ambivalences that are as characteristic of Forster's representations of England as the patriotic desire to locate an essential nation and redress an ailing nationality.

By situating Hall and Scudder's refuge in England's embattled greenwood, Forster again affirms rural England over suburbia, urbanism, and modernity:

They must live outside class, without relations or money . . . But England belonged to them. That, besides companionship, was their reward. Her air and sky were theirs, not the timorous millions' who own stuffy little boxes, but never their own souls.   (*M*, p. 207)

This vocabulary of ownership works to authorise Hall and Scudder's natural life of love and to connect it to rural England. But the internal exile they accept as social outlaws queries the fantasy that England 'belongs' to this new English family and that the countryside will survive modernity's relentless spread. On the evidence of *Maurice*, indeed, the fictive therapy Forster's earlier novels prescribe seems to have failed to cure modern England's ills. *Maurice*'s nation of 'timorous millions' remains as immune as Harriet Herriton to Forster's lessons of tolerance, passion, and love.

The endings of a number of Forster's later homosexual stories refuse Hall and Scudder's refuge of pastoral fantasy and intensify the pessimistic implications lurking in *Maurice*'s conclusion. In 'Arthur Snatchfold' (written in 1928), a brief and satisfying sexual encounter between the older, urban businessman, Sir Richard Conway, and the young country milkman, Arthur Snatchfold, results in Snatchfold's arrest and conviction for indecency, a fate Conway – like Hall and Scudder – narrowly avoids. And in one of Forster's last fictions, 'The Other Boat' (written around 1957–8), a race-crossing, homosexual love affair ends tragically as the result not of intolerant authorities, but of a young gay Englishman's internalisation of the English antipathy to homosexuality. The shipboard affair between the young English officer, Lionel March, and his mixed-race lover, Cocoanut, eventually provokes within March a psychic backlash. Overwhelmed by guilt, he terminates the affair, inciting Cocoa to bite back (literally) and March to strangle his lover and throw himself overboard. Together, 'Arthur Snatchfold' and 'The Other Boat' interrogate the crossing of different types idealized in the English novels, exposing doubts and ambivalences alive in all Forster's national allegories. (Both stories are in *LC*, pp. 97–112 and 166–97 respectively.)

Despite their pastoral-idealistic conclusions, their fantasies of national reconciliation, Forster's English novels are riddled with anxiety, violence, and death. In late 1906, Foster delivered a lecture to The Working Men's College, concerning 'Pessimism in Literature', on modern literature's distrust of optimism and rejection of the happy endings typical of eighteenth- and nineteenth-century fiction. Forster explains this literary pessimism to his audience of culturally ambitious working men – among whom Leonard Bast might sit – as a result of modern writers' conviction, derived from their saturation with 'the idea of evolution', that 'all things change'. Such a world-view makes 'separation' the only convincing way to end a modern fiction

(*AE*, pp. 136–8). This view clarifies why Forster's English novels paradoxically resist the reconciliations they render. Death, disconnection, and failure are as common in them as marriage, connection, and success. So while *The Longest Journey* promotes the Wonham family as a paradigm for a rehabilitated England, the narrative journey toward that nation is littered with literal and figurative corpses: Gerald Dawes, Rickie's public-school nemesis and Agnes Pembroke's first fiancé, dies of a broken back suffered in a football match; later, after the marriage of Rickie and Agnes turns sour, their newborn daughter, weak and lame like her father, dies after a brief illness; soon after their daughter's death, Rickie and Agnes's marriage breaks apart; and, in the novel's closing pages, Rickie himself is killed by the train from which he saves his half-brother. Similarly, while *Howards End* optimistically positions Margaret and her nephew as England's true inheritors, the novel leaves its own casualties: the freedom of Charles Wilcox, incarcerated for accidentally killing Bast; the ambition and willpower of Henry Wilcox, devastated by his son's incarceration; and, most significant, the lives of Mrs Wilcox, whose sojourn in London drains her life away, and Bast, whose weak heart fails under Charles's onslaught and the bookshelf he grabs hold of as Charles strikes him. In this light, the ending of *Maurice*, despite being relatively free of figurative or literal corpses, appears less 'happy' than Forster's 'Terminal Note' insists. The union of Hall and Scudder requires, after all, their total withdrawal from English society.

Forster's plots struggle to construct a freer, more natural, and healthier Englishness and preserve a mystical rural England from modernity's relentless expansion. But the recurrence of failure, violence, and death raises serious questions about the price and efficacy of Forster's reformist fantasies. Paradoxically, Forster aggravates the problem, exerting as much narrative effort interrogating the English novels' fantastic endings as defending them:

> Howards End, Oniton, the Purbeck downs, the Oderberge, were all survivals, and the melting-pot was being prepared for them. Logically, they had no right to be alive. One's hope was in the weakness of logic . . .
>
> 'Because a thing is going strong now, it need not go strong for ever,' [Margaret] said. 'This craze for motion has only set in during the last hundred years. It may be followed by a civilization that won't be a movement, because it will rest on the earth. All the signs are against it now, but I can't help hoping, and very early in the morning in the garden I feel that our house is the future as well as the past.' (*HE*, p. 337)

Margaret Schlegel argues idealistically against modern civilisation's relentless, colonising logic. But Forster refuses to deny, 'all the signs are against it', emphasising the illogicality of her dream that Howards End 'is the future as well as the past'. Accordingly, Margaret's hope evades an important fact threatening the novel's edenic conclusion, its pastoral fantasy of national regeneration: neither Henry's legal transfer of Howards End to Margaret, nor his eldest son Charles's jail term, inhibits Charles's literal inheritance of Mrs Wilcox's Howard blood (English rural gentry) and the perpetuation of the Howard line through his proliferating offspring ('they breed like rabbits' says Miss Avery – one of Forster's mythic country folk – upsetting Margaret (*HE*, p. 271)). Given Mrs Wilcox's mystic significance to the novel and its rendering of her link with Howards End and rural England as mythic, the spectre of this growing brood of Wilcox competitors for the inheritance of the (English) earth exerts further pressure on the fantasy that England's future lies in a return to rural life and a reconciliation of England's classes and class factions. Similarly, Stephen Wonham's belief at the end of *The Longest Journey* that he guides the future of the English 'race', that his thoughts and passions will 'triumph in England' (*LJ*, p. 289), is menaced by the ongoing presence of the novel's reviled suburbanites, Herbert Pembroke, who becomes a clergyman, and his sister Agnes, who remarries after Rickie's death and starts producing children. And while Hall and Scudder's homosexual union in *Maurice* may endure 'for the ever and ever that fiction allows' (*M*, p. 216), Forster informs readers that the lovers are condemned by society to live as outlaws and by 'Nature' to 'go the way of all sterility' (*M*, p. 78), unable to reproduce their love, as can intolerant English heterosexuals like Charles Wilcox and Agnes Pembroke.

In the end, I want to stress this aesthetic and political ambivalence at the centre of Forster's allegories of England and Englishness: their refusal to resolve competing desires to confront and escape modernity, to assail and restore England, to prosecute and rehabilitate Englishness. This ambivalence may explain why readers find neither Forster's realist diagnoses of England and Englishness, nor his fantastic prescriptions for their ailing condition wholly convincing. But it also explains why Forster's national allegories are worth reading and thinking about. For they articulate with particular honesty and interest the aesthetic and political complexities and contradictions of Forster's moment, confirming him as one of the most fascinating and important English writers of the early twentieth century.

Notes

1. See, for example, the essays in *Englishness: Politics and Culture 1880–1920*, ed. Robert Colls and Philip Dodd (London: Croom Helm, 1986).
2. Peter Widdowson, *E. M. Forster's 'Howards End': Fiction as History* (London: Chalto and Windus for Sussex University Press, 1977), pp. 21–36; Daniel Born,

'Private Gardens, Public Swamps: *Howards End* and the Revaluation of Liberal Guilt', *Novel*, 25:2 (1992), 141–59.

3. Ian Baucom, *Englishness, Empire, and the Locations of Identity* (Princeton University Press, 1999), pp. 116–34.
4. Lionel Trilling, *E. M. Forster* (New York: New Directions, 1943); Frederick Crews, *E. M. Forster: The Perils of Humanism* (Princeton: Princeton University Press, 1962), pp. 19–36; Michael Levenson, *Modernism and the Fate of Individuality: Character and Novelistic Form from Conrad to Woolf* (Cambridge: Cambridge University Press, 1990), pp. 78–93.
5. Dodd, 'England, Englishness, and the Other in E. M. Forster', in *The Ends of the Earth: 1876–1918*, ed. Simon Gatrell (London: Ashfield, 1992), p. 213.
6. Dodd, 'Englishness and the National Culture,' in Colls and Dodd, *Englishness: Politics and Culture*, pp. 4–7.
7. Trilling, *E. M. Forster*, pp. 76–99; Wilfred Stone, *The Cave and the Mountain: A Study of E. M. Forster* (Stanford: Stanford University Press, 1966), pp. 184–215.
8. Benedict Anderson, *Imagined Communities: Reflections on the Origin and Spread of Nationalism* (London: Verso, 1983), p. 82.
9. Trilling, *E. M. Forster*, pp. 38–56; Stone, *The Cave and the Mountain*, pp. 122–61.
10. Samuel Hynes, *The Edwardian Turn of Mind* (London: Pimlico, 1991), pp. 33–53.
11. See, for example, N. C. Macnamara, *Origin and Character of the British People* (London: Smith, Elder & Co., 1900), esp. pp. 211–13.

4

ANN ARDIS

Hellenism and the lure of Italy

[Dr Johnson] said, 'A man who has not been to Italy, is always conscious of an inferiority, from his not having seen what is expected a man should see. The grand object of traveling is to see the shores of the Mediterranean.

All our religion, almost all our law, almost all our arts, almost all that sets us above the savages, has come to us from the shores of the Mediterranean.'
Boswell, *Life of Johnson*[1]

When Forster sends his characters to Italy, he invokes a complex tradition of representing English travel to southern Europe. Italy epitomises the 'sacredness of old European beauty and aspiration'.[2] Its monuments and artefacts were a staple component of the Grand Tour, the eighteenth-century tradition of travel to the Continent that functioned as the finishing stage in a young English gentleman's education. As Dr Johnson's comment suggests, a young gentleman 'ritually joined himself to the "Classical Mind" by visiting the sites made famous by the texts he had studied'.[3] As the Continental tour became more accessible to a broader range of English travellers in the nineteenth century, however, the value of this kind of travel could no longer be taken for granted. Rather than offering a chance to commune with the 'Classical Mind', English travel to Italy in the post-Romantic period could actually exacerbate a sense of cultural and historical belatedness. It could expose rather than resolve a sense of emotional and sensual alienation.

Schooled in the cultural ideals of the Grand Tour, Forster is both familiar with nineteenth-century re-visionings of that tradition and acutely sensitive to the crass banalities and cross-cultural *faux pas* of early twentieth-century English middle-class tourists. He appreciates the opportunities that travel provides for new kinds and dimensions of contact among English travellers of different classes. He also values the transformative potentialities of cross-class, cross-cultural contacts between 'natives' and English men and women. He is, in other words, a writer who works both within and against a tradition of English travel writing as he – through his depiction of travel to southern Europe – attempts to renegotiate class and sexual identity issues at home in England.

'Cambridge men' and the Grand Tour

'He speaks of travelling after Cambridge. He wants me to go.'
'I trust you will – but not Greece, Mr Hall. That is travelling for play. Do
dissuade him from Italy and Greece.'[4]

Most of Forster's travellers to southern Europe do not fit the eighteenth-
century model of the Grand Tourist. First and foremost, they are not typically
young upper-class gentlemen. They are the Miss Abbotts and Miss Bartletts
of small-town southern England who are surprised that the drawing room of
their Italian pension is decorated 'to rival the solid comfort of a Bloomsbury
boarding-house' and that their Signora speaks with a Cockney accent (*RV*,
p. 7). They are inclined to note with distaste that the company at meals
includes men such as Mr Emerson and his son George, who typify the 'ill
bred people whom one does meet abroad' yet from whom their lives are safely
insulated back at home (*RV*, p. 3). They grumble at the elaborate protocols
of chaperonage that govern their movement through Italy, even though their
travel is possible precisely because of these protocols. That is, their travel is
possible because a burgeoning tourist industry has established 'contact zones'
that anglicise Italy just enough that it is 'safe' for young English women
and their chaperones.[5] Its landscape is to be appreciated, though both its
starker mountainscapes and its opulent flora lie disturbingly, excessively,
beyond the norm of English pastoral ideals. Its architectural and historical
splendours are to be admired with the help of an ever-handy Baedeker, or a
gentleman relative who has previously travelled in Italy. And one's English
chaperone can usually be counted on to keep one from any inappropriate
contact with the natives, who may or may not speak English, may or may not
appreciate the subtleties of English class dynamics, may or may not recognise
the cultural superiority of their English visitors.

Before saying anything more about Forster's gentle (yet nonetheless
barbed) satires of English middle-class tourists, though, it will be useful
to look closely at his characterisation of young gentlemen travellers, since
his critique of 'Cambridge men' serves as a backdrop for his representations
of other English tourists in Italy. As the comment by Mrs Durham quoted
above might suggest, the Grand Tour does not carry, in Edwardian England,
the cultural weight and authority that it could in the eighteenth century. Mrs
Durham views such a tour as 'play'. She expects her son to graduate from
Cambridge and follow his father into local politics. She does not, however,
assume that a Continental tour will make Clive either a better citizen of the
world or a more responsible landowner and politician. As the heir apparent
of a failing English estate, he would be better served by a tour of America,

in her view. 'Anyone sensible' would prefer that destination, she notes (*M*, p. 95). Missing from her comments entirely is an appreciation of Italy or Greece as 'the spiritual fatherland of us all', to borrow Rickie Elliot's phrasing in *The Longest Journey* (*LJ*, p. 126).[6] Absent as well is any recognition of the practical value of a classical Oxbridge education for a politician or landowner.[7] Instead, a Continental tour represents nothing more than an unnecessary postponement of Clive's accession to adult responsibility. He is 'a student – a dreamer', Mrs Durham quips to Maurice, and she is anxious that he get on with the business of life. '[H]e must take his place, he must fit himself', she insists (*M*, p. 95).

For strikingly different reasons Maurice's attitude toward Clive's impending tour of Greece is equally negative. '[I]n spite of the food and the frescoes', he had enjoyed his post-graduation trip to Italy with Clive (*M*, p. 111). Yet he 'ha[s] no use for Greece': 'his interest in the classics had been slight and obscene, and had vanished when he loved Clive. The stories of Harmodius and Aristogeiton, of Phaedrus, of the Theban Band were well enough for those whose hearts were empty, but no substitute for life' (*M*, pp. 110–11). Clive agrees in part with Maurice: 'Greece had been clear but dead', he notes upon his return to England. Indeed, Greece was '[h]orrible', he tells Maurice's sister, distressing her with his vehemence (*M*, pp. 121, 125).

What is at issue in these very distinct but equally critical characterisations of English travel to southern Europe is alternately the social 'usefulness' of a Grand Tour and the status of Hellenistic values in Edwardian England. Mrs Durham's utilitarian attitude toward travel as a means of acquiring economic know-how is probably self-explanatory, invoking as it does a very familiar turn-of-the-twentieth-century characterisation of America as both the site and the engine of modern industrial and economic ingenuity. Forster's critique of English Hellenism is complicated enough, however, to require careful unpacking and historical contextualisation.

Hellenism – the systematic study of Greek history, literature, and philosophy – served as a crucial means of both liberalising political discourse and establishing the basis for a homosexual 'counterdiscourse' that was able to justify homosociality in ideal terms during the great age of English university reform in the mid-Victorian period. On the one hand, the revisionary Greek ideal lying at the centre of nineteenth-century English Hellenism was 'the purest model of Victorian liberalism itself', promising to 'restore and reinvigorate a nation fractured by the effects of laissez-faire capitalism and enervated by the approach of mass democracy'. On the other hand, English Hellenism provided 'the means of sweeping away the entire accumulation of negative associations with male love which had remained strong through the beginnings of the nineteenth century'.[8] The triumph as well as the ultimate downfall of the New Hellenism in this regard was Oscar Wilde's passionate defence of male love as 'pure' and 'perfect' and 'intellectual' in the final days of his third trial in 1895.[9] Although the courtroom erupted immediately in wild applause, the cultural backlash sparked by Wilde's trials and imprisonment was enormous, and reverberated for decades.[10] It is within the long and complex history of English Hellenism that exchanges such as the above in *Maurice* need to be situated.

As critics have noted, Hellenism held a position 'of central importance' in Forster's thought and writings and is closely aligned to that of late-Victorian Hellenists such as John Addington Symonds, Walter Pater, Samuel Butler, and G. Lowes Dickinson.[11] Stemming largely from his study of Classics at Cambridge with Nathaniel Wedd, Forster's Hellenism has been aptly described as the 'simple idealizing sort in which the ancient world is invoked as a standard to set off the deficiencies of modern civilization.[12] This intellectual training prompts Forster to argue in *Alexandria* that 'the Greece that is a spirit' died in the fifth century: 'the Greece that tried to discover truth and create beauty and that had created Alexandria' has no relationship whatsoever with modern Greece.[13] It also powers his gentlemen travellers' contemptuous attitudes toward tourists who lack a classical education, and therefore are unlikely, as Philip Herriton fears will be the case with his sister-in-law Lilia and her companion, Miss Abbott, for example, to appreciate properly the glories of Italy.

Notably, though, Forster is highly critical of Hellenism when it becomes an arid, deadening intellectualism: when intellectual inquiry is de-coupled from sensual and emotional experience and a classical Platonic modelling of a continuum between physical and intellectual stimulation is abandoned in favour of the crassest kind of homophobic attachment to class privilege, masked as idealised, disembodied intellectual inquiry.[14] The exchanges between Maurice Hall and Clive Durham on the subject of Greece are exemplary in this regard. Although Clive concedes to Maurice's sister that Greece is 'dead', he fails to acknowledge fully the betrayal of Platonic idealism that he enacts himself in his attempt to 'reconstruct his life from the bottom' while in Greece (*M*, p. 125). Going to Greece is, importantly, an excuse for withdrawing from his relationship with Maurice, an excuse, moreover, for characterising this relationship with his college friend as an adolescent attachment that can now be superseded by adult hetero-normativity. But what kind of life will this be? His marriage to Anne, the society woman he meets while in Greece, is full of compromised intimacies. Their sexual relationship 'ignore[s] the reproductive and the digestive functions', and it is conducted silently 'in a world that bore no reference' to their daily lives (*M*, p. 164). This 'secrecy', the narrator notes, 'drew after it much else in their lives' (*M*, p. 164).

Secrecy suited him, at least he adopted it without regret. He had never itched
to call a spade a spade, and though he valued the body the actual deed of
sex seemed to him unimaginative, and best veiled in night. Between men it
is inexcusable, between man and woman it may be practiced since nature
and society approve, but never discussed nor vaunted. His ideal of marriage
was temperate and graceful, like all his ideals, and he found a fit helpmate in
Anne, who had refinement herself, and admired it in others. They loved each
other tenderly. Beautiful conventions received them – while beyond the barrier
Maurice wandered, the wrong words on his lips and the wrong desires in his
heart, and his arms full of air. (M, p. 165)

By the end of this passage, what has been exposed as 'wrong' is not Maurice's
desire for a fully sexual relationship with Rick or his 'gift of listening beneath
words' to achieve 'an access of intimacy' (M, p. 122). Rather, what is 'wrong'
are both Clive's attitude toward sex and his support for the 'beautiful conventions' of hetero-normativity that enable him to function, he would like to
think, so effectively in his social world. At the end of the novel, when Clive
turns against Maurice, he does so with the full force of social convention:

Clive sprang up with a whimper of disgust. He wanted to smite the monster, and
flee, but he was civilized, and wanted it feebly. After all, they were Cambridge
men . . . pillars of society both; he must not show violence. And he did not; he
remained quiet and helpful to the very end. But his thin, sour disapproval, his
dogmatism, the stupidity of his heart, revolted Maurice, who could only have
respected hatred. (M, pp. 243–4)

As is hinted at elsewhere in his work but never so boldly stated, Forster
is highly critical of 'Cambridge men': they are known by the 'stupidity'
of their hearts, their interest in tamping down or disguising any show of
emotion in the name of 'civilization', and an intellectuality that deliberately
and relentlessly divorces itself from both emotional and sensual registers
of experience. Rather than being able either to embrace the full continuum
of sexual, emotional, and intellectual intimacy modelled in ideal Hellenic
relationships between men or to move beyond Platonism to a more positive
epistemology of sexuality, they deny, repress, or simply fail to recognise
their homosociality, opting instead either for celibate bookishness or the
compromised intimacies of conventional heterosexual marriages such
as Clive and Anne Durham's or Rickie and Agnes Elliot's. They are,
additionally, entrapped by their understanding of 'proper' class relations.
In Clive Durham's case, for example, 'intimacy with any social inferior
was unthinkable' (M, p. 242). He recoils from Maurice after the latter has
announced his relationship with Alec Scudder not only because of the kind
of relationship it is but also because of *who* Alec is.

Maurice's relationship with Alec will deserve further attention in the final section of this essay. I want now, though, to consider how the thematics and plot of *Maurice* – specifically, the critique of intellectualised Hellenism and a plot that turns upon the choice of sexual and emotional intimacy with a social inferior – are anticipated by an important late Victorian precursor text: George Eliot's *Middlemarch*.

Blood and photographs, Baedekers and 'yaller dog[s]'

Ruins and basilicas, palaces and colossi, set in the midst of a sordid present, where all that was living and warm-blooded seemed sunk in the deep degeneracy of a superstition divorced from reverence; the dimmer but eager Titanic life gazing and struggling on walls and ceilings; the long vistas of white forms whose marble eyes seemed to hold the monotonous light of an alien world: all this vast wreck of ambitious ideals, sensuous and spiritual, mixed confusedly with the signs of breathing forgetfulness and degradation, at first jarred [Dorothea Brooke] with an electric shock, and then urged themselves on her with that ache belonging to a glut of confused ideas which check the flow of emotion.   George Eliot, *Middlemarch*[15]

'So, Miss Honeychurch, you are travelling? As a student of art?'
'Oh, dear me, no – oh, no!'
'Perhaps as a student of human nature,' interposed Miss Lavish, 'like myself?'
'Oh, no. I am here as a tourist.'
  'Oh, indeed,' said Mr Eager. 'Are you indeed? If you will not think me rude, we residents sometimes pity you poor tourists not a little – handed about like a parcel of goods from Venice to Florence, from Florence to Rome, living herded together in pensions or hotels, quite unconscious of anything that is outside Baedeker, their one anxiety to get "done" or "through" and go on somewhere else. The result is, they mix up towns, rivers, palaces in one inextricable whirl. You know the American girl in *Punch* who says: "Say, Poppa, what did we see at Rome?" And the father replies: "Why, guess Rome was the place where we saw the yaller dog." That's travelling for you. Ha! ha! ha!' (*RV*, pp. 59–60)

Scholars have often noted Forster's deep familiarity with George Eliot's work. The connections I would emphasise here involve their characterisations of travellers to Italy who lack a gentleman's education and their interest in relationships that challenge social class conventions. In Forster's novels, as in *Middlemarch*, middle-class English travellers come to Italy thinking that an experience of unity with the 'Classical Mind' is what is expected of and for them. Instead, however, travel becomes both an occasion for increasing alienation from that classical tradition and an opportunity for experiences unmediated by it. Mr Casaubon would have Dorothea's first trip to Italy function as a turning point in her young life, as it had in his own:

> 'I will remember that I considered it an epoch in my life when I visited [Rome] for the first time; after the fall of Napoleon, an event which opened the Continent to travellers. Indeed I think it is one among several cities to which an extreme hyperbole has been applied – "See Rome and die:" but in your case I would propose an emendation and say, See Rome as a bride, and live thenceforth as a happy wife.' *(Middlemarch*, p. 148)

Rather than providing an initiation into both the sexual, emotional, and intellectual (she hopes) intimacies of marriage and the public glories of classical culture, though, Dorothea's Grand Tour results in a different kind of epiphany. Having dreamed of finding 'large vistas and wide fresh air' in her husband's mind, she now realises there are only 'anterooms and winding passages' leading nowhere *(Middlemarch*, p. 145). Having married her ideal of classical education, she now recognises his vapid pedantry: 'What was fresh to her mind was worn out to his; and such capacity of thought and feeling as had ever been stimulated in him by the general life of mankind had long shrunk to a sort of dried preparation, a lifeless embalmment of knowledge' *(Middlemarch*, p. 146). As she stands in the Vatican Museum – eyes 'fixed dreamily on a streak of sunlight', oblivious to the 'antique beauty' *(Middlemarch*, p. 140) around her, focused solely on a newly bleak internal vision of the life ahead of her, back at home in England, with the man she now knows her husband to be – she is observed by Will Ladislaw and his German friend. Dorothea's Grand Tour (and Book I of the novel) thus culminates in a negative epiphany about her husband's Hellenism, and with the reader's (if not Dorothea's) recognition of Will's attractiveness to her, his more appropriate partnering with her.

Forster takes the fullest possible advantage of the precedents set by Eliot in re-scripting the traditional Grand Tour. Instead of functioning as the finishing stage in a classical education, his travellers, like Eliot's, are shocked into the life of the senses by their experiences there. The 'flow of emotion' long since checked 'by a glut of confused ideas' about high culture and intellectual tradition is made possible when things happen on tour that are not anticipated by their formal education, their guidebooks, or their English chaperones *(Middlemarch*, p. 145). Consider, for example, 'The Story of a Panic', Forster's short story about Eustace, a fourteen-year-old boy whom his aunts think of as 'delicate' and whom the narrator considers 'peevish', unhealthy, and utterly lacking in social graces, who is transformed by the mysterious happenings on the picnic in the Vallone Fontana Caroso he takes with his aunts, the curate Mr Sandbach and the unnamed narrator and his wife and daughters.[16] Prior to their panic-stricken flight down the valley, his companions argue more or less pleasantly about whether the view is beautiful, or whether it would make a good picture, or whether '[a]ll the poetry is going from Nature' through commercialisation and development (p. 7). Although Mr Sandbach is 'endeavouring to fit him for one of our great public schools' (p. 2), Eustace remains wilfully unengaged by this polite yet transparently semi-educated conversation, responding only with an 'irritable frown' to Mr Sandbach's attempt to engage him in a sidebar discussion about whether or not the narrator's daughter Rose will find ancient history 'worth [her] notice' (p. 8). His companions return, however, to find him curiously and inexplicably 'improved' by his experience in their absence (p. 19). Although he still withholds himself from their conversation, he races about 'like a real boy' (p. 19), 'stepp[ing] out manfully, for the first time in his life, holding his head up and taking deep draughts of air into his chest' on their return to the hotel (p. 18). What has happened to him can't be explained, can't be categorized rationally – and certainly doesn't represent the culmination of a young English gentleman's classical education. Rather, this particular young gentleman's version of a Grand Tour results in eruptions of physical energy and emotion that the narrator, as the voice of English convention in this story, finds entirely unseemly: first his gallantry to the old peasant woman they meet on the roadside, then his effusive public display of affection toward Gennaro, the 'clumsy, impertinent fisher-lad' (p. 20) serving temporarily as a waiter in the hotel, then his midnight rant about 'the great forces and manifestations of Nature', and finally his escape into the countryside following Gennaro's untimely death in their leap from the garden wall (p. 30).

A similar trajectory drives the plot of *A Room with a View*, as Forster orchestrates Lucy Honeychurch's development into a woman who can defy English social convention by marrying the 'ill-bred' young man that 'the better class of tourist' is initially surprised to find sharing their pension in Florence (*RV*, p. 3). Lucy is perfectly willing to describe herself as a tourist, not a student of art or human nature (i.e., not a traveller on a Grand Tour in the traditional sense). Yet her experiences don't fit the pattern Mr Eager mocks so pointedly through his reference to the *Punch* cartoon in the paragraph that serves as the second epigraph to this section. Instead of remaining 'quite unconscious of anything that is outside Baedeker', Lucy is placed, time and again, in situations that are not mediated by guidebooks of any kind. Travelling distills and sharpens her sensory experiences only when she finds herself 'off the map', so to speak, in situations for which she has no prior referent.[17]

Her first real experience of Italy is thus the 'ravishing moment' in the Square of the Annunziata when she sees 'in the living terra-cotta those divine babies whom no cheap reproductions can ever stale' (*RV*, p. 18). Though Miss Lavish had just instructed her *not* to look at her Baedeker – 'We will simply drift', she had announced at the outside of their 'adventure' – Miss Lavish is curiously incapable of sharing Lucy's pleasure in this sight, declaring with dismay 'that they were out of their path now by at least a mile' (*RV*, p. 18). After her companion abandons her on the steps of Santa Croce, Lucy initially wanders through the building, 'unwilling to be enthusiastic over monuments of uncertain authorship or date. There was no one even to tell her which, of all the sepulchral slabs that paved the nave and transepts, was the one that was really beautiful, the one that had been most praised by Mr Ruskin' (*RV*, pp. 19–20). Quickly, however, 'the pernicious charm of Italy worked on her, and instead of acquiring information, she began to be happy' as she wanders through the church, reading the notices in Italian about not spitting or allowing dogs in the building, coming to the rescue of the Italian toddler who trips on the foot of a sepulchre (*RV*, p. 20).

Lucy's evening walk in the Piazza Signoria later that same day is also ventured *sans* Baedeker. Knowing that it would be considered inappropriate for her to take a ride on the electric tram without a chaperone, she opts instead to visit a shop where she can purchase photographs of well-known Italian artworks. George Eliot's Dorothea Brooke stands desolate in front of the masterpieces in the Vatican Museum, unable to see the beauty that surrounds her because of her internal turmoil regarding her deadening marriage. In contrast, Forster's Lucy extends 'uncritical approval to every well-known name' represented in the photographs on display in the tourist shop; yet 'the gates of liberty seemed still unopened' to her, the narrator notes (*RV*, p. 40). '"The world," she thought, "is certainly full of beautiful things, if only I could come across them."' But '[n]othing ever happens to me', she reflects – just before she witnesses the knife fight between the two Italians over a petty debt and faints into George Emerson's arms (*RV*, p. 40).

The sequence of events here is crucial. Living sixty-odd years after Dorothea Brooke, Lucy's experience of great art is always already mediated by its mechanical reproduction for mass circulation.[18] She can't visit Santa Croce without wondering how Baedeker *and* Ruskin would have her appreciate its frescos and statuary. She can't purchase the photograph of Botticelli's 'Birth of Venus' without hearing Miss Bartlett's commentary about Venus's nudity being a 'pity' (*RV*, p. 40). The violent exchange she witnesses between the two Italians, over a sum of money less than the amount she has just spent on souvenir photographs, is a catalyst for change – in George Emerson if not yet in Lucy herself. The blood that covers her souvenirs not only frightens him; it also forces him to acknowledge that 'something tremendous has happened' (*RV*, p. 43). 'It was not exactly that a man had died; something had happened to the living' (*RV*, p. 45). 'I shall want to live', he tells her. When Lucy's photographs of great art float down the Arno and George determines, 'without getting muddled', to face the reality that 'something tremendous has happened' (*RV*, p. 43), Forster's version of a Grand Tour functions not, as Samuel Johnson had argued, as an occasion for seeing 'what is expected a man should see', but instead as an opportunity for exposure to entirely unanticipated dimensions and categories of experience. Unlike the tourists Mr Eager mocks through his reference to the *Punch* cartoon about the American and her father, Forster's tourists aren't anxious 'to get "done" or "through" and go on somewhere else'. Nor are they so overwhelmed and disoriented by the glut of sights they have taken in that they identify Rome only by the 'yaller dog' they saw there. Instead, Italy functions as an occasion for getting beyond 'the muddle' of English social convention and traditional cultural values. It is a site for identifying what it might really mean 'to live'.

Re-circuiting desire, re-imagining England

Dear Miss Morland, consider the dreadful nature of the suspicions you have entertained. What have you been judging from? Remember the country and the age in which we live. Remember that we are English, that we are Christians. Consult your own understanding, your own sense of the probable, your own observation of what is passing around you. Does our education prepare us for such atrocities? Do our laws connive at them? Could they be perpetrated without being known, in a country like this, where social and literary intercourse is on such a footing, where every man is surrounded by a neighbourhood of voluntary spies, and where roads and newspapers lay everything open? Dearest Miss Morland, what ideas have you been admitting?

Jane Austen, *Northanger Abbey*[19]

[*Maurice*] belongs to an England where it was still possible to get lost. It belongs to the last moment of the greenwood . . . There is no forest or fell to escape to today, no cave in which to curl up, no deserted valley for those who wish neither to reform nor corrupt society but to be left alone. (*M*, p. 254)

With the speech in Jane Austen's *Northanger Abbey* that serves as the first epigraph for this section, Catherine Morland's Gothic fantasies about Henry Tilney's family home are exposed, once and for all, as delusions inspired by reading too many Gothic novels like Anne Radcliffe's *The Italian*. This is England; that is, this *isn't* Italy, Henry scolds her; and it is more than time to behave as a proper English gentlewoman. Henry Tilney upholds an ideal of England as a civilized world 'where roads and newspapers lay everything open'. By contrast, the England that Forster loves best retains its untameable heart, persists in being a 'greenwood' that can never be entirely eradicated or civilised. In this ideal England of Forster's imagining, it would still be 'possible to get lost'. I would like to explore in this section the connection to be made between Forster's investment in England as a greenwood, his characterisation of travel to southern Europe as a means of learning how 'to live', and the value he places on 'getting lost'. Austen's Catherine Morland has not had a gentleman's education, has not been on a Grand Tour, and must shed her appetite for lurid Gothic fantasies before she can marry Henry Tilney. Her maturity is marked by her relinquishment of her fictional adventures in Italy in favour of English domesticity. Forster's characters, by contrast, are transformed in a positive way by their actual travels to southern Europe, provided that they can relinquish their investment in class distinctions, their assumption of moral, intellectual, and social superiority, and their confidence in 'civilization' while abroad. Sometimes they even achieve this kind of transformation without travelling abroad. In either case, the goal for Forster's travellers is to come home – to an England that holds new possibilities because their experiences have enabled them to imagine different patterns and parameters of intimacy, different ideals and values of 'home'.

Consider, for example, the double triangulation of desire in *Where Angels Fear to Tread* that is set in motion when Philip Herriton follows his sister-in-law to Italy, where he intends to rescue her from an unseemly engagement to the son of an Italian dentist. Surprised to find Lilia married to Gino Carella, Philip is even more surprised to find himself charmed by both Caroline Abbott, Lilia's travelling companion, and Gino. He had long since dismissed Miss Abbott as one of his parish's dutiful, dull spinsters; what his sister Harriet refers to as his 'Italy mania',[20] his bookish appreciation of Italian history and art, had kept him confident of his superiority to any of his mother and sister's acquaintances. Yet his interaction with Miss Abbott in the course of their failed attempt to kidnap Lilia's son eradicates this sense of confidence, leaving him vulnerable to his own emotional needs: 'He had known so much about her once – what she thought, how she felt, the reasons for her actions. And now he only knew that he loved her, and all the other knowledge seemed passing from him just as he needed it most' (pp. 271–2). Initially, he wants desperately to believe that Gino is a cad and a lout for taking advantage of his sister-in-law. Yet he relishes the ebullient male comraderie that Gino and his motley friends proffer to him at the opera, and by the end of the novel he is struggling to assimilate what he has just learned about Miss Abbott's passionate attachment to Gino (though he can't quite acknowledge his own). *Where Angels Fear to Tread* unapologetically orientalises the Italian male, romanticises his 'primitive' sensuality and non-English social habits and attitudes. The point to emphasise here, though, is that the traditional marriage plot has been re-circuited several times over through Gino: in spite of '[c]enturies of aspiration and culture' (p. 280), as Philip notes, Lilia, Miss Abbott, *and* Philip cannot escape the appeal of Gino's dark animality. Philip and Miss Abbott both return to England to dedicate themselves to work – but Miss Abbott's life will be 'endurable' (p. 283) only because she will be able to speak with Philip occasionally about Gino. The child they had hoped to rescue has died tragically, and Philip's flippancy is no match for the other brutal reality he and Miss Abbott have both acknowledged: Gino returns with them to England as an awareness of bodily sensations and emotions that lie beyond the pale of polite conversation.

As is so often the case in Forster's fiction, Philip's classical education and intellectuality are a handicap rather than an asset to him in understanding what has transpired in Italy. If *A Room with a View* ends on a happier note, it is not least because Lucy Honeychurch and George Emerson have never had the advantage of that kind of education. By marrying her Will Ladislaw, Lucy will avoid the deathtrap represented by her 'Cambridge man', her Mr Casaubon, the aptly named Cecil Vyse. But it is in *Maurice* rather than *A Room with a View* that the critique of arid classicism, of a Hellenism in which intellectual inquiry is totally divorced from sensual and emotional experience, that I have been tracing through Forster's representations of travel to Italy and Greece, will culminate. In closing, I turn briefly to the scene that transpires in the British Museum as Alec and Maurice's relationship pivots from one involving the potential of blackmail and social scandal to one involving the possibility that England might still be a greenwood.

In *Maurice*, the veil of heterosexuality that Forster throws over so many relationships in his earlier fiction falls away entirely.[21] Instead of using a male–female relationship as a screen for the projection of homosexual desire, the novel confronts quite directly the homophobia that is so deeply rooted both in the English educational system and in class relations. After Maurice receives Alec's letter, announcing that he "*know[s] about you and Mr Durham*" (*M*, p. 216) and accusing Maurice of treating him unfairly, Maurice asks Alec to meet him at the British Museum before he sails for South America. The British Museum: repository of so many cultural treasures that British imperialists have taken from sites across the globe and returned for 'safe keeping' to England. The British Museum: a cultural institution that is open to all, and especially to those whose formal education has been minimal. '[A] place round which one could take – er – the less fortunate,' as Maurice's old public-school teacher notes when he meets Maurice and Alec peering at a model of the Acropolis (*M*, p. 224). Mr Ducie mis-identifies Maurice, misreads Maurice's relationship with Alec – and is called away by his wife, looking precisely the 'old fool' he had determined not to be when he launched into his mini-lecture on the British Museum to cover his embarrassment at both mis-remembering Maurice and observing Maurice's gesture of physical intimacy to Alec (*M*, p. 224). The exchange between the three men is brief, yet it alters the dynamic between Maurice and Alec, inviting the one to a confession of love and the other to renounce his charge of blackmail. Full resolution of their situation won't be reached until they meet in the boathouse at Penge, the Durham family's country estate. But the scene in the British Museum is a pivotal point in their relationship.

Dorothea Brooke realises fully the limitations of Casaubon as she stands in the Vatican Museum, oblivious to the cultural treasures that surround her. Similarly, Maurice Hall recognizes the 'endless inaccuracy' (*M*, p. 223) of the British public-school system and everything it stands for as he leans over a model of the Acropolis, that icon of classical culture, talking to his old teacher while touching the neck of his working-class lover. The possibility that England can still function as a greenwood, can harbour a richness and a range of sexual and emotional experience unsanctified by society, opens out in this moment, when Forster takes George Eliot's re-visioning of the Grand Tour and rewrites it still more radically. Maurice has been to Italy. It is this exchange on English soil, however, that exposes the radical discontinuity between the homosocial continuum of sexual and emotional experience he is finally embracing and the intellectual idealism epitomised by a classical education culminating in a Grand Tour. It is this exchange, too, that not only propels the novel toward a utopian conclusion but also guides Forster's further experiments in the narrative representation of relationships between men. Forster's own travels will take him to Alexandria and elsewhere in north Africa; characters in his later fiction will travel to northern Europe, north Africa, India, and beyond. Yet his subsequent efforts to write about relationships unscripted either by classical Platonism[22] or compulsory heterosexuality take their cue from these early works about travel to southern Europe and the deadly, deadening intellectualism entombed in Edwardian Hellenism.

Notes

1. James Boswell, *Life of Johnson*, ed. R. W. Chapman (new edn, corr. J. D. Fleeman, Oxford: Oxford University Press, 1980), p. 742.
2. D. H. Lawrence, *Studies in Classic American Literature* (1923; Harmondsworth: Penguin, 1977), p. 45.
3. James Buzard, *The Beaten Track: European Tourism, Literature, and the Ways to Culture, 1800–1918* (Oxford: Clarendon Press, 1993), pp. 110, 130. Subsequent references to this study will be cited parenthetically in the text.
4. E. M. Forster, *Maurice* (New York: W. W. Norton, 1971), p. 95. Subsequent references to this edition will be cited parenthetically in the text.

5. 'Contact zones' is Mary Louise Pratt's term, as developed in *Imperial Eyes: Travel-Writing and Transculturalism* (London and New York: Routledge, 1992).
6. Rickie Elliot describes Italy alone in this manner, but Mrs Durham's association of Greece with Italy is worth repeating here, and will be important later in my argument.
7. See Buzard, *The Beaten Track*, pp. 97–101, for more detailed discussion of the motives and expectations for a gentleman's European travel.
8. Linda Dowling, *Hellenism and Homosexuality in Victorian Oxford* (Ithaca and London: Cornell University Press, 1994), pp. xiii, 79, 31, 79.
9. H. Montgomery Hyde, *The Trials of Oscar Wilde* (London: William Hodge, 1948), p. 236; Dowling, *Hellenism and Homosexuality*, pp. 1–5, 148–53.
10. Joseph Bristow, *Effeminate England: Homoerotic Writing After 1885* (New York: Columbia University Press, 1995); Richard Dellamora, *Masculine Desire: The Sexual Politics of Victorian Aestheticism* (Chapel Hill: University of North Carolina Press, 1990); Michael S. Foldy, *The Trials of Oscar Wilde: Deviance, Morality, and Late-Victorian Society* (New Haven, CT: Yale University Press, 1997); Alan Sinfield, *The Wilde Century: Effeminacy, Oscar Wilde, and the Queer Movement* (New York: Columbia University Press, 1994).
11. David Roessel, 'Live Orientals and Dead Greeks: Forster's Response to the Chanak Crisis', *Twentieth-Century Literature*, 36:1 (Spring 1990), 43.
12. G. D. Klingopoulos, 'E. M. Forster's Sense of History and Cavafy', *Essays in Criticism*, 8 (1958), 160–1.
13. E. M. Forster, *Alexandria: A History and a Guide* (1922; repr. New York: Oxford University Press, 1986), p. 56. See Roessel's discussion of this text ('Live Orientals and Dead Greeks', 57–8) and Peter Jeffreys, 'Cavafy, Forster, and the Eastern Question', *Journal of Modern Greek Studies*, 19 (2001), 61–87.
14. For an important discussion of Forster's critique of classical epistemology and its negative characterisations of sexuality, see Debrah Raschke, 'Breaking the Engagement with Philosophy: Re-envisioning Hetero/Homo Relations in *Maurice*', in *Queer Forster*, ed. Robert K. Martin and George Piggford (Chicago and London: University of Chicago Press, 1997), pp. 151–66.
15. George Eliot [Mary Anne Evans], *Middlemarch*, ed. Gordon S. Haight (1871–2; Boston: Houghton Mifflin Co., 1968), p. 144. Subsequent references to this edition will be cited parenthetically in the text.
16. E. M. Forster, 'The Story of a Panic', *The Celestial Omnibus and Other Stories* (New York: Alfred A. Knopf, 1927), pp. 3, 14.
17. See Buzard for discussion of Forster's 'considerable critical engagement' with the guidebook industry supported by English tourism, *The Beaten Track*, pp. 285, 285–331.
18. Although published in the 1870s, *Middlemarch* is set in 1832 – i.e., before the development of photography. Buzard's treatment of Forster's familiarity with guidebook culture and its importance in his work is excellent, but could productively be further complicated by more detailed consideration of the development of new technologies of visuality like photography and film. I can only gesture toward that kind of analysis here as I invoke Walter Benjamin's 'The Work of Art in the Age of Mechanical Reproduction', in *Illuminations* (New York: Schocken Books, 1968), pp. 217–52.

19. Jane Austen, *Northanger Abbey* (1816; Orchard Park, NY and London: Broadview Press, 1996), pp. 194–5.

20. E. M. Forster, *Where Angels Fear to Tread* (1905; New York: Knopf, 1920). All subsequent page references have been incorporated into the text.

21. See Margaret Goscilo, 'Forster's Italian Comedies: Que(e)rying Heterosexuality Abroad', in *Seeing Double: Revisioning Edwardian and Modernist Literature*, ed. Carola M. Kaplan and Anne B. Simpson (New York: St. Martin's Press, 1996), pp. 193–214; Lois Cucullu, 'Shepherds in the Parlor: Forster's Apostles, Pagans, and Native Sons', *Novel, A Forum on Fiction*, 32:1 (1998), 19–50; and Cucullu, '"Only Cathect": Queer Heirs and Narrative Desires in *Howards End*', in *Imperial Desire: Dissident Sexualities and Colonial Literatures*, ed. Richard Ruppel and Philip Holden (Minneapolis: University of Minnesota Press, 2003), pp. 195–222.

22. See Jesse Matz's '"You Must Join My Dead": E. M. Forster and the Death of the Novel', *Modernism/Modernity*, 9:2 (2002), 303–17, for a powerful reading of Forster's unpublished writings about his relationship with Mohammed el Adl. Matz associates the memoir Forster writes in the form of a letter to his lover after his death from tuberculosis with his 'desertion of fiction' as an enterprise (p. 304).

5

DOMINIC HEAD

Forster and the short story

Forster's short stories are commonly held to be insubstantial, lacking the sophistication associated with other twentieth-century practitioners of the form. They are deemed to be governed by a whimsical fascination with the supernatural, and to represent light relief from the novels. Without making excessive counter-claims, this essay seeks to demonstrate that Forster's stories are, on occasion, more technically interesting than is sometimes assumed, revealing some affinities with the work of other modernist writers, and betraying some intriguing points of contact with the novels.

Forster's reputation as a short story writer rests, principally, on the two volumes of stories published during his lifetime, *The Celestial Omnibus* (1911) and *The Eternal Moment* (1928). These twelve stories were combined in 1947 to form the *Collected Short Stories*; the same twelve published in the Abinger Edition as *The Machine Stops and Other Stories*.[1] In his editorial introduction to the Abinger Edition, Rod Mengham correctly observes that 'Forster's decision in the question of what should, or should not be collected was a significant act that needs to be recognized' (*MS*, p. vii); but Mengham also points out that the title *Collected Short Stories* was 'grossly inaccurate' (*MS*, p. vii), even though sanctioned by Forster. The stories collected in 1947 were all written before the First World War, and omit all of those (complete) stories published posthumously as *The Life to Come and Other Stories* (1972). Introducing this posthumous collection, Oliver Stallybrass indicates that the stories cover the whole extent of Forster's career, 'ranging, probably, from 1903 to 1958, with some revision as late as 1962' (*LC*, p. vii). The reason why the stories in *The Life to Come* had to await posthumous publication, along with the novel *Maurice*, is simple: their homosexual content, which would have made it impossible for an editor to accept them when they were written, and impossible for Forster to offer them for publication. In addition, a few unfinished stories and fragments remain. These are published in *Arctic Summer and Other Fiction*, a volume that 'spans Forster's entire career as a writer – from his early twenties to his eighties' (*AS*, p. vii).

The fact that Forster continued to write shorter fiction puts a fresh complexion on his announcement, in the introduction to the *Collected Short Stories* (1947), that 'these fantasies . . . represent all that I have accomplished in a particular line' (*MS*, p. xv). The 'particular line', which might once have seemed to suggest that Forster gave up writing short stories before 1914, seems with hindsight to denote the fantastical properties of the particular stories Forster sanctioned for publication, which comprise a series of reflections on paganism, mythology, and the afterlife. The preoccupation with the fantastic suggests that Forster has affinities with Kipling as a short story writer, rather than with the technically more innovative modernists, such as Joyce, Mansfield, and Woolf. Mansfield's comments on 'The Story of a Siren' are instructive, here:

> There is a certain leisureliness which is of the very essence of Mr Forster's style – a constant and fastidious choosing of what the unity shall be composed – but while admitting the necessity for this and the charm of it, we cannot deny the danger to the writer of drifting, of finding himself beset with fascinating preoccupations which tempt him to put off or even to turn aside from the difficulties which are outside his easy reach.[2]

Mansfield's stories are noted for their sophisticated structure and disruption of linear chronology, as well as for their innovations in the use of narrative voice. The relativism associated with modernist writing is amply illustrated by Mansfield's use of alternative (sometimes multiple) perspectives, and the careful patterning of stories like 'Prelude', 'Daughters of the Late Colonel', and 'The Garden Party' demonstrates the controlled 'collage' effect – the impressive use of juxtaposition and montage – that is a rightly celebrated feature of modernist expression. Narrative perspective becomes crucial in such stories, where an emphasis on internal mood (rather than external action) makes the effect peculiarly vulnerable to authorial clumsiness or intrusiveness. In her story 'Miss Brill', Mansfield claimed that she chose 'not only the length of every sentence, but even the sound of every sentence . . . the rise and fall of every paragraph to fit her, and to fit her on that day at that very moment'.[3] One can extrapolate from the alien 'leisureliness' Mansfield detects in 'The Story of the Siren' to say that Forster's stories are quite unlike hers, driven more by the pursuit of ideas than by an ideal of technical virtuosity.

Of course, Forster's modernism is of a quite different hue to that of Joyce, Mansfield, or Woolf; or, at least, it manifests itself in different ways. For David Medalie, it is Forster's treatment of liberal humanism that points up a particularly significant relationship to modernism (rather than, as is sometimes assumed, denoting his distance from it). In both *Howards End* and *A Passage to India*, suggests Medalie, 'the implication, albeit couched in wistfulness, is unflinchingly clear: liberal-humanism is no longer tenable; there are no longer viable contexts for its articulation'. These major novels can then be seen to be about 'the legacy of loss, its shape and its possibilities'. In this reading, Forster emerges as a 'reluctant modernist', embracing the 'sorrows born of newness', since 'the admission that new times compel new tellings is not necessarily an exuberant one'. Neither is it merely the major novels that contribute to this assessment; for Medalie, Forster's story 'The Eternal Moment' bears the stamp of his modernism, being 'one of his most interesting deliberations, within a humanistic focus, upon meagreness and plenitude, loss and salvaging'.[4]

'The Eternal Moment' is one of Forster's best stories. It is set in an area bordering Italy, and it recounts the return of a novelist, Miss Raby, to a town called Vorta, which she visited as a girl twenty years before, and which she made famous with tourists by using it as a setting for her first novel, also called 'The Eternal Moment'.[5] Miss Raby is travelling with her maid (Elizabeth), and Colonel Leyland, with whom she has an uncertain attachment. They are returning to the scene where a young man, then a porter, had fallen in love with her twenty years before. This is the agreeable memory with which the story opens, and which was part of the inspiration for Miss Raby's first novel, 'written round the idea that man does not live by time alone, that an evening gone may become like a thousand ages in the courts of heaven' (*MS*, p. 164).

The treatment of time, however, is far from the celebration of the enduring revelatory episode that seems to be implied in the title of Miss Raby's novel. What she finds on her return to Vorta is a town ruined by the greed and infighting that its commercial success seems to have brought with it; and Miss Raby feels that she is to blame. Inevitably, she finds the porter, Feo, who had once declared his love for her, now tending to fat, working as the concierge at the hotel from which the town's bad blood seems to emanate. Driven by her unconventionality, she determines to confront Feo with the episode from their youth (which he has apparently forgotten) in order to see if she can prompt a 'spark of life' in him (*MS*, p. 176). Feo's first thought is that she is trying to ruin him (the exchange occurs in the presence of Colonel Leyland), but realising this is not the case, he contrives a private wink for her benefit, thus provoking Miss Raby's central revelation:

> It was a ghastly sight, perhaps the most hopelessly depressing of all the things she had seen at Vorta. But its effect on her was memorable. It evoked a complete vision of that same man as he had been twenty years before. She could see him to the smallest detail . . . She could hear his voice, neither insolent nor diffident,

never threatening, never apologizing, urging her first in the studied phrases he had learnt from books, then, as his passion grew, becoming incoherent, crying that she must believe him, that she must love him in return, that she must fly with him to Italy, where they would live for ever, always happy, always young. She had cried out then, as a young lady should, and had thanked him not to insult her. And now, in her middle age, she cried out again, because the sudden shock and the contrast had worked a revelation. 'Don't think I'm in love with you now!' she cried.

For she realized that only now was she not in love with him: that the incident upon the mountain had been one of the great moments of her life – perhaps the greatest, certainly the most enduring: that she had drawn unacknowledged power and inspiration from it . . . Never again could she think of it as a half-humorous episode in her development. There was more reality in it than in all the years of success and varied achievement which had followed, and which it had rendered possible. (*MS*, pp. 178–9)

This complex reassessment of the past has something of the power one asso-ciates with Proust's ability to evoke the passage of time in the appearance of a character. (The story predates *Le temps retrouvé*, which was published posthumously in 1927.) Beyond this, there is an extraordinary element of defeat in the literary theme. Miss Raby's eternal moment turns out to be irreducibly ambivalent: the worth of her life, she now realises, has been bestowed by the fleeting (and repressed) experience of love. But her youthful literary sense of the eternal moment was evidently more artificial: the novel that launched her career took its inspiration from the arrested moment of love, packaged as a familiar fantasy of the exotic. And while her fantasy moment granted her comfort and status, the locale that inspired it was ren-dered mean by the packaging of the fantasy. Now the altered reality impinges on the fantasy, revealing its true personal worth, and (by implication) the comparative worthlessness of the writer's life.

The story conveys an extraordinary sense of parasitism; this, apparently, is what drives Miss Raby, 'seeing a path of salvation', to the desperate expedient of trying to make Feo agree to give her his youngest son to raise, so that the child can learn that 'rich people . . . are not the vile creatures he supposes' (*MS*, p. 180). Would such 'salvation' be a genuine and selfless atonement for the failed social interaction of the tourist relationship, imposed on Vorta by her writing? Or would it also be a personal, and partly selfish redemption for the childless writer, becoming step-mother to the son of the only man she had ever loved? Ultimately, it seems a confused gesture, tainted by her tribal desire to champion the 'rich people' who seem unable to free themselves from a pervasive mean-spiritedness. Miss Raby then progresses to another moment of personal revelation, which seems to take her beyond the nihilism of the earlier one:

> In that moment of final failure, there had been vouchsafed to her a vision of herself, and she saw that she had lived worthily. She was conscious of a triumph over experience and earthly facts, a triumph magnificent, cold, hardly human, whose existence no one but herself would ever surmise. From the view terrace she looked down on the perishing and perishable beauty of the valley, and, though she loved it no less, it seemed to be infinitely distant, like a valley in a star.
>
> (*MS*, p. 83)

The final isolation of Miss Raby carries a hint of redemption, especially in a world dominated by the 'automatic conventionality' of the tourists on the one hand (*MS*, p. 162), and the 'vast machinery' of profit-making that determines the behaviour of the locals on the other (*MS*, p. 174). But, ultimately, the withdrawal seems an expression of exhaustion and defeat, rather than a convincing moment of transcendence; we cannot so easily let the writer off the hook for being 'the making of Vorta' (*MS*, p. 180).[6]

The story, then, fences in the idea of the eternal moment with ambivalence: it evokes false literariness; complex (and destructive) self-knowledge; and ignoble isolation. But, as a sophisticated short story element – and here we can think of Forster's eternal moment as opposed to Miss Raby's – it becomes significant. This is one piece that sees Forster writing in the spirit of those modernist short story writers, like Joyce and Mansfield, who cultivate an ironic and opaque use of the revelation or epiphany to condense a rich sense of contingency in a very few words. (The hazy or ironic epiphanies of Joyce's *Dubliners* are the most obvious touchstone.)

'The Eternal Moment', however, is something of an oddity in Forster's writing. It is the only one of the stories published in his lifetime that refrains from a fantastic or supernatural treatment. Technically, the other stories tend to take Forster in alternative directions. On one issue, however – the explicit distrust of the machine age – his stories seem very much of their time, and, to a degree, in tune with another strand of modernist thinking: 'for Yeats, Lawrence, Forster, and others', suggests Tim Armstrong, 'the technological, rationalist, and utilitarian worldview derived from Newton, Hobbes, and Locke was the enemy of art, and to be opposed by a return to the sources of life'.[7] Armstrong cites Forster's well-known science fiction story 'The Machine Stops', a future dystopia in which humanity's reliance on technology has reached its logical conclusion: life is controlled by a single, global machine which orders a subterranean existence in honeycomb cells, lit artificially, governed by a cerebral existence that is lacking in distinction. The machine, rather like an early internet, facilitates the acquisition of a banalised general knowledge, and the means of its transmission. One character, the rebellious Kuno, desires to rediscover the surface of the earth (where he has seen 'homeless' figures, waiting for the underground civilisation to end). It is he who foretells the stopping of the machine before the story's apocalyptic end (*MS*, p. 118).

The rediscovery of nature and a suspicion of bookishness or false intellectualism are dominant elements in the stories in *The Machine Stops*. It would be wrong to equate this with the primitivism of a Lawrence, though there is some affinity, here; and, generally, Forster's stories, with their fabulistic orientation, are closer to Lawrence's than to Mansfield's. 'The Story of a Panic' is representative of this impulse, the story of an encounter with Pan, and the transformation of the boy, Eustace, who has summoned him 'in the chestnut woods above Ravello' (*MS*, p. 1). As he does in several of his stories, Forster deploys the device of an unimaginative and prejudiced narrator, the better to highlight the extraordinary nature of those events that are beyond the narrator's comprehension. The 'panic' that drives the benighted English tourists from their picnic in the woods, also leaves Eustace alone, to be discovered lying on his back with a goat's footmarks on the earth nearby (*MS*, p. 8). Eustace now swaps his listlessness for a passionate desire to be outdoors, and for the company of the young waiter Gennaro. The story ends with the death of Gennaro, but with the shouts and laughter of Eustace, who has foiled attempts to incarcerate him, resounding 'far down the valley towards the sea' (*MS*, p. 22).

There is also a hint in this story that a proper engagement with nature might combine with an appropriate intellectual life. The story begins with the announcement that 'Eustace's career – if career it can be called – certainly dates from that afternoon in the chestnut woods above Ravello' (*MS*, p. 1). The idea that we should read 'career' as denoting the character's later (and perhaps professional) life (rather than simply denoting the story's significant episode), is suggested by the narrator's observation of Eustace after his apparent encounter with Pan:

> I have often seen that peculiar smile since, both on the possessor's face and on the photographs of him that are beginning to get into the illustrated papers. But, till then, Eustace had always worn a peevish, discontented frown; and we were all unused to this disquieting smile. (*MS*, p. 8)

The indication that, in later life, Eustace has gone on to enjoy a degree of notoriety that is linked to the afternoon of the panic (and his continuing happiness) is a rare moment of affirmation in Forster's shorter fiction.

A more characteristic treatment of the confrontation between the worldly and the spiritual is found in 'The Road From Colonus', another story of the benighted English abroad, this time in Greece. The ageing Mr Lucas, in the story's central scene, is overcome by the revelation that comes to him upon discovering an enormous hollow plane tree, still living, with 'an impetuous spring' gushing through the trunk, that also houses a shrine, cut by 'simple country folk' wishing to pay tribute to 'beauty and mystery' (*MS*, p. 77). Although it is quite impractical to change the party's travel plans, Mr Lucas determines to stay in the nearby khan, or inn, convinced that this place is his salvation. His daughter Ethel and their fellow travellers, however, contrive to bundle him ignominiously back on to his mule, undermining his plan to stay, together with his dignity (*MS*, p. 82).

In the second section of the story, Mr Lucas and his daughter are back in England, some time later. He has reverted to type, an old man obsessed with his own domestic comforts. The arrival of a parcel, wrapped in old Greek newspaper, brings a twist in the tale redolent of Maupassant: Ethel translates an article in which are reported the deaths of the inhabitants of the khan, crushed by a 'large tree' which blew down on them on the very night that Mr Lucas had determined to stay there (*MS*, p. 85). Mr Lucas is oblivious, however, and can think only of the letter of complaint he plans to send to their landlord (*MS*, p. 86).

The supernatural element is ambiguous: does the collapse of the plane tree denote the collapse of some human/natural harmony violated by the insensitive English travellers, unable to respond to the tree-shrine in the way the elderly Mr Lucas does? Or was this probable death somehow *intended*, an apposite end for him at his visionary moment, and of which he is cheated? Certainly his mean existence in England does not indicate the lucky escape that the surprise ending implies, structurally.

But how are the cruel deaths of the Greeks explained by the supernatural motif? If we are meant to believe, in the logic of the story, that the actions of the English have somehow incurred the wrath of the gods, then the locals emerge as unlucky bystanders; and if Mr Lucas has been whisked away from his intended end, it is an end that is cruel in sweeping up the innocent locals in its path of destruction. In either case, the implied supernatural element obliges us to condemn the very presence of these English people in Greece, including Mr Lucas: all seem party to the wreaking of a havoc that goes far beyond their individual actions or insensitivities. There is a parallel with Miss Raby in 'The Eternal Moment', returning to Vorta twenty years on to discover her fictionalised account of the place has destroyed the life of the community in her absence. Like the tourists encouraged by Miss Raby, the visitors to Greece in 'The Road From Colonus' are party to a collective cultural vandalism that is larger than any individual transgression, and which delivers its destructive force after they have gone.

Reading through the supernatural motif, we discover a parable about the evils of tourism.

There is, then, a degree to which Forster uses the supernatural or the fantastic that is sceptical in its implications, revealing a more self-conscious literary focus, as in the subtly enriched stock device of the surprise revelation at the end of 'The Road From Colonus'. A related treatment is found in 'The Curate's Friend', in which a priest recollects the day a Faun appeared to him, evidently saving him from a marriage to which he was not suited. A joyful communion with nature, and a bachelor existence with a career in the Church, are instigated by the apparition:

> Though I try to communicate that joy to others – as I try to communicate anything else that seems good – and though I sometimes succeed, yet I can tell no one exactly how it came to me. For if I breathed one word of that, my present life, so agreeable and profitable, would come to an end, my congregation would depart, and so should I, and instead of being an asset to my parish, I might find myself an expense to the nation. Therefore in the place of the lyrical and rhetorical treatment, so suitable to the subject, so congenial to my profession, I have been forced to use the unworthy medium of a narrative, and to delude you by declaring that this is a short story, suitable for reading in the train.
>
> (*MS*, p. 74)

If we accept the narrator's words at face value, we are asked to rate narrative fiction as an inferior form of expression, inadequate to the religious intensity of his feeling of oneness with the world – the short story offers the only acceptable way of expressing it. At the same time, however, the narrator insists that this is not simply a fiction, that it has a vitality that cannot be openly admitted. The Faun, and the awareness the Faun makes possible, suggests a homosexual theme: the narrator's true nature and happiness, revealed to him at the moment he is diverted from marrying, has to be shrouded in secrecy, lest he should become 'an expense to the nation'. In this case, giving credence to the fantastic is an allegory of the dawning of homosexual awareness. There is also an implicit lament about the inadequacy of fiction, which, if publishable, and 'suitable for reading on the train' has to work to conceal this kind of sexual content.

There are various ways, then, in which the fantastic and mythological content of the stories in *The Machine Stops* can be seen as a veneer, concealing recognisably grounded social and cultural themes beneath the surface. This is a redeeming feature, because one could not make too large a claim for Forster as a convincing writer of the fantastic or supernatural. There is something perfunctory about this aspect of the stories; neither can one make a claim for Forster's originality in this direction. John Colmer suggests that one significant strand of short story writing, in the period of its rapid growth as a new literary form in the late nineteenth and early twentieth century, was its peculiar fascination for writers who wished to combine realism and fantasy, the natural and the supernatural. Consequently, in writing stories about Pan and the supernatural, Forster was in part conforming to a current literary fashion.[8]

The element of social and cultural rootedness identifiable in some of the stories, beneath the supernatural or fantastic surface narratives, with their mythological references, is not immediately apparent, and not always acknowledged. Indeed, there is a prevailing view that the stories lack a certain balance in this connection.

For Frederick Crews, a way of accounting for Forster's use of mythology is helpfully established by reference to Nietzsche's distinction, in *The Birth of Tragedy*, between the Apollonian and Dionysian principles. The Dionysian is 'the spirit that feels the oneness of all things', and which 'shares in all the pain and ecstasy in the universe'. In opposition to this 'involvement in excess', the spirit of Apollonianism establishes 'measure and morality' and 'imposes the image of finite humanity upon the disorder of experience', by recognising 'forms, borders, and categories'. Working on the assumption that a vital form of art 'draws its Apollonian images from a Dionysian intoxication with the primal unity', Crews finds a way of articulating the essence of Forster's importance, with reference to his most prominent novel, *A Passage to India*. Here the tone is characterised as being 'more "Apollonian" than ever in its sober dismissal of romantic illusions', even though 'this is also the most poetic of his novels'. Forster achieves a kind of balance by showing 'the relative insignificance of morality against a background of total disorder', thus giving 'the Dionysian principle its due', and 'turn[ing] over his art, for the first and apparently the last time, to a single controlling vision, which, though it eclipses his humanism, finally produces a novel with something of the power and wholeness of a myth itself'.[9]

This establishes a principle of balance that is transformative, but which also invokes the quintessential twentieth-century liberal dilemma of self-doubt. (It is also another way of articulating that wistfulness about the shortcomings of liberal humanism that may be a distinctive feature of Forster's modernism.)

The principle of balance, however, can also make the short stories seem inadequate. Where the Dionysian principle is in the ascendancy – as in 'The Story of a Panic', with its equation between 'freedom' and 'wild excess' – an incomplete vision is presented. Crews is clear that the better known short stories – 'The Story of a Panic', 'The Other Side of the Hedge', 'The Story of the Siren', 'Other Kingdom', 'The Curate's Friend', 'The Road From

Colonus' – are at one, at least in intention, 'with Forster's total ethical ideal', which is 'the Apollonian one of proportion, but of *vital* proportion, between body and soul, passion and intellect'. But the fact that this is not seemingly *achievable* in the short stories, may point to a formal limit. Unlike *The Longest Journey* and *Howards End*, where Forster 'has the leisure to bring his central characters to this balance', the short stories 'must confine themselves to a single psychological reversal', involving an initial 'confronting of the passionate side of one's nature', rather than clear progression 'toward a final harmony'. For Crews, this means that 'Forster's tales rest on a rather conventional antithesis between naturalness and inhibition, paganism and suburban Christianity'. The most that can be claimed for the stories is that 'the Dionysian identification with nature points dimly ahead toward the Apollonian ideal of self-knowledge'.[10] And if Crews is right that 'the gradual disappearance of allusions to Greek mythology' in Forster's work 'marks a growing independence from a certain current of shallow moralism', then the early stories, with their overt mythological references, would seem to be the embodiment of Forster's immature vision.[11]

The readings offered above of 'The Eternal Moment', 'The Road From Colonus', and 'The Curate's Friend' suggest a more sophisticated use of revelation than is implied in that 'shallow moralism'. These stories also betray an element of unresolved debate about the function of literature, very much in the spirit of the liberal writer's dilemma. Nevertheless, Crews's formulation pinpoints the kind of insubstantiality that many readers of the stories have identified, and which all serious readers of them must address.

One answer to the perceived shortcomings of Forster's short stories is to assess them as vehicles for ideas in a way that is not constrained by the usual conventions of the plot-driven story. In the view of Judith Scherer Herz, it is profitable to consider Forster's essays and stories together as 'short narratives', since both modes offer a freedom from convention, a freedom that suited Forster.[12]

In the fiction, a significant aspect of this freedom, for Herz, stems from the fact that 'the short story can shelter in the realms of fantasy and prophecy'. Capacities such as these locate a retreat from 'story' in the simple sense of a plot-driven narrative; and it was not Forster's particular forte to produce striking or original narratives in this sense. Instead, Herz finds a striking alternative rationale. Picking up on Forster's (semi-apologetic) references to Hermes in the introduction to the *Collected Short Stories* (*MS*, pp. xv–xvii), Herz makes an intriguing suggestion: that 'the Hermetic presence is . . . felt in the shaping of the narrative', so that Hermes 'informs the controlling point of view, which is often distinct from the teller of the tale'.[13]

'The Celestial Omnibus' presents an interesting example for consideration, here. The celestial journey that the mysterious sunrise and sunset omnibus affords, is an imaginative flight. The various drivers – Sir Thomas Browne, Austen, Dante – are facilitators for those, like the boy in the story, who are open to the transforming imaginative experience. By contrast, the smug Mr Bons ('snob' backwards),[14] despite presiding over 'the Literary Society' (MS, p. 29), has failed to cultivate the right kind of responsiveness, and plunges to a symbolic death. The story thus seems to be a straightforward parable about how to read, and a lament for contemporary 'literacy' in the sense that Forster intends it here: the hourly service of the omnibus has been suspended 'owing to lack of patronage' (MS, p. 31).

The story is an uncoloured third-person narrative, related from the point of view of the boy. Herz's contention, however, is that this is one of those stories where 'Hermes functions as the mythic analogue of the authorial presence'. The claim is that this device 'diminishes the necessity for direct intervention, or, rather, turns such intervention into a species of masquerade, where, in the person of the god, the narrator can manifest truths'. Consequently, 'the short story, in Forster's hands, becomes literally an epiphany', since 'the god himself inhabits there'.[15]

There is nothing, at a technical level, that clinches this; but one can see some substance in the claim when one thinks of the experience of reading the series of stories in *The Machine Stops*. A sequence of stories with the quality of parable, exploring the theme of spiritual development in opposition to the pettiness of the everyday, inevitably suggests a higher plane of organisation; and we may find the project is lent greater dignity, and seriousness, by the device of Hermes as mediator between author and reader.

However, there is also a sense in which Hermes is surely used ironically. Hermes was the god of roads: a messenger, the protector of travellers, and the bringer of luck.[16] Clearly, Hermes cannot be said to preside effectively over the journeys depicted in 'The Road From Colonus' and 'The Eternal Moment', where travelling itself is a focus of condemnation.

The noteworthy stories in *The Life to Come* – the posthumous collection of unpublished (but finished) material written throughout Forster's career – create effects that are related to the question of travel. The recurring theme of repressed homosexuality in the collection can be seriously limiting, producing moral tales directed fairly straightforwardly at social hypocrisy or restriction, as in 'Arthur Snatchfold' or 'Dr Woolacott'. There are two more interesting stories, however, where the denial or suppression of homosexuality is interestingly linked to colonialism. 'The Life to Come' recounts the story of a missionary, Pinmay, who seduces – or is seduced by – an indigenous

Chief called Vithobai. The attraction is evidently mutual, but the element of self-division is entirely Pinmay's: Vithobai believes from the start that the 'love of Christ' to which he is introduced is sexual. Finally, as Vithobai is dying, Pinmay seeks atonement for 'the dark erotic perversion that the chief mistook for Christianity' (*LC*, p. 76). Because it is not the custom of his ancestors to die in a bed, Vithobai has retired to the roof of his dwelling. Questioning Pinmay on the Christian understanding of the life to come, Vithobai is persuaded that they will meet again, and that there will be 'real and true love'. Impatient for this eternal life, he stabs the missionary 'through the heart' before throwing himself off the roof (*LC*, pp. 81–2).

The piece is richer than some of the other pieces in the volume, since the theme of sexual repression is linked to the issue of ideological control. Forster shows how the strictures of colonialism are mutually damaging to coloniser and colonised; but he also indicates how the colonialist's ideas can be appropriated to unleash unexpected counter-forces. This is economically achieved and, although these ideas have become familiar aspects of postcolonial writing, the presentation seems particularly insightful for 1922, when the story was written (*LC*, p. xii).

'The Other Boat' (written 1957–8) is a related piece, and the other noteworthy story in the collection.[17] Again, the theme is the repression of homosexuality; and again, this becomes more than a personal preoccupation since it is made to speak to the question of colonialism and the psychological damage it may be responsible for.[18] A relationship develops between Captain Lionel March and the 'half caste' Moraes, though Moraes (nicknamed 'Cocoanut') has contrived to 'catch' March by arranging things so they would have to share a cabin on this passage to India.[19] Caught between his desire for this 'excellent kid', and his sense of propriety and status, March finally murders Cocoanut during a frenzied sexual act before throwing himself into the sea (*LC*, pp. 195–6).

The combination of repulsion and attraction is skilfully evoked, and in a manner that recalls the hypnotic relationship between the officer and the orderly in Lawrence's 'The Prussian Officer'; here, the ambivalence requires us to unpack some of the prejudices, since the confused response is based on the elision between different taboos. March seems to fear being caught with someone not of his 'caste' (*LC*, p. 192), as much as he fears the scandal that a homosexual affair would involve, and it is that double marginalisation of Cocoanut which makes him doubly desirable, 'other' in two senses. The threat to March's colonial career, as a military man posted to India, and planning marriage, comes from his repressed desires, and the external manifestation of these in the person of Cocoanut: the murder and self-destruction is evidently emblematic of colonial hypocrisy.

Perhaps the most characteristic element of Forster's stories is indicated by 'The Life to Come', with its attempt to define an alternative kind of religious intensity, which is inclusive in ways that he feels organised Christianity is not. In the spirit of Lawrence's 'The Man Who Died', Forster uses Vithobai's misunderstanding of Christian theology to suggest that the Divine should embrace the sexual.

The deliberation about salvation is probably the key feature of Forster's stories. In 'Mr Andrews' he makes his boldest and most positive statement about what this might mean. In the story, an English Christian (Mr Andrews) and a Turkish Moslem, fly up to Heaven, each convinced of their own righteousness and the other's unworthiness, and are admitted for their act of praying on behalf of the other (*MS*, p. 136). Their rapid disillusionment stems from the discovery that Heaven is a place where 'their expectations were fulfilled, but not their hopes'. Mr Andrews summarises the experience: 'we desire infinity and we cannot imagine it. How can we expect it to be granted?' (*MS*, p. 138) Both choose to depart, and experience a personal dissolution:

> As soon as they passed the gate, they felt again the pressure of the world soul. For a moment they stood hand in hand resisting it. Then they suffered it to break in upon them, and they, and all the experience they had gained, and all the love and wisdom they had generated, passed into it, and made it better.
>
> (*MS*, p. 139)

The opening of the story seems an apt illustration of Forster's much-quoted assertion that 'two people pulling each other into salvation is the only theme I find worthwhile'.[20] However, the benign effects of personal dissolution, projected at the end, seem to imply something beyond personal salvation. If this is a 'post-Christian' sentiment, it also implies something secular and communal that is related to Forster's ambivalence about the adequacy of liberal humanism in the twentieth century. If he cannot describe a state beyond personal co-operation and tolerance, he does imply, in the gesture that concludes 'Mr Andrews', that these qualities should lead us on to the higher plane that we cannot imagine.

Notes

1. The six stories originally from *The Celestial Omnibus* are: 'The Story of a Panic', 'The Other Side of the Hedge', 'The Celestial Omnibus', 'Other Kingdom', 'The Curate's Friend', and 'The Road From Colonus'; the six originally from *The Eternal Moment* are: 'The Machine Stops', 'The Point of It', 'Mr Andrews', 'Co-ordination', 'The Story of the Siren', and 'The Eternal Moment'. This is the order in which they appear in both the *Collected Short Stories* and in the edition

used here, *The Machine Stops and Other Stories*, Abinger Edition, vol. 7, ed. Rod Mengham (London: André Deutsch, 1997), cited in the essay as *MS*.

2. Katherine Mansfield, 'Throw them overboard!', *Athenaeum*, 4711 (13 August 1920), 209–10, repr. in *E. M. Forster: the Critical Heritage*, ed. Philip Gardner (London: Routledge and Kegan Paul, 1973), pp. 184–6. Quote from pp. 184–5.

3. *The Letters and Journals of Katherine Mansfield: A Selection*, ed. C. K. Stead (Harmondsworth: Penguin, 1981), p. 213.

4. David Medalie, *E. M. Forster's Modernism* (Basingstoke and New York: Palgrave, 2002), pp. 4, 2, 38.

5. Rod Mengham indicates that Forster had Cortina d'Ampezzo in mind as the basis for Vorta: at the time the story is set, Cortina was part of 'Italia Irredenta' (with a mostly Italian population), though it is now in the Alto Adige (*MS*, p. 189).

6. An alternative perspective on the ethics of fiction writing is offered in *A Room with a View*, where the novel by Miss Lavish plays a chance role in bringing the lovers together – in the spirit of that novel's 'comic muse'.

7. Tim Armstrong, 'Technology: "Multiplied Man"', in *A Concise Companion to Modernism*, ed. David Bradshaw (Oxford: Blackwell, 2003), pp. 158–78. Quote from p. 167.

8. John Colmer, *E. M. Forster: The Personal Voice* (London and Boston: Routledge and Kegan Paul, 1975), p. 29. Colmer indicates that the theme of Pan 'may be found in Yeats's poetry of the 1890s, in Meredith's novels (much admired by Forster when he first began to write), in the nature writing of Richard Jefferies (who also celebrates the spirit of place and the eternal moment), and, at a much more popular level, in Saki and in Kenneth Grahame's *The Wind in the Willows*'.

9. Frederick Crews, *E. M. Forster: The Perils of Humanism* (Princeton: Princeton University Press, 1962), pp. 124–5, 140–1.

10. Ibid., pp. 129–31.

11. Ibid., p. 124.

12. Judith Scherer Herz, *The Short Narratives of E. M. Forster* (Basingstoke and London: Macmillan, 1988).

13. Ibid., pp. 8, 30.

14. Other readers will have been more observant than me and will have spotted this detail, brought to my attention by John Colmer's book. See *E. M. Forster: The Personal Voice*, p. 34.

15. Herz, *The Short Narratives of E. M. Forster*, p. 35.

16. Adrian Room, *Room's Classical Dictionary: The Origins of the Names of Characters in Classical Mythology* (London: Routledge and Kegan Paul, 1983), p. 157.

17. In the estimation of Norman Page, 'The Other Boat' is 'the finest story in the volume . . . an impressively tragic tale, masterly in its sureness of touch and a worthy pendant to *A Passage to India*'. See *E. M. Forster* (Basingstoke and London: Macmillan, 1987), p. 124.

18. One might contrast this with the less convincing treatment of homosexual attraction in 'Ralph and Tony' where Forster tries to find some resolution and acceptance between his characters, hinted at by the unconventional responses of the 'martyred Margaret' who seems to give her benediction to Ralph and Tony at the end (p. 92).

19. The ethnicity of Cocoanut is uncertain. He has two passports, one Portuguese, one Danish. The narrator, rendering March's train of thought, gives the speculation that 'half the blood must be Asiatic, unless a drop was Negro' (*MS*, p. 181). Earlier, the narrator indicates that he 'belonged to no race' (*MS*, p. 174). Nevertheless, his treatment by the English as a racial inferior has a colonial flavour. Indeed, Colonel Arbuthnot considers the arrangement by which March is obliged to share a cabin with the 'resident wog' to be damaging to 'our prestige in the East' (*MS*, p. 194).

20. E. M. Forster, *Commonplace Book*, ed. Philip Gardner (Stanford: Stanford University Press, 1987), p. 55.

6

ELIZABETH LANGLAND

Forster and the novel

The intensely, stifling human quality of the novel is not to be avoided; the novel
is sogged with humanity; there is no escaping the uplift or the downpour,
nor can they be kept out of criticism. We may hate humanity, but if it
is exorcised or even purified the novel wilts; little is left but a bunch of words.
(*AN*, pp. 15–16)

In the course of his lifetime, Forster wrote six novels, but that simple state-ment conceals more than it reveals. Those novels were penned during a period of only twenty years in what was a very long life extending over ninety years. Born in 1879, at the height of the late Victorian period, Forster died in 1970 in a post-modern England. The novels themselves cluster in the first two decades of the twentieth century; the first, *Where Angels Fear to Tread*, appeared in 1905 and the last written, *A Passage to India*, was published in 1924. One novel, *Maurice*, was not published until 1971, but, as Forster notes, it was begun in 1913 and finished in 1914. Its subject – homosexuality – determined that it would wait almost half a century before publication made it available to a general readership.

In addition to the fact that his novels cluster into a short period of his life, Forster also penned his ultimate word on the subject, *Aspects of the Novel*, as a series of lectures delivered in the spring of 1927, published in the same year, and unaltered in subsequent reissues of the volume. Forster's work is helpfully illuminated both by examining that short work on the novel and by recognising his distinctive position as a novelist, bridging the late Victorian and early modern periods.

Forster is a difficult novelist to approach because he appears simple, in part due to his temperamental allegiance to the Victorian period. About himself he wrote in 1946: 'I belong to the fag-end of Victorian liberalism' (*TCD*, p. 54). He seems to have had recourse to a nineteenth-century liberal humanism in resolving his novels, an emphasis that sets at naught the complexities of literary modernism. Further, his work presents none of the stylistic resistance and technical virtuosity characteristic of his notable contemporaries such as James Joyce and Virginia Woolf. For most of his novels, Forster employs an omniscient and somewhat intrusive narrator, a narrative technique more characteristic of high Victorianism than of modernism. In addition, Forster's novels remain rigorously focused on the struggles of characters in conflict with their own societies and other cultures. As his contemporaries were turning attention inward, focusing increasingly on consciousness itself and society as immanent in that consciousness, Forster, like his Victorian predecessors, kept his eye on individuals' varied relationships to societies external to themselves. So, at best, Forster claims a precarious stake in the twentieth-century canon.

He was aware of his somewhat anomalous position in his century. He engaged in long discussions about the nature of fiction with Virginia Woolf, like himself a member of the Bloomsbury circle. Whereas she famously claimed that, 'On or about December 1910, human character changed',[1] and championed an art form more experimental and self-sufficient, Forster consciously argued for a very different aesthetic. He insisted that the claims of life were primary, she the claims of art. He objected to her singleness of vision as a denial of life, she to his double vision as a failure of art.[2] Together, Forster and Woolf present for us the modernist conflict.

Clear evidence of Forster's determination to take a tack different from many of his contemporaries emerges in *Aspects of the Novel* when he refuses the kind of historical approach characteristic of other theorists and critics who have attempted to say something comprehensive about the genre. In a long introductory chapter, Forster juxtaposes novelists from different periods, centuries, and cultures, stating that 'This idea of a period of a development in time, with its consequent emphasis on influences and schools, happens to be exactly what I am hoping to avoid during our brief survey . . . Time, all the way through, is to be our enemy' (*AN*, p. 5). Defining '[c]lassification by chronology' as a crime and 'classification by subject matter' as 'sillier still' (*AN*, p. 7), Forster adopts the image of a 'circular room, a sort of British Museum reading-room', peopled by English novelists 'all writing their novels simultaneously' (*AN*, p. 7). His self-styled 'ramshackly course' (*AN*, p. 8) allows Forster to pair novelists like Samuel Richardson and Henry James, Charles Dickens and H. G. Wells, and, more unusual, Laurence Sterne and Virginia Woolf, and he concludes his introduction with the claim that 'Principles and systems may suit other forms of art, but they cannot be applicable here – or if applied their results must be subjected to re-examination. And who is the re-examiner? Well, I am afraid it will be the human heart' (*AN*, p. 15). In this grand gesture, Forster has staked out the ground not only for his series of lectures but also for his own novels, those 'spongy tract[s], those fictions in prose of a certain extent which extend so indeterminately' (*AN*, p. 15).

This essay on Forster and the novel has two primary goals: first, to understand Forster's own aesthetic of the novel and to explore its capacity to illuminate the emphases and techniques of his canon; and second, in the context provided by that examination, to reconsider Forster's stature as a novelist and his contributions to the form of the novel in the early twentieth century.

The pivot of Forster's theory of the novel and the pivot of his novels is the human heart, more specifically love and the complications that love engenders. He gives short shrift to 'story', which he acknowledges is 'the fundamental aspect of the novel' but regrettable because it appeals atavistically to simple curiosity. Story is only 'the life in time' that provides a framework for Forster's other aspects of the novel – people, plots, fantasy, prophecy, pattern, and rhythm – that create the 'life by values' (*AN*, p. 19).

Notably, Forster devotes two lectures of nine to what he calls 'People' – not character, but people, and the difference between the terms is telling. In part, Forster wants to insist on the importance of creating credible individuals not mere technical devices, an implicit critique of some of his more experimental contemporaries. Forster reserves the concept of a 'character' to mean, essentially, a human being confronting the dictates of material life in ways that reveal values. Forster fears the aestheticism that characterises some modernist works; for him, ethics must be wedded to aesthetics. The inclusion of human beings in novels provides opportunities to introduce values into the crude enterprise of eliciting curiosity through the means of a story.

What is surprising, and certainly controversial as a proposition, is Forster's next claim that the 'main facts in human life are five: birth, food, sleep, love, and death' (*AN*, p. 33). Four of these are fundamental to existence: one must be born and die, one must have nourishment and rest for the body. Then there's love, which term Forster says he is using in its 'widest and dullest sense' (*AN*, p. 34). It comprehends mere sex and the highest aspirations of the spirit: 'All I suggest is that we call the whole bundle of emotions love, and regard them as the fifth great experience through which human beings have to pass. When human beings love they try to get something. They also try to give something, and this double aim makes love more complicated than food or sleep. It is selfish and altruistic at the same time' (*AN*, p. 35). The priority Forster gives to this whole complex of emotions he terms 'love' helps us to understand how he conceives and develops his novels.

Because Forster's first, less frequently read novel, *Where Angels Fear to Tread*, establishes techniques, patterns, and themes that reverberate throughout his later works, I will invest time in outlining its plot, which hinges on love. Philip Herriton, from whose point of view the story emerges, has a passion for Italy that leads him to persuade his widowed and relatively unsophisticated sister-in-law, Lilia, that she should immerse herself in the culture of that southern country because 'Italy really purifies and ennobles all who visit her' (*WAFT*, p. 4). The family deplores Lilia's manners and propensities – she has the 'knack of being absurd in public' (*WAFT*, p. 4) – and they want to remove Lilia's influence from her daughter, Irma, and her person from the snares of potential suitors. To ensure her respectability, the family provides Lilia with a chaperone, 'sober Caroline Abbott', who is herself ten years younger than her 33-year-old charge (*WAFT*, p. 6). Of course, Italy works its own kind of magic on the mind and heart of Lilia, and she marries an Italian adventurer, Gino, and then dies in giving birth to their son. Once again, the Herriton family decides to intervene and claim the child, who is a half brother to Irma, tragically underestimating the charismatic power of Gino and the depth of his involvement with his young son. The rescue party of three – Philip, his sister, Harriet, and Caroline Abbott – precipitates a disaster that costs the life of the child and culminates in the painful revelation for Philip, who has come to love Caroline deeply, that she, in turn, passionately loves Gino. Philip, the first of many ascetics who people Forster's novels, has reached his passion via a spiritual path: 'her thoughts and her goodness and her nobility had moved him first, and now her whole body and all its gestures had become transfigured by them' (*WAFT*, p. 141). But Caroline, who believes Philip to be without passion, is oblivious to his heart, and confesses to him that she is now in love, body and soul, with Gino. She has left Gino forever, but her motive for betraying her secret is that she must be able to speak of him sometimes or she 'shall die' (*WAFT*, p. 146).

Central themes and characteristic techniques emerge: the association of asceticism with aestheticism, a revelation of the muddle experienced by people coerced by social convention and alienated from the life and 'truth' of the body, and the use of a travel experience to foreign countries as a way of clarifying what is English. At least in the early novels, the muddle is resolved through an ultimate affirmation of life and love in the body. In his last two published novels – *Howards End* and *A Passage to India* – the prophetic mode infuses and informs the resolution in crucial ways that I will elaborate shortly. In *Where Angels Fear to Tread*, the resolution punctuates loss – Caroline's of Gino and Philip's of Caroline – even as Philip has his epiphanic recognition that 'For her [Caroline] no love could be degrading; she stood outside all degradation. This episode, which she thought so sordid, and which was so tragic for him, remained supremely beautiful' (*WAFT*, pp. 147–8). Forster's next novel, *The Longest Journey* (1907), struggles with the same tensions and longings for a more inclusive reality but also reaches a resolution that accepts fragments.

A Room with a View (1908) presents the most satisfactory transcendence of the muddle, which it links to a full embrace of Italy and the Italian experience, which symbolise, in their turn, the characters' transcendence of the crippling aspects of their Englishness. Forster's third novel allows a fulfilment in the body that is only glimpsed or intuited in the two earlier novels, but that fruition is precarious. Lucy Honeychurch's emotions have long been stifled and cannot be nourished by what is offered by a church veering to hypocrisy on the one side and asceticism on the other. She reveals untapped depths in part through her playing the piano, particularly the works of Beethoven, which persuades Reverend Beebe that 'if Miss Honeychurch ever takes to live as she plays, it will be very exciting – both for us and for her' (*RV*, p. 31). But Lucy fears what her music discloses to her. Although counselled by Mr Emerson, a fellow pensioner in the Bertolini, to 'let yourself go. You are inclined to get muddled . . . Pull out from the depths those thoughts that you do not understand, and spread them out in the sunlight and know the meaning of them' (*RV*, p. 26), she veers away from that disturbing sunlight toward the certainty of established convention even as she cries out: 'I want not to be muddled' (*RV*, p. 79).

The novel is split into two parts: Italy and England. The Lucy who returns to England for the second half has been superficially improved by Italy without succumbing to the deeper, and threatening, possibilities it has revealed. Her new-found cultivation has attracted Cecil Vyse, another of Forster's ascetics, who shares the tendencies of Philip Herriton to turn a woman into an aesthetic object or object of worship. But Lucy resists being treated as a work of art because Italy has offered her the chance to fathom herself and be true to her emotions. In a pattern reminiscent of *Where Angels Fear To Tread*, Cecil, like Philip, becomes a better man when stirred out of his asceticism by passion for a living, breathing woman no longer conceived as aesthetic and spiritual. For Cecil, as for Philip, it is too late, but not for Lucy, who penetrates her own muddle to accept the truth of her love for George Emerson.

Maurice echoes *A Room with a View* in both its patterns and its thematic resolution – although the novel's setting at Cambridge University, its focus on men, and its representation of homosexuality may interfere at first with our recognising the similarities. Maurice, like Lucy, loves first somewhat ideally and abstractly – his will is in thrall to Clive's, which permits spiritual mingling between the men while denying or ignoring bodily desire. Alec, who, as a servant and gamekeeper, is even more ineligible and unacceptable than was George Emerson as a railway employee, ultimately offers to Maurice that redemptive holiness and sanctity of direct bodily desire and its consummation.

Forster distinguishes in *Aspects of the Novel* between fantasy and prophecy, and in *Maurice*, as in *The Longest Journey*, fantasy is the dominant mode and makes possible an improbably happy ending to Forster's novel about homosexual love and fulfilment. Both novels depict an England where escape was still possible; Maurice and Alec can simply disappear. As Clive is counselling Maurice about needing to silence a potentially extortionate Alec, 'Maurice had disappeared thereabouts, leaving no trace of his presence except a little pile of the petals of the evening primrose' (M, p. 214). In his ominously entitled 'Terminal Note' to Maurice, written forty-six years later, Forster acknowledges that the book 'certainly dates' for the 'vital reason' that 'it belongs to the last moment of the greenwood', a sylvan zone of freedom outside of social law and convention. Forster adds that 'The Longest Journey belongs there too, and has similarities of atmosphere. Our greenwood ended catastrophically and inevitably . . . There is no forest or fell to escape to today, no cave in which to curl up, no deserted valley for those who wish neither to reform nor corrupt society but to be left alone' (M, pp. 219–20).

Although this essay employs the concepts of fantasy and prophecy in analysing the techniques and effects of Forster's novels, it is important to acknowledge that Forster himself does not introduce an explicit discussion of either concept into any of his own novels. Indeed, he seems to preclude considering his work in the light of 'prophecy' by declaring that D. H. Lawrence is 'as far as I know, the only prophetic novelist writing today – all the rest are fantasists or preachers' (AN, p. 99). Nonetheless, Forster's fiction *does* engage with these terms in very illuminating ways, and they tell us something important about Forster's methods and techniques in the novel. Two-thirds of the way through his series of lectures – having completed discussions of story, people, and plot – Forster reaches a moment of summary: 'The idea running through these lectures is by now plain enough: that there are in the novel two forces: human beings and a bundle of various things not human beings, and that it is the novelist's business to adjust these two forces and conciliate their claims' (AN, p. 73). This summation becomes a platform for considering what 'more' might exist in the novel: 'And by "more" . . . I mean something that cuts across them like a bar of light, that is intimately connected with them at one place and patiently illumines all their problems, and at another place shoots over or through them as if they did not exist' (AN, p. 74). Forster not only concludes that something more exists, but decides that 'we shall give that bar of light two names: fantasy and prophecy' (AN, p. 74), both suggesting access to a deeper knowledge beyond the quotidian.[3]

By the time Forster was writing his two great novels – *Howards End* and *A Passage to India* – he was consistently and subtly pursuing that something more, that bar of light that cuts across the human and the non-human. The illuminating light of fantasy that asks us to 'pay something extra' (AN, p. 76) emerges most powerfully in the elusive figure of Mrs Wilcox, whose first

ELIZABETH LANGLAND

words in *Howards End* point to realms of knowledge beyond the quotidian: 'Charles, dear Charles, one doesn't ask plain questions. There aren't such things' (*HE*, p. 19). Through her connection with Howards End, for which she seeks a spiritual heir, and the wych-elm that stands by it, Mrs Wilcox emerges as a unifying force linking past, present, and future in a fable of England. It is she who 'knows everything . . . is everything . . . is the house, and the tree that leans over it' (*HE*, p. 311).

'Love', that motive force in the early novels, still drives the characters of *Howards End*. The novel begins with the debacle of a sudden passion between Margaret's sister, Helen, and Mrs Wilcox's son Paul, and concludes with the birth of a 'love child', the progeny of another short-lived passion – Helen again and the lower-middle-class Leonard Bast. Yet even when the joining of man and woman is tinged with the sordid or mercenary, something grander and more mysterious beckons, a radiance bequeathed by love, a sense that life is dangerous and unmanageable not because it is a battle but 'because it is a romance, and its essence is romantic beauty' (*HE*, p. 105).

Pivotal as love is to the novel's story and plot, the prominence of Howards End, and, at Mrs Wilcox's sudden death, the question of its inheritance, gesture to larger questions of who properly should inherit England herself. '"Does she belong", the narrator asks, 'to those who have moulded her and made her feared by other lands, or to those who had added nothing to her power, but have somehow seen her, seen the whole island at once, lying as a jewel in a silver sea, sailing as a ship of souls, with all the brave world's fleet accompanying her toward eternity?' (*HE*, p. 172). Conflicts that had been represented in Forster's earlier novels as between persons (Gino and Philip) or perhaps between cultures (Italy and England) have now acquired the mythic, prophetic dimension of an illumination that shoots over them or through them as if they did not exist and, in so doing, gestures toward connection and reconciliation.

'Only connect', the epigraph to *Howards End*, demands reconciling seeming opposites: the seen and unseen, the prose and the passion, the beast and the monk, the joys of the flesh on one side and the inconceivable on the other, the transitory and the eternal. But the truth or proportion that is achieved through connection cannot begin with the average: '[T]ruth, being alive, was not halfway between anything. It was only to be found by continuous excursions into either realm, and though proportion is the final secret, to espouse it at the outset is to insure sterility' (*HE*, p. 192).

Forster's grasp of what it means to be muddled – which is a failure of connection, a tendency to live in fragments – finds powerful representation in Margaret Schlegel's condemnation of her new husband, Henry Wilcox, who had been Ruth Wilcox's husband and had earlier betrayed her with Jacky:

'You shall see the connection if it kills you, Henry! . . . Stupid, hypocritical, cruel – oh, contemptible! – a man who insults his wife when she's alive and cants with her memory when she's dead . . . These men are you. You can't recognize them, because you cannot connect . . . All your life you have been spoilt . . . No one has ever told you what you are – muddled, criminally muddled' (*HE*, p. 305). And against the anodyne of criminal muddledom, Forster posits a vision of connection and wholeness, a vision possible from the perspective, so to speak, of Howards End: 'In these English farms, if anywhere, one might see life steadily and see it whole, group in one vision its transitoriness and its eternal youth, connect – connect without bitterness until all men are brothers' (*HE*, p. 266). The characters or 'people' in Forster's novel ultimately recede, shadow-like, behind the prophetic light of connection and universal brotherhood that illumines the whole.

The composition of *Maurice* succeeded *Howards End* and, with its completion, Forster was to wait almost ten years before publishing *A Passage to India*, a novel that removed him from England and Europe and allowed him to grapple with the great questions of Empire, India, and Britain's complex relationship to the subcontinent in general. In structure, Forster's last novel is his most experimental and his most modern. Although always impatient with the demands of 'story' ('Yes – oh dear yes – the novel tells a story' (*AN*, p. 17)), Forster's fiction has previously relied upon the sequence of events, particularly the causal sequence of events that he gives the higher designation of 'plot', to generate the narrative instabilities that are then resolved in the events of a novel's conclusion. Unsurprisingly, birth, death, and sleep, three of the other five 'main facts' in human life, join with love to resolve fairly traditionally the primary instabilities that Forster's actions have introduced and to bring his fictions to a close. In *Howards End* Leonard Bast dies, but Helen gives birth to his child, who will inherit the farm and, implicitly, all of England. *Where Angels Fear to Tread* closes with the debacle of the child's death, whereas *Maurice* and *A Room with a View* conclude with love consummated. Finally, *The Longest Journey* culminates with sleep and an augury of waking to a new life with salvation for the next generation.

What distinguishes the plot of *A Passage to India* from that of Forster's earlier fictions is that primary instabilities in the action are resolved two-thirds of the way through the novel. In short, the gathering tensions and frustrated attempts to find common ground between the British and Indian populations – both Hindu and Muslim – lead inexorably to the Marabar Caves, Adela Quested's accusation of attempted rape, the trial of Aziz, the tumult of Adela's recantation and Aziz's acquittal, and Adela's return to England. Arguably, at this point in the narrative the momentum generated by plot has largely dissipated, yet the novel is far from over.

Although highly unusual, it is interesting – both for similarities and signif-icant differences – to compare *A Passage to India* with what has been called the first novel in English, Samuel Richardson's *Pamela* (1740–1). There, too, primary instabilities in the plot, signified by servant Pamela's unequal rela-tionship to her gentleman master, Mr B, are resolved two-thirds of the way into the novel, in this case by the characters' marriage. Yet, Richardson has left loose ends generated by Pamela's substantial elevation in status and the uncertainty about whether she will be accepted by Mr B's family and by other members of his class, and he spends the last third of the novel resolving those issues. Whereas Richardson's structure has been seen as accidental and prob-lematic and has been attributed to challenges still to be met in this new form, Forster's structure is deliberate. And rather than having been criticised for a flawed plot, Forster has been praised for his vision.

While I have pointed backwards to Richardson to clarify a point about plotting, I would now pair Forster with his contemporary Virginia Woolf to make a point about the modernist aesthetic of *A Passage to India*. In this novel, the kinds of clarifications that typically follow the resolution of major plot instabilities all unravel, and more confusion results. The Englishman Fielding, who has won the trust of the Indians by defending Aziz's innocence, is compromised in their minds by chivalrously hosting Adela Quested in the wake of the trial until she can depart safely for England. Mrs Moore, the Englishwoman who had earlier befriended Aziz and with whom he feels a deep spiritual bond, withdraws in the aftermath of the debacle of the Marabar Caves, leaves for England, and dies at sea. And although Fielding ultimately meets and marries Mrs Moore's daughter, Stella, Aziz becomes persuaded that Fielding is marrying his accuser Miss Quested, an illusion deliberately fostered by his friend Mahmoud Ali, and Aziz withdraws and refuses all communication with his former friend.

Thus, further division and rupture strew the narrative path leading away from the trial. No event or sequence of events can resolve these narrative instabilities: they are born of a clash of cultures, a conflict of values, and the impossibility of some kind of connection that transcends the individual. We note a connection, for example, with Virginia Woolf's *To the Lighthouse* (1927). There, the plot instabilities generated by Mrs Ramsay's death can be completed only by an evanescent gesture, Lily Briscoe's brushstroke as Mr Ramsay reaches the lighthouse with Cam and James. Nonetheless, Woolf preserves throughout the novel the narrative drive of the characters' quest to reach the lighthouse. Forster dispenses with that kind of narrative drive and focuses his attention exclusively on the lyrical and prophetic modes. At the end of *A Passage to India*, Fielding asks Aziz, 'Why can't we be friends now? . . . It's what I want. It's what you want.' The narrator, not

Aziz, provides the response: 'But the horses didn't want it – they swerved apart; the earth didn't want it, sending up rocks through which the riders must pass single file; the temples, the tank, the jail, the palace, the birds, the carrion, the Guest House, that came into view as they issued from the gap and saw Mau beneath: they didn't want it, they said in their hundred voices, "No, not yet," and the sky said, "No, not there"' (*PI*, p. 312). Both Woolf and Forster represent consciousness immanent in the universe, adopting a more lyrical than narrative mode to resolve their novels. This distinctively modernist gesture must figure into our understanding of Forster's novelistic canon even if we hesitate to claim Forster as a modernist.

If one goal of this essay was to consider Forster's novels and novelistic techniques in his own terms, then the second goal must be to assess his work and its significance within a larger context provided by his period and peers. Despite his experimental conclusion to *A Passage to India*, Forster does not shake himself free of certain Western ideologies, and critics who assess Forster's novelistic canon are troubled by back currents of values and beliefs working against the innovative techniques and prophetic gestures, so that the visions Forster presents inevitably remain caught up in ideologies and contradictions of his period. Edward Said uses the conclusion to *A Passage to India*, cited above, to illuminate his thesis in *Orientalism* that, although Asia is brought 'tantalisingly close' to the West, 'we are left at the end with a sense of the pathetic difference separating "us" from an Orient destined to bear its foreignness as a mark of its permanent estrangement from the West'.[4] For Said, the West's gestures of friendship must be accepted only in their own terms, and so the imperialism that has been challenged reasserts itself. And my own earlier article arguing for Forster's transformative feminist perspective in *Howards End* has to grapple uneasily in its conclusion with how definitive is Margaret Schlegel's triumph over the imperialist, patriarchal mode represented by Henry Wilcox and his sons.[5] It's not clear that Forster's gestures toward an unspoken knowledge can finally evade the patriarchal hierarchies that Margaret's 'only connect' seeks to transcend. We need to consider whether the fantastic and prophetic modes as they exist in Forster require from him a more rigorous and systematic analysis of the structures of oppression to which he himself has contributed. It is, perhaps, a limitation of his work that his liberalism and focus on the individual human stop him short of grasping fully the predations of imperialism, patriarchism, chauvinism, and sexism. Nonetheless, his analyses of sexuality, gender, class, and nationality constitute some of the more modern aspects of his novels.

Readers might expect that Forster's homosexuality would have given him a more trenchant insight into the operations of power, but we must recall in this context the 'fantasy' with which his explicitly homosexual novel,

Maurice, concludes. Fantasy by other names might be known as escapism or nostalgia for things as they are not, never were, and never will be. By allowing Maurice and Alec to escape into the greenwood, is Forster simply turning his eyes away from historical reality? Certainly, such an evasion would not be contradictory to the aesthetic spirit of *Aspects of the Novel* in which Forster espouses both fantasy and prophecy as avenues to a higher truth. The question arises: when Forster wants to be visionary is he thwarted by a reactionary nostalgia?

Perhaps Forster glimpsed the shortcomings of his own fiction in diagnosing the limitations of the English as a people. In his 1926 essay 'Notes on the English Character', Forster comments that the English must act in a world 'of whose richness and subtlety they have no conception. They go forth into it with well-developed bodies, fairly developed minds, and undeveloped hearts'. The Englishman 'is afraid to feel' (*AH*, pp. 4–5). Further, he argues that although 'No national character is complete', the 'English character is incomplete in a way that is particularly annoying to the foreign observer. It has a bad surface – self-complacent, unsympathetic, and reserved' (*AH*, p. 13). Muddle, he implies, is the most characteristic condition of the English man or woman, and it is that single concept that echoes through all of Forster's novels. Tellingly, Forster is impelled by a sense of urgency to make what he calls 'this feeble contribution' to understanding the English character: 'The nations *must* understand one another, and quickly . . . for the shrinkage of the globe is throwing them into one another's arms' (*AH*, p. 13). This perceptive observation about the tendency of the world informs all of Forster's novels.

I would like to end with some reflections provoked by these insights. Writing when he did and positioned canonically where he is, Forster is a pivotal figure in the history of the novel. Although he employs some modernist themes and techniques, detailed above, his impulses and values did not allow him to espouse a modernism that lacked both a strong ethical grounding and a commitment to illuminating human life in society. Forster's ongoing dialogue about the novel with Virginia Woolf diagnoses the unease he felt. Although clearly allied to writers like John Galsworthy and Arnold Bennett in his commitment to representing individuals in society, Forster is also drawn to suggesting the beauty, the mystery, the meditative, mythic, and numinous quality of human life that inhabits the ordinary and, in so doing, he approaches instead the realms of Woolf and Joyce. Virginia Woolf could not say of Forster, as she did of Galsworthy and Bennett, that the insistent first-person pronoun 'I' falls like a bar across the page.[6] Like Thomas Hardy, who quit writing novels in 1896 and turned thereafter to poetry, Forster was never fully at home with the dispositions and novelistic conventions of his age. He did not write another novel after *A Passage to India*. But Forster's novels have never been consigned to the literary attic as 'period' pieces; they are instead important documents of the transition into modernism.

That Forster's novels remain relevant today is testified by their rebirth as popular movies. They retain their immediacy for us, in part, because they bring before our eyes the spectres of homophobia, sexism, patriarchism, and imperialism with which we grapple, and force us to acknowledge the seemingly intractable restrictions of national character, of muddle, in transcending our limitations in order to achieve understanding and harmony. All of Forster's characters – whether Maurice Hall or Margaret Schlegel or Fielding – aspire beyond themselves and genuinely yearn for some kind of integrative, transformative connection. However, even Fielding, who 'had no racial feeling' (p. 62), cannot transcend the divide of national character. Existing only as an intuition, connection eludes Forster's characters: 'Not yet, not now.' And if not yet and not now, then when? And how long can we afford to wait when the 'shrinkage of the globe' is 'throwing [us] into one another's arms'? Forster may exhibit nostalgia as he looks backwards, but we can forgive that nostalgia because he also glances without sentimentality into the void opening up in the future.

Notes

1. Virginia Woolf, "Mr Bennett and Mrs Brown", *The Death of the Moth and Other Essays* (New York: Harcourt, 1942).
2. Ann Henley, 'But We Argued About Novel-Writing: Virginia Woolf, E. M. Forster and the Art of Fiction', *Ariel*, 20:3 (July 1989), 74.
3. Forster leaves a final chapter of *Aspects of the Novel* to discuss pattern and rhythm, which I have omitted from my discussion here because they are less germane to my argument.
4. Edward Said, *Orientalism* (New York: Pantheon Books, 1978), p. 224.
5. Elizabeth Langland, 'Gesturing Towards an Open Space: Gender, Form and Language in E. M. Forster's *Howards End*', in *Out of Bounds: Male Writers and Gender(ed) Criticism*, ed. Laura Claridge and Elizabeth Langland (Amherst: University of Massachusetts Press, 1990), pp. 252–67. Quote from pp. 261–4.
6. Virginia Woolf, *A Room of One's Own* (New York: Harcourt, 1929), pp. 103–5.

7

CHRISTOPHER LANE

Forsterian sexuality

I should have been a more famous writer if I had written or rather published
more, but sex has prevented the latter.
(Forster, diary entry, 31 December 1964, quoted *LC*, p. xiv)

'What do you want for yourself?' When D. H. Lawrence asked Forster this
question, early in 1915, the writers had known each other barely a week.[1]
They had met and talked amiably just a few days earlier, at a dinner party
hosted by Lady Ottoline Morrell. Books and letters soon crossed in the mail,
followed by an invitation for Forster to stay with Lawrence at Greatham,
Sussex. Both men had by this point won acclaim (Forster rather more than
Lawrence) and each hoped to cement what he thought would be an important friendship. But the visit did not go well. On the second day, Lawrence
launched into a tirade about Forster's work, life, and philosophy that ended,
hours later, with Forster asking plaintively, 'How do you know I'm not
dead?'[2]

Readers might prefer to draw a veil over this exchange, convinced that
it points more to Lawrence's aggression than to Forster's reticence. But the
exchange has different value, I believe, in showing how Forster sometimes
tried to transpose desire into nonsexual forms, including literary depictions
of marriage and what he called 'democratic *affection*'.[3] This chapter will
examine the creative tensions informing this transposition and its implications for readers and critics, especially those wanting to assess sexuality's
influence on Forster's life and work. For with startling perception, Lawrence
broached a set of issues, sexual and creative, that Forster had huddled defensively and privately berated himself for, and throughout the 1910s could find
no simple way to resolve. 'You with your "Only Connect" motto . . . reach
the limit of splitness here', Lawrence cried after reading 'The Story of a
Panic', reprinted in *The Celestial Omnibus*, which Forster had sent him.
'You are bumping your nose on the end of the cul de sac'.[4] Forster was
'perverse[ly] pushing back' his creative 'waters to their source',[5] complained
Lawrence, who then appealed to Bertrand Russell and others to share his
exasperation: 'Forster . . . is bound hand and foot bodily. Why? . . . He tries
to dodge himself – the sight is painful. But why can't he act?'[6] Forster, he
added insightfully, 'knows that self-realisation is not his ultimate desire. His

ultimate desire is for the continued action which has been called the social passion – the love for humanity – the desire to work for humanity'.[7]

That Lawrence was at the time trying to crystallise his own philosophy about love and friendship doubtless is one reason he competed with and bristled over Forster's maxim in *Howards End*, 'Only connect the prose and the passion, and both will be exalted' (*HE*, p. 183). As Lawrence noted disparagingly, this connection was one that Forster increasingly couldn't make – an outcome affecting the older man's creativity, sexual happiness, and state of mind in the 1910s, which also determines how we read and interpret Forster today. It is worth asking, then, whether the latter's 'ultimate desire' was not in fact 'self-realisation' but something else instead: perhaps a nonsexual ideal like 'social passion – the love of humanity', because at the time other options did not strike him as socially or creatively viable.

Forster's thoughts and letters shed some light on this internal conflict, but, as with Lawrence's claims, none of these is an exhaustive or completely reliable guide to his fiction, a point to which I will return. Despite the acclaim greeting *Howards End* in 1910, he soon felt stymied, uncertain what form and direction his fiction should take. His earlier novels had received favourable reviews, though some commentators carped about the number of deaths in *The Longest Journey* and viewed Cecil Vyse in *A Room with a View*, doubtless correctly, as but a caricature of late-Victorian aestheticism. They also pointed to an increasingly stale motif in these works, whereby protagonists are torn in allegiance between stuffy English conventions and their own desire for spontaneity and freedom, the latter invariably represented as non-English, or at least not middle class. Flouting her in-laws' scorn and disapproval, for instance, Lilia Herriton in *Where Angels Fear to Tread* initially enjoys emotional freedom with Gino Carella in rural Italy. And when, in *A Room with a View*, George Emerson kisses Lucy Honeychurch in the countryside beyond Florence, he alters the course of her affections and their own future when they return to England.

Italy for Forster's male and female protagonists evidently symbolizes more than a reprieve from the familiar and the known. It releases their romantic yearnings – ones for which their own customs leave almost no room. The result is a generic, almost impersonal conflict between 'the tame' and 'the savage', in which the former designates a family or 'clan' that's cheerlessly servile to English customs, while the 'savage' becomes a wide umbrella term for everything the clan opposes:[8] catholic taste in culture, cross-cultural understanding, spontaneity and hospitality, racial diversity, and unorthodox sexual pleasure. After *Howards End*, too, 'the tame' and 'the savage' assume stronger homoerotic inflection in Forster's fiction. Especially at the end of *Maurice*, Maurice Hall is shown less as shuttling between these worlds or trying to resolve the gulf separating them than as fundamentally committed to Alec Scudder's world, and thus implicitly disloyal to his own. Because of sexuality's power in Forster's later writing, moreover, the gulf dividing these classes forms one basis for betrayal, whereby friendship (at least in theory) is meant to prevail over the dictates of clans and nations.[9] Whether it finally does, however, is open to question: sexuality in stories like 'The Other Boat' and 'The Life to Come' is often so volatile, as we'll see, that it destroys characters, relationships, and the principles Forster invoked to guide them, and what is betrayed, poignantly, is the sexual relationship itself.

Signs of this tension manifest quite early in Forster's writing, but they generally dissipate before a crisis ensues. In 'The Story of a Panic', for instance, Eustace Robinson and Gennaro form a brief friendship surpassing their national and class differences as, respectively, 'a young English gentleman and . . . a poor Italian fisher-boy' (*MS*, p. 13). Considering such 'promiscuous intimacy . . . perfectly intolerable', their affronted adult witnesses seek every possible way of ending it, including by confining Eustace (*MS*, p. 12). The fourteen-year-old tries to escape with Gennaro, but when the latter dies inexplicably from shock, Eustace flees alone to the woods in delirious laughter. This equivocal outcome – combined with Pan's hinted appearance as a figure sweeping over Eustace, whose name resonates quietly with 'ecstasy' – let Forster transpose his ending without countenancing a physical affair between Eustace and Gennaro. A *deus ex machina* like Pan becomes a strategic clinamen, that is, in allowing Forster to swerve away from one erotic conclusion to which his narrative points.

Some of Forster's readers hinted at the time at this potential evasion. Indeed, he was 'horrified' and 'disgust[ed]' to learn from a 'chirrupping' Maynard Keynes that Charles Sayle, a librarian at Cambridge, was busy spreading his own reading of the story: 'Buggered' – or, as Forster puts it, 'B by a waiter at the Hotel, Eustace commits bestiality with a goat'.[10] More intriguing still is Forster's admission, in the 1920s, that although he wrote the story with 'no thought of sex for [the characters, for] no thought of sex was in my mind', he'd come round to seeing that 'in a stupid and unprofitable way [Sayle] was right and that this was the cause of my indignation' (*LJ*, p. 302).

Another example of Forster's early fiction illustrates his almost tenacious use of triangular patterns of desire among men and women to avert possible couplings between men. In the unfinished fragment 'Ralph and Tony', written during the summer of 1903, a 'decadent' Ralph tries to propose to Margaret, Tony's sister. But when Tony rejects Ralph's friendship, disgusted by the latter's almost religious devotion to Italy, Ralph perceives that he's 'failed' in all respects, and – radically enervated – his health declines rapidly (*AS*, p. 80). Tony then rescues Ralph from what appears to be attempted suicide. What Ralph has wanted, it transpires, is a quasi-romantic union among all three characters; his ardor for Margaret cannot tolerate or outshine Tony's 'prefer[ence] to be left in the cold' (*AS*, p. 80):

> 'I want to marry your sister'.
> Tony did not speak.
> 'And I want to live with you'.
> He did not speak.
> 'Can I?' trembled out.   (*AS*, p. 80)

Tony attracts Ralph, we learn, because he epitomises the easy physicality that Forster previously had attributed only to Italian men:

> [Tony] was in fact a pure pagan, all the more complete for being uncon-scious, living the glorious unquestioning life of the body, with instinct as a soul. Intellect he had, and also that nameless residue which some suppose will be immortal, but it was still far in the background, and he had made only the physical parts truly his own . . . [T]he body was the man.   (*AS*, pp. 89–90)

The fragment ends with Margaret's confused speculation about Tony and Ralph's volatile friendship, but when they patch things up she assents rapidly to a marriage in which, presumably, she'll share her husband with her brother.

Until he finished *Howards End*, Forster generally succeeded in keeping 'that nameless residue' of homoeroticism 'far in the background' of his fiction. Thereafter, he seemed to lose interest in these triangular structures, tending either (as in *Maurice*) to substitute a man for the position he had assigned an intervening clan or woman, or (as in 'The Other Boat' and, to a lesser degree, *Arctic Summer* and *A Passage to India*) to make the clan and woman subordinate to a stronger narrative interest in male friendship.

These complex negotiations, pointedly described in Forster's diary and letters, signal both his frustration with the marriage plot as a stylistic cliché and his grasp of its frequently limited satisfaction for women and men yearn-ing for alternative experiences. For complex biographical and intellectual reasons, then, the resulting difficulties are worth investigating. 'Are the sexes really races, each with its own code of morality', the narrator of *Howards End* asks in combined archness and exasperation, 'and their mutual love a mere device of Nature's to keep things going? Strip human intercourse of the proprieties, and is it reduced to this?' (*HE*, p. 237). The narrator implies that the sexes' 'mutual love' is also a stale plot 'device' that no longer inspires. Unable to compose a word of fiction on 16 June 1911, moreover, Forster lamented in his diary a growing 'weariness of the only subject that I both can and may treat – the love of men for women & vice versa'.[11]

Yet despite or even because of his growing interest in failed connections between men and women, Forster resisted publishing – and, at times, even writing – one alternative to which they repeatedly pointed: the extension of male friendship into a fully sexual affair. Instead, he tried settling on a nonsexual compromise, 'democratic *affection*', and set out to write a novel with 'plenty of young men and children in it, and adventure. If possible pity and thought. But no love-making – at least of the orthodox kind, and perhaps not even of the unorthodox' (quoted *AS*, p. xiv).

The result, *Arctic Summer* (1910–12), is named after the 'new era . . . [with] no dawn' for which Martin Whitby, the protagonist, earnestly yearns (*AS*, p. 125). 'Dawn implies twilight', he tells his pallid wife, Venetia, when describing his imagined transformation through endless epiphany, 'and we have decided to abolish both'. A civil servant in his thirties, Whitby is urbane and progressive yet stuck in a rut; his marriage characteristically obtains from an 'orderly love' (*AS*, p. 132). 'By the time Martin went to Italy', the narrator explains with comparable banality, 'his inner life was complete, and he is submitted as an example of a civilized man' (*AS*, p. 133). His counterpoint is Lieutenant Clesant March, a younger man who is formal and less cultivated, but unconsciously chivalric and yearning as well for a Romantic epiphany. The fragment ends before either man grasps what form this might take, but the narrator offers hints from Whitby's malaise: He 'never knew what it is to be split in two, for reason to drag one way and passion the other until the victim is red with shame and perhaps black with mud' (*AS*, p. 132).

March saves Whitby's life on a platform of Basle station, appropriately on the way to Italy; yet while friendship between them is wanted it proves strangely impossible, in ways recalling Tony's incipient contempt for Ralph. Unlike in 'Ralph and Tony', moreover, which ends with both men reconciled as friends, Whitby and March's friendship flounders because the narrator insistently punctures the older man's attraction to the younger 'warrior' (*AS*, p. 121). In saving Whitby's life, March apparently 'had merely done for him what he would have done [revised to: 'hoped to do'] for anyone else; and it was nonsense to elevate him into a hero; unfair besides' (*AS*, p. 121).

Whereas March's action is meant to be spontaneous but galvanic, the narrator's intervention – on the work's second page – is carefully bathetic, as if Forster were at pains to dampen Whitby's excitement. Jarred by his near-death experience and, later, 'strangely . . . touched' by discovering March's likeness in a fresco near Milan (symbolically, a battle scene), Whitby settles into despondency (*AS*, p. 148). Failing to act when his chauffeur implausibly is trapped and killed in a fire in an Italian cinema, Whitby (like Conrad's

Jim) confronts his cowardice through implacable guilt. 'But it was too late for Martin', the narrator overexplains. 'The primitive man in him had been roused, and he could not still it. He broke loose and ran like a criminal, shaken by tearless sobs. "Oh my God, I've been a coward," he repeated. "Oh my God you can't forgive that – you never did – you never will"' (*AS*, p. 157). The transformation Whitby wanted generates neither pleasure nor a release of courage comparable to March's. Instead, the novel bogs down in the protagonist's self-recrimination and inertia, never to recover.

Doubtless an interesting principle, 'democratic *affection*' let Forster juxtapose two slightly recast perspectives on 'tame' life. Still, as Whitby's goal remains abstract and disembodied, *Arctic Summer*'s direction proves almost necessarily vague. The novel tries to reunite Whitby and March in impulsive defence of the latter's younger brother, Lance, who in ways hinting at displaced erotic conflict is expelled from Cambridge University for having sex with a woman. The manuscript ends melodramatically with Lance killing himself in shame. But after dithering over narrative possibilities, including giving the novel an alternative section (the 'Tripoli Fragment' of November 1911) and a brand-new beginning (the 'Radipole Version' from the summer of 1912), Forster ran out of steam. 'My novel awful', he privately admitted that spring.[12] Five months earlier, on New Year's Eve, 1911, his rueful self-assessment helps explain why:

> Literature, very bad. One good story – The Point of It – one bad unpublished play – The Heart of Bosnia. That is all. I seem through at last, & others begin to suspect it. Idleness, depressing conditions, need for a fresh view of all life before I begin writing each time, paralyse me. Just possible I may finish Arctic Summer, but see nothing beyond. Like writing erotic short stories, some of which may be good.[13]

As Lawrence guessed several years later, this creative and psychological paralysis wasn't new to Forster, who lamented that he had 'grind[ed] out' *Howards End* and found the results unimpressive: 'tired and discontented at the slightness of my work'.[14] Alluding to Freud's intriguing words, just over five years later, about those 'wrecked by success', P. N. Furbank adds that Forster viewed 'the spectacle of success and literary professionalism . . . with dismay' and reacted to the praise and celebrity following *Howards End* with concerns about 'going smash'.[15] Yet Forster's private remarks indicate as well that other, intellectual worries besieged him, including how 'to work out: – The sexual bias in literary criticism, and perhaps literature . . . in its ideal and carnal form', as he put it in a diary entry about another unfinished manuscript, an essay provisionally entitled 'On pornography and sentimentality'.[16]

By 1911, these self-assessments imply, Forster had exhausted the formal and narrative arrangements organising his earlier fiction. Virginia Woolf would assert (with deliberate tendentiousness) that 'on or about December 1910 human character changed',[17] but foremost in her mind was Roger Fry's exhibition 'Manet and the Post-Impressionists', not the novels and short stories of Forster, which (despite the authors' avowed affection) she privately dubbed 'impeded, shrivelled and immature'.[18] Formal and philosophical innovations in art, literature, music, cinematography, psychology, physics, economics, and a host of other fields were at the time momentous and seemingly inexhaustible, yet for intriguing reasons Forster was stymied, unable to point his fiction in a viable direction. 'What is going to happen?', he asked his audience blankly when reading a revised version of *Arctic Summer* at the Aldeburgh Festival in June 1951, a situation hinting that, forty years later, he had little additional material to share and was – even after publishing *A Passage to India* – haunted by this earlier, crucial impasse (*AS*, p. 162). 'I had got my antithesis [between the civilized and heroic man] all right. But I had not settled what was going to happen, and that is why the novel remains a fragment. The novelist should I think always settle when he starts what is going to happen, what his major event is to be' (*AS*, p. 162). That Forster in all senses could not 'settle' in the 1910s invites us to reconsider Lawrence's claim that he 'tries to dodge himself', because 'self-realisation is not his ultimate desire'.[19]

Self-realisation, Forster hinted several times, isn't possible without a full integration of sexuality – without, as the narrator of *Howards End* puts it, connecting 'the prose and the passion' (*HE*, p. 183). Yet, as the above details show, his attempts at forging this connection were a mixed success, and it's important to assess why. Accompanying (and perhaps undermining) his efforts at completing *Arctic Summer* was a newfound interest in writing homoerotic stories, which, Forster hoped, would release his creativity. At the time, he had no intention of showing these stories even to close friends, and wrote them, as he later put it, 'not to express myself but to excite myself'.[20] This emphasis on avoiding or surpassing self-expression is worth taking seriously, though Forster's full assessment of these works remains clouded by ambiguity. Despite his telling Edward Garnett in November 1910 that he thought them 'better than my long books',[21] around 1922 he decided to 'burn . . . my indecent writings or as many as the fire will take. Not a moral repentance, but [from] the belief that they clogged me artistically. They . . . were a wrong channel for my pen'.[22] While stories like 'The Life to Come' were published posthumously, then, the other erotic fiction that Forster wrote – for the most part composed after *Howards End* and destroyed just before he finished *A Passage to India* – has an intriguing, almost galvanic relation to his major works, as if it were an inadmissible supplement to his Edwardian novels and a constitutive, if largely repressed, ingredient to the friendship between Fielding and Aziz, which concludes, after all, with Aziz 'half kissing' the Englishman (*PI*, p. 312).

Yet Forster's commentary on his writing in the early 1910s still doesn't quite add up, or is at least counterintuitive. Can 'excit[ation]' really 'clog', especially when diffidence about writing fiction long preceded this period? Previously viewed as the solution to his writing-block, these stories later seemed to crystallise in his mind as a chief cause of his problems. Excitement, we might say, generated its own creative paralysis, and displacing self-expression clearly wasn't the answer.

When Forster therefore began looking for 'the sexual bias in . . . perhaps literature . . . [but] not in experience which refuses',[23] paradoxically he retreated once more, recording in 1910 a personal statement that displays rather less bravado: 'However gross my desires, I find I shall never satisfy them for the fear of annoying others. I am glad to come across this much good in me. It serves instead of purity'.[24] Here, ascesis stands as a virtue and an imagined path to sublimation, which surely made Forster's thwarted creativity and partial reliance on erotic fiction all the more galling to him.

The final words of 'The Feminine Note in Literature' are, I think, the clearest sign of – and another explanation for – these conceptual difficulties with sexuality and embodiment. Forster presented the paper in October 1910 to the Cambridge Apostles and again, on 9 December that year, to Vanessa Bell's 'Friday Club'. It has two endings, the latter probably written for the Bloomsbury group, and there one finds the following succinct, if debatable, claim: 'Men have an unembodied ideal. Women embody their ideal in some human being, be it a woman or a man'.[25] The first idea recalls Forster's characterisation of Whitby in *Arctic Summer*. A variation on Milton's notorious aphorism about men and women's different relationships to God, Forster's distinction between embodiment and disembodiment also let him gauge intellectually whether he should try producing 'literature . . . in its ideal and carnal form' or whether, as a man, he might plausibly avoid the latter by pursuing the type of disembodiment that Meredith, for one, allegedly had sanctioned in *The Egoist*.[26]

These formulations reproduce succinctly the problems besetting Forster at the time. That he produced two endings and two beginnings for his paper, based largely on its differently gendered audiences, implies that his argument was partly contingent on those who heard it. Yet his distinction between embodiment and disembodiment began to fray and, by the end of the paper, to seem unsustainable. In the opening paragraph for the all-male Apostles, Forster asserts: 'Men are men, women are women, and in a discussion like the present it is impossible quite to keep one's eye off the other end of the plank. We are going to talk about women; and very fortunately, none of them are in the room' (AS, p. 16). One imagines a burst of male laughter after this shared joke. But the second version is more tentative, adding a flurry of questions and mixed metaphors that dissipate the argument:

> What is the feminine note in literature? <Is there firstly a feminine note in literature? If so, what is it? If so, what is the masculine note? Second,> Intelligence and sympathy can only limit the field. They can as it were decrease the impetus of the see saw of sex, they cannot stop it surging altogether, and in a discussion like the present, it is impossible to keep one's eye off the other end of the plank. (AS, p. 17)

Despite lessening the effects of sex, however, neither intelligence nor sympathy can dampen it entirely, a veiled indication of Forster's ongoing hopes that they might. When likened to a 'see saw', or polarising binary, 'sex' in this passage implies what we now call 'gender'. Yet Forster's mixed metaphor of 'surging', in the next clause, suggests that he had begun discussing sexuality (for how, logically, can 'the impetus of [a] see saw . . . surg[e]'?). Similar contortions recur in his fiction, as we've seen. Still ensnared by this drama ten days later, for example, he explained in his diary that *Arctic Summer* should contain 'no love-making – at least of the orthodox kind, and perhaps not even of the unorthodox'.[27] 'It would be tempting to make an intelligent man feel towards an intelligent man of lower class what I feel', he added, 'but I see the situation too clearly to use it as in *Mon Frère Yves*, where the author is either deceiving the public or himself'.[28]

In Pierre Loti's 1883 novel, which Forster invokes here, an admiring naval officer (also called 'Pierre', who doubles as the narrator) forms a chaste attachment to a younger sailor, Yves Kermadec, over whom he keeps a 'brotherly' eye, and with whom he arguably is besotted. Adept at masking this emotion, the older man is canny at voicing through indirect free speech the struggle that other sailors experience from protracted isolation:

> The warm darkness brought thoughts of love which were not of [the sailors'] seeking. There were moments when they came near to weakening again in a troubling dream; they felt the need of opening their arms to some desired human form, of clasping it with a strong and forceful infinite tenderness. But no, no one, nothing . . . It was necessary to pull themselves together, to remain alone, to turn over on the hard planks of the wooden deck, and to think of something else, to begin to sing again. . .[29]

'Opening their arms to some desired human form': despite this lyrical communication of unvoiced and provocatively ungendered desire, Forster thought Loti's novel too reticent and even dishonest in its aims. His response is notable – and, I think, questionable – because Loti used *disembodied* objects of desire to extraordinary effect, leaving room for homoerotic possibility precisely by refusing to specify the gendered object of his sailors' fantasies. Why didn't Forster adopt a similar tack? Since in 'The Feminine Note' he also thought men 'have an unembodied ideal' while privately doubting 'whether ['democratic *affection*'] has any strength', Forster concluded that the fiction he'd written, with its 'swish of . . . skirts and . . . non-sexual embraces', needed greater affective conflict to spark readerly and even authorial curiosity (*AS*, p. xiv). Had he adopted Loti's impressionist emphasis, or even a related stress on the nebulousness of objects of fantasy (following Woolf, Joyce, Mansfield, and many other contemporaries), he would have extended not depleted this effect by increasing the narrative mobility of his characters' desires. Forster, however, hewed a more conventional, tortuous path.

The story of his eventual, if short-lived, release from this period of creative paralysis is well known. By his lights, too, the precipitate was physical, and even quasi-erotic. While visiting Edward Carpenter and his lover George Merrill at their home, Forster was overwhelmed by both the sensual atmosphere and that Merrill 'touched my backside – gently and just above the buttocks'.[30] 'The sensation was unusual', he added in his 'Terminal Note' to *Maurice*. 'It seemed to go straight through the small of my back into my ideas, without involving my thoughts' (*M*. p. 215).

Despite sounding a bit far-fetched, this memory signals Forster's release from the repression and self-censorship that had hamstrung him for several years; for three months, at least, he banished self-doubt and wrote most of *Maurice* with unusual freedom and exuberance. True, his progress was checked when G. Lowes Dickinson read and found appalling one of his erotic stories, which he mistook for the novel, but the inspiration Forster discovered after visiting Carpenter and Merrill buoyed him up for a while and doubtless helped transform Maurice's guarded eroticism into a physical affair with Scudder.

Put another way, *Maurice* is an advance in that it embodies Whitby and March's halting, sexless dynamic in *Arctic Summer*; yet by refusing to consider releasing the novel ('Publishable – but worth it?' was Forster's now-famous query (quoted *M*, p. xlvii)), he could suspend anxiety about imagining how readers (like his mother) who expected a follow-up to *Howards End* would greet a romance involving only men. Nevertheless, writing *Maurice* also compounded his difficulties, because to all appearances the manuscript, though finished, added to his pile of unpublished and incomplete works, doing little to alter public assessments that he was 'played out'.[31]

Above all, and again counterintuitively, *Maurice* exacerbated rather than solved Forster's quandary about how to integrate sexuality and embodiment into his fiction. 'I do want to raise these subjects [including homosexuality] out of the mists of theology', he told Forrest Reid in March 1915, in an intriguing allusion to the ineffable,[32] but the novel's allusions to *morbidity* and *perversion* voice retrograde shades of sexological judgement from Havelock Ellis and others that exasperated Bloomsbury friends like Lytton Strachey:

> The absence of the suburb-culture question was a relief [. . . but t]here remains the general conception – about which I don't feel at all certain . . . It's difficult to distinguish clearly your views from Maurice's sometimes, but so far as I can see, you go much too far in your disapproval of [copulation]. For instance, you apparently regard the Dickie incident with grave disapproval. Why? Then, à propos of Maurice tossing himself off (you call it a 'malpractice') (Ch. xxxii), you say – 'He knew what the price would be – a creeping apathy towards all things'. How did Maurice know that? And how do you?[33]

Strachey's blunt questions were not only warranted but also difficult for Forster to answer. An earlier draft of the novel had ended with Kitty, Maurice's sister, discovering Alec and Maurice living and working together contentedly as woodcutters in Yorkshire; Strachey and others found this scenario so weak and improbable that Forster took their advice and cut it.[34] All the same, as Strachey insisted, the Maurice–Alec affair remains 'very wobbly . . . partly because the ground isn't enough prepared: and Alec's feelings I don't quite seize . . . I should have prophesied a rupture after 6 months – chiefly as a result of lack of common interests owing to class differences'.[35] Especially when we consider Forster's narrative difficulties integrating embodiment into his work, his assertion 'that in fiction anyway two men should fall in love and remain in it for the ever and ever that fiction allows' (*M*, p. 216) implies that, even to him, the ending offered really an illusion of permanence to compensate for the obstacles besetting such relationships in everyday life.

Nevertheless, the clearest sign of sexuality's ongoing volatility in Forster's fiction, after he set *Maurice* aside, is the violent deaths terminating interracial homoerotic affairs in stories like 'The Other Boat' (1915–16) and 'The Life to Come' (1922). The latter ends with Vithobai stabbing Paul Pinmay in delirious passion while on the verge of his own death; the former story largely reverses this violence, as Lionel March, an English officer (with a name echoing Clesant March's in *Arctic Summer*), strangles his secret lover, Cocoanut, an Indian naval secretary and childhood acquaintance, on a boat. This last scenario hints that Forster revisited both his own unfinished manuscript and Loti's novel while overwriting both with his own erotic fantasies, but the violence in these stories is gratuitous not redemptive, and extends a set of questions about the stakes and status of intimacy that haunts all of Forster's work. 'The sweet act of vengeance followed, sweeter than ever for both of them', the narrator says as Lionel strangles Cocoanut in revenge for being bitten by him; 'and as ecstasy hardened into agony his hands twisted the throat. Neither of them knew when the end came, and he when he realized it felt no sadness, no remorse' (*LC*, pp. 195–6). Immediately thereafter, Lionel bursts out of his cabin, 'and naked and with the seeds of love on him . . . dive[s] into the sea' to his death (*LC*, p. 196). Melodramatic endings like these doubtless corroborate Forster's admission, in 1920, that 'nothing is more obdurate to artistic treatment than the carnal'.[36]

These difficulties with carnality recur throughout Forster's mature fiction, where he tried adding sexuality to 'democratic affection' in hopes of harmonising both with his political values, yet the sexuality generates curious, unforeseen effects that undermine his fraternal ideals. The 1930s fable 'What Does It Matter? A Morality' doesn't sustain its title's insouciant question, for instance, and ends, as I've explained elsewhere, by foreclosing on sexuality precisely when it tries advancing a vision of equanimity.[37] Betrayal is also a piquant theme in 'Arthur Snatchfold' (1928), a story that sets out to substitute an almost blasé acceptance of homosexuality for prejudice. My final example, however, is a curious, little-discussed, and rather weak story called 'Little Imber', which Forster wrote in 1961 as he was approaching his eighty-third birthday. 'In its fantastic dissolution of the obstacles to fatherhood ordinarily raised by homosexuality', writes Elizabeth Heine, the tale

> echoes back to the ambivalences of *Arctic Summer*. Set in the future after a period of devastating warfare, the story once again tests ideas of sexual morality, gentlemanliness and heroism as the civilized Warham, virile but no longer young, is attracted despite his prejudices to Imber, both young and virile.
>
> (*AS*, p. xxvi)

What's startling – and potentially 'grotesque' – about the story, as Heine concedes (*AS*, p. xxvii), is that both men are hired to procreate with women in order to correct a 'growing unbalance between the sexes' ('imber' means 'fertilizing shower' in Latin, as one of the characters observes) (*AS*, pp. 231, 228). Women far outnumber men in this future society, and one of the characters is quick to speculate why: 'male and female had got tired of each other without knowing it and refused to breed because of boredom' (*AS*, p. 231).

If we can set aside that Warham and Imber could never determine the sex of their offspring, the tale – capturing some of the spirit of the 1960s – certainly alters our perception of Forster's earlier reticence:

> 'We were not expecting you, I fear', cries the Abbess [in charge of the Birth House]. 'Why do you visit us just now?'
> 'To fuck'.
> 'Oh! Oh yes I see. I should not have asked you that'. (AS, p. 228)

Warham and Imber conduct their mission with inexhaustible efficiency, yet their hostility and competition soon burgeon into desire as they wrestle in near-Lawrentian fashion, then contemplate the professional and erotic effects of their fight's 'obscene . . . outcome': some surplus semen they cannot use for impregnation (AS, p. 232). They end up cuddling after having sex together.

The story is 'remarkably free from death and violence and guilt', Heine says, before calling it 'oddly moving in the simplicity of its desire for progeny' (AS, p. xxvii). That's one way of looking at Forster's strange and clearly ironic story, yet its weaknesses are also impossible to ignore. Both men view their job so perfunctorily that any affective desire for children is muted by their bland professionalism. The story arguably excited Forster (he called it 'remarkable' in his diary (quoted AS, p. xxvii)), because it views homosexuality as an irrepressible, guiltless supplement to heterosexuality, perhaps because the former surfaces only when procreation is assured. Representing in its return to 'democratic *affection*' the end of a long arc in Forster's work, too, the story finally aligns homosexual desire with sensual pleasure, rather than – as in various stories in *The Life to Come* collection – with murder and suicide.

The larger point, though, is that even when Forster represented sexuality forthrightly – as he did in later years, using uncharacteristic verbs like 'fuck' – he extended rather than resolved earlier dilemmas in his fiction. Readers and critics therefore must assess – as I shall in closing – how to approach (without distorting) these dilemmas and whether we think candour or full disclosure in his earlier writing could have resolved them.

Throughout this chapter I have paired Forster's writing with his often-unpublished commentary in order to bring out his intense personal struggles with sexuality and embodiment. In doing so, I hope to have shown that these struggles involve but also surpass psychobiography, since stylised accounts of courtship and marriage lost some of their lustre in the Edwardian age when writers like Forster grappled with more diverse forms of intimacy. In these struggles one witnesses broader intellectual arguments, that is, about how writers could represent sexuality when aspects of its force belie sense and meaning. So in quoting Forster's frequent bafflement about his creative difficulties with 'the carnal', I have used his statements less as reliable guides to his fiction than as running commentary on what, of the sexual, is over-wrought, volatile, or simply ineffable.

We should note, however, before disputing, quite different assessments of these topics. When earlier critics read the manuscripts of *Maurice* and *The Life to Come* collection soon after Forster's death in 1970, they embarked on a wholesale revision of his corpus, either fiercely protecting the earlier work from the alleged tarnish of his homosexual 'pornography'[38] or reinterpreting all of his marriage plots as thwarted attempts at representing a different kind of love. Reviewing *Maurice* and J. R. Ackerley's memoir of Forster in 1971, for instance, Samuel Hynes opined: 'Most obviously, Forster could not imag-ine any aspect of the range of experience between men and women – hetero-sexual attraction, heterosexual relations, marriage were mysterious to him. No wonder he resented having to write "marriage novels" – the subject was quite beyond his range'.[39] For Hynes, Forster's women are simple foils for as-yet-unrepresentable male couplings, and every narrative difficulty in his work gestures to a homosexual secret that Forster's suppressed manuscripts apparently ratify. Indeed, Hynes assumed that the problems Forster revealed as *ensuing from* heterosexuality explain all of his incoherence as a writer: 'One must conclude that Forster was incapable of recording deep currents of feeling – sexual feeling most obviously, but other deep feeling as well . . . *Ordinary emotional states were beyond Forster.*'[40]

Because this argument insists on a formal correspondence – and even a per-ception of repressed transparency – between Forster and his work, it leaves almost no room for fantasy or the imagination, to say nothing of stylistic difficulty – a well-known facet of early modernist fiction (including works by Meredith and Conrad) that influenced Forster. In asserting, moreover, that texts reproduce their authors' biographical concerns and that fiction unfailingly represents desires that fall conclusively on one or another side of a clear sexual binary, Hynes and other critics adopted an antimodernist stance that leaves little space for Forster's inchoate forms of sexuality.

I have argued against these presumptions, because sexual desire plays a much more nebulous, if sometimes volatile role in Forster's fiction, and because, tired of Edwardian conventions but uncertain how to recast or dis-solve them, he tried transposing sexuality's effects into new forms, includ-ing 'democratic *affection*'. If his letters and diary entries tell us anything, then, it's that authors often cannot supply the last word about their creative endeavours. As Lawrence perceived, moreover, the gaps and dilemmas shap-ing Forster's writing suggest provocatively that, concerning sexuality, self-realisation wasn't always his final goal. Put another way, Forster's struggle to represent sexuality brought to the fore other narrative and philosophical dilemmas that are worth considering in their own right. These include how to render appropriately the inner lives of characters and how to coax narrative into capturing the difficulties and opportunities that arise from all forms of intimacy. It remains for us to ask whether we can accept Lawrence's observations on these terms without viewing them solely about Forsterian reticence and evasion, and whether we can view narrative difficulty in Forster's work as a phenomenon that arises independently of his and his characters' sexual secrets.

Notes

1. D. H. Lawrence to Forster, 28 January 1915, *The Letters of D. H. Lawrence*, ed. George J. Zytaruk and James T. Boulton (8 vols., Cambridge: Cambridge University Press, 1979–2000), vol. II, p. 266.
2. Forster, quoted in P. N. Furbank, *E. M. Forster: A Life* (New York: Harcourt Brace Jovanovich, 1978), vol. II, pp. 9–10.
3. Forster, 'Desire for a book', diary entry for 19 December 1910, quoted *AS*, p. xiv.
4. Lawrence to Forster, 3 February 1915, *The Letters of D. H. Lawrence*, vol. II, p. 275.
5. Ibid., p. 276.
6. Lawrence to Bertrand Russell, 12 February 1915, ibid., vol. II, p. 283.
7. Ibid.
8. See June Perry Levine, 'The Tame in Pursuit of the Savage: The Posthumous Fiction of E. M. Forster', *PMLA*, 99:1 (1984), 72. The word 'clan' is the narrator's sardonic term for this group in *WAFT*, p. 25.
9. See Forster, 'What I Believe' (1938), *TCD*, p. 66 and my chapter, 'Betrayal and Its Consolations in Forster's Writing', in *The Burdens of Intimacy: Psychoanalysis and Victorian Masculinity* (Chicago: University of Chicago Press, 1999), pp. 197–223.
10. Forster, 'My Books and I' (a paper read to the Bloomsbury Memoir Club in the early 1920s), reproduced as Appendix B to *LJ*, p. 302.
11. Forster, diary entry, 16 June 1911, quoted in Furbank, *E. M. Forster*, vol. I, p. 199.
12. Forster, diary entry, 12 May 1912, quoted *AS*, p. xx.
13. Forster, diary entry, New Year's Eve, 1911, quoted in Furbank, *E. M. Forster*, vol. I, p. 204.
14. Forster, diary entry in 1910, quoted in ibid., p. 185.
15. Furbank, *E. M. Forster*, vol. I, p. 185; Forster, quoted in ibid., p. 199. The Freud reference is to 'Some Character-Types Met with in Psycho-Analytic Work (II): Those Wrecked by Success' (1916), *The Standard Edition of the Complete Psychological Works of Sigmund Freud*, ed. and trans. James Strachey (24 vols., London: Hogarth, 1953–74), vol. XIV, pp. 316–31.
16. Forster, '[On pornography and sentimentality]', an unfinished manuscript, described in a diary entry of 25 October 1910, quoted in Heine's introduction to *AS*, p. xvi.

17. Virginia Woolf, 'Character in Fiction' (1924), in *The Essays of Virginia Woolf*, ed. Andrew McNeillie (3 vols., New York: Harcourt Brace Jovanovich, 1988), vol. III, p. 421.
18. Woolf to Ethel Smyth, 21 September 1930, *The Letters of Virginia Woolf*, ed. Nigel Nicolson and Joanne Trautmann (6 vols., London: Hogarth, 1975–80), vol. IV, p. 218. See also *The Diary of Virginia Woolf*, ed. Anne Olivier Bell and Andrew McNeillie (5 vols., New York: Harcourt, 1977–84), vol. III, p. 152, for her account of Forster's wounded reaction to her fairly critical review of *Aspects of the Novel* in *Nation & Athenæum* (12 November 1927), pp. 247–8. Finally, see Woolf's essay 'The Novels of E. M. Forster', in *The Death of the Moth and Other Essays* (New York: Harcourt, 1942), pp. 162–75.
19. Lawrence to Bertrand Russell, 12 February 1915, *The Letters of D. H. Lawrence*, vol. II, p. 283.
20. Forster, quoted in Furbank, *E. M. Forster*, vol. I, p. 200.
21. Forster, letter to Edward Garnett, 12 November 1910, *Selected Letters of E. M. Forster*, ed. Mary Lago and P. N. Furbank (2 vols., London: Collins, 1983–5), vol. I, p. 117.
22. Forster, diary entry, 8 April 1922, quoted in Donald Salter, 'That Is My Ticket: The Homosexual Writings of E. M. Forster', *London Magazine* (February–March 1975), 6.
23. Forster, '[On pornography and sentimentality]', quoted in Heine's introduction to *AS*, p. xvi.
24. Forster, diary entry in 1910, quoted in Furbank, *E. M. Forster*, vol. I, p. 183.
25. Forster, *The Feminine Note in Literature: A Hitherto Unpublished Manuscript*, ed. and introd. by George Piggford (London: Cecil Woolf, 2001), p. 33.
26. Forster, '[On pornography and sentimentality]', quoted in Heine's introduction to *AS*, p. xvi; Forster, *The Feminine Note*, p. 33.
27. Forster, 'Desire for a book', quoted *AS*, p. xiv.
28. Ibid.
29. Pierre Loti, *A Tale of Brittany (Mon frère Yves)*, trans. W. P. Baines (1883; London: T. Werner Laurie Ltd., 1924), pp. 270–1; original ellipses.
30. Forster, 'Terminal Note' to *M*, p. 215.
31. Forster, diary entry, 17 December 1913, quoted in Furbank, *E. M. Forster*, vol. I, 258.
32. Forster to Forrest Reid, 13 March 1915, quoted in ibid., vol. II, p. 14.
33. Lytton Strachey to Forster, 12 March 1915, quoted in ibid., vol. II, pp. 15–16.
34. This epilogue is reprinted as an appendix to *M*, pp. 221–4.
35. Lytton Strachey to Forster, 12 March 1915, quoted in Furbank, *E. M. Forster*, vol. II, p. 15.
36. Forster, letter to Siegfried Sassoon, 11 October 1920, *Selected Letters of E. M. Forster*, vol. I, p. 316. The sentence ends: 'but it has got to be got in, I'm sure: everything has got to be got in'.
37. Lane, *The Burdens of Intimacy*, pp. 212–23.
38. Salter, 'That Is My Ticket', p. 16.
39. Samuel Hynes, 'A Chalice for Youth', *TLS* (8 October 1971), 1215.
40. Ibid., my emphasis.

8

JANE GOLDMAN

Forster and women

'I prayed you might not be a woman'
(*LJ*, p. 73)

'You can't drag in a woman'
(*M*, p. 109)

What is the status and relevance of the word 'woman' in Forster's writing? The first quotation above is spoken by a man to the woman he disastrously marries in a novel that takes its title from Shelley's epithet for marriage but which is dedicated to brotherhood. The second is spoken, ironically enough, by a man opting for marriage and forsaking (platonic) love between men, to a sexually braver man, in a novel that openly explores homosexual relationships in a regime of compulsory heterosexuality. Is the word 'woman' functioning differently in each case? This chapter considers Forster's representations of women and, more broadly, the changing understanding of what such representation might involve.

Most of Forster's novels and many of his short stories include strongly realised women protagonists or characters. George Watson finds Margaret Schlegel, for example, 'the most fully realised Englishwoman in the fiction of her century', while Rose Macaulay finds all Forster's women characters, old and young, 'alive with [. . .] imaginative actuality',[1] and there is a rich and continuing seam of criticism exploring Forster's typology of women. Moreover, 'Forster and Women' may in some ways appear a limited if not obsolete topic, suggesting (1970s) vintage feminist criticism and ignoring its unspoken (and, for many, the now more relevant) topic of 'Forster and Men'. But the sense of obsolescence may not be due merely (and somewhat crudely) to the acknowledgement of biographical information concerning Forster's homosexuality. Feminist criticism has moved on from charting 'images of women' in male-authored texts; and Forster criticism has moved on in a number of directions with the posthumous publication of his explicitly homosexual writings encouraging a rethinking of gender in the rest of his *œuvre*. Such factors, of course, complicate rather than render obsolete the topic of women and prompt a network of interconnected critical questions, including whether it is possible to represent women at all.

As for understanding 'Forster and Women' with regard to his life, bio-graphical studies also show contradictions and paradoxes in Forster's rela-tionships and attitudes to women. In youth he comes across as something of a misogynist, happily initiated into the higher privileges of patriarchy (includ-ing the exclusive order of the Cambridge Apostles), of limited sexual knowl-edge and experience, dominated by his mother, shaped by other matriarchs; and in older age he emerges as a semi-closeted gay man, with declared masochistic tendencies, who paradoxically comes to a close friendship with his lover's wife, dying in her arms. Biography, however, is not the main concern of this chapter, except where critical issues are thrown up by the cross-referencing of his life, and his homosexuality in particular, with his fictional work.

Feminists looking to Forster's literary and social milieu come to quite dif-ferent thoughts on his treatment of women in life and letters. While some see Forster as an anti-patriarchal ally of his Bloomsbury colleague and feminist, Virginia Woolf, others align him squarely with the homosocial patriarchy itself. Jane Marcus, for example, finds Woolf comes to dispel the 'illusion' that 'homosexual and bi-sexual men of Bloomsbury', Forster included, were 'women's natural allies and fellow outsiders' in patriarchy: 'patriarchy pro-tects its own'.[2] Christopher Reed blames Phyllis Rose's (1978) biography of Woolf for this line of criticism, and her view of male Bloomsbury and Forster's gay novel, *Maurice*, as misogynist.[3] Elaine Showalter thinks 'we must accept the fact that Forster saw women as part of the enemy camp. While not precisely antagonistic to them, he believed them to be allied with the forces and institutions of repression.'[4] Yet she is at pains to dis-agree with those critics (Lionel Trilling and Wilfred Stone, for example) who (uncritically) have found his fiction contemptuous of women. Rae H. Stoll finds Forster's fiction misogynous.[5] Elizabeth Langland, on the other hand, attempts to see beyond the complexities of Forster's misogy-nist life to a radical sexual politics in his texts. In her helpful exploration of gender in *Howards End*, she acknowledges 'Forster's homosexuality and outspoken misogyny', but argues that Forster's tortured confusion over his sexuality while composing this novel 'also fuelled a desire for something other than the classical opposition between male and female, masculine and feminine'; and she identifies 'a radical sexual politics that has been obscured by psychobiographies'.[6] Forster's positive, and liberating, treatment of the body, and his challenge to Platonism's devaluing of the body, has also been well received by feminist critics.[7] There is more to 'Forster and Women', however, than deciding on whether or not he meets, in life or in letters, with feminist approval. But rather than plunge into either the life or the novels, it would be useful to begin by considering Forster's own literary criticism where it touches on women.

'The Feminine Note in Literature'

In Forster's literary criticism, women seem marginalised, despite his declared admiration for Jane Austen. In *Aspects of the Novel*, he passes acerbic comment on critics who have found 'an organic connection' between the English novel and 'the Women's Movement': 'As women bettered their position the novel, they asserted, became better too. Quite wrong. A mirror does not develop because an historical pageant passes in front of it' (*AN*, p. 13). His warm, constructive appreciation of Woolf is tempered by abhorrence of her feminism, which he finds to disfigure her writing: 'There are spots of it all over her work, and it was constantly in her mind' (*TCD*, p. 249). Yet he did acknowledge her feminist tract, *A Room of One's Own* (1929), as 'brilliant' (*TCD*, p. 249). He also appears to have had a formative influence on her thinking about women and fiction, the subject of this very tract.

Forster's paper, 'The Feminine Note in Literature', was first delivered to the Cambridge Apostles, and then to the Bloomsbury Friday Club (of which Woolf was a founding member) in 1910. Indeed Woolf heard Forster's paper in December 1910, the precise month, according to her famous declaration, when 'human character changed'.[8] The extant drafts of the paper have only recently been published. This illuminating piece, written 'at the height of his pre-war fame' following the acclaimed publication of *Howards End*,[9] provides helpful insights into Forster's own fictional treatment of women, and into his explorations of gender, sexuality, and aesthetics.

'The Feminine Note in Literature' shows a sophisticated understanding of the complicated issues facing women as writers. Forster also addresses various critical attempts to distinguish the formal qualities of men's and women's writing: 'When you are reading a book can you tell instinctively whether it is the work of a man or a woman?' (pp. 16–17). The 'feminine note in literature', Forster avers, 'must be felt'; the question of authorial gender is an 'emotional' one (p. 17). Men and women may, of course, read as well as write differently, and Forster shows great sensitivity to the gender of his audience in providing two versions of his paper, one addressed to his exclusively male Cambridge colleagues, the other to the mixed company of Bloomsbury. 'We are going to talk about women; and very fortunately, none of them are in the room', he tells the first audience (anticipating Woolf's playful allusions to her all-women audience in *A Room of One's Own*). To his mixed audience, he begins instead by declaring the paper to be 'self-conscious', that it 'would like not to be chivalrous, and it would like not to be insulting' (p. 17), echoing the critique of medieval chivalric gender codes expounded in *A Room with A View* two years earlier (See Chapters 8 and 20: 'Medieval', and 'The End of the Middle Ages').

The drafts of 'The Feminine Note in Literature' show the paper to bifurcate at certain other points to accommodate Forster's two different audiences. Forster comes tentatively to define the feminine note as 'ethical' (p. 32), as the creation of characters showing 'a preoccupation with personal worthiness' (p. 33). He differentiates between men and women novelists by arguing that 'men have an unembodied ideal', which he finds illustrated by Conrad's *Lord Jim* (the hero 'falls away from courage and honesty'). Women, on the other hand, 'embody their ideal in some human being, be it a woman or a man' (p. 33). Such characters exemplify the 'strong practical vein' in women novelists, 'this desire to set up a sensible, visible standard of righteousness' (p. 34). He seems to find such personification of ideals, or personal worthiness, a flaw or 'limitation' in some women's writing. But, he concedes, it is possible to transcend such gender limitations: 'the question of the feminine note is not really important in great literature. There personality dominates' (p. 19). This model of personality and creativity transcending sex and gender seems to anticipate Woolf's theory of androgyny, propounded in *A Room of One's Own* (and developed from Coleridge). Forster, like Woolf after him, apparently finds great writers, male or female, beyond gender categorisation: 'Jane Austen is more an Austen than a Jane <, even as Molière is more Molière than John>' (p. 19). Also, like Woolf, he grounds his discussion of women and fiction in a materialist analysis of women's social, political, and economic status. The paper begins by reminding his Cambridge audience of previous papers on 'the Subjection of Women', and coyly placing the present one 'as a frivolous footnote' (p. 16) to such discussions. But Forster presents the two different spheres as linked oppositional forces. This is the realm of 'feeling' rather than 'reason', and he draws on John Stuart Mill when he concludes:

What you mistake for the masculine or the feminine will disappear, and personality, and nothing besides personality will remain. For think of the past. Think how, until <the last century> \ lately/, women were <mostly> the servants or playthings of men. On such rare occasions as they did acquire culture, their outlook was too conventionalised and limited to win them immortality. Time has changed much of this, and will change more. A freer atmosphere is at hand, and the artificial products of the past – <the Hetaira,> the Châtelaine, the Grande Dame, \ the Bluestocking/ – will be blown away and give place to the individual, of whom Emily Brontë is a type, the individual, distinguished only by personal qualities.   (*The Feminine Note in Literature*, p. 20)

This passage is startling in its anticipation of Woolf's comparative analysis, in *A Room of One's Own*, of woman in history and in poetry. But Woolf goes further than Forster in seeking to identify a set of aesthetics to serve women writers, a set of feminist aesthetics, in fact. However, both Forster and Woolf share a common ideal of androgynous writing, and agree that women rarely achieve this ideal. The goddess Demeter is Forster's androgynous ideal, according to his earlier essay 'Cnidus' (1904), 'for she has transcended sex' (*AH*, p. 168). But Forster is not concerned, as Woolf is, with working out a detailed prospectus for women writers. He identifies the differences in women's writing as something to be ironed out before the ideal can be achieved, whereas Woolf seems paradoxically to advocate the pursuit of a different aesthetic form adapted to women in order to arrive at androgyny. Forster does, nevertheless, exploit in his writing a similar analysis of the gender politics of representation.

'The Feminine Note in Literature', then, shows that Forster, at the height of his literary career, is conscious of the material impact of the rise of the New Woman and feminism on fiction; that he is also conscious of gender and sexuality in relation to formalism and symbolism, and in relation to the politics of reading. Forster's ability here to address the same text to two differently gendered audiences may also be evident in his fiction. His paper also shows his concern for an ideal of humanity, and of writing, that is beyond gender categorisation, while grounded in gendered individualism and particularity. We can see how his analysis of gender and aesthetics coincides in many respects with Woolf's, and where it falls short. Woolf's outline, furthermore, of how fiction might address both the historical, material realities of women's lives as well as their co-option in the traditional symbolic order of aesthetics is useful in an analysis of Forster's treatment of women. 'What one must do', she urges in considering the representation of woman, 'to bring her to life was to think poetically and prosaically at one and the same moment, thus keeping in touch with fact – that she is Mrs Martin, aged thirty-six, dressed in blue, wearing a black hat and brown shoes; but not losing sight of fiction either – that she is a vessel in which all sorts of spirits and forces are coursing and flashing perpetually.'[10] Forster's writing does indeed seem to think both 'poetically and prosaically' about women, and to foreground these simultaneous and contradictory representations of the feminine. Indeed, like Woolf's, his writing acknowledges the problem of representing the feminine using an aesthetics of representation which is itself gendered (feminine). The aesthetic self-consciousness that marks both writers' work as 'modernist' is inflected with a similarly self-reflexive gender-consciousness.

Woman as art

We can see Forster's modernist technique at work, and inflected by such a self-reflexive gender-consciousness, in his portrayal of women characters. In *Where Angels Fear to Tread*, Philip's 'surprise [. . .] improvement', which Forster identifies as the 'object of the book' (*WAFT*, p. 149), is in effect a modernist moment of aesthetic epiphany, one that precedes by a number of years Joyce's more celebrated epiphanies in *A Portrait of the Artist as a Young Man*. Philip comes to feel 'saved' (*WAFT*, p. 139) as a result of looking at Miss Abbott as if she were a goddess. But in the description that follows she becomes, under his gaze, not merely a divinity, but one represented in great, Renaissance art. Almost motionless, she is caught in his aestheticising gaze, then, as work of art, in the tradition of the *pietà*, in an almost fixed gesture of maternal comforting, where her slight and gentle movements are described as appropriate to the pictorial design. Forster's slippery indirect narrative leaves it open as to whether or not this 'seemed fitting' to the narrator as well as to Philip:

> All through the day Miss Abbott had seemed to Philip like a goddess, and more than ever did she seem so now. Many people look younger and more intimate during great emotion. But some there are who look older, and remote, and he could not think that there was little difference in years, and none in composition, between her and the man whose head was laid upon her breast. Her eyes were open, full of infinite pity and full of majesty, as if they discerned the boundaries of sorrow, and saw unimaginable tracts beyond. Such eyes he had seen in great pictures but never in a mortal. Her hands were folded round the sufferer, stroking him lightly, for even a goddess can do no more than that. And it seemed fitting, too, that she should bend her head and touch his forehead with her lips. (*WAFT*, pp. 138–9)

But at the centre of Philip's 'composition' is the head of the beautiful young man, Gino, embraced and framed by the reifying figure of Miss Abbott. Just as Miss Abbott has become unfixed, slipping between mortal, goddess, and work of art, part of the system of representation itself, so too have the 'boundaries' of Philip's composition: is the object of his gaze Miss Abbott or Gino? Are the two genders becoming blurred, or is one doing the representational work of the other? There are many such moments in Forster's fictional writing, where women are represented with a textual self-consciousness concerning their symbolic and signifying status *as women*. In the case of Lucy Honeychurch, she is represented as herself conscious of these unstable boundaries of the feminine, between life and representation. Her much cited desire 'to drop the august title of the Eternal Woman, and go there [the real world] as her transitory self' (*RV*, p. 40), comes just as she buys a reproduction of Botticelli's *Birth of Venus*, a celebrated Renaissance nude, epitomising the mythic, aesthetic order to which the feminine has been consigned. It is at the moment of Lucy's contemplation of this and other Renaissance images, that an Italian youth is knifed in front of her, as if marking the violence of rupture between the symbolic order of Art inhabited by the Goddess of Love and the real world in which Lucy has encountered her future husband.

The visual, visceral language of the body is communicated by the dying man who appears to have 'an important message for her. He opened his lips to deliver it, and a stream of red came between them and trickled down his unshaven chin' (*RV*, p. 41). This graphic image imposes a figure of menstruating female genitalia on the man's face. It is now that George Emerson appears. But is Lucy Honeychurch any different to Botticelli's Venus, as part of the novel's symbolic order, any more real, any less part of an eternal order of art? Forster represents her as conscious of such questions, but this does not prevent her from being understood in turn as an aesthetic convention, the personification of a sophisticated aesthetic quandary over representation. Indeed, Forster seems to encourage such an understanding. But his novel also clearly and wittily celebrates Lucy's escape from the prison of Cecil's aestheticising and deadening vision of herself as a Renaissance masterpiece by Leonardo (*RV*, pp. 88–9), when later 'she had failed to be Leonardesque' (*RV*, p. 116); 'she had become a living woman, with mysteries and forces of her own, with qualities that even eluded art' (*RV*, p. 171). If, as Forster suspects, women are caught up in a deadening aesthetic order, while men traditionally enjoy inhabiting the real world – 'Men, declaring that she inspires them to it, move joyfully over the surface, having the most delightful meetings with other men, happy, not because they are masculine, but because they are alive' (RV, p. 39) – Forster seems to be inverting tradition by inscribing the dying Italian youth as a sign and portent, particularly by the striking feminising of his face. Is there also something subversive in the gender and sexual politics of George Emerson's encounter with Lucy Honeychurch, triangulated with the violent death of another man? It is a pattern that recurs in Forster. Compare, for example, *The Longest Journey*'s triangulation of Rickie, Agnes, and her dead fiancé, Gerald.

It is not difficult to find women linked to the aesthetic in Forster's writing. Chapter 9 of *A Room with a View*, for example, is facetiously entitled 'Lucy as a Work of Art'. There seems always to be a picture or photograph or other representation in close proximity to his women. So, Forster's fictional writing not only offers a variety of representations of women and the feminine, but it also opens up questions of how women and the feminine are caught up in the literary and cultural processes of representation. What is represented by these processes, in Forster's writing and the so-called historical, sociological, or psychological accuracy of his representations, is perhaps of less interest than the processes themselves. Indeed, what women represent in Forster may not be women at all. To recognise this is not to condemn him. For one thing, Forster cannot be singled out for exploring or exploiting patriarchal language, for self-consciously re-inscribing, as feminist theorists have recognised, woman or the feminine merely as a mark of her absence, an allegorical marker of masculine presence. Indeed Forster's self-conscious textuality, conversely, may be read as politically subversive. Some of the most interesting feminist readings of Forster are by critics influenced by deconstructive theory and French feminism. Frances L. Rusticcia, for example, while acknowledging that 'gynesis and misogyny [. . .] often turn up as strange bedfellows', warns: 'a feminism that either ignores or flees from the gynesis of [*A Passage to India*], reading it solely as politically objectionable, runs the risk of reducing a work of genius and (more important to feminism) losing out on the subversive power that it has to offer.'[11] Brenda Silver, drawing on Foucault, also tenders a sympathetic feminist reading of *A Passage to India*, which she finds 'a study of what it means to be *rapable*, a social position that cuts across biological and racial lines to inscribe culturally constructed definitions of sexuality within a sex/gender/power system.'[12] But there is also a specifically gay tenor to Forster's feminine narrations. Perhaps his experimentalism extends only as far as consolidating gay men in patriarchy while still excluding women as other. If gay readings of Forster tend to erase women's presence further from his texts, perhaps queer readings enable a return of sorts. Is it possible to arrive at positive, feminist readings of 'Forster and Women'? Or to read women in Forster without the obligatory, dull, taxonomy of female stereotypes? Or to read Forster's women as more than allegories of philosophical or ideological positions? These thoughts and questions are explored further below. But it is to the simple, admiring recognition elicited by some of Forster's fictional women that we now turn.

Forster as a women's writer

From his earliest critical reception, Forster has been considered, somewhat naïvely, a women's writer, praised by critics, adored by film actresses, for his empathetic and powerfully drawn women characters. Lucy Honeychurch and Margaret Schlegel, for example, emerge from page and screen as among the most beloved exemplars of the modern 'Englishwoman'. And Forster's reputation in this respect is only enhanced by anecdotes of his actually having been mistaken for a woman himself – in life and in print. He recalls how

Elizabeth von Arnim, who employed him as a tutor to her children, 'confused [him] for one of the housemaids';[13] whereas Elia W. Peattie, reviewing *Howards End* for the *Chicago Tribune*, formed the impression that 'the writer is a woman of a quality of mind comparable to that of the Findlater sisters or to May Sinclair'. Her 'feeling the book is feminine' somehow authenticates his fiction as women's, but Peattie herself had a stereotyped view of how 'the feminine mind' should be represented, 'with its irrational yet dramatic succession of moods'.[14] Cyril Connolly characterised Forster as 'the Sacred Maiden Aunt of English Letters',[15] suggesting a lack of insight into the mind of either gender. Gore Vidal finds he dispenses irony 'with an old auntie-ish twinkle'.[16] Going beyond the fiction, readers and critics have harvested details of Forster's personal effeminacy, his closeness to his mother, his debt to his matriarchal benefactress, and biographical tribute to her, his scrutiny of the lot of Indian women, and so on, to amplify the sense of Forster's positive feminine disposition; and his homosexuality and homosociality are here apparently not seen as contradictory of this disposition, nor to harbour misogyny.

Approaching 'the attenuated Forster'[17] through the autobiographical writings of Virginia Woolf, on the other hand, perhaps it is possible to be mystified by the unproblematic construal of this 'half a monk' and 'elderly bugger'[18] as a woman's writer at all, or indeed, in so far as it has become a matter of critical relevance, a woman's man. 'I always feel him shrinking sensitively from me, as a woman, a clever woman, an up to date woman', Woolf confided to her diary in 1919.[19] She also records his clearly expressed misogyny: 'One night we got drunk, & talked of sodomy, & sapphism, with emotion – so much so that next day he said he had been drunk [. . .] He said he thought Sapphism disgusting: partly from convention, partly because he disliked that women should be independent of men.'[20] Forster roused her to great anger when in 1935, 'Woolf met [him] on the steps of the London Library where he had just come from a committee meeting. She thought for a moment that he was going to invite her to join the Board, but he told her the committee had agreed that "ladies are impossible" [. . .] In November 1940, Woolf got great satisfaction from turning down Forster's invitation to join.' Yet Woolf considered him her 'best critic'.[21] According to Michael J. Hoffman and Ann Ter Haar, 'the ties between Forster and Woolf seem extraordinarily positive and long-lasting.'[22] Recourse to biography, whether in support or refutation of Forster as a women's writer, furnishes mixed messages.

Yet, returning to the fiction, and its reception, we might also wonder whether it is the writing or in fact the man that Katherine Mansfield and Frieda Lawrence are criticising in their early, much cited, negative responses to Forster's portrayal of women and heterosexual relations. Although Frieda

Lawrence claims to 'love' *The Longest Journey* for its depiction of 'man-to-man love instead of bloodrelationship', which pleases her because it refutes the bonds of motherhood, she also remarks on Forster's misogyny: 'now for the man-to-man [. . .] Your women I don't understand, *you* seem to dislike them *much*!'[23] She claims the universal application of 'man-to-man' (speaking as one human to another) to make the point that Forster's novel in fact excludes women from his universal vision of humanity, something we might unambiguously discern from the book's dedication to the brotherhood of Cambridge Apostles. May Sinclair, on re-reading *Howards End*, similarly found she 'disliked his women all through'.[24]

Mansfield, on the other hand, finds the same novel 'not good enough' because Forster fails to convincingly depict heterosexual relations: 'I can never be perfectly certain whether Helen was got with child by Leonard Bast or by his fatal forgotten umbrella. All things considered, I think it must have been the umbrella.'[25] Contemplating the line of criticism initiated by Mansfield's causticity, J. H. Stape is concerned that since 'Forster's homosexual nature has been revealed, some would find reasons for the novel's "inadequate" or "unconvincing" portrayals of heterosexual relations as deriving not only from a lack of personal experience, but from an inability of imagination to present relationships between men and women that are convincing psychological and social realism'.[26] He rightly dismisses as 'facile' the idea 'that Forster's homosexuality prevented him from describing physical relationships between men and women'.[27] Stape goes to the manuscripts to prove that Forster was indeed capable of more realistic representation, showing that in earlier drafts of *Howards End* his 'initial descriptions of these sexual relationships were more concretely presented and that various physical encounters were consistently muted or altogether deleted in revision' (although the differences that he indicates are subtle). He suggests that the revisions were made for a number of reasons, including a desire to emphasise 'comradeship between sexes' and 'a reluctance to offend', but also a choice of 'thematic rather than realistic emphasis'.[28] Stape's pointing up of the symbolic aspects of Forster's characterisation of women seems a polite reminder to Forster's readers, critics (and actresses), whether they love or loathe his heroines, that it would be foolish to read his fiction as realist, or his characters as real people.

If we are to make sense of women in Forster's fiction, then, we must acknowledge that Forster is a modernist writer. Some confusion may still occur, particularly if one has been schooled to think of the narrative experimentalism of high modernism as a more sophisticated, even more accurate, form of realism. But the elements of textual self-consciousness, metanarrative, poetic or lyric discourse, and myth, for example, in much modernist fiction (including Forster's), make such doctrine untenable. Woolf identifies in Forster's novels a developing 'contrast between poetry and realism', show- ing how the realist elements in Forster's fiction are balanced by lyric ones, which prevent us from reading him simply as a realist: 'His old maids, his clergy, are the most lifelike we have had since Jane Austen laid down the pen. But he has into the bargain what Jane Austen had not – the impulses of a poet. The neat surface is always being thrown into disarray by an outburst of lyric poetry.'[29] In showing how Forster 'makes the change from realism to symbolism', Woolf identifies a 'hesitation' she considers to be 'fatal': 'For we doubt both things – the real and the symbolical: Mrs Moore, the nice old lady, and Mrs Moore, the sybil.'[30] Forster's writing is flawed, according to Woolf, because it allows the reader to 'see two separate parts'.[31] Forster's realist aspect throws off balance the symbolic: 'He has recorded too much and too literally. He has given us an almost photographic picture on one side of the page; on the other he asks us to see the same view transformed and radiant with eternal fires [. . .] The Marabar caves should appear to us not real caves but, it may be, the soul of India. Miss Quested should be transformed from an English girl on a picnic to arrogant Europe straying into the heart of the East and getting lost there.'[32] And, when it comes to his women characters, if Forster at times fails to convincingly 'think poetically and prosaically at one and the same moment', to repeat Woolf's dictum, then so too do many of his readers.

A strange cultural need to read literature as documentary leads some read- ers, actors, film directors, and critics (who should know better) to understand Margaret Schlegel as a convincing portrayal of a real woman, or George Emerson as a real man. The mechanistic clunking of Forster's symbolic armature is hardly hidden by the selection of the name Schlegel, 'as the countryman of Hegel and Kant, as the idealist' (*Howards End*), suggesting the minor German aesthetic philosopher(s); nor by that of Emerson, the American 'nature' poet-philosopher. Forster's text knows you, the reader, should have spotted these allusions, but more importantly, *pace* Woolf, it wants you to know that it knows that you know. And while it is possible to find, as the case of Emerson suggests, both genders co-opted into allegorical systems in Forster's work, it is also possible to discern a distinct gender pol- itics operating, whereby women are nevertheless more closely aligned with aesthetics and systems of representation.

Hegel seems to be Forster's guiding philosopher (like Stewart Ansell, 'he's read too much Hegel' (*LJ*, p. 197)): his fiction readily maps on to the Hegelian, triadic, model of thesis, counter-thesis, and synthesis/trans- cendence;[33] and perhaps his treatment of gender follows suit, synthesising and/or transcending masculinity and femininity. This is possibly personified, in *The Longest Journey*, by Stephen Wonham, whose surname, a rearrangement of 'woman' and 'h[e]', may suggest a synthesis of man and woman. Rae H. Stoll also finds the name 'phonetically close to "womb"';[34] and he is certainly a kind of man-mother by the end of the novel. The identification of Hegelian triads in Forster's narrative design again undermines readings of his characters as real people, his women as real women. His writing draws attention to this, as Miss Pembroke's 'neat little resumé' serves to remind: 'Allegory. Man = modern civilization (in bad sense). Girl = getting in touch with Nature.' (*LJ*, p. 119). If Forster's apparent realism, then, deludes some readers into thinking only prosaically of his women characters as real women, his modernist symbolism tends to turn readers and critics who follow it into diagram-makers or puzzle-solvers, deciphering his women as personifications of philosophical tenets. The Schlegel sisters, for example, may personify western aesthetics, or be read as 'the repository of cultured liberal humanitarianism'.[35] In representing such abstract values, or social forces, they are not real women; but nor are they simply functioning as allegory. Forster's seems to be allegory that knows it is so; and it is a mode of representation that also draws attention to its own gender politics. Such intricate self-consciousness is some distance from simplistic views of Forster's strongly realised women characters. Yet there persists the cultural myth that Forster is quite simply a women's writer by virtue of such characters.

Typologies of Forster's women

His reputation for empathy with the feminine aside, 'Forster and Women', as I have already mentioned, may be considered a somewhat 1970s topic. It fits neatly with the project of 'feminist critique', famously outlined in retrospect by Elaine Showalter (in 1979), as the kind of feminist criticism 'concerned with *woman as reader* – with woman as the consumer of male-produced literature', and with examining 'the images and stereotypes of women in literature, the omissions of and misconceptions about women in criticism, and the fissures in male-constructed literary history. It is also concerned with the exploitation and manipulation of the female audience, especially in popular culture and film; and with the analysis of woman as sign in semiotic systems.'[36] And there is certainly a wealth of feminist scholarship from the 1970s providing such insights, although critical focus was often on 'images and stereotypes of women' sometimes at the expense of considering 'woman as sign'. But feminist criticism is not alone in categorising Forster's women.

Following Forster's declared passion for Demeter, G. S. Amur finds Forster's women characters not to be 'archetypal like Joyce's Molly Bloom . . . But, like the "flappers" in Scott Fitzgerald or the "bitches" in Hemingway, they do suggest a typology.'[37] He identifies three types: the 'saved', Lucy Honeychurch and Margaret Schlegel; the 'lost', Mrs Herriton, Lady Turton, Agnes Pembroke, and 'even Mrs Failing'; the 'sexless angels', Caroline Abbott, Adela Quested, and Helen Schlegel. Evelyn Hanquart focuses on the 'mother-figure' and the 'lex materna' (law of the mother) in Forster's *œuvre*, of which Ruth Wilcox is the high point. With *A Passage to India*, the hero's 'relationship with his or her mother, has then ceased to be crucial'. But the 'castrating mother' returns with Mrs March in 'The Other Boat' where Forster 'leads us back to an aggressive, frightening and threatening vision of the mother-figure'.[38] Hanquart ignores *Maurice*. Masako Hirai's (1998) chapter on sisters in *Howards End*, intelligently deflects critical interest from Forster's mother-figures, but perpetuates the mythical reading of the Schlegel sisters through the *Antigone* of Sophocles. Bonnie Finkelstein, in *Forster's Women: Eternal Differences* (1975), argues: 'Forster's greatest characters are women; and his novels closely examine the problems of women in society; but his overall theme is a larger one in which women function as representatives of all humanity.'[39] Finkelstein identifies in Forster a 'humanist, androgynous vision [that] remains radical',[40] and she provides chapter-length studies of the women in each novel. But such readings seem narrow in focus, given the sophisticated and self-conscious explorations not only of images and misconceptions of women as characters in Forster's writing, but also of the cultural inscriptions of woman as sign, and the self-conscious exploration of gender and representation.

Forster's women as gay ciphers

A concern with 'woman as sign in semiotic systems', however, prompts a second thought on 'Forster and Women': perhaps it is in fact an irrelevance, a critical anachronism. Since public acknowledgement of the open secret of Forster's homosexuality, and the posthumous publication of the 'elderly bugger's' openly homosexual writing in the 1970s (at the very time when feminist critique of his women characters was under way), the reading of Forster's women as women must surely be revised. 'A central paradox about E. M. Forster as a writer', remarks one critic, 'is his overwhelming interest in women, an interest difficult to reconcile with his homosexuality'.[41] I am not sure I understand this 'paradox'. Why should a writer's sexuality be considered something to 'reconcile' with his or her writing? Why should not an 'elderly bugger' write about women? But Forster, certain arguments go, was obliged to write about women, having been prevented by law from writing openly on homosexuality. And this means that the *œuvre* should be re-read 'with the hindsight given by *Maurice*'.[42]

When I consulted an academic colleague who knew Forster in his latter years at Cambridge, he offered me the following proposition: 'No woman under the age of fifty-five in Forster's work is a woman at all; over the age of fifty-five, some of them are.' It may be that Forster's fictional world is in truth entirely populated by gay men and the odd mother-goddess crone. But is it productive to read Forster's heterosexual couples as allegories of homosexuals? Certainly it adds another level of irony to his already irony-laden dialogue. For example, when Agnes asks Rickie 'Did you take me for a Dryad?' (*LJ*, p. 73), she opens up Forster's heavily underlined theme of women's doubleness, their simultaneous occupation of a mythological, symbolic status and of their real, historical, and material existence. Rickie's reply may be taken to mean that he wishes for the mythological version of the feminine, the Dryad: 'I prayed you might not be a woman' (*LJ*, p. 73); but there is a Wildean bite to his reply suggesting he hopes not for a woman at all, mythical or real, but a man. The textual foregrounding of woman as Dryad points up her allegorical function here in standing as vehicle for the masculine. In this reading, Agnes's relationship with her doomed first suitor, Gerald, would also be understood as homosexual. When Rickie tells her 'What he gave you then is greater than anything you will get from me', Agnes is 'frightened. Again she had the sense of something abnormal' (*LJ*, p. 74). But she seems to refuse to partake in the process of allegorisation, even if she cannot quite identify it, and even as she enacts it by embracing and containing her lover: 'Then she said, "What is all this nonsense?" and folded him in her arms' (*LJ*, p. 74). This exchange anticipates the 'symbolic moment' when Wonham confronts Rickie for his impetus to allegorise, to co-opt others as symbols:

> 'You talk to me but all the time you look at the photograph' . . . The man was right. He did not love him, even as he had never hated him. In either passion he had degraded him to be a symbol for the vanished past. The man was right, and would have been lovable. He longed to be back riding over those windy fields, to be back in those mystic circles, beneath pure sky. Then they could have watched and helped and taught each other, until the word was reality, and the past not a torn photograph, but Demeter the goddess rejoicing in the spring.   (*LJ*, p. 255)

The exchange leads to Agnes's invocation of the dead Gerald, to the feeling that 'Agnes had absorbed the passion out of both of them', as if she were the degraded symbolic receptacle of their emotions; and it leads to the rejection of allegory and masquerade: '"Come with me as a man," said Stephen, already out in the mist' (*LJ*, p. 257).

Finding that the 'true relationships between Rickie and Stephen Wonham in *The Longest Journey* and between Aziz and Fielding in *A Passage to India* are of course homosexual ones', Francis King argues that Forster's writing is improved by his self-censorship:

> [G]iven the fact of his homosexuality . . . the deliberate suppression of any overt reference to it in the writings published during his lifetime caused Forster to write, not with less, but with an even greater intensity. He was obliged to find a whole series of metaphors for his real sexual preoccupations and it is in these metaphors that so much of the power of his writing resides.[43]

But King does not offer a satisfactory account of how, precisely, women function in such a reading of Forster's fiction. Are they merely metaphors for men? This line of thinking would make it difficult to account for the presence of women at all in Forster's openly homosexual novel, *Maurice*. It is worth noting Lytton Strachey's observation to Forster on the unpublished text: 'you really do make a difference between affairs between men and men and those between men and women . . . (So that when [Clive] said to Maurice "I love you as if you were a woman", he was telling a lie.)'[44] Strachey seems to be referring to (an earlier draft of?) the moment when Clive tells Maurice: 'I feel to you as Pippa to her fiancé' (*M*, p. 73). That Clive's feelings for Maurice may be represented by Pippa's to her fiancé, however, is contradicted by his identification of 'a particular harmony of body and soul that I don't think women have even guessed. But you know' (*M*, p. 73). Are women in Forster's fiction perhaps a little more than empty signifiers; are they present at least in Strachey's sense of acting as foils to Forster's all-male relationships? Or may we take the proposition that Strachey extrapolates ('I love you as if you were a woman') as the key to decoding Forster's women in the rest of his fiction?

Forster's queer women

Eve Kosovsky Sedgwick's account of homosocial triangles of desire, in *Between Men*, informs Robert K. Martin's fascinating queer reading of Forster's women. He argues that in *Where Angels Fear to Tread*, for example, 'Philip's apparent love for Caroline is in fact a displacement of his desire for Gino; if Caroline (and Lilia) had held Gino, then Philip can achieve his goals, indirectly, as part of a homosocial triangle . . . embracing Gino *through* Caroline.'[45] Martin examines similar triangular relationships in other works, including *The Longest Journey* and the posthumously published story 'Ralph and Tony'. Martin draws on another of Sedgwick's illuminating theories, that of 'the avunculate', to show how Forster's fiction explores alternative family structures to that of the dominant patriarchal and compulsory heterosexual. He defends Forster's account of a 'perfunctory' sexual relationship between Helen and Leonard, in *Howards End*, as serving Forster's desire 'to establish a new kind of relation outside physicality', and he finds Margaret and Helen to form 'a female sacred family assuring continuity'. Helen and Leonard's relationship, he argues, should be viewed 'in the context of a search on Forster's part for a queer kind of begetting that can lead to the construction of a queer "family"'.[46]

In this reading women are not effaced as such, but they may well be returned to personifying sacred fertility, maternalism. This returns us to Forster's passion for Demeter and other goddesses, and his reliance on or manipulation of stereotyped mythic representations of women, his patriarchal reinscriptions of the feminine in representational economies. Martin points up the significance of the photograph of Stockholm in *The Longest Journey*, which represents 'the testimony, along with Stephen himself, to Mrs Elliot's moment of romantic rebellion . . . it is Mrs Elliot whose spirit prevails at the end, not as a physical parent but as a guide to passions that defy convention'.[47] On this view, the woman, Mrs Elliot, of course, disappears even as a mother, co-opted as a symbol of queer rebellion. Yet, as we have seen, it is this very business of co-option as symbol that her son (whose surname queers the word woman to Wonham) rebels against. Forster's representation of woman and Wonham is far too sophisticated, or too slippery, to allow for such easy allegory.

Notes

1. George Watson, 'Forever Forster: Edward Morgan Forster (1879–1970)', *Hudson Review*, 55:4 (Winter 2003), 626–32. Quote from p. 626; Rose Macaulay, 'Women in the East' (1924), quoted in *E. M. Forster: The Critical Heritage*, ed. Philip Gardner (London: Routledge and Kegan Paul, 1973), p. 197.
2. Jane Marcus, *Virginia Woolf and the Languages of Patriarchy* (Bloomington: Indiana University Press, 1987), p. 183.
3. Christopher Reed, 'The Mouse that Roared: Creating a Queer Forster', in *Queer Forster*, ed. Robert Martin and George Piggford (Chicago and London: Chicago University Press, 1997), pp. 75–88. Quote from p. 84.
4. Elaine Showalter, '*A Passage to India* as "Marriage Fiction"', *Women and Literature*, 5:2 (1977), 3–16. Quote from p. 7.
5. Rae H. Stoll, '"Aphrodite with a Janus Face": Language, Desire, and History in *The Longest Journey*', in *E. M. Forster: Contemporary Critical Essays*, ed. Jeremy Tambling (Basingstoke and London: Macmillan, 1995), pp. 30–50. Quote from p. 46.

6. Elizabeth Langland, 'Gesturing Towards an Open Space: Gender, Form, and Language in E. M. Forster's *Howards End*', in *Out of Bounds: Male Writers and Gender(ed) Criticism*, ed. Laura Claridge and Elizabeth Langland (Amherst: University of Massachusetts Press, 1990), pp. 252–67. Quote from p. 253.

7. For example, Debrah Raschke, 'Breaking the Engagement with Philosophy: Re-envisioning Hetero/Homo Relations in *Maurice*', in *Queer Forster*, ed. Martin and Piggford, pp. 151–65. Quote from p. 154.

8. Virginia Woolf, 'Character in Fiction' ['Mr Bennett and Mrs Brown'] (1924), in *The Essays of Virginia Woolf*, ed. Andrew McNeillie (London: Hogarth Press, 1988), vol. III, p. 421.

9. George Piggford, 'Introduction' to Forster, *The Feminine Note in Literature* (London: Cecil Woolf, 2001), p. 7. Further page references are embodied in the text.

10. Woolf, *A Room of One's Own* (London: Hogarth Press, 1929), pp. 56–7.

11. Frances L. Rusticcia, '"A Cave of My Own": E. M. Forster and Sexual Politics', *Raritan*, 9:2 (1989), 110–28. Quote from p. 127.

12. Brenda Silver, 'Periphrasis, Power, and Rape in *A Passage to India*', *Novel*, 22 (1988), 86–105. Quote from p. 88.

13. Francis King, *E. M. Forster and his World* (London: Thames & Hudson, 1978), p. 40.

14. Elia Peattie, review, *E. M. Forster: The Critical Heritage*, ed. Gardner, p. 160.

15. Cyril Connolly quoted King, *E. M. Forster*, p. 57.

16. Gore Vidal, *United States: Essays 1952–1992* (London: André Deutsch, 1993), p. 255.

17. *The Letters of Virginia Woolf*, ed. Nigel Nicolson and Joanne Trautmann (London: Hogarth Press, 1975), vol. I, p. 499.

18. *The Letters of Virginia Woolf*, ed. Nigel Nicolson and Joanne Trautmann (London: Hogarth Press, 1977), vol. III, p. 352.

19. *The Diary of Virginia Woolf*, ed. Anne Olivier Bell (London: Hogarth Press, 1977), vol. I, p. 263.

20. *The Diary of Virginia Woolf*, ed. Anne Olivier Bell assisted by Andrew McNeillie (London: Hogarth Press, 1980), vol. III, p. 193.

21. *The Letters of Virginia Woolf*, ed. Nigel Nicolson and Joanne Trautmann (London: Hogarth Press, 1978), vol. IV, p. 126.

22. Michael Hoffman and Ann Ter Haar, '"Whose books once influenced mine": The Relationship between E. M. Forster's *Howards End* and Virginia Woolf's *The Waves*', *Twentieth Century Literature* (Spring 1999), 46–64. Quote from p. 46.

23. Frieda Lawrence, letter to Forster, Gardner, *E. M. Forster: The Critical Heritage*, p. 97.

24. May Sinclair, journal entry, 22 June 1923, quoted King, *E. M. Forster*, p. 41.

25. Katherine Mansfield, *Journal of Katherine Mansfield*, ed. J. Middleton Murry (London: Constable, 1954), p. 121; Gardner, *E. M. Forster: The Critical Heritage*, p. 162.

26. J. H. Stape, 'Leonard's "Fatal Forgotten Umbrella": Sex and the Manuscript Revisions to *Howards End*', *Journal of Modern Literature*, 9:1 (1981–2), pp. 123–32. Quote from p. 123.

27. Ibid.

28. Ibid.
29. Woolf, 'The Novels of *E. M. Forster*' (1927), *The Essays of Virginia Woolf*, ed. Andrew McNeillie (London: Hogarth, 1994), vol. IV, p. 494.
30. Ibid., p. 496.
31. Ibid., p. 497.
32. Ibid., p. 496.
33. See Robert K. Martin, '"It Must Have Been the Umbrella": Forster's Queer Begetting', in Martin and Piggford, *Queer Forster*, p. 255; and Wilfred Stone, *The Cave and the Mountain* (1966), pp. 189–90.
34. Stoll, '"Aphrodite wth a Janus Face"', p. 48.
35. Anne Wright, *Literature of Crisis, 1910–1922: Howards End, Heartbreak House, Women in Love and The Waste Land* (Basingstoke and London, Macmillan, 1984), p. 27.
36. Elaine Showalter, 'Toward a Feminist Poetics' (1979), in *The New Feminist Criticism: Essays on Women, Literature and Theory*, ed. Elaine Showalter (London: Virago, 1986), p. 128.
37. G. S. Amur, 'Hellenic Heroines and Sexless Angels: Images of Women in Forster's Novels', in *Approaches to E. M. Forster. A Centenary Volume*, ed. Vasant A. Shahane (New Delhi: Arnold Heinemann, 1981), pp. 24–34. Quote from p. 26.
38. Evelyn Hanquart, 'The Evolution of the Mother-Figure in E. M. Forster's Fictional Work', in Shahane, *Approaches to E. M. Forster*, p. 68.
39. Bonnie Blumenthal Finkelstein, *Forster's Women: Eternal Differences* (New York and London: Columbia University Press, 1975), p. vii.
40. Ibid., p. viii.
41. Amur, 'Hellenic Heroines and Sexless Angels', in Shahane, *Approaches to E. M. Forster*, p. 24.
42. Oliver Stallybrass, Editorial Note, *HE*, p. 352.
43. King, *E. M. Forster*, p. 113.
44. Lytton Strachey, letter to Forster (12 March 1915), quoted in Gardner, *E. M. Forster: The Critical Heritage*, p. 431.
45. Martin, '"It Must Have Been the Umbrella"', p. 256.
46. Ibid., p. 272.
47. Ibid., p. 266.

9

JUDITH SCHERER HERZ

A Room with a View

What is the story? How does one tell it, understand it? Does one read it as one would a Jane Austen novel with the heroine Lucy Honeychurch, like Emma Woodhouse or Elizabeth Bennet, coming to learn who she is and what she wants through false starts and confusions, both internal and imposed by society, finally rewarded by the right husband (not her mistaken first choice) at the end? That is certainly one way of reading the novel, and for many years following its 1908 publication, it was read as a cheerful *Bildungsroman*, its heroine's education unfolding as social comedy inflected by social satire, although marred in the eyes of some by too much whimsy or fantasy or sentimentality or downright eccentricity. But that story, even as it organises the plot, is not the whole story. Threaded through a comic tale of tourism and its discontents, built on the scaffolding of the standard marriage plot, is a darker, more complex, less end-determined narrative.

To a degree, that story was heard by the novel's early readers, but for the most part with puzzlement rather than pleasure. Why does Mr Emerson preach so much? What motivates the Reverend Beebe? Why is George so unrealised as a character? These questions recur through the century but from the publication of James McConkey's study in 1957 onwards, they more often become the means to enter Forster's novel with varying degrees of sympathy. They are seen less as pointing to flaws in the novel than as constituting its interest. This version of Forster's text tests its plot elements against a set of abstractions, utopic ideals, and beliefs about truth and passion, about comradeship and the call of the blood, rather than against the social conventions and public expectations of the realist novel. As Claude Summers argued in his 1983 study, 'With considerable artistic daring, Forster translates the materials of romantic comedy into a novel of ideas'.[1] As a result, we pay more attention to the narrative voice (or voices) than to the imperatives of plot.

A Room with a View is several novels in one – social comedy, mythic romance, novel of ideas, shifting in modes from realism to romance to

138

polemic, at once light and dark, celebratory and melancholy. It is structured throughout on intricately linked antitheses – rooms/views, inside/outside, medieval/classical, the ascetic/the fruitful, dark/light, lies/truth, earth/sky, blood/water. These, however, are not seen in simple either/or terms; rather they are woven into a dense narrative fabric. Formal preoccupations are central to the text, even though Forster may have been 'an ambivalent formalist', in David Medalie's phrase.[2] Painting, architecture, sculpture, and music offer analogues for character, setting, and argument. Visual motifs are worked through in a musical pattern. The end of the crucial fourth chapter, for example, is echoed in the novel's last line. In Chapter 4 the water of the river washes the blood from the postcard as George comes to his recognition that he wants to live at the same time as the roar of the river 'suggest[ed] some unexpected melody to [Lucy's] ears' (*RV*, p. 45); at the novel's close, 'The song died away; they heard the river, bearing down the snows of winter into the Mediterranean' (*RV*, p. 209).[3]

A Room with a View is also several novels in the sense that it carries within it the two other novels that Forster wrote over the five or six year period of its gestation and composition. Begun before *Where Angels Fear to Tread* (1905) and *The Longest Journey* (1907), it was the last completed, and it can serve as a prism through which to read the two novels, *Howards End* and *Maurice*, that closely followed it. The Italy of Forster's first published novel and the green and expansive English landscape of his second are its two staging grounds. As it combines them, it creates, in Wilfred Stone's formulation, '*Angels* with the breath of *The Longest Journey* blowing through it'.[4] But it also contains a much earlier design deriving from his experiences as a tourist in 1901–2, visiting Italy in the company of his mother, who seems to have been an improbable combination of Charlotte Bartlett and Mrs Honeychurch. He began writing about these experiences in diaries and letters and then in an early run at *A Room with a View* in the fragment called 'Old Lucy'.[5]

It is the only one of his novels – and this includes drafts of the early, unfinished 'Nottingham Lace' and the unfinished 'Arctic Summer' – to have chapter titles. The titles contribute to the overall comic effect. They are jocular and detached as they specify scene, lay out the cast of characters, and identify thematic strands and symbolic motifs. The most extreme example is the title of Chapter 6, in which nearly all the characters thus far assembled are listed as in a *dramatis personae* of a play. The lengthy title concludes in a comic anticlimax: '[they] drive out to see a view; Italians drive them'; but even here the symbolic pattern is maintained. It is significant, however, that the two chapters that function as the emotional and symbolic pivots of the novel in each section, Chapters 4 and 12 – the murder in the piazza and the bathing scene at the Sacred Lake – have no titles, suggesting that they belong to a different kind of novel, that they cannot be reduced to clever phrases in a satiric scheme.

A Room with a View works and reworks the characters, moments, and methods of the first two novels and benefits from the lessons learned while writing them. Thus there are no sudden deaths among the major characters, although in 'New Lucy', George is killed just at the climax of the marriage plot, almost with the same weird abruptness as Gerald's death in *The Longest Journey*. However, plotting was never Forster's strong suit. He would simply introduce some unexpected event to alter the course of narration.[6] Thus death strikes suddenly in *Howards End* when it is necessary to remove Leonard Bast from the novel's cast, although that move is a much more fraught and symbolically complex event than the *Journey's* more convenient deaths. In *A Room with a View*, the murder in the piazza is also a fraught event that echoes through the text but the death is external to the characters' lives even though it is crucial to the novel's symbolic design. It functions in much the way the Giotto fresco in Santa Croce does, as something that the characters must look at, react to, and then try to understand.[7]

The cast of characters, the relations among them, the world they move through and the narrator's relationship to them are very similar in all three early novels. George is part Stephen Wonham, part Stewart Ansell from *Journey* and he points toward *Howards End's* Leonard Bast with some subtle class adjustments. Mr Emerson is a more fully elaborated Mr Failing, here a socialist journalist rather than a gentlemen philosopher. Cecil is a much less sympathetic Philip Herriton from *Angels*, and Charlotte Bartlett is drawn from the same materials as his sister, Harriet.[8] Lucy follows from that novel's Caroline Abbott and points to the Schlegel sisters of *Howards End*, but especially Helen. However, she is probably best aligned with *Journey's* Rickie as she follows the same trajectory of ignoring her instincts, letting muddle prevail and joining the ranks of the benighted until, unlike Rickie, '[t]he scales f[a]ll from [her] eyes' (*RV*, p. 168) and she is saved.

While the characters are also in some measure reprises of earlier characters, what most distinguishes *Room* from its predecessors is Forster's desire to have it all work out, to arrive at a happy ending, shadowed, precarious, and tentative as that ending may be. 'It's bright and merry and I like the story', he wrote to Robert Trevelyan while working on it in 1907; 'Yet I wouldn't and couldn't finish it in the same style . . . The question is akin to morality' (*RV*, p. xiii). An index of that tentativeness, one of the markers of the shadows cast over the conclusion, is the one character that has no precedent in the two other novels, that is, the Reverend Mr Beebe. His role opens crucial issues for the novel's interpretation: Who tells the story? That is what is and where is the narrative point of view, the site of focalization? Who desires whom? That is, how do sex and gender circulate in the text? And how are the questions of desire and narration related?

In the most obvious sense the narrator is an observer, one who sets the scene, commenting sometimes wryly, sometimes ruefully at what his characters do and say. He is, however, often very close to their point of view; the opening of Chapter 2, for example, has the narrator in Lucy's room, looking out of the window with her, even though we are not aware of Lucy in the room for two and a half paragraphs. Gradually we realise that the observations, feelings, and thoughts described are part hers, part his. But as the scene moves to the pension breakfast room, the narrator draws back and the characters are set in motion by a ventriloquising puppet master who allows himself a few asides: 'Miss Honeychurch would remember the story. The men on the river were fishing' (*RV*, p. 16), the free indirect discourse carrying Miss Lavish's conversation, which is followed by the parenthetical remark, '(Untrue; but then, so is most information)' (*RV*, p. 16). This inside/outside narrative point of view organises, reports, indeed often is the novel's action. As with much of Forster's fiction, it is the telling more than the tale to which we attend.

Nonetheless, other characters often speak through and alongside the narrator: Mr Beebe and Mr Emerson between them both bring about crucial events in the novel and carry its underlying polemic, and Cecil, in the second part, in his double role as unsuitable suitor and comic muse,[9] controls much of the plot, functioning, too, as its commentator. Of these, Mr Beebe is the most complex. He is introduced at the start as a genial, enabling presence, one who recognises folly, and seems, on the whole, on the side of truth and youth. Listening to Lucy play Beethoven on the Pension piano on a wet afternoon, he recalls the time when he had first heard her play when she had visited her cousin, now her chaperone on the Italian journey, in Tunbridge Wells. It was Beethoven's Opus 111 and he was startled not only by the choice but by the execution. 'If Miss Honeychurch ever takes to live as she plays, it will be very exciting – both for us and for her' (*RV*, p. 31).[10] He understands the Beethoven, able to hear in her playing of it 'the hammer strokes of victory', echoing the narrator's comment that her playing possessed a passion, 'not easily labelled. . . . she was tragical only in the sense that she was great, for she loved to play on the side of Victory' (*RV*, p. 29). But even as Mr Beebe responds once again to her music and the narrator allows us to see her through his interested eyes, he withholds full sympathy from her. Indeed he will become as much antagonist as friendly interpreter, although it will take some time for that to become fully evident. Of Lucy's Santa Croce visit, for example, when alone without Baedeker or Miss Lavish she found herself looking at the Giotto 'Ascension of St John' through the conflicting responses of Mr Emerson and George, and as a result being brought to see the world from their point of view, he was disapproving. '[H]e did not wish their cause to be championed by a young girl; he would rather it should fail' (RV, p. 37).[11] Embedded in that comment is the basic conflict on which the entire novel turns.

Mr Emerson does not use music as a way of understanding our place in the world, but he articulates the novel's controlling system of values and offers a variant on the theme of victory: 'Pull out from the depth those thoughts you do not understand', he says to Lucy, 'and spread them out in the sunlight, and know the meaning of them . . . [A]ll life is perhaps a knot, a tangle, a blemish in the eternal smoothness. But why should this make us unhappy? Let us rather love one another, and work and rejoice' (RV, pp. 26–7). To live as she plays, to look at her thoughts in the clear sunlight: these are the two ethical imperatives offered by the narrator and his surrogates. But these abstractions – love, victory – can be variously understood. The Lucy character carries a good deal of their meaning, certainly much of what Forster hoped his book expressed even though he knew he could not simply 'write down, "I care about love, beauty, liberty, affection, and truth," although I should like to' (December 1908 letter to Malcolm Darling, quoted RV, p. xi). But what is the truth about love? Indeed who loves whom in this text? How interested is Forster in the courtship of Lucy and George? How does the shadow of a homosexual romance shape our reading of the heterosexual marriage plot?[12] Is it not, in Margaret Goscilo's terms, 'a richly queer text'?[13]

Much recent criticism has emphasised the textual homoerotics. From the throbbing tower in the scene of the murder in the piazza to the bathing scene in the Sacred Lake, the novel has been read more in terms of the writer's desire for George than George's desire for Lucy.[14] Markley argues, for example, that 'by switching the gendered object of the male gaze from female to male, and by disrupting the progress of his narratives at important moments during which the reader is invited to gaze on a tableau in which the male body is the central point, Forster invented a kind of narration that powerfully expresses male homoerotic desire while shrewdly maintaining the veneer of heterosexual conventionality'.[15] It is on George's body, Markley argues, that 'the gaze is chiefly concentrated'. Further, to the degree that Forster might not have been able fully to imagine desiring a woman, the force of attraction in the text surely moves from narrator to George rather than to Lucy. 'Girls like Lucy were charming to look at', the narrator remarks, 'but Mr Beebe was, from rather profound reasons, somewhat chilly in his attitude towards the other sex, and preferred to be interested rather than enthralled' (*RV*, p. 32). It is for these 'profound reasons' that he is 'conscious of some bitter disappointment' (*RV*, p. 93) at the prospect of her marriage to Cecil and becomes the outright enemy of her marriage to George. George, he says scornfully to Mr Emerson, 'no longer interests me. Marry George, Miss Honeychurch. He will do admirably' (*RV*, p. 203).

This is not to say that Mr Beebe (secretly) loves George, although the bathing scene brings him to the brink of that possibility.[16] But it does suggest that Forster 'loved' George, that is, created him out of his own desires. Mr Beebe, however, until he is made an active antagonist, remains the 'sensitive gentleman', the Victorian bachelor, understood as a distinct cultural type, whose 'psychic constitution' in Eric Haralson's argument 'opens onto homosexual panic, if not homosexual possibility'.[17] The bathing scene carries a sexual charge in its language, in the space it opens in the narrative for other longings, other resolutions. Here Forster writes homosexual desire without giving it either a name or an action. As desire circulates it connects man to man. However, the bathing scene, which stages this desire most emphatically, is carefully keyed to the heterosexual plot, for 'to the degree that the episode advances George's conquest of Lucy, the lake reprises the riverine bed of violets in which they first kissed in Italy'.[18]

Many critics have given this scene careful attention, locating it in a range of interrelated contexts: nineteenth-century paintings by Eakins and Tuke of boys bathing, Whitman's *Song of Myself*, Housman's *Shropshire Lad*, as well, as Edward Carpenter, Nietzsche, Carlyle, and Symonds.[19] Haralson reads this edenic moment as a variant of the greenwood fantasy that will conclude *Maurice*. It is a staged moment, a *tableau vivant*,[20] with George and Lucy's brother Freddy, and Mr Beebe swimming, running, and playing football with their clothes. They 'played at being Indians' (*RV*, p. 131); they 'rotated in the pool breast high, after the fashion of the nymphs in Götterdämmerung' (*RV*, p. 130). In that 'call to the blood and to the relaxed will' (*RV*, p. 133), they found 'a social space where not only anticorporeality but also heterosexist presumption and regulation are put in suspense'.[21] But it is temporary. The piles of discarded clothes 'proclaim . . . [w]e are all that matters. Without us shall no enterprise begin. To us shall all flesh turn at the end' (*RV*, p. 131).

The three play, but George, the figure the scene is constructed around, the one most looked *at* as he stands 'Michaelangelesque on the flooded margin' (*RV*, p. 130), remains only lightly looked *into*. He enters the novel with a question mark pinned to the wall of his pension room. The implied questions – why live? what is life worth? – are then somehow answered by the death in the piazza when he decides, yes, he will live. Except for his response to the Giotto fresco, when in contrast to his father's sceptical criticism he sees it depicting the right way to get to heaven, that is, by oneself and being greeted there by friends, he is largely inaudible. A few appearances, a few remarks, and a sudden kiss in a field of violets (the landscape given a sexual potency far stronger than the depiction of the kiss: 'this terrace was the well-head, the primal source whence beauty gushed out to water the earth' (*RV*, p. 68)) constitute his role in Part I. In Part II, after the immersion in the Sacred Lake (primal source and gushing beauty are part of that scene's conception, too), he returns as the replacement suitor. There is a second sudden kiss and then, Phaethon-like, he carries off his Persephone, completing the set of symbolic patterns around the motifs of life and death, earth, water, and sky.

There is a kiss at the Sacred Lake, however, but it is Cecil who gives it, absurdly, awkwardly, wishing as 'he approached [Lucy] . . . that he could recoil' (*RV*, p. 108). Always clothed, mostly seen in a room, he interests Forster as both individual and type, but he has a human complexity even if he is chiefly the object of the narrator's satire. He is an Edwardian rather than Victorian bachelor. His asceticism is aestheticised, given a Paterian gloss.[22] In the ethical/sexual accounting of the novel he is consistently on the negative side – medieval (he is described as a gothic statue), celibate, hypocritical, mocking. If George appears as the passionate heterosexual created out of a closeted gay man's desire, Cecil is the repressed homosexual, created out of a gay man's bemused disdain. He is much too proud of his physical unfitness ('I don't play tennis – at least, not in public', he annoyingly protests (*RV* p. 97)) to be admired by one whose imagination is filled with the images and statuary of ancient Greece. He is 'like a Gothic statue' we are told in the first description of Cecil, and that 'implies celibacy, just as a Greek statue implies fruition' (*RV*, p. 87). It is worth recalling Forster's meditation in his essay, 'Macolnia Shops', on the athletes depicted on the *cista ficoroni*, the cylindrical bronze toilet case that he saw on his first Italian journey. The essay was written at the same time as the Lucy drafts: 'Pollux the boxer has unsealed the spring . . . It is a good thing to satisfy the body . . . cherish the body and you will cherish the soul'.[23] Or as Mr Emerson phrases it: 'We shall enter [the Garden of Eden] when we no longer despise our bodies' (*RV*, p. 126).

However, despite (or because of) Cecil's languor and indifference, much of what happens in the second part of the novel happens through and around him. It is his mockery, his patronising condescension, and bloodless amusement at other peoples' words and actions, both the silly and the serious, that create the turns of plot and inadvertently send his bride-to-be into the arms of his unsuspected rival. His collusion with the comic muse in displacing the Miss Alans and bringing the Emersons to Summer Street provides the counterpart to the pension satire in Part I. But this is balanced by something unexpected. Although Forster may have examined Lucy's inner life more intellectually than emotionally, he created the world she lived in, the object of much of Cecil's scorn, with considerable emotion. It was a world he knew and loved, however much he made fun of its preoccupation with '[e]ggs, boilers, hydrangeas, maids' (*RV*, p. 141).

Both place and persons are important here. The opening scene of Part II is the drawing-room, Windy Corner, the Honeychurch home, its curtains drawn, letting in a filtered and varied light, disclosing a human space, so that while the sun is shut out, 'within, the glory, though visible, was tempered by the capacities of man' (*RV*, p. 82). It is filled with imperfect furniture but inhabited by people who know how to live in it, to talk to one another. Brother Freddy, studying anatomy, leaves a bone on a chair; Cecil is dismayed. 'For Cecil considered the bone and the Maple's furniture separately; he did not realize that taken together, they kindled the room into the life he desired' (*RV*, p. 90). The room is intimately connected to its view; indeed inside and outside blend here as nowhere else in the novel: 'Lucy, who was in the little seat, seemed on the edge of a green magic carpet which hovered in the air above the tremulous world' (*RV*, p. 86). The descriptions of place are closely aligned to the development of the characters. Hence Cecil's inability to respond to Windy Corner and the small village of Summer Street is an index of his failure to know her. 'He did not realize that Lucy had consecrated her environment by the thousand little civilities that create a tenderness in time . . . Nor did he realize a more important point – that if she was too great for this society she was too great for all society' (*RV*, p. 110).

Nearly a half century later, in his biography of his great aunt, Marianne Thornton, Forster described the house that gave him so strong a sense of place. It was the house that was to become Howards End, but his attachment to it infuses this text as well. 'The garden, the overhanging wych-elm, the sloping meadow, the great view to the west, the cliff of fir trees to the north . . . the impressions received there remained and still glow – not always distinguishably, always inextinguishably – and have given me a slant upon society and history.'[24] What also gives emotional force to the scenes in Windy Corner is the figure of Mrs Honeychurch. A note on her character in 'New Lucy' holds as well for her role in the finished novel: 'Always boasted of being commonplace: in reality no one less.'[25] She was modelled, he wrote in the copy of the book he gave to the painter Paul Cadmus, on Louise Whichelo, his beloved maternal grandmother. One gets a glimpse of this in *Marianne Thornton*: 'How I adored my grandmother! – we played for hours together . . . It is with her – with them [the Wichelos] – that my heart lies' (*MT*, p. 250).

But it is this very attachment to person and place that complicates the resolution of the novel.[26] Lucy and George are together at the Bertolini, gazing
out the window but their happiness is not complete. '[T]he Honeychurches
had not forgiven them; they were disgusted at her past hypocrisy; she had
alienated Windy Corner, perhaps forever' (*RV*, pp. 206–7). On one level this
is hard to understand. Mrs Honeychurch had never liked Cecil, keenly aware
of his sneering, his coldness, and neither had Freddy. Why had she not con-
sented to the marriage? Mr Beebe's influence is offered as a possible reason,
but it hardly seems adequate. Possibly class distinctions account for it, but
these had never weighed in the design earlier, except in the pension gossip.
It is as if Forster did not entirely trust the novel he was writing or trust his
characters to carry its belief system adequately. Does not domesticity enter
into that final scene too emphatically as Lucy darns George's socks, treating him as a mother would a child?[27] Can they really be comrades, those
two?

If Mr Beebe and Mr Emerson fight over Lucy's soul within the text, is there
not another contention outside it: Louise Whichelo, the adored grandmother,
as the presiding spirit of the domestic, the rooted and placed, versus the
spirit of the open road, a composite deity, part Carpenter, Whitman, Butler,
Housman, and Thoreau? Of course, this opposition is less stark; indeed in
much of Forster's writing it is elided so that domestic space and pastoral
space merge, but it might account for one's sense of incompletion, of the
tentative and precarious in that final scene. For another voice is heard there
that would call them out from the room. It belongs to the cabman, who is
the same and yet not the same 'Phaethon' who drove them in Chapter 6 in the
novel's Austen-like expedition scene. Then he had lost his own Persephone
but yet set up the circumstances for George to embrace his. Now his words,
'domani faremo un giro', recur like a refrain as Lucy and George talk at the
window. But there will be no ride tomorrow, for, as Lucy gently calls to him,
'Siamo sposati'. The cabman, his task completed, 'drove away singing . . .
[T]he song of Phaethon announced passion requited, love attained' (*RV*,
p. 209). The married couple stay inside.

But Forster does not leave it at that. There is, the last line of the novel
proclaims, 'a love more mysterious', figured in 'the river, bearing down the
snows of winter into the Mediterranean'. What is this mysterious love? In
its immediate context it might refer, in part, to the strange, unconscious
impulse that led Charlotte Bartlett to allow for the fateful conversation with
Mr Emerson that last evening in the Rectory. But the language makes a
greater claim than that. It suggests the close of Dante's *Paradiso* in its final
vision of 'the love that moves the sun and other stars'. Forster had been
reading Dante while writing the novel, giving a lecture on Dante at the

Working Men's College in November 1908 that conveyed a complex ambivalence toward his subject. Dante 'made the impossible credible', he wrote, but he found something inhuman, too distant in Dante's view 'upon the Empyrean . . . and though his words are full of love and beauty, they gather a certain terror as they pass through the interspaces' (*AE*, p. 168). Despite this protestation, one might argue that something of the same thing seems to happen in Forster's text. As the scene opens out, inscribing the emotions of his characters in natural cycles far larger than they, Lucy and George seem almost to disappear. They are at once within those pension walls and out in the interstellar spaces beyond. Possibly too much is being asked of these young lovers. They are asked to inhabit too many kinds of novels, too many kinds of love.

It is a novel that will 'gratify the home circle, but not those whose opinions I value most', Forster wrote to a friend when he had just completed it. (Letter to Wedd, 25 June 1908, quoted *RV*, p. xiv.) Exactly fifty years later in an essay published in the *Observer* and the *New York Times Book Review*, and included as an appendix in the Abinger Edition of the novel, Forster described it as 'not my preferred novel – *The Longest Journey* is that – but it may fairly be called the nicest' (*RV*, p. 210). I am not sure that Forster is the best reader of his own work in these statements. Of course, *The Longest Journey* would be his preferred, but there is more of that novel contained in *Room* than these remarks allow. Still, what they do underline is his inability or unwillingness to look at his characters once the plot design has been completed. They remain fixed figures in a landscape and since he is not interested in their 'nice' marriage, it is the symbolic pattern towards which our attention is directed at the novel's close. Thus, while his 1958 predictions about their future life are amusing enough, albeit melancholy, the focus is external. It is on the changing world they were to inhabit as the Great War broke out and idyllic spaces like Windy Corner disappeared.

However, one character remained vivid in Forster's imagination in those retrospective remarks: Cecil, here removed from the novel and placed directly in Forster's world. Forster tells a story, possibly true, that offers a fitting retrospective glance at our text: the scene is a party in Alexandria sometime after 1914; someone wanted a little Beethoven, although the hostess worried that 'Hun music might compromise us. But a young officer spoke up. "No it's all right," he said, "a chap who knows about those things from the inside told me Beethoven's definitely Belgian." The chap in question must have been Cecil. That mixture of mischief and culture is unmistakable. Our hostess was reassured, the ban was lifted, and the Moonlight sonata shimmered into the desert' (*RV*, p. 212). Culture, mischief, but also Beethoven. '[T]hat some sonatas of [his] are written tragic no one can gainsay; yet they can triumph or despair as the player decides' (*RV*, p. 29), a fair description of the reader's position at the end of this novel.

Notes

1. Claude Summers, *E. M. Forster* (New York: Frederick Unger, 1983), p. 82.
2. David Medalie, *E. M. Forster's Modernism* (Basingstoke and New York: Palgrave, 2002), p. 99.
3. Medalie, examining the use of music in the novel (which he reads as a pre-modernist text), argues that Forster employs the *leitmotif* rather than 'the ever-widening reference', the 'rhythmical recurrences' that mark his subsequent more modernist writing (p. 124). Brian May in *The Modernist as Pragmatist: E. M. Forster and the Fate of Liberalism* (Columbia and London: University of Missouri Press, 1997) also looks at the liberalism/modernism divide, arguing that in *Room*, Forster had not yet found 'a way to split the difference between liberalism and modernism' (p. 14).
4. Wilfred Stone, *The Cave and the Mountain: A Study of E. M. Forster* (Stanford, CA: Stanford University Press, 1966), p. 217.
5. See Oliver Stallybrass's 'Introduction' and notes to E. M. Forster, *The Lucy Novels: Early Sketches for 'A Room with a View'*, ed. Oliver Stallybrass, The Abinger Edition of E. M. Forster, vol. 3a (London: Edward Arnold, 1977) for a detailed discussion of the evolution of the novel. The volume contains all the materials that constitute 'Old Lucy' and 'New Lucy'.
6. In a 1904 letter to his friend Robert Trevelyan, Forster wrote, 'If you could also provide one of them something to do and something to die of, I should also be grateful', *Selected Letters of E. M. Forster*, ed. P. N. Furbank and Mary Lago, vol. 1 (Cambridge, Mass.: Harvard University Press, 1983), p. 61.
7. In 'Old Lucy' only George (then called Arthur) is present. See *The Lucy Novels*, p. 36.
8. Harriet's remark after removing a 'smut' from her eye that 'foreigners are a filthy nation', was originally given to Charlotte Bartlett in 'Old Lucy': see *The Lucy Novels*, p. 23.
9. 'I have won a great victory for the Comic Muse. George Meredith's right – the cause of Comedy and the cause of Truth are really the same', Cecil proclaims (*RV*, p. 115), referring to Meredith's *An Essay on Comedy and the Uses of the Comic Spirit* (1897).
10. The complex use of music in the novel has been frequently noted. See John Beer, *The Achievement of E. M. Forster* (London: Chatto and Windus, 1962), ch. 3; Frederick P. W. McDowell, *E. M. Forster* (rev. edn) (Boston: Twayne Publishers, 1982), pp. 22–3; John Lucas, 'Wagner and Forster: *Parsifal* and *A Room With a View*,' *ELH*, 33 (1966), 92–117.
11. A quite different reading of Mr Beebe is offered by Nigel Rapport, *The Prose and the Passion: Anthropology, Literature, and the Writing of E. M. Forster* (Manchester: Manchester University Press, 1994). Rapport understands Beebe's role 'as both *in loco auctoriensis* and *in loco lectoriensis*' (p. 106).
12. The first critic to identify a homosexual subtext in the novel was Jeffrey Meyers whose essay was written before the publication of *Maurice*. '"Vacant Heart and Hand and Eye": The Homosexual Theme in *A Room with a View*', *English*

Literature in Transition, 13 (1970), 181–92. See also Judith Scherer Herz, 'The Double Nature of Forster's Fiction: *A Room with a View* and *The Longest Journey*', *English Literature in Transition*, 21(1978), 254–65; see also Summers, *E. M. Forster* (1983), for early explorations of this issue, and James Buzard, 'Forster's Trespasses: Tourism and Cultural Politics' (1988), repr. in *E. M. Forster*, ed. Jeremy Tambling (Basingstoke and New York: Palgrave, 1995), pp. 14–29, who examines how Forster 'investigate[s] existence within the state of tourism', arguing that 'as a homosexual man seeking some sanctioned vehicle for his own desires . . . he is unable to free himself from the tourist state' (pp. 18–19).

13. Margaret Goscilo, 'Forster's Italian Comedies: Que(e)rying Heterosexuality Abroad', in *Seeing Double: Revisioning Edwardian and Modernist Literature*, ed. Carola M. Kaplan and Anne B. Simpson (New York: St. Martin's Press, 1996), pp. 193–214; quote from p. 211. She argues that Forster 'interweaves feminist and homoerotic agendas . . . by redistributing the gender and nationality of the figures seeking or offering Mediterranean erotic-spiritual salvation' (p. 203).

14. Parminder Kaur Bakshi argues in *Distant Desire: Homoerotic Codes and the Subversion of the English Novel in E. M. Forster's Fiction* (New York: Peter Lang, 1996) that Forster was not interested in his female protagonist, but rather in George's 'latent homosexuality' (p. 139). For Tariq Rahman, 'The Double-Plot in E. M. Forster's *A Room with a View*, *Cahiers victoriens et édouardiens*, 33 (1992), 43–62, 'the development of the relationship of George and Lucy is a metaphor for the quest for sexual happiness by homosexuals in a homophobic society' (p. 43), with Forster portraying Lucy as if he is 'thinking of her as if she were a boy' (p. 48).

15. A. A. Markley, 'E. M. Forster's Reconfigured Gaze and the Creation of a Homoerotic Subjectivity', *Twentieth Century Literature*, 47:2 (Summer 2001), pp. 268–92; quote from p. 268.

16. This is essentially Meyers's argument. A scene in 'New Lucy', which Meyers had not seen, suggests that something like this might have been part of Forster's initial thinking about Mr Beebe. It's a scene of cross purposes in the woods at night; Mr Beebe and George misunderstand each other, but Mr Beebe's feelings are clear enough (*The Lucy Novels*, pp. 106–12).

17. Eric Haralson, '"Thinking about Homosex" in Forster and James', in *Queer Forster*, ed. Robert K. Martin and George Piggford (Chicago and London: University of Chicago Press, 1997), pp. 59–73; quote from p. 68. Haralson uses Eve Sedgwick's terms in this argument (see Sedgwick, *Epistemology of the Closet* (Berkeley: University of California Press, 1990)).

18. Haralson, '"Thinking about Homosex"', p. 69.

19. Summers has shown how through allusion, quotation, and the books he put in the Emersons' bookcase, Forster was consciously creating a homosexual literary tradition, an argument also developed by Haralson. For the importance of Edward Carpenter for Forster, see Robert K. Martin, 'Edward Carpenter and the Double Structure of *Maurice*,' *Journal of Homosexuality*, 8 (1983), 35–46; see also Nicola Beauman, *E. M. Forster: A Biography* (New York: Alfred A. Knopf, 1994), pp. 207–10.

20. Mike Edwards in his study, *E. M. Forster: The Novels* (Basingstoke and New York: Palgrave, 2002), emphasises the theatricality of the text, how Forster sets scenes as in a play, using the encounter as his organizing principle.

21. Haralson, '"Thinking about Homosex"', p. 70.
22. Joseph Bristow, 'Against "Effeminacy": The Sexual Predicament of E. M. Forster's Fiction,' *Effeminate England: Homoerotic Writing after 1885* (New York: Columbia University Press, 1995), describes Cecil looking at Lucy 'through the aesthete's Paterian lens. Here the vampirism of La Gioconda, haunting the stylized cadences of Walter Pater's *Studies in the History of the Renaissance* (1873), displays the cold misogyny invested in the sphinx-like secrecy that so many fin-de-siècle writers ascribed to female sexuality' (p. 72).
23. E. M. Forster, *Abinger Harvest* (New York: Harcourt Brace, 1964), p. 172.
24. E. M. Forster, *Marianne Thornton: A Domestic Biography* (London: Edward Arnold, 1956), pp. 269–70.
25. *The Lucy Novels*, p. 90.
26. P. J. M. Scott in *E. M. Forster: Our Permanent Contemporary* (New York: Barnes and Noble, 1984) asks why the marriage is understood as being in defiance of the world. He argues that it is because the marriage is a stand-in for something left unarticulated (p. 72).
27. See Bristow, 'Against "Effeminacy"', p. 73.

10

DAVID BRADSHAW

Howards End

Chalky cheese

No reader of the opening chapters of *Howards End* could fail to gather that the Schlegels and the Wilcoxes are meant to be contrasted. But whether these families are really as different as chalk and cheese is a conundrum that grows in significance as Forster's fourth novel unfolds. And even if a reader still thinks that the two households are fundamentally unalike in their conduct and convictions on completing the book, the thornier question of where Forster's deepest sympathies lie, with his heavy-handed idealists or his sports-mad philistines, may well remain unsettled. For despite its narrator's poise and its assured (if sparse) social comedy, not to mention the clear overlap between Forster's interests and those of the Schlegels, it is not *Howards End*'s certainties that catch the eye but its hesitations, tensions, 'rich ambiguity . . . [and] fundamental *irresolution*'.[1] Like Charles Wilcox and Aunt Juley on their fateful journey from Hilton station to Howards End, Forster can seem at 'cross-purposes'[2] in this novel 'composed of contraries',[3] yet that only makes it all the more intriguing in the context of his contrast-driven work as a whole and all the more absorbing in its own right. 'Whatever the flaws, weaknesses and contradictions we may perceive in Forster's own ideological position', Peter Widdowson comments astutely, '[*Howards End*], by containing them, gains rather than loses'.[4]

The narrator must be reckoned with from the beginning of *Howards End* and not least because his first utterance ('One may as well begin with Helen's letters to her sister') suggests either a curious indifference to form or a weary, Tibby Schlegel-like disinclination to 'begin' the novel at all; possibly both. But no matter how we gloss his opening words, the narrator's role is accentuated at the start of the book and it is impossible to ignore him from then on. Time and again, he turns audaciously from story-telling and underscores his sizeable presence in the text, either by making direct reference to himself or by assuming the flamboyantly characterful yet oddly effacing, frequently skittish yet withal rather earnest, here sagacious there facetious, at times magniloquent and often magnificent, maxim-wielding yet far from emphatic manner which is the hallmark not just of Forster's companionable narrators but also (if to a lesser extent) the signature style of his essays, lectures, broadcasts, reviews, and criticism. In *Howards End*, however, Forster's unmistakable voice is particularly audible. The narrator tells us, for example, of his spats with his grocer about 'the quality of his sultanas' (p. 184); he speaks disparagingly (and seemingly from personal experience) about 'those who coquet with friendship' (p. 89); he notes despondently that 'man is an odd, sad creature as yet, intent on pilfering the earth, and heedless of the growths within himself' (p. 273), while in Chapter 5 he extols the unrivalled pleasures of Beethoven's Fifth Symphony and the meaning of its constituent parts, rubbishing *en passant* both the Queen's Hall in London and the Free Trade Hall in Manchester (pp. 44–5). Earlier in the novel, having waxed lyrical about the railway stations of London, the narrator informs us that Margaret Schlegel thinks King's Cross 'always suggested infinity' and its 'situation – withdrawn a little behind the facile splendours of St Pancras – implied a comment on the materialism of life'. 'If you think this ridiculous', the narrator continues, 'remember that it is not Margaret who is telling you about it' (p. 27). How could we possibly forget? With the notable exceptions of the novels with a purpose that H. G. Wells wrote after *The History of Mr Polly* (1910), and Lawrence's novels of the 1920s, such as *Kangaroo* (1923), obtrusive narrators are more or less absent from modernist literature, unless their function, like Marlow in Conrad's *Heart of Darkness* (1902), is to draw attention to their own untrustworthiness. But the narrator of *Howards End* is both conspicuous and (it seems) dependable, his chatty ubiquity only reinforced by his frequently quirky diction. As Barbara Rosecrance has remarked:

> The narrator's techniques of omniscience and engagement are familiar, but his voice goes further in self-dramatization, in manipulation of the reader, in the frequency and length of intervention than in any other Forster novel. The tendency of the narrator to step out of the action to formulate its larger significance also reaches its height in *Howards End*. No other Forster narrator establishes so personal a hegemony.[5]

Furthermore, while he may be as reliable as he is approachable, the narrator must be treated with considerable caution because it is far from easy, here and there, to reconcile the tolerant, live-and-let-live values on which Forster's wider reputation rests with the occasional tartness and unflagging class bias of his 'commentator' (p. 107). It is all too easy to fall for the narrator's charm, to be won over by his verbal idiosyncrasies, his appealing eccentricities, and his amiable, off the cuff judiciousness, but such captivation needs to be resisted (as well as savoured), because when he is at his most disarming the narrator can also be at his most disquieting. So much so, in fact, that some readers might wish to reconsider whether, on the evidence of *Howards End*, Forster's status as a liberal icon is really as secure as some critics would have us believe. One way or another, questions of 'contrast'[6] dominate *Howards End*, the criticism it has generated and the challenges it presents.

The cleavage between the *Weltanschauung* of the Schlegels and the Wilcoxian worldview is something about which every critic of the novel has had something to say. 'It is the story of a conflict between two points of view', the *Athenaeum*'s reviewer declared with assurance in 1910. 'The Schlegels are clever, sensitive, refined; they have a feeling for beauty and truth, a sense of justice and of proportion; they stand for what is best in modern civilization: the Wilcoxes are vulgar, blatant and brutal; such time as they can spare from money-making they devote to motors and bridge and suburban society; they stand for all that is worst.'[7] The Ismail Merchant and James Ivory film adaptation of 1992 only lent further weight to this time-honoured view that each family is the converse of the other, and, of course, there is a great deal in the text to support such an interpretation. The motoring Wilcoxes, for example, are undoubtedly driven by the 'blatant' values of the market-place – so much so, in fact, that they comprise more of a business concern than a family unit, with Charles Wilcox filling 'the post of chairman' (p. 109). Charles, his sister Evie, and their father Henry disregard the handwritten and 'unbusinesslike' (p. 108) note by means of which Ruth Wilcox had hoped to leave Howards End to Margaret because such an act of generosity would have failed to take account of their material 'improvements' to the property, such as the addition of a garage (p. 108) and a kitchen extension (p. 205). In addition, their commercial mindset is clearly allied to a 'brutal' (picking up another of the *Athenaeum*'s terms) streak in the Wilcoxes. Henry is adept at '*bullying porters*' (p. 19) and will be casually responsible for Leonard abandoning his relatively safe job at the Porphyrian Fire Insurance Company and indifferent to his being 'turned out' (p. 223) of Dempster's Bank, just as Charles is peremptory with a railway porter at Hilton (p. 31) and gives Crane, his chauffeur, a thorough dressing-down in Chapter 11, having previously 'got rid of the little Italian beast' (p. 103) who preceded him. In fact, Charles's inadvertently lethal assault on Leonard in Chapter 41 is but the tragicomic nadir of his bullying and bad-tempered stomp from one chapter to the next. Sentenced to three years in prison, the only things Charles is likely to miss behind bars are 'money-making', motoring, and games, for, like the rest of his family (apart from his mother), Charles is obsessed with sport. Evie does '*callisthenic exercises on a machine that is tacked on to a greengage tree*' (p. 20), and she, her brother, and father are all observed either playing or practising croquet, bridge, tennis, golf or cricket or are known to be devoted to them: Helen recalls that 'Evie talked cricket averages till I nearly screamed' (p. 40) during her first visit to Howards End. When the Wilcoxes are not whacking balls or playing cards they spend their time fishing, swimming, and shooting. Interestingly, the Schlegels see the Wilcoxes as having 'their hands on all the ropes' (p. 41), as if the family were engaged in nothing less than a consummate gymnastics display.

But *are* the Schlegels the *antithesis* of the Wilcoxes? In some obvious ways they are, but in other, more interesting ways they are not. Tibby, for example, is a perfect match for the Wilcox men in his indifference to Leonard, yet this sedentary, 'dyspeptic and difficile' (p. 44) egghead could not be further removed from their milieu of unthinking stretching and striving. His sisters (especially Margaret), on the other hand, reveal unexpected affinities with it. When Henry travels down to Swanage with an engagement ring for Margaret, for example, the two lovers greet each other with 'a *hearty* cordiality' (p. 179; emphasis added), while Margaret says at another point that she desires 'activity without civilization' (p. 119), as though she aspires to nothing more than a good round of golf. In a similar manner, when Helen visits Howards End at the beginning of the novel she falls not just for Paul but for the relentless 'energy' (p. 37) of his family as a whole, the 'robust ideal' (p. 38) they embody. '*Men like the Wilcoxes would do Tibby a power of good*' (p. 19), Helen reports back to Margaret not irrelevantly.

Initially, Helen enjoys being browbeaten by the Wilcox men, 'being told that her notions of life were sheltered or academic; that Equality was nonsense, Votes for Women nonsense, Socialism nonsense, Art and Literature, except when conducive to strengthening the character, nonsense' (pp. 37–8), but whereas she soon sets herself against the Wilcoxes, Forster repeatedly stresses Margaret's growing attraction to their view of life, how 'collision with them stimulated her . . . they had grit as well as grittiness, and she valued grit enormously' (pp. 111–12). The more intimate Margaret becomes with Henry, the closer she gets to the 'depths of his soul' (p. 185), the more she approves of what she finds there – at least before she finds out about his liaison with Jacky. Margaret's susceptibility to the sheer drive of Henry and their fundamental compatibility is the principal reason why readers are best advised to probe the juxtaposition of the two families rather than simply taking it as read. Even the core distinction between the Wilcoxes' 'outer life of telegrams and anger' (p. 176; see also p. 112) and a Schlegelian inner world of 'Literature and Art' (p. 23) is not as clear-cut as it seems. Certainly, the Wilcoxes are no bookworms, and Charles is recalled from his Naples honeymoon by the telegram which informs him of his mother's death (p. 101). Similarly, an angry telegram is sent by Henry to his unsatisfactory tenant,

Hamar Bryce (p. 197), and Paul Wilcox sends a (presumably congratulatory) 'cablegram' (p. 254) to his father and Margaret on their wedding day and one to Evie on hers (p. 208). But the Schlegels dispatch telegrams even more promptly – pp. 27, 35, 40 (twice), 247, 270, 271, 274 – and it is important to bear in mind that the first time the 'telegrams and anger' phrase (a favourite Wilcoxian duality with many commentators on the novel) occurs, it applies not to the twin poles of the Wilcoxian world, but to the telegrams which Helen and Margaret exchange at the beginning of the novel and the upset they cause (p. 41).

Likewise, although Leonard wants to 'improve [him]self by means of Literature and Art' (p. 65), these cultural agencies have a lot to answer for in *Howards End*. 'Books', according to Margaret, is a 'holy word' (p. 259), but a 'shower' of books (p. 315) plays a hefty role in Leonard's death, while the London clerk would never have ended up on the gravel of Howards End in the first place had it not been for his fetishization of such authors as Ruskin and Stevenson and his devotion to the 'Art' of Beethoven. Of course, it is just possible that Forster wishes us to *disapprove* of the Schlegels' blinkered immersion in Literature and Art – even the narrator concedes that 'the world would be a gray bloodless place were it entirely comprised of Miss Schlegels' (p. 42) – but it is rather unlikely.

With their professed interest in theosophy (pp. 158, 257, 323), socialism, feminism, and egalitarianism, and their liberated disdain for society's petty conventions, Helen and Margaret's progressive credentials could not be more blatant. From a modern-day perspective, however, they harbour a number of less open-minded attitudes and an aptitude for gross insensitivity which make them seem at times anything but advanced or enlightened. The 'impetuous' (p. 24) and 'impulsive' (p. 26) Margaret, for example, dispatches a well-meaning but discourteous letter to Ruth Wilcox (p. 77) and shortly afterwards snubs her suggestion that they travel down to Howards End together (p. 93), while even Aunt Juley (Mrs Munt) has a capacity for 'imprudence' (p. 37), as her 'hideous blunder' (p. 33) in mistaking Charles for Paul all too clearly reveals. Rashness and clumsiness, we soon realise, run in the Schlegel family (the grotesquely inactive and self-sufficient Tibby excepted), and although they claim to think 'personal relationships' 'supreme' (as did Forster), they are at times staggeringly badly handled by them. Above all, the main blame for Leonard's death (as well as Jacky's off-stage but inevitable plunge into destitution) may be laid squarely at the feet of the 'ramshackly' (p. 54) Helen. She and Leonard first meet because she absent-mindedly walks off with his brolly. 'I do nothing but steal umbrellas' (p. 54), she airily admits when Leonard calls to collect his own, before offering him a selection from the horde she has thoughtlessly accumulated over the years:

'I steal umbrellas even oftener than I hear Beethoven', Helen confesses later in the novel (p. 123). And when rummaging around for Leonard's umbrella, Helen reminds Margaret that she cannot simply stand by and tut-tut with disapproval, as at some previous date Margaret 'stole an old gentleman's silk top-hat', mistaking it for a muff (p. 54). Are the Schlegel sisters refreshingly emancipated from the bridles of convention, the reader might ask, or are they simply careless and self-centred (like their appalling younger brother)?

According to Margaret, Helen is 'too relentless. One can't deal in her high-handed manner with the world' (p. 183) and many readers might well be inclined to agree. When Helen bursts into Evie's wedding party with the Basts in tow, for example, Margaret angrily condemns her 'perverted notion of philanthropy' (p. 223). Having gone on to convince herself later that night that 'she loved [Leonard] absolutely, perhaps for half an hour' (p. 308), Helen leaves him a note in the morning 'intended to be most kind' but which 'hurt' him 'terribly' (p. 308). 'The expedition to Shropshire crippled the Basts permanently', we are told. 'Helen in her flight forgot to settle the hotel bill, and took their return tickets away with her; they had to pawn Jacky's bangles to get home, and the smash came a few days afterwards . . . He turned to his family, and degraded himself to a professional beggar. There was nothing else for him to do' (p. 309). The contrast between Leonard's slump into 'unemployable' (p. 309) idleness and the self-indulgent indolence of Tibby, who is asleep after a 'good lunch' when Leonard calls at Wickham Place a little further on in the novel (p. 312), is hard to overlook. Earlier, the narrator has referred to the Schlegel household's 'life of cultured but not ignoble ease' (p. 115), but his qualification becomes increasingly difficult to swallow. 'Tibbikins', in particular, is little more than a 'frigid' (p. 274) *rentier*, as gluttonous in his craving for food as he is for bookish absorption; in Chapter 30, for example, as Helen weeps before him, he simply carries on eating his lunch before taking up his Chinese grammar. It is Henry's conviction that '[l]ack of education makes people very casual' (p. 203), but in *Howards End* the most casual characters by some distance are the far from uneducated Helen and Tibby Schlegel.

Following Jacky's desperate visit to Wickham Place (when she interrupts Helen in full spate on the topic of social reform) Helen makes fun of her for the enjoyment of Margaret and Tibby (p. 120). She calls Jacky 'Mrs Lanoline' (p. 120) – that is, 'Mrs Wool-fat' – accuses her of having a 'face like a silk-worm' and claims she is not 'capable of tragedy' (p. 121). Further on in the novel, we are told that Margaret, too, finds Jacky 'repellent' (p. 229). Indeed, for two women supposedly committed to feminism and social justice, both sisters possess some distinctly snobbish and objectionable social attitudes.

Margaret, notably, refers not to the 'lower orders' (p. 34) as does the narrator, but to the 'lower animals' (p. 94). She pens an odious letter to Helen about Leonard and Jacky – '*The Basts are no good . . . The Basts are not at all the type we should trouble about*' (p. 239) – and is 'distressed . . . by odours from the abyss' when Leonard visits Wickham Place in pursuit of his wife (p. 124). The nightmarish horrors of the social 'abyss', so alarmingly laid before the reading public in such volumes as C. F. G. Masterman's *From the Abyss* (1902) and Jack London's *The People of the Abyss* (1903), haunted the genteel mind, and it is this profound anxiety which lies just beneath Margaret's comment above and her remark about Jacky trailing 'odours from the abyss' (p. 229) when she appears at Oniton. By the end of the novel, Margaret is relieved that she and her sister have crossed over 'the black abyss of the past' and are living 'a new life . . . gilded with tranquility' (p. 326), but she seems oblivious to the fact that Jacky, at that very moment, must either be teetering on the edge of a far from figurative abyss or, more likely, already well on her way to the bottom of it. This further evidence of the Schlegels' blindness, crassness, hypocrisy, and bigotry might be parcelled together in support of the view that Forster never intended us to be as favourably disposed towards them as the first few chapters of the novel seem to encourage us to be. Forster's aim may have been to discredit the Schlegels by exposing them as merely skin-deep progressives. And in making the siblings and their aunt dependent on unearned income from railway stock and other shares (beneficiaries, in other words, of successful entrepreneurs like Henry Wilcox), Forster appears to underline the Schlegels' *kinship* with the Wilcoxes, not the gulf between the two families. After all, one of the 'Foreign Things' (p. 28) in which Margaret so successfully invests may well be Henry's highly profitable Imperial and West African Rubber Company (see below).

The woman problem and the prig problem

Although he calls Leonard a 'chap' (p. 130) at one point, Forster's 'commentator' has an obvious distaste for the clerk. For instance, after Leonard has retrieved his threadbare umbrella and returned to his lodgings, the narrator proceeds to describe his sitting-room with a sickly relish, fitting it up, among other things, with 'one of the masterpieces of Maude Goodman' (p. 60). Had this object been described more simply as a print or some other kind of reproduction after the intensely sentimental but hugely popular Maude Goodman (d.1938), the narrator might have been thought to be doing no more than portraying Leonard and Jacky's lowly accommodation as realistically as possible. But 'masterpieces' sneers both at Goodman's saccharine

DAVID BRADSHAW

scenes of domestic bliss and her basement-bound admirers. Again, it might
be argued that the narrator's disdain is targeted not at Leonard's poor taste,
but Jacky's. But when he adds that the whole 'amorous and not unpleasant
little hole . . . struck that shallow makeshift note that is often heard in the
modern dwelling-place. It had been too easily gained and could be relin-
quished too easily' (p. 60), he seems to condemn *both* Jacky and Leonard
for being unable to afford anything better or more permanent of their own.
Elsewhere, the narrator speaks of Leonard's 'cramped little mind' (p. 127)
and gives him a top hat which is too big for him, 'the ears bending outwards
at the touch of the curly brim' (p. 131), suggesting that he also thinks of
him as having a cramped little head.

Forster's unease with Leonard comes across just as clearly in the treatment of his voice: his attempts to represent the language of the clerk just
don't sound convincing ('It really is too bad when a fellow isn't trusted.
It makes one feel so wild' (p. 65); 'I say, Jacky, I'm going out for a bit'
(p. 313)). Now, it could be that Forster burdens Leonard with the idiom of
his 'betters', equips him with the words of a man who has gobbled up Ruskin
and feels intimidated by the polish of the Schlegels, in order to emphasise
the nasty discordance of the class system. But his portrayal of Leonard's
partner makes this reading rather less plausible. Jacky is first encountered
through her beaming photographic likeness: 'Teeth of dazzling whiteness
extended along either of Jacky's jaws, and positively weighed her head side-
ways, so large were they and so numerous' (pp. 60–1). Intentionally or not,
Forster's words evoke the myth of the *vagina dentata* (vagina with teeth),
the age-old association of women 'with orality, digestion and incorporation;
and with women's (fantasised) jealousy of and power over men'.[8] But when
Jacky enters the room shortly afterwards, she could not be less vampiric,
being merely, we are told, a 'woman . . . of whom it is simplest to say that
she was not respectable' (p. 63). By employing this common-or-garden put-
down, the narrator simply betrays his genteel class prejudice: it is just the
kind of priggish slight that Aunt Juley might be expected to come out with.
Moreover, in spite of himself, the narrator does go on to detail Jacky's gaudy
apparel at some length, but 'her hair', we are informed, 'or rather hairs . . .
are too complicated to describe' and her 'face does not signify. It was the
face of the photograph, but older, and the teeth were not so numerous as the
photograph had suggested, and certainly not so white. Yes, Jacky was past
her prime, whatever that prime may have been. She was descending quicker
than most women into the colourless years' (p. 63). While these words may
or may not be misogynistic, they most certainly lack compassion, and this
impression is only reinforced when the narrator goes on to tell us that Jacky
is 'on the shelf' at thirty-three, invoking a music hall ditty to that effect.

Furthermore, although Jacky is hard of hearing, the narrator chooses to refer to her '*degraded* deafness' (p. 67; emphasis added), while at Oniton she is said to be 'so *bestially* stupid that she could not grasp what was happening' (p. 224; emphasis added). By employing intensifiers such as these, the narrator assumes a position of contemptuous superiority over Jacky and for the modern reader this can be jarring to say the least. Something similar occurs when a young woodcutter is described as descending from a tree '[w]ith a grunt' in Chapter 11, 'for he was mating', and when Charles's wife Dolly is dismissed as 'a rubbishy little creature, and she knew it' (p. 101). As Michael Levenson has pointed out, 'these colloquialisms – "rubbishy," and "she knew it . . ."' ensure that the narrator's attitude to Dolly has 'more the tone of a personal crotchet than an Olympian edict'.[9] Awkwardly, Aunt Juley is not the only person in *Howards End* in whom '[e]sprit de classe' is 'strong' (p. 34).

But it is not just the treatment of Dolly and Jacky that raises eyebrows. Henry Wilcox '*says the most horrid things about women's suffrage*' (p. 21) to Helen and some readers may wonder whether the narrator is in cahoots with his 'masterly ways' (p. 185). At the beginning of Chapter 18, for example, when Margaret receives a letter from Henry announcing his willingness to let his Ducie Street house to the Schlegels, we are told that, should the sisters be in favour of his proposal, 'Margaret was to come up *at once* – the words were underlined, as is necessary when dealing with women – and to go over the house with him' (p. 161). Does the parenthesis convey Henry's point of view (presented as indirect discourse) or the author's (as filtered through the narrator)? Similarly, when Henry's Cyprian 'episode' (p. 255) with Jacky comes to light Margaret feels justifiably angry with him, but only a little further on, as she undresses for bed, her irritation has collapsed into forgiveness. 'Pity . . . is at the bottom of woman', the male narrator opines. 'When men like us, it is for our better qualities . . . But unworthiness stimulates woman. It brings out her deeper nature, for good or evil' (p. 240). By the following morning Margaret has entirely absolved Henry: 'She played the girl, until he could rebuild his fortress and hide his soul from the world' (p. 243). But if Margaret is only 'play[ing]' on this occasion, by the time of her Austrian honeymoon she has become little more than a literate plaything. Henry enjoys watching her 'reading poetry or something about social questions', but he only has 'to call, and she clapped the book up and was ready to do what he wished. Then they would argue so jollily, and once or twice she had him in quite a tight corner, but as soon as he grew really serious she gave in. Man is for war, woman for the recreation of the warrior, but he does not dislike it if she makes a show of fight. She cannot win a real battle, having no muscles, only nerves' (p. 255). Soon afterwards Henry says patronisingly (but meaning to be tender), 'What a practical little woman it is! What's it been reading?' (p. 257). After her marriage, Margaret effectively cuts herself off from new ideas and defers entirely to a husband who symbolically infantilises her, calls her (even though she is in her thirties) his 'girl' (pp. 276, 281, 296, 297), and who is convinced that all women are unteachably illogical (p. 278). By the end of the novel, of course, Henry has been neutered and is shut up in a dark room with hay fever (p. 326) while Margaret and Helen rule the roost at Howards End, but it is difficult to misremember the compromises Margaret has had to make, the psychological and ideological elisions which have had to be enforced by the author, in order for this idyll to come into being. Does the final sentence's bumper 'crop of hay' (p. 332) really compensate for all that has had to be scythed down to make way for it? *Howards End* was written at a time when 'The Woman Question' was a matter of grave and growing concern in England. The first imprisonment of suffragettes occurred in 1905 and it is difficult to read the novel's negative representations of and comments about women without bringing that disturbed context of prejudice, militancy, and repression into play.

Eugenics and the looming big one

Eugenics, another of the novel's underlying concerns, filled many newspaper columns during the Edwardian period, with the Eugenics Education Society being founded in 1907 to fight what it saw as two threats to national survival.[10] The first was a drop in the birth rate, which alarmed eugenicists because it contrasted with a rising birth rate in competitor nations, such as Germany. This anxiety looms large in Chapter 6 when Leonard is hailed by a fellow clerk outside his lodgings in Camelia Road. 'Very serious thing this decline of the birth rate in Manchester' (p. 59), Cunningham remarks. Leonard is taken aback by his comment and Cunningham repeats it, this time 'tapping at the Sunday paper in which the calamity in question had just been announced to him' (pp. 60–1). The second, related threat was internal, in that the eugenics lobby argued that the fall in the British birth rate was far steeper among the affluent and educated classes than among those deemed to be less socially meritorious, giving rise to widespread fears about the so-called 'multiplication of the unfit'.

While the decline in the birth-rate is referred to only once, the racial degeneration of which it was thought to be indicative is brought into focus whenever Leonard tittups into view. 'The population still rose', the narrator muses at one point, 'but what was the quality of the men born?' (pp. 116–17). If Leonard is typical, it is not impressive. His bent spine and narrow chest (p. 122) bespeak his membership of the dysgenic underclass and he is said to be a 'colourless, toneless' man who has 'already the mournful eyes above a drooping moustache that are so common in London . . . one of the thousands who have lost the life of the body and failed to reach the life of the spirit' (p. 122). 'During the second half of the nineteenth century the majority of the British people began to live and work in cities', Derek Fraser has noted. 'By the Edwardian years that majority had become overwhelming – 77 per cent in 1901 and 80 per cent in 1911.'[11] It was widely believed, however, that modern city life was by its very nature dysgenic and Leonard's feeble, deformed, and undernourished body is the incarnation of all that dread. A curious aspect of this aspect of the novel, though, is that the puny Leonard has to carry Forster's degenerationist forebodings almost on his own. London is said to be growing ever more populous, but the 'satanic' (p. 94) megopolis the reader encounters is surprisingly deserted, with, it appears, only Leonard and one or two other lower-middle-class clerks stalking its streets. The seething masses of Victorian fiction are nowhere to be seen, never mind the even more multitudinous hosts of the Edwardian city.[12]

The weak-hearted Leonard is contrasted with two sturdier models of British manhood, the well-nourished yeoman and the 'Imperial' type. 'Healthy, ever in motion, [the Imperial type] hopes to inherit the earth. It breeds as quickly as the yeoman, and as soundly; strong is the temptation to acclaim it as a super-yeoman, who carries his country's virtues overseas' (pp. 314–15). Despite the narrator going on to say that 'the Imperialist is not what he thinks or seems. He is a destroyer. He prepares the way for cosmopolitanism' (p. 315), his grudging admiration for the Imperial type comes across so strongly in the novel that it is as if the narrator, too, has fallen for the 'temptation' of the 'super-yeoman'. The narrator's observations have been prompted by an embodiment of the 'Imperial' type (probably Charles) driving past Leonard as he walks towards Howards End and his death. Charles, a 'robust man' (p. 81), is the eugenically sound and fecund offspring of Henry Wilcox, a man with a 'robust' complexion (p. 165) and no need of Eustace Miles' 'body-building dishes' (p. 161). By Chapter 21, in sharp contrast to the increasingly sterile men of Manchester (and 'Auntie Tibby' (p. 55)), Charles has emulated Henry in fathering three children and by Chapter 33 Dolly is expecting their fourth. Evie, too, is 'built firmly' (p. 154), and the 'broad-shouldered' (p. 40) Paul goes out to Africa both in fulfilment of his national 'duty' (p. 119) and to forge his manhood, while Margaret's admiration for the Wilcoxes' dynamism, her belief that they 'keep England going' (p. 268), only increases as the novel progresses. Miss Avery upsets her by observing, uninhibitedly, 'Ay, they breed like rabbits' (pp. 268–9), but the truth is that from a novel haunted by the spectre of degeneration, the virile and fruitful Wilcoxes emerge with a lot of eugenic credit. What is more, when

Charles fells Leonard he enacts the eugenicists' most cherished fantasy, the eradication of the unfit by the fit, and while it would be going much too far to suggest that this kind of wish-fulfilment was at the front of Forster's mind when he conceived his novel, it is quite possible that it was not as firmly filed away at the back of his mind as we might like to imagine.

In spite of his unimpressive physique, Leonard is Jacky's protector and without him, as Helen points out in Chapter 30, she is likely to 'sink' as countless women had done before her and were likely to do in her wake, 'till the lunatic asylums and the workhouses are full of them, and cause Mr Wilcox to write to the papers complaining of our national degeneracy' (p. 249). Her comment sounds like a fiery retort to the eugenicist preoccupations of Edwardian England and William Greenslade has argued that Forster, too, shows himself:

> to be contemptuously hostile to the discursive apparatus which, with such facile certainty, separated the healthy from the weak, the fit from the unfit, the normal from the tainted.
>
> Forster's achievement is to give full play to the most socially and ideologically arrogant of these discourses at this period with a telling raid on the territory of masculinity with its coercive discourses of power, its command of social and economic space, its emotional hollowness and deep repressions: the fortress that Henry Wilcox inhabits in *Howards End*.[13]

Greenslade may be right and some readers will tune into Forster's subversive hostility more easily than others. But it is also possible that Forster's own fear of 'the people of the abyss' and his anxieties about the dysgenic effects of city life led him to admire Henry Wilcox and his family rather more than the liberal *bien-pensant* within him would have cared to acknowledge. Indeed, far from being the villains of *Howards End*, the impressively fit and fertile Wilcoxes might be its unlikely heroes. This is certainly the impression D. H. Lawrence picked up, writing to Forster in 1922: 'I think you *did* make a nearly deadly mistake glorifying those *business* people in *Howards End*'.[14]

Nor is it just the urban masses that have lost their evolutionary thrust. 'I think . . . that our race is degenerating', Margaret sighs in exasperation when her brother and sister are unable to decide whether they want to live in Ducie Street or not. 'We cannot settle even this little thing; what will it be like when we have to settle a big one?' (p. 162), she continues with reference to the ominous state of European relations and the impending 'big one' against Germany which would finally arrive in 1914. *Howards End* emerged from Forster's pen as Anglo-German tensions – 'England and Germany are bound to fight' (p. 74) – plumbed new depths, and these frictions shade the novel in a number of ways. There are passing references to the precarious state of Anglo-German relations in *Where Angels Fear to Tread* (Chapter 6) and *The Longest Journey* (Chapters 8 and 33), but in *Howards End* they burst forth in Fräulein Mosebach's 'patriotic' determination to marry Helen to a German in Chapter 12 and Aunt Juley's conviction that Britain, rather than Germany, has been 'appointed by God to rule the world' (p. 43), while Henry makes it clear that one of the principal reasons why Paul is in Nigeria is because 'England will never keep her trade overseas unless she is prepared to make sacrifices. Unless we get firm in West Africa, Ger – untold complications may follow' (p. 137). In Simpson's, a well-known London restaurant, a bellicose clergyman declares (with Kaiser Wilhelm II in mind), 'The Emperor wants war; well, let him have it' (p. 158), while Mrs Wilcox observes that 'people do not seem quite to like Germany' (p. 86) following Margaret's 'patriotic' words in favour of 'things Teutonic'.

Anglo-German rivalry is epitomised in Aunt Juley's and Herr Liesecke's competitiveness about music (Elgar versus Beethoven) in Chapter 5, and so Forster's celebrated account of the sublimity of Beethoven's Fifth Symphony could be read as a defiantly anti-jingoistic gesture, just as the narrator has been quick to emphasise that the Schlegels are not 'Germans of the dreadful sort' (p. 42). But like so many other facets of the novel, nothing is simply black or white. Is it the case that Forster is being bold and provocative in 1910 when he represents Beethoven's 'Hun music'[15] as incomparable and half-Germans sympathetically, engaging head on with the popular prejudice against 'things Teutonic'? Or is he suggesting, in the Schlegel sisters' blundering insensitivity, that a kind of Prussianism is already at large in Liberal England? If so, is it significant that a *German* sword is instrumental in Leonard's death? And who hands the sword to Charles when he asks for 'a stick'? One of the Schlegel sisters, presumably (p. 315).

England, the empire, and the rubber boom

Though set in London, Hertfordshire, Dorset, and Shropshire, the British Empire casts its long shadow over *Howards End*, and while it seems likely that Forster set out to critique imperialism as unequivocally as he wished to pillory the materialistic Wilcoxes, yet again the situation turns out to be more complex than we might have anticipated in view of the opening chapters. Two 'Anglo-Indian ladies' attend Evie's wedding (p. 208) and one of them describes it as 'quite like a Durbar' (p. 221), while another guest, Mrs Warrington, has just come 'back from the Colonies' (p. 211). Similarly, though 'rubbishy', Dolly is the daughter of a retired Indian Army officer (p. 80) and her brother is currently serving in the subcontinent, just as Charles is a Boer War (1899–1902) veteran (p. 167). Most notably of all, of course, the Wilcoxes' family business is the *Imperial* and West African Rubber Company, which, according to the map in the antechamber to Henry's office, owned 'a helping of West Africa . . . Another map hung opposite, on which the whole continent appeared, looking like a whale marked out for blubber' (pp. 196, 276; emphasis added).

The latter map no doubt reflects the carving up of Africa which the Congress of Berlin (1884–5) sanctioned and it was the escalating demand for rubber in particular which made that carving, in places, all the more ferocious. Within a few years, rubber had become nothing less than the raw material of modernity, insulating the ever increasing range of electrical goods and enabling the burgeoning number of bicycles and cars to speed along ever more rapidly. In fact, between 1880 and 1910 'rubber became the most important, most market-sensitive, most sought-after new commodity in the world'.[16] Demand for it took off exponentially precisely at the time when Forster was writing *Howards End* (1908–10) and its price boomed in a manner 'reminiscent of the railway mania before 1845'.[17] 'Hardly a week went by in 1909 without the formation of a new rubber plantation company being announced in the London press. Often it was more than one a week' and by 20 April 1910, the price of rubber on the London Stock Exchange peaked at twelve shillings a pound.[18] No wonder Margaret tells Helen that the Wilcoxes' company is 'a big business' (p. 114), and it is against this background of feverish speculation and mushrooming profits that Henry Wilcox's fortune swells to such an extent that within two years of his wife's death he has 'almost doubled his income' (p. 137) and become a near millionaire (p. 139), nothing remarkable by today's standards but a formidable level of wealth in the Edwardian period.

But African rubber was also a deeply tainted commodity by the time Forster began writing *Howards End*. In 1904, a shocking exposé of the systematic barbarity which attended the exploitation of rubber in Leopold II's Congo territory had been published by Roger Casement[19] and this resulted, four years later, in the international community insisting on a major reorganisation of Belgian rule there. Nigeria was not mired in scandal like the Congo when Forster sat down to write his novel, but many of its first readers may well have placed particular stress on the words 'African' and 'Rubber' and drawn their own conclusions about the lucrative exploits of the Imperial and West African Rubber Company. Indeed, they may have eyed Henry Wilcox in the same kind of way (if not quite with the same level of disapproval) that we now view the ivory-grabbing Kurtz and his colleagues in *Heart of Darkness*. Tellingly, when Henry, Margaret, Tibby, and Charles are discussing Helen's strange and elusive behaviour in Chapter 34, Henry's genial demeanour suddenly slips away 'and they saw instead the man who had carved money out of Greece and Africa, and bought forests from the natives for a few bottles of gin' (p. 277).

All the more noteworthy, then, that Margaret thinks the kind of imperialist qualities that Henry possesses in such abundance have also been responsible for the suppression of savage customs at home. 'If Wilcoxes hadn't worked and died in England for thousands of years, you and I couldn't sit here without having our throats cut. There would be no trains, no ships to carry us literary people about in, no fields even. Just savagery . . . Without their spirit life might never have moved out of protoplasm' (pp. 177–8). She sees the Wilcoxes, in other words, as an efficient evolutionary organism, perfectly adapted to succeeding in the capitalist jungle either at home or abroad. But Henry's overseas activities also lead to his downfall. Britain had occupied Cyprus following an earlier Congress of Berlin (1878), and it was on that island, ten years prior to Evie's wedding, that Henry's fling with Jacky took place in 'a garrison town' (p. 243). With the elapse of almost a century since the publication of the novel, it is unlikely that many modern readers will be as anxious as Margaret to extol Henry's capitalist and imperialist qualities, and his patriarchal womanising is likely to be viewed as equally unappealing.

'Imperialism', we are told at one point, 'had always been one of [Margaret's] difficulties' (p. 197), but this does not prevent her, during her Christmas shopping expedition with Mrs Wilcox, buying 'a golliwog' for a girl of her acquaintance (p. 90). In 1910 such a purchase had none of the unsavoury significance it would have today, but even so it suggests a degree of blinkeredness on Margaret's part. Or perhaps it indicates her real attitude towards black people. For although Margaret claims to be out of sympathy with the Empire, at times she sounds very much like a typical imperialist. She belittles Nigeria and Nigerians, for example, in words which she may well have picked up in the Wilcox household – 'dull country, dishonest natives, an eternal fidget over fresh water and food' – adding, with Paul in mind, 'A nation who can produce men of that sort may well be proud. No wonder England has become an Empire' (p. 119). And although she and Helen 'would at times dismiss the whole British Empire', they do so, significantly, 'with a puzzled, if *reverent*, sigh' (p. 42; emphasis added). Indeed, it is Margaret, not the Wilcoxes, who introduce imperialist rhetoric into Howards End. She is aware on first entering the house, for instance, that she 'would *double her kingdom* by opening the door that concealed the stairs' (p. 202; emphasis added) before thinking immediately, among other things, 'of the map of Africa; of empires' – presumably because she knows the home improvements she has in mind would be funded by the overflowing coffers of the Imperial and West African Rubber Company. Oddly, given its peaceful location, the heart of the house beats 'martially' (p. 202), yet if *Howards End is* a synecdoche for England as a whole, as some critics have argued, what could be more appropriate? A martial spirit, after all, was one of the main factors which brought the Empire into being.

Another contrast worth highlighting is that between the idealised rural England which the narrator evokes and the real state of the English countryside at the time the novel was written. Standing on the Purbeck hills at the beginning of Chapter 19, for instance, the narrator apostrophises the Isle of Wight in terms which link it with the novel's broader concern with good breeding and racial fitness. He exalts it as 'the island that will guard the Island's purity till the end of time . . . It is as if a fragment of England floated forward to greet the foreigner – chalk of our chalk, turf of our turf, epitome of what will follow' (p. 170). His words amount to nothing less than an encomium to his native land in which 'the imagination swells, spreads and deepens, until it becomes geographic and encircles England' (p. 171), with the chapter as a whole culminating in a crescendo of national pride: 'England was alive, throbbing through all her estuaries, crying for joy through the mouths of all her gulls . . . For what end are her fair complexities, her changes of soil, her sinuous coast? Does she belong to those who have moulded her and made her feared by other lands, or to those who have added nothing to her power, but have somehow seen her, seen the whole island at once, lying as a jewel in a silver sea, sailing as a ship of souls, with all the brave world's fleet accompanying her towards eternity?' (p. 178). A cluster of literary allusions, the most obvious to John of Gaunt's famous speech in Shakespeare's *Richard II* (II.i), are set in train during this passage, but it may come across as distinctly chauvinistic to contemporary ears, even though Forster was almost certainly trying to achieve the opposite effect by acting as a spokesman for those who had 'added nothing' to England's power. Something similar happens when the narrator turns his attention to London's 'various railway termini', which he says 'are our gates to the glorious and the unknown. Through them we pass into adventure and sunshine . . . In Paddington all Cornwall is latent and the remoter west; down the inclines of Liverpool Street lie fenlands and the illimitable Broads; Scotland is through the pylons of Euston; Wessex behind the poised chaos of Waterloo' (p. 27). Here the narrator mixes the real and the mythical rhapsodically, while at another point in the novel he laments the absence of 'a great mythology' of England (p. 262), his own heightened discourse, quite possibly, being an attempt to set that right.

Beneath the narrator's soaring words, however, the first readers of *Howards End* would have known that all was not well in rural England. They would have known, as Henry knows, that 'the days for small farms are over' (p. 205). From around 1875 to 1895 England experienced a severe agricultural depression caused by the importation of cheap American wheat, a succession of poor summers, and livestock epidemics, and on the back of these catastrophes came bankruptcy, evictions, and rural depopulation. Between 1881 and 1911 the agricultural population of England fell by nearly 20 per cent.[20] So although the narrator might claim (with an authority borrowed from Matthew Arnold[21]) that on farms such as the Averys' 'one might see life steadily and see it whole . . . connect without bitterness until all men are brothers' (p. 264), by this point in the novel we sense that all is not right even on this particular farm, never mind the farms of England in general. Miss Avery's niece, Madge, for instance, despite being a farmer's wife, is 'mortified by innumerable chickens, who rushed up to her feet for food, and by a shameless and maternal sow. She did not know what animals were coming to' (p. 264). Madge's discomfort with her own livestock tells us far more about the true state of things in rural England than the narrator's nostalgia for a pre-motorcar-and-suburbia golden age.

In Chapter 41, when Leonard makes the final journey of his life, he observes agricultural labourers who have 'been up since dawn'. The narrator expands on this passing encounter, building it into a quasi-eugenicist *cri de cœur*: 'they were men of the finest type . . . They are England's hope. Clumsily they carry forward the torch of the sun, until such time as the nation sees fit to take it up. Half clodhopper, half board-school prig, they can still throw back to a nobler stock, and breed yeomen' (p. 314). Yet at Oniton, a shamefaced Leonard tells Helen that his grandparents were precisely such 'agricultural labourers' (p. 234) from Lincolnshire and Shropshire, a biographical tit-bit that emphasises just how much physical damage city life has inflicted on England's manhood in just two generations. Once again, Leonard is made to stand before the reader as a scapegoat, the personification of a degenerate, less 'noble' kind of Englishman.

Ruth Wilcox, on the other hand, is more a genius loci than a mother of three, the frail personification of Forster's stand against the noisy new England of movement, motoring, and materialism. Having been born at Howards End, Mrs Wilcox glides 'noiselessly', over the lawn in Chapter 3, with 'a wisp of hay in her hands' (p. 36), an allusion to Ceres, the Roman corn goddess. She can sniff hay without any adverse effect (p. 20), whereas Henry, Charles, Evie, and Tibby are all hay-fever sufferers. And if Mrs Wilcox is a kind of high priestess of the fields with extraordinary powers of communion, her life-long home is nothing less than a 'sacred place' (p. 325). Howards End was based on a house near Stevenage in Hertfordshire called Rooksnest where Forster lived from 1883 to 1893, and a good deal of the significance the narrator attaches to the fictional dwelling reflects the author's nostalgia for the only childhood home in which he appears to have been truly happy. According to Margaret, Howards End has 'wonderful powers . . . It kills what is dreadful and makes what is beautiful live' (p. 293) and, like Rooksnest,[22] it is protected by a wych-elm with teeth embedded in it (pp. 19, 191, 206). But the house where Forster lived as a child was surrounded by extensive meadows, whereas the location of Howards End, in the words of Paul, is 'not really the country, and it's not the town' (p. 330). Situated only an hour from London by train, it will not be long before Howards End and nearby Hilton are consumed by suburban sprawl. Even Henry notices that the neighbourhood's 'getting suburban' (p. 141), with a 'stream of residences . . . thickening up' (p. 199) towards it. Hilton High Street is really no more than a settlement 'strung upon the North Road, with its accreting suburbs' (p. 97) and Hilton station strikes 'an indeterminate note. Into which country will it lead, England or Suburbia? It was new, it had island platforms and a subway, and the superficial comfort exacted by businessmen' (pp. 29–30). The answer to the narrator's question could not be clearer and at the end of the novel 'London's creeping' ever nearer, with the 'red rust' of suburbia visible only a few meadows away (p. 329). Nor is London only spreading northwards. When Leonard attempts to escape southwards from the city by walking at night into Surrey, it is just as impossible to shake off the suburbs: after Wimbledon, 'It was gas lamps for hours' (p. 126). Leonard pitches up among 'suburban hills' (p. 131) before travelling back to the city by commuter train.

Pollution, panic, and emptiness

Forster's acute unease with modernity is most evident in his treatment of the motorcar. Like many Edwardian intellectuals, he was appalled by the racket and 'stench' (p. 29) of the automobile and he regarded its intrusive and newfangled power as symptomatic of the 'brutal', speeded-up and money-orientated culture which he loathed so intensely, a 'culture as is implied by the advertisements of anti-bilious pills' (p. 29). Even Charles, a man whose language is peppered with the jargon of motoring ('tooling' (p. 31); 'a longer spin' (p. 32)), whose idea of a perfect holiday is a 'motor tour in England' (p. 81), and who receives a car from his father as a wedding present (p. 81), gets a headache when he is unwise enough to go 'motoring before food' (p. 319). Forster's anti-car position anticipates latter-day concerns about the environmental impact of exhaust emissions and the alienating effects of noise pollution, of course, and Nicholas Royle has even suggested that 'Howards End might in fact be called the first modern ecological novel in English'.[23]

It is also worth noting that the car is not only associated with noise, stink, and discharge, but also with blunders, accidents, and low comedy. Henry and Evie return early from Yorkshire not only because 'police [speed] traps' (p. 94) are unsportingly pervasive in that county but also because their 'vermilion giant' (p. 164) has been involved in a 'motor smash' with a horse and cart near Ripon (p. 96), just as Albert Fussell's vehicle flattens 'a rotten cat' (p. 213) in Shropshire and a similar fate nearly befalls baby 'Porglywoggles' in Chapter 35. When cars pass through Summer Street, we read at the beginning of Chapter 12 of *A Room with a View*, 'they raised only a little dust, and their stench was soon dispersed by the wind and replaced by the scent of the wet birches or of the pines' (*RV*, p. 124), but by the time he wrote *Howards End* Forster clearly felt the car problem had become far more intrusive, disruptive, and indelible. '[M]onth by month', the narrator tells us at the beginning of Chapter 13, 'the roads smelt more strongly of petrol, and were more difficult to cross' while 'human beings . . . breathed less of the air, and saw less of the sky' (p. 115). 'The dust problem caused great resentment and was a factor in political debate on automobilism', comments Peter Thorold.[24] A speed limit of twenty miles per hour was in force between 1903 and 1930, though it was widely disregarded,[25] and when cars thunder by in *Howards End*, lungs and gardens fill with dust (pp. 32–3), just as when they are stationary their engines 'ooz[e] grease on the gravel' (p. 308). Yet when Charles accelerates past the 'lower orders' at one point in his father's 'throbbing, stinking car' (p. 36) – with a heedlessness reminiscent of that more notorious Edwardian road-hog, Toad of Toad Hall – and they vanish 'in a cloud of dust' (p. 34), the reader might wonder whether, like Leonard's elimination and the fairy-tale close of the novel, this is not another moment of wish fulfilment on Forster's part. The car is undoubtedly a loud and filthy menace, but its colonisation of England seems to offer a radical solution to the nation's social and demographic problems: they disappear from sight in an instant.

The epigraph to *Howards End*, 'Only connect . . .', is almost as well known as the novel itself. It most obviously refers to Margaret's efforts to unite the (supposed) spirituality and culture of the Schlegels with the grounded commercial nous of the Wilcoxes and it turns out to be an abbreviation of the novel's most heartfelt *donnée*: 'Only connect! That was the whole of [Margaret's] sermon. Only connect the prose and the passion, and both will be exalted, and human love will be seen at its highest. Live in fragments no longer' (p. 188). By Chapter 22, however, Margaret thinks she has failed to achieve such a fusion because of Henry's 'obtuseness' and by Chapter 38 she turns her full fury on her husband:

You shall see the connection if it kills you, Henry! You have had a mistress –
I forgave you. My sister has a lover – you drive her from the house. Do you
see the connection? Stupid, hypocritical, cruel – oh, contemptible! – a man
who insults his wife when she's alive and cants with her memory when she's
dead. A man who ruins a woman for his pleasure, and casts her off to ruin
other men. And gives bad financial advice, and then says he is not responsible.
These men are you. You can't recognise them, because you cannot connect . . .
No one has ever told you what you are – muddled, criminally muddled.

(p. 300)

'It is those who cannot connect who hasten to cast the first stone' (p. 304),
the narrator pronounces with kind of Biblical authority soon afterwards,
but could it be that he himself is the novel's principal stone-caster, in that he
cannot connect with the likes of Leonard and Jacky? By Chapter 31, the narrator is referring to Henry and Margaret as 'our hero and heroine', but many
readers may wish to resist such tags and the novel's improbably optimistic
conclusion. The 'time for telegrams and anger was over' (p. 321) the narrator
observes, but there will be readers unable or unwilling to banish the time of
'telegrams and anger' so readily from their minds. Margaret has straightened
out the 'tangle' (p. 329) which Henry's involvement with Jacky and Leonard's
with Helen has brought about, and Margaret and Henry (who seems not only
tired but moribund at the end) have 'learned to understand one another and
forgive' (p. 328), just as there has been a rapprochement between Helen and
Henry: but some readers will feel that the heaped-up 'muddledom' (p. 310) of
the past few years cannot be ironed out so easily. Like the melding of the spiritual and the commercial which Margaret and Henry's marriage represents,
Helen's child is literally the offshoot of a connection (albeit fleeting) between
England's gentlefolk and her urban masses, between England and Germany,
but is this contrast-defying mongrelism any more than a fantasy on Forster's
part? A more fitting epigraph, perhaps, might have been 'panic and emptiness', a phrase which is repeated on a number of occasions throughout the
novel (pp. 40, 46, 47, 102, 175, 232) and which is generally applied to the
high-octane vacuity of Wilcoxdom. However, behind the Wilcoxes' 'wall
of newspapers and motor-cars and golf-clubs' (p. 40), as this chapter has
tried to show, are to be found not only 'panic and emptiness' but also traits
which Forster seems to have found rather more attractive.

If Forster's original intention was to write a 'Condition of England' novel
focusing, among other things, on how the mercantile bourgeoisie was fast
superseding the aristocracy and rural gentry as the nation's most powerful
social group (as Henry informs Margaret as they look out of one of Howards
End's upper windows, 'Most of the land you see . . . belongs to the people

at the Park – they made their pile over copper – good chaps' (p. 205)), it did not end up that way. Just as Helen tells Margaret at the beginning of the novel that Howards End is not *'going to be what we expected'* (p. 19), so *Howards End* does not quite turn out as the reader might have anticipated on the strength of its early chapters. Rather it turns into a far more enthralling novel which spotlights not the sturdiness of Forster's liberal values, but their relative frailty. Patently a novel of contrasts, *Howards End* is no less fundamentally a novel of contradictions.

Notes

1. Peter Widdowson, *E. M. Forster's 'Howards End': Fiction as History* (London: Chatto and Windus for Sussex University Press, 1977), p. 12.
2. E. M. Forster, *Howards End* (London: Penguin, 2000), p. 33. All further page references are embodied in the text.
3. John Sayre Martin, *E. M. Forster: The Endless Journey* (Cambridge: Cambridge University Press, 1976), p. 110.
4. Widdowson, *E. M. Forster's 'Howards End'*, p. 12.
5. Barbara Rosecrance, *Forster's Narrative Vision* (Ithaca, NY, and London: Cornell University Press, 1982), p. 131.
6. This is Forster's own term. See *Selected Letters of E. M. Forster*, ed. Mary Lago and P. N. Furbank vol. 1. (1879–1920), (London: Collins, 1985), p. 187.
7. Anonymous review, *Athenaeum*, 4336 (3 December 1910), p. 696.
8. Elizabeth Grosz,'Animal Sex: Libido as Desire and Death', in *Sexy Bodies: The Strange Carnalities of Feminism*, ed. Elizabeth Grosz and Elspeth Probyn (London and New York: Routledge, 1995), p. 281; see also pp. 284, 293.
9. Michael Levenson, 'Liberalism and Symbolism in *Howards End*', in *Modernism and the Fate of Individuality: Character and Novelistic Form from Conrad to Woolf* (Cambridge: Cambridge University Press, 1991), pp. 78–101. Quote from p. 84.
10. For an overview of the origins and literary appeal of eugenics in the period c.1880–1939, see David Bradshaw 'Eugenics: "They Should Certainly be Killed"', in *A Concise Companion to Modernism*, ed. David Bradshaw (Oxford: Blackwell, 2003), pp. 34–55. See also Dan Stone, *Breeding Superman: Nietzsche, Race and Eugenics in Edwardian and Inter-war Britain* (Liverpool: Liverpool University Press, 2002).
11. Derek Fraser, 'The Edwardian City' in *Edwardian England*, ed. Donald Read (London and Canberra: Croom Helm in Association with the Historical Association, 1982), pp. 56–74. Quote from p. 56.
12. For a subtle contextualisation of the novel's engagement with inter-related anxieties about the mushrooming city of London, the state of England, its growing population and modernity, and Forster's position with regard to New Liberal thinking on these matters, see David Medalie, *E. M. Forster's Modernism* (Basingstoke and New York: Palgrave, 2002), pp. 1–25.
13. William Greenslade, *Degeneration, Culture and the Novel, 1880–1940* (Cambridge: Cambridge University Press, 1994), p. 213.

14. *The Letters of D. H. Lawrence*, ed. Warren Roberts, James T. Boulton, and Elizabeth Mansfield, vol. IV (June 1921–March 1924) (Cambridge: Cambridge University Press, 1987), p. 301.

15. This is a phrase Forster twice uses in 'A View without a Room' (1958), a short essay in which he speculates about what might have happened to George and Lucy Emerson in the years following their marriage, including Lucy 'continuing to play Beethoven. Hun music!' during the First World War. ('Appendix', *A Room with a View*, ed. Oliver Stallybrass (1908; London: Penguin Books, 2000), pp. 232, 233.)

16. Henry Hobhouse, 'Rubber: Wheels Shod for Speed', in *Seeds of Wealth: Four Plants that Made Men Rich* (Basingstoke and Oxford: Macmillan, 2003), pp. 125–85. Quote from p. 130.

17. Hobhouse, *Seeds of Wealth*, p. 161.

18. Austin Coates, *The Commerce in Rubber: The First 250 Years* (Singapore, Oxford, and New York: Oxford University Press, 1987), pp. 144, 154.

19. *Correspondence and Report from His Majesty's Consul at Boma Respecting the Administration of the Independent State of the Congo* (London: HMSO, 1904). See also 'The King and the Congo', ch. 7 of John Loadman, *Tears of the Tree: The Story of Rubber – A Modern Marvel* (Oxford: Oxford University Press, 2005), pp. 108–42.

20. See Christabel S. Orwin and Edith H. Whetham, *History of British Agriculture* (Newton Abbot: David and Charles, 1964), pp. 258–386.

21. According to Matthew Arnold in his poem 'To a Friend' (1848), the Greek poet Sophocles 'saw life steadily, and saw it whole'. There are further allusions to this famous Arnoldian phrase on pp. 67, 165, and 314.

22. See 'Rooksnest', an appendix to the Penguin edition, pp. 333–43, esp. p. 338.

23. Nicholas Royle, *E. M. Forster* (Plymouth: Northcote House in Association with the British Council, 1999), p. 49. See also Wilfred H. Stone, 'Forster, the Environmentalist', in *Seeing Double: Revisioning Edwardian and Modernist Literature*, ed. Carola M. Kaplan and Anne B. Simpson (Basingstoke and London: Macmillan, 1996), pp. 171–92.

24. Peter Thorold, *The Motoring Age: The Automobile and Britain 1896–1939* (London: Profile Books, 2003), p. 38.

25. Sean O'Connell, *The Car and British Society: Class, Gender and Motoring 1896–1939* (Manchester and New York: Manchester University Press, 1998), p. 115.

11

HOWARD J. BOOTH

Maurice

When *Maurice*, the latecomer among Forster's completed novels, was published posthumously in 1971, many reviewers saw the book as a failure. Time and again the text was seen as 'simple' and dated in its treatment of homosexuality.[1] Often behind the negative assessment of the novel was the view that a text addressing male–male desire could not be good art. Philip Toynbee, writing in the *Observer*, found *Maurice* 'novelettish, ill-written, humourless and deeply embarrassing'. He argued that among the 'special restraints' that made Forster's other novels a success was that 'he should *not* express his homosexual feelings directly'. Forster's talents were best confined by a 'millrace', and it was the very channelling of his energies through the exclusion of homosexuality that gave his other work its force. For Toynbee, homosexual experience was best left on the bank, outside representation and the creative process.[2] Subsequent critics reacted strongly to the initial reception to the novel, exploring it in the context of 1913–14, when it was first drafted. However, the view of the text as straightforward and unsophisticated has remained in place. It is that position that I want to challenge here, and to make the case for *Maurice* as a thoughtful adaptation of the novel form to the subject matter and a strong intervention in debates of the time.

Maurice can be seen as highly conventional, combining two of the main masterplots of the novel as a genre, the *Bildungsroman* and the 'marriage plot'. It is, though, also a new departure for the novel, as Forster had to meet the technical challenge of writing a *Bildungsroman* where the result of the protagonist's engagement with society is the decision to live outside it, and a 'marriage plot' where the lovers are two men. What the novel calls the '[b]eautiful conventions' (*M*, p. 141) of heterosexual love and marriage are not available to Forster. When compared with earlier literature addressing maturation and male–male relationships in this period, *Maurice* was a marked advance. Gregory Woods has noted that 'at the end of the nineteenth century male homosexuality (and lesbianism less often and less emphatically) starts to be written about as an essentially tragic condition':[3] the project of *Maurice*, though, is to recast earlier texts as comedy. In 1908, Forster listed a number of authors in his diary which, as Robert K. Martin has argued, can be seen as an effort to construct a homosexual canon.[4] Alongside artists from the past are authors of contemporary schoolboy and university fiction. In this published work of the preceding twenty-five years only platonic love between two boys or undergraduates is represented. The love is doomed, and so are many of the main characters. In A. W. Clarke's *Jaspar Tristram* (1899), for example, schoolboy affairs are the main subject matter as Jaspar (known to his intimates at school as Rosie) falls in love with Els (Elsie) before being rejected in favour of Orr, an older boy. Jaspar's search for an 'ideal friend' sees him switch from Els to Els's sister, Nina. Orr reappears as Jaspar's rival for Nina, and Jaspar's love is again frustrated. Nina dies at the end of the novel, reinforcing the permanence of the failure to find love. In the fiction of H. M. Dickinson and Howard Overing Sturgis, too, those who do not adopt conventional heterosexual roles become passive: distortion of personality, unhappiness, and, often, illness and death result.[5] Writing about homosexuality often involved depicting damage and withdrawal.

With *Maurice*, Forster embarked on a different trajectory. The aim was to address individual maturation with the outcome of comedy, while remaining attentive to the wide range of homosexual experience. Forster wanted a more active central figure, and was prepared to approach homosexuality directly. The difficulties for a novelist abounded. Controlling the narrative is a problem when, early on in the novel, it is difficult to imagine opportunities for dialogue; the main character engages only with those who hold homosexuality to be taboo. Initial scenes are brief and tongue-tied and the novel has a pared-down quality. While there may, in the second half of the novel, be more scope for dialogue and developed scenes, Forster then had the challenge of handling the transition to a more conventional style of narrative.

The novel is carefully organised to convey Maurice's isolation and loneliness while still depicting a network of social relations. This sense of separation occurs even though Maurice is ostensibly part of such powerful social units as the suburban household, the public school, an old university, the City, and the country house. The narrative voice, authoritative and apart, is usually focalised through Maurice, but we do revisit key events to see how they were viewed by other characters. The focus of the narration is on what was felt at that particular time, and on relating what happens to Maurice to the general experience of growing up. Maurice is treated very differently from the pathologising case histories of homosexuals found in sexology texts, with the emphasis falling on the normality of his responses.

The mode of narration has been compared unfavourably to *Howards End* and *A Passage to India* – even in one case to *Arctic Summer*[6] – but it needs instead to be seen as a set of necessary modifications to the novel form in order to undertake a specific task.

Maurice's crisis late in Part 1 of the novel can be used as an example of the way the text is narrated and responses described. He has rejected Clive and is on the edge of acknowledging his sexuality to himself,

> Madness is not for everyone, but Maurice's proved the thunderbolt that dispels the clouds. The storm had been working up not for three days as he supposed, but for six years. It had brewed in the obscurities of being where no eye pierces, his surroundings had thickened it. It had burst and he had not died. The brilliancy of day was around him, he stood upon the mountain range that overshadows youth, he saw. (*M*, p. 46)

The tone is authoritative yet involved, and the imagery has the major role in conveying meaning. What we see here is just part of the pattern of imagery in the text that is used to measure Maurice's progress. His advance towards a homosexual relationship is linked to things the culture traditionally views negatively, including rain, the outside, and darkness. On leaving his preparatory school he is called 'brave' by the other students, but 'A great mistake – he wasn't brave: he was afraid of the dark' (*M*, p. 3). Night terrors are found in other *Bildungsroman*; they play a central role, for example, in Compton Mackenzie's *Sinister Street*, the first volume of which was published on 1 September 1913, just before Forster began work on *Maurice*.[7] This is shaped to Maurice's situation with precision. Going to bed back at home he is troubled by a very particular light effect, though also fascinated by it. The shadow of the streetlight reflected in the mirror represents the alternate world of his sexuality. The thought of George the garden boy allows him to 'overc[o]me the spectral' and go to sleep – the love of a friend, then, is the reality that will overcome the illusion that he belongs in the everyday world (*M*, p. 10). Later in the text 'going through the looking-glass' is Clive's pejorative term for a homosexual lifestyle (*M*, pp. 150, 211). When the earlier scene is remembered it becomes much more than a clichéd reference to a Lewis Carroll text.

The novel uses different places and topographies to help Forster depict the unfolding experiences of a socially isolated protagonist. The major locations accrete meaning through the text, though often their expected meaning is 'inverted'. For example, the Halls' house represents suburban values, but it is also linked to the turn in Maurice's relationship with Clive, when Clive suffers his relapse there. When Clive returns to the Halls' house to tell Maurice of his reorientation to heterosexuality, he sees the street lights as forming chains, which is a sign of his new wish to knit himself back into the social fabric through marriage (*M*, p. 102). London becomes the place where Maurice and Alec reach an understanding, a victory for the greenwood won in the metropolis. As well as the novel's stress on place there is also the topography of mental development. Maurice's adolescence and growth towards manhood and the acceptance of his homosexuality is represented in terms of his leaving a deep valley and moving upwards. The use of landscape to provide a language for development was written into the original choice of name for the central character – not Maurice Hall, but Maurice *Hill*. It was only changed when, late in life, Forster became concerned that a Cambridge academic had the same name as his protagonist (*M*, pp. liii–liv).

Forster's use of symbol and image to provide a structure against which the events and characters are measured can be compared with his other novels and modernist writers such as Lawrence and Woolf. Lawrence would go further than Forster in his critique of Western culture and its underlying structures, but he was committed to identifying as heterosexual.[8] With a less benign view of nature he would not have shared Forster's belief that trusting to nature and the body would necessarily lead to positive intervention from some external force, that Alec would be out there in the rain to respond to Maurice's cry. *Maurice* does not look like a text of the modernist period in its positive, and some might say 'old-fashioned', resolution. However, the text can be seen as addressing self-formation in a way that anticipates the era of 'identity politics'.

As well as ways of plotting same-sex love and the use of imagery, Forster also takes and reshapes elements from the ideas of the time. The critic J. H. Stape has explored the 'generic hybridism' of the novel, its recasting of late Victorian texts and ideas, and especially Walter Pater's *Marius the Epicurean*.[9] Given the stress on Maurice's ordinariness the character and the text could not be made too overtly intellectual or literary, but the intellectual underpinning for the project is clearly signalled. Though Maurice does not engage with the radical thinkers of the age, he is suspected of being in sympathy with them. Anne asks whether he is a disciple of Nietzsche, to which Maurice's response is 'Ask me another!' (*M*, p. 144). In a move characteristic of modernism, the complex present is explored by reference to underlying structures believed to be revealed in ancient myth. While Clive is associated with Pallas Athene, Maurice is linked to myths around disruption, nature, and passion through Dionysus. With the evening primrose pollen in his hair Maurice is said to be 'quite bacchanalian' (*M*, p. 162) and in descriptions of Alec there is also an element of the Pan figure that had fascinated Forster (among other early twentieth-century writers) in 'The Story of a Panic'.[10]

The novel depicts Maurice as someone presented with different possible ways of living, including socially imposed 'normality', the relationship with Clive that proves to be a wrong turn, and the relationship with Alec. He learns to deal with setbacks, to learn from situations, and to grow stronger. The narrative structure of *Maurice* follows the stages on the way to maturity, where the key incidents correspond to the chapter unit. A view of the novel's structure in terms of a developing set of associations differs from the influential account of Robert K. Martin. He sees the text as having a 'double structure', with Parts I and II dominated by the relationship with Clive, Hellenism, and a view of male–male love that excludes sex. Martin argues that this can be linked with the nineteenth-century writer John Addington Symonds. This position cannot be sustained for the later Symonds, who was more relaxed about homosexual sex after his crisis in Cannes in January 1868. The second half of the text is dominated by the cross-class relationship with Clive, where the attitude to sex and society follows the views of Walt Whitman and Edward Carpenter.[11] While Martin's article was the first significant reading, useful in beginning to describe how the imagery works in the novel, he gives a sense of the novel that is too static, and says little about the text as process.

More than simply showing Maurice in relation to various models, the novel debates whether the precedents for various social roles help or hinder development. Though a line on this is proposed, the issue remains a problem for the text, a faultline opens up. As precedents for same-sex desire provide the novel with narrative material and a vocabulary, this is also an issue of form. The psychoanalytic term 'identification' can help open out the issues here and provide a terminology for Forster's treatment of maturation, though the drafting of the novel predates by a few years Freud's development of the term, as he turned to explore ego formation. For Freud, identification is the explanation of how character is formed. Individuals form links with another person, on whom they begin to model their behaviour. Freud's focus was on the early identification with the parents as part of the Oedipus complex, but he also argued that 'secondary' identifications – social forces such as education and the law – help to reinforce the model provided by the father. What Freud did not explore is how the male child who desires his own sex, though he would not find models for a homosexual lifestyle in the family or supported by the secondary paternal identifications, could locate precedents for his desires in culture and history. These could be termed secondary maternal identifications. For Freud, identification is an unconscious process. It cannot necessarily be willed, and the child growing up homosexual may well, after refusing many possible sites of identification, find it difficult to suddenly start identifying when they discover someone to identify with.[12] In

Maurice, the eventual rejection of convention runs across sexuality, family, class, and work. If one way of thinking about identification is as the pull towards an external object that mediates between a present and future version of the self, then it is difficult to imagine what within the culture can support the sundering of the self from social life, and the adoption of a place somehow outside language and representation.

In the exploration of these issues in *Maurice* it is not simply a matter of the homosexual hitting on a storehouse of identifications. They can constrict and lead astray. Clive finds Plato to be very important – 'Never could he forget his emotion at first reading the *Phaedrus*' (M, p. 55) – and he makes his declaration of love to Maurice by referring to reading Plato's *Symposium*. However this provokes the reaction 'Oh rot' and the narrative voice says of Clive's feelings that 'books meant so much for him he forgot that they were a bewilderment to others. Had he trusted the body there would have been no disaster, but by linking their love to the past he linked it to the present, and roused in his friend's mind the conventions and the fear of the law' (M, p. 58). At the end of Chapter 16, Clive discusses the influence of desire on aesthetic judgement, comparing the way he responds to Michelangelo and Greuze, but Maurice cannot follow the quick flow of his ideas. Clive comments 'These private roads are perhaps a mistake' (M, p. 74), and what comes next does indeed take a different view of the past, one that asserts the benefits of the absence of all homosexual identifications,

> And their love scene drew out, having the inestimable gain of a new language. No tradition overawed the boys. No convention settled what was poetic, what absurd. They were concerned with a passion that few English minds have admitted, and so created untrammelled. Something of exquisite beauty arose in the mind of each at last, something unforgettable and eternal, but built of the humblest scraps of speech and from the simplest emotions.   (M, p. 75)

The difference between this passage and the preceding discussion of art and desire could suggest that the relationship will fail, and in particular that Clive is too concerned with imposing a particular shape on the relationship. While *Maurice* condemns the stultifying effects of some identifications, they are also, as we shall see, depicted as necessary for personal development, and so to the narrative. The novel does not fully resolve the tension between the thoughtful and cultural, and the instinctual and new.

The phrase 'humblest scraps of speech' acknowledges that the difficulty of representing this instinctual form of desire, one not constrained by past models and history, centres on language. In the opening scene of the text Maurice is given a talk about sex by Mr Ducie. The marks in the sand explaining heterosexual sex mean, in Mr Ducie's view, that Maurice 'need never be puzzled or bothered now' (*M*, p. 5). The signs, though, are unstable, and not just because they are drawn in the sand. Maurice feels that Ducie is a 'liar' when he worries that women will see the images, and a world of hypocrisy, guilt, and complexity opens up that Ducie said he was removing (*M*, p. 6). Later, homosexuality is introduced by means of its very unmentionability, following the old legal way of referring to sodomy (in Latin) as 'the crime that cannot be mentioned among Christians'.[13] The Dean says to his students, 'Omit: a reference to the unspeakable vice of the Greeks' (*M*, pp. 37–8), and Maurice asks the young doctor, Jowitt, 'I say, in your rounds here, do you come across unspeakables of the Oscar Wilde sort?' (*M*, p. 131). When Mr Ducie reappears in the British Museum chapter, issues of language are again to the fore. Maurice is recognised by the sound of his voice while towering over a scale model of the Acropolis saying 'I see, I see, I see' (*M*, p. 193). Where Clive once led by reference to Greece, Maurice now stands above and understands. When Ducie misremembers his former pupil's name, Maurice claims to be 'Scudder', taking charge of issues of naming and identity. Though Alec then claims to have a 'serious charge' to bring against Maurice, he does not carry it through, and a crisis of threatened blackmail passes (*M*, p. 194). From the child under instruction, and an adult with an unnameable sexuality, Maurice has become the accomplished operator in and between the signs, able to play situations to his benefit.

Though the narrative voice says that Maurice is sceptical about identifications – which, in an echo of the scene on the beach with Ducie, are described as 'scratches in the sand' (*M*, p. 48) – he becomes adept at recognising and utilising those that are genuinely helpful. These are often linked to the figure of Risley – based, Forster acknowledged, on Lytton Strachey. At first Maurice finds Risley a 'queer fish' (*M*, p. 23). Maurice himself is never going to become an intellectual and an aesthete, but he recognises that Risley might be useful to him in his development:

> He was not attracted to the man in the sense that he wanted him for a friend, but he did feel he might help him – how, he didn't formulate. It was all very obscure, for the mountains still overshadowed Maurice. Risley, surely capering on the summit, might stretch him a helping hand. (*M*, p. 23)

The 'surely' here is a characteristically deft touch, suggesting the confidence Maurice has, without evidence, that Risley must have the answers and be happy. Clive, on the other hand, is described as leading 'the beloved up a narrow and beautiful path' before they became 'equal' (*M*, 80). Following Clive is like going 'up the garden path', only in the particularly well-kempt and civilised form of Hellenism.

The first effort Maurice makes to follow up the acquaintance with Risley leads to a dead end. Walking up the dark corridor to Risley's room he crashes into the door, and finds Clive within. They strike up a friendship over the piano rolls of Tchaikovsky's Sixth Symphony that Clive is borrowing from Risley. (Later, Clive's London flat, where Maurice and Clive spend their last night together before Clive goes to Greece, is said to have a similar approach to that to Risley's rooms at Cambridge (*M*, p. 93).) When Maurice considers getting married after his consultation with Dr Barry he goes to a concert, to find that the same symphony is being performed:

> [Risley] informed his young friend that Tschaikowsky had fallen in love with his own nephew, and dedicated his masterpiece to him. 'I come to see all respectable London flock. Isn't it *supreme*!'
>
> 'Queer things you know,' said Maurice stuffily. It was odd that when he had a confidant he didn't want one. But he got a life of Tschaikowsky out of the library at once. The episode of the composer's marriage conveys little to the normal reader, who vaguely assumes incompatibility, but it thrilled Maurice. He knew what the disaster meant and how near Dr Barry had dragged him to it. Reading on, he made the acquaintance of 'Bob', the wonderful nephew to whom Tschaikowsky turns after the breakdown, and in whom is his spiritual and musical resurrection. The book blew off the gathering dust and he respected it as the one literary work that had ever helped him.
>
> (*M*, pp. 137–8)

The book is not dusty, rather it blows the dust off Maurice. He does not want to talk about his life to Risley, but the proffered source of identification does help.[14]

Maurice develops a habit of listening 'underneath the words' (*M*, p. 192) and also attending to possible external objects that will be useful. These do not have to be of immediate and obvious benefit, and can take different forms. Maurice's conversation with his dying grandfather about his strange cosmology leads Maurice to abandon thoughts of committing suicide. He is struck by the phrase 'let it out, but not yet, not till the evening' (*M*, p. 119). The element of solar myth in the cosmology convinces Maurice that it may be worth waiting for his life to change, things may turn round just as winter gives way to spring. When he does let out his cry into the night, Alec responds. Though the reason for visiting the hypnotist is that he may be able to reorientate Maurice's desires towards women, the actual effect is to open him to the relationship with Alec. In time Maurice is not simply led by identifications, but fixes on those that accord with the trajectory of his own development. The tension remains, however, as to whether this is achieved through conscious reflection or as a matter of pure instinct.

Maurice finds a source of identification that is known precisely because it is somehow 'external' to, and challenging, society. His isolation means that he can only speak about it to the hired ear of Lasker-Jones:

> 'England wasn't all built over and policed. Men of my sort could take to the greenwood.'
> 'Is that so? I was not aware.'
> 'Oh, it's only my own notion,' said Maurice, laying the fee down. 'It strikes me there may have been more in that Robin Hood business than meets the eye. One knows about the Greeks – Theban band – and the rest of it. Well, this wasn't unlike. I don't see how they could have kept together otherwise – especially when they came from such different classes.' (*M*, p. 183)

This reference to Robin Hood was omitted due to an eye-slip from the 1959 typescript and the 1971 edition of *Maurice* and only restored in the Abinger edition (*M*, 276 n. to p. 183, ll. 27–9). It draws on the view of Robin Hood established in the Romantic period, which saw him as a political radical and an outsider. Victorian and Edwardian writers had also focused on the homosocial aspects of the group.[15]

It is perhaps the stress on what thought and the external object can do, in addition to the body and the physical world, which took Forster away from the influence of Edward Carpenter. The final entries in his so-called 'Locked Diary' for the years 1913 and 1914 show the initial force of Forster's identification with Carpenter and the start of its decline. On 31 December 1913 he ended his entry with 'Edward Carpenter! Edward Carpenter! Edward Carpenter!'. On 31 December 1914 he wrote, 'E. C. He too is less important. What I owe him, though!' (*M*, pp. x, xiv). In the 'Terminal Note' that Forster later wrote to the novel he said of Carpenter that 'For a short time he seemed to hold the key to every trouble' (*M*, p. 215).

Attending to Forster's own exploration of issues of homosexual maturation helps when it comes to discussing perhaps the major article on *Maurice*, by John Fletcher, which was published in 1992. Fletcher sees the novel as 'the one explicitly homosexual *Bildungsroman* produced within the mainstream English literary tradition by a canonical author'. However, he keeps in place the view that the text is straightforward, finding interest instead in what it excludes. He views Forster as 'essentially timorous', a view of the novel based on Forster's refusal to publish it in his lifetime.[16] Surely, though, eliding decisions about publication with the content of the novel is an unsatisfactory move. Fletcher assumes that publishing the book would have been possible in Britain before Forster's old age. In his 1960 Terminal Note Forster argued that the positive ending was a key factor in whether it was publishable in Britain (*M*, p. 216). This had been accurate up until then, though things were changing with the Obscene Publications Act of 1959 and the *Lady Chatterley's Lover* trial (at which Forster was a witness).[17] As Fletcher contends, had the book been published earlier it might indeed have done much good, but care should be taken before we condemn Forster for actions in a different social, legal, and historical context.

Fletcher questions Martin's 'double structure' argument because it offers a simple binary opposition and fails to recognise Symonds's own indebtedness to Whitman. (That said, Symonds, too, is attacked for 'closeted timidity'.[18] Fletcher sets a standard for homosexual conduct in Victorian and Edwardian times that few lived up to.) Though he does see the novel as moving from a Greek and Platonic relationship to one influenced by Carpenter and Whitman, what interests Fletcher are the traces in the book of what the happy resolution of the Maurice and Alec narrative seeks to excise. Insightfully, he argues that the narrative in the 'Terminal Note' on the novel's conception is its 'primal scene', and looks at what tensions and difficulties that fantasy construction seeks to resolve. The absences from the novel include: Forster himself, effeminacy, the reasons for Clive's reorientation to heterosexuality and father-figures. While Fletcher notices things that deepen and extend our reading of the novel, there are problems with his construction of Forster as a novelist seemingly devoid of intelligent self-awareness, and of *Maurice* as a text which has a transparent, timid, and constricted surface one can quickly step past.

Though the text has the ending of comedy, for Fletcher it has an undertow of loss and exclusion. He is particularly perceptive in raising the return of narrative focus at the end of the novel to Clive, and his regret in old age at the loss of Maurice. That said, we can now read, as an appendix to the Abinger edition of the novel, the ending where Maurice and Alec are discovered years later working in a forest by Maurice's sister Kitty (*M*, pp. 221–4). There may have been practical problems that led Forster to drop this ending, not least the fact that it seems he no longer had a copy of it. The effect of the First World War on the main characters would need to be explained, and it was clearly difficult to imagine and represent the future of the Maurice–Alec relationship. The extra chapter tells us more about Kitty than it does about the two lovers. In the final version of the text, the return to Clive can be seen in terms of a different kind of loss than Fletcher suggests. It perhaps constitutes the return of the possibility of love between those with similar class backgrounds. At this time the two main forms of desire saw a difference in age or class. Though the gender of the lovers was the same it was as if difference had to be written into the relationship in other ways.

Fletcher stresses the exclusion of the feminine from the depictions of homosexual masculinity. He argues that Forster and other homosexual writers responded to the position that desire for the same sex was the result of sexual inversion by trying to create a manly homosexuality, something we see with the character of Maurice. One can indeed go further here, and say that the text not only excludes the feminine from its male characters but has no positive depictions of women.[19] Joseph Bristow has expanded Fletcher's argument into a reading of Forster's entire output in terms of an anxious rejection of an effeminate England.[20] There are surely dangers though in suggesting that the exclusion of inversion theory from the novel is simply the result of an accommodation on Forster's part between models of inversion and societal pressure to be manly. It can also be argued that Forster consciously produces a text that does not interpret homosexuality through the main sexological models, unlike the lesbian novel *The Well of Loneliness* which draws heavily on theories of inversion. Neither does Forster draw on degeneration to explain same-sex love, the view that homosexuality is some kind of inherited weakness and infirmity. A rejection of degenerationist approaches can be seen when *Maurice* is compared with *The Longest Journey*. The earlier text, as Elizabeth Heine has shown, connects Rickie Eliot's lameness with degeneration and homosexuality (*LJ*, pp. xviii–xxvi). As I have sought to argue here, *Maurice* often 'inverts' what the reader expects to find. The novel's lack of interest in the inversion of the sexes is perhaps itself another of these inversions.

The main problem with Fletcher's assumptions around Forster's constrained timidity in *Maurice* is that he misses the novel's tough and serious consideration of an issue that is often ignored – that there must have been many drawn to their own sex who did not act upon their own desires or form same-sex relationships. The reorientation of Clive can be seen as part of the novel's concern with the attractive and yet deadening effects of social convention which prevent many from acting on their desires. A large number of those who make the attempt draw back, and the novel reaches to explain this in terms of order and (necessary) mess. Clive's stress on purity is part of his constricted, fastidious way of seeing the world. He condemns Maurice's preparedness to engage with dirt, saying that he stands for 'Dirt at all costs' (*M*, p. 93). The difference between the two is shown when Maurice nurses Clive during his illness, cleaning the chamber pot when Clive has diarrhoea. This only leads Clive to recoil further from Maurice as he moves back towards the centre in society. The shift from homosexual to heterosexual love was an important issue for Forster, as he had to account for the marriage and increasing distance of his sometime lover, H. O. Meredith (*M*, pp. xv–xvi). His effort to understand this seems to have involved the view that people could change the way they lived their lives due to fear and a sense of what social conformity offered. The 'return to Clive' at the end of the novel and Clive's passionless marriage casts doubt on how thoroughgoing such reorientations were.

The novel explores the view that homosexuality was not very rare, rather that often it did not break surface and find expression in words and acts. The concern with a wide range of homosexual experience can be seen with the figure of Maurice's father. Also called Maurice (*M*, p. 16), he was on his way to becoming a 'pillar of Church and Society when he died, and other things being alike Maurice would have stiffened too'. The father did not go to Cambridge, and did not hear Risley's injunction to speak and debate. We learn that 'where his father would have kept canny silence [Maurice] began to talk, talk' (*M*, p. 33). The Maurice who had been told by his mother to 'grow up like your dear father in every way' (*M*, p. 8) has begun to identify elsewhere. The father's role in the text is that of the close relative whose life moved back in line with convention:

> As [Maurice] sat in his office working, he could not see the vast curve of his life, still less the ghost of his father sitting opposite. Mr Hall senior had neither fought nor thought;[21] there had never been any occasion; he had supported society and moved without a crisis from illicit to licit love. Now, looking across at his son, he is touched with envy, the only pain that survives in the world of shades. For he sees the flesh educating the spirit, as his has never been educated, and developing the sluggish heart and slack mind against their will.
>
> (*M*, p. 128)

We can question here whether for Maurice it is always only 'the flesh educating the spirit', or whether cerebral reflection is also seen as necessary. The view that only a few homosexuals succeed in forming relationships in this society is expressed through the flower imagery when Maurice drives away from Penge on the way to his consultation with Lasker-Jones:

> Not far from the lodge there was a nasty little climb, and the road, always in bad condition, was edged with dog roses that scratched the paint. Blossom after blossom crept past them, draggled by the ungenial year: some had cankered, others would never unfold: here and there beauty triumphed, but desperately, flickering in a world of gloom. Maurice looked into one after another, and though he did not care for flowers the failure irritated him. Scarcely anything was perfect. On one spray every flower was lopsided, the next swarmed with caterpillars, or bulged with galls. The indifference of nature! And her incompetence! He leant out of the window to see whether she couldn't bring it off once, and stared straight into the bright brown eyes of a young man.
>
> (*M*, p. 154)

The poor weather refers not only to the English summer but, by extension, to the prevailing conditions for homosexual love. Many blossoms fail, just as many lives are not fulfilled. The eyes of Alec, though, are like the perfect flowers Maurice is watching for. The language of Darwinian natural selection is appropriated to describe the homosexual who finds a life partner. While Maurice has acted in ways that have increased his chances of this happening, we are made acutely aware that the 'happier year' mentioned in the novel's dedication is a long way off. The events in the novel take place in an 'ungenial year'.

In the decades after first drafting the text Forster's changes were mainly technical in nature. Though he asked Christopher Isherwood 'Does it date?', he wisely resisted attempts to try and update the text (*M*, p. xxxvi). He worked on how Maurice and Alec meet after Maurice sees the boat leave Southampton without his lover on board. Though Alec does send a message telling Maurice that he will go to Clive's estate, Maurice does not receive it. Forster placed enough references to the boathouse at Penge earlier in the novel for the reader to accept that Maurice's journey there was undertaken instinctively, that he simply assumes that this is where one would go to find Alec (*M*, p. 208). The words of the lovers in Chapter 45, when they do meet up again, are part of the final changes Forster made to the novel. As well as dealing with a problem in the plotting, it is also, as Philip Gardner has pointed out, Forster's farewell to novel writing. It runs, 'And since Maurice did not speak, indeed could not, [Alec] added, "And now we shan't be parted no more, and that's finished."' (*M*, pp. xliii, 209) These last additions from Forster appear to constitute the wholly clear statement of permanent love from a working-class man that he so wanted to hear himself. However, the way the emotion chokes off Maurice's words can be linked to Forster's own move into silence, and the novel's interest in instinct and language. The sleepy 'that's finished' appears to be a positive resolution, but there is a deep ambivalence. It is also an echo of Christ's last words on the cross, which suggests that both homosexual love and the act of writing are a form of crucifixion. Even when it appears otherwise, *Maurice* is not simple and straightforward.

Notes

1. C. P. Snow (*Financial Times*, 7 October 1971) said that 'The novel is very short, and the story simple'. Walter Allen in the *Daily Telegraph* for the same day said 'The plot is simple'. Nigel Dennis (*Sunday Telegraph*, 10 October 1971) argued that the 'theme is homosexuality – too taboo for words when it was written, but perhaps too dated for words when it is read today'. Cyril Connolly felt that 'the element of dating is fatal'. All these responses to the novel are reprinted in Philip Gardner (ed.), *E. M. Forster: The Critical Heritage* (London: Routledge and Kegan Paul, 1973), pp. 433, 437, 465, 459.

2. *Observer*, 10 October 1971. Reprinted in Gardner, *E. M. Forster: The Critical Heritage*, pp. 463–4. David Lodge in *The Tablet* (23 October 1971) argued that the claim that the novel's failings in terms of 'complexity, interest, humour, and rhetorical skill' could be put down to its subject matter 'would be far too crude, but it had, one must feel, *something* to do with the subject'. He also argued that 'Structurally, *Maurice* is less complex than Forster's other novels. It is a *Bildungsroman* which follows the hero's fortunes in a straightforward and often summary way.' Reprinted in Gardner, *E. M. Forster: The Critical Heritage*, pp. 474–5.

3. Gregory Woods, *A History of Gay Literature: The Male Tradition* (New Haven and London: Yale University Press, 1998), p. 217.

4. Robert K. Martin, 'Edward Carpenter and the Double Structure of *Maurice*', *Journal of Homosexuality* 8:3–4 (1983), 35–46, quote from p. 37.

5. A. W. Clarke, *Jaspar Tristram* (1899; New York: Garland, 1984), pp. 177, 207–8. H. M. Dickinson, *Keddy: A Story of Oxford Life* (London: William Heinemann, 1907). Two of the three novels by Howard Overing Sturgis are relevant here *Tim* (Leipzig: Bernhard Tauchnitz, 1891) and *Belchamber* (1904; Oxford: Oxford University Press, 1986).

6. See Paul Binding in his review of the Hesperus Press edition of *Arctic Summer*. 'While *Maurice* is, in style if not in subject, a rather unForsterian work, in its concentration on the psychology of one central character, *Arctic Summer* is, from its first sentences, in the unique and idiosyncratic idiom of the author of *Howards End*, with its deft movement from humorous observation of social mores to some disturbing, intimate generalisations about the human world.' *The Guardian* (11 October 2003) at http://books.guardian.co.uk/review/story/0,12084,1060162,00.html

7. In *Sinister Street*, Michael Fane's dream about walking down a disturbing street at night-time prefigures his later engagement with the sub-cultures of London that he finds both fascinating and abhorrent. Compton Mackenzie, *Sinister Street* (1913–14; London: Penguin, 1960), pp. 42–7.

8. See my 'D. H. Lawrence and Male Homosexual Desire', *Review of English Studies*, 53 (2002), 86–107.

9. J. H. Stape, 'Comparing Mythologies: Forster's *Maurice* and Pater's *Marius*', *English Literature in Transition, 1880–1920*, 33:2 (1990), 141–53. A sustained comparison between *Maurice* and Samuel Butler's *The Way of All Flesh* is also needed.

10. See Walter Pater, 'A Study of Dionysus', *Greek Studies* (London: Macmillan, 1895), pp. 1–48. On the connections between Dionysus and Pan see pp. 7–10.

11. Martin, 'Edward Carpenter and the Double Structure of *Maurice*', pp. 35–46. On Symonds's crisis at Cannes and what followed see Phyllis Grosskurth, *John Addington Symonds: A Biography* (London: Longmans, 1964), pp. 124ff.

12. See J. Laplanche and J-B. Pontalis, *The Language of Psycho-Analysis*, trans. Donald Nicholson-Smith (London: The Hogarth Press and the Institute of Psycho-Analysis, 1973), pp. 205–8, and Sigmund Freud, *The Ego and the Id*, *The Complete Psychological Works of Sigmund Freud*, vol. xix, trans. James Strachey et al. (London: The Hogarth Press and the Institute of Psycho-Analysis, 1961), pp. 28–39.

13. Sir William Blackstone, *Commentaries on the Laws of England* (4 vols., Oxford: Clarendon Press, 1769), vol. IV, pp. 215–16. See also Ephesians 5:3 'But fornication, and all uncleanness, or covetousness, let it not be once named among you, as becometh saints.'

14. See also Bret L. Keeling, '"No Trace of Presence": Tchaikovsky and the Sixth in Forster's *Maurice*', *Mosaic*, 26:1 (March 2003), 85–101.

15. See Stephen Knight, *Robin Hood: A Mythic Biography* (Ithaca, NY: Cornell University Press, 2003), pp. 94–149. Knight has argued that *Maurice* is part of a 'definite Robin Hood renaissance' in the Georgian period. See Stephen Knight, *Robin Hood: A Complete Study of the English Outlaw* (Oxford: Blackwell, 1994), pp. 201–17, quote from p. 214.

16. John Fletcher, 'Forster's Self-erasure: *Maurice* and the Scene of Masculine Love', in *Sexual Sameness: Textual Differences in Lesbian and Gay Writing* ed. Joseph Bristow (London: Routledge, 1992), pp. 64, 65.

17. The 1959 Act allowed a defence of artistic merit. In the earlier legal context the view taken of homosexuality seems to have been crucial. The fate of Radclyffe Hall's *The Well of Loneliness* in 1928 can be compared to that of Compton Mackenzie's *Extraordinary Women* from the same year, which was not the subject of legal action. See Michael Baker, *Our Three Selves. A Life of Radclyffe Hall* (London: GMP, 1985), pp. 201–57 and Compton Mackenzie, *My Life and Times: Octave Six* (London: Chatto and Windus, 1967), pp. 147–9.

18. Fletcher, 'Forster's Self-erasure', p. 66.

19. It would be difficult to sustain a reading that Forster was showing the constricted and limited range of identities available to women at this time, as there are few signs of sympathy for the women in the novel. Indeed, they are presented as part of the problem.

20. Joseph Bristow, *Effeminate England: Homoerotic Writing After 1885* (Buckingham: Open University Press, 1995), pp. 55–99.

21. The Abinger edition reads at this point: 'Mr Hall senior had neither fought not thought;' but this is clearly a typographical error.

12

PETER CHILDS

A Passage to India

Introduction

A Passage to India is the most controversial of Forster's novels. The majority of critics regard it as his finest work yet no consensus has emerged about its meanings, partly because the book has proven highly responsive to so many approaches. Despite literary criticism's changing focal points over the decades, from politics and spirituality through to ethnicity and sexuality, it has always kept *A Passage to India* firmly in its sights because Forster's novel offers fertile ground for the broadest range of analytical and theoretical perspectives. This, in turn, is precisely because of the narrative's simultaneous breadth of reference and radical indeterminacy.

After *Howards End*, and after producing four novels in six years, Forster appeared to the general reading public to lie largely dormant for fourteen years, until *A Passage to India* appeared in 1924. Yet, in that time, despite the intervention of the war years, he had published three books: *The Celestial Omnibus* (1911), *Alexandria: A History and a Guide* (1922), and *Pharos and Pharillon* (1923), a book of literary and historical sketches. He had also finished a play, 'The Heart of Bosnia', written *Maurice*, and begun another novel ('Arctic Summer') which he was never to finish, exploring friendship and the Renaissance ideal of the 'complete' individual. Most importantly for *A Passage to India*, during these years Forster travelled twice to India. He visited the subcontinent for the first time in October 1912 with R. C. Trevelyan and Goldsworthy Lowes Dickinson. On setting out, Forster conjectured whether his trip might kill off his projected novel and indeed it did contribute to that book's termination. But it led to two other novels, both of which, like the aborted 'Arctic Summer', centred on the subject of friendship.

In India, Forster visited the Barabar Caves near Gaya (the model for the Marabar Caves), Bankipore (Chandrapore), and the princely state of Chhatarpur.[1] He began developing his new Indian novel in the summer of

1913 but soon broke off to write *Maurice* in September, which occupied most of his time for writing fiction until the following summer. The outbreak of war in August 1914 also put Forster's Indian novel on hold, by which time he had still managed to write most of the first section, 'Mosque', and the first chapters of the second, 'Caves'. Forster also spent three years from 1915 to 1918 working for the Red Cross in Alexandria, and in several ways Egypt became for him, personally and culturally, the bridge or passage between Europe and India – a perspective reinforced by his late decision to name *A Passage to India* after Walt Whitman's 1871 poem celebrating the opening of the Suez Canal.

Forster returned to India in March 1921 as Private Secretary to the Maharajah of Dewas State Senior (the model, with Chhatarpur, for Mau) and stayed until November. There is consequently a small irony attaching to the fact that in *A Passage to India* Ronny 'did not approve of English people taking service under the Native States, where they obtain a certain amount of influence, but at the expense of the general prestige' (*PI*, p. 83). In all, Forster spent about eighteen months in India pre- and post-war, witnessing a full calendar year of weather, as does his novel. *A Passage to India* itself takes place neither before nor after the war. It is instead an amalgam of Forster's impressions on his two visits, with the British-Indian characters, for instance, retaining pre-war attitudes despite the novel's publication in the 1920s; for example, Forster's observation in an article of 1922 about a 'lady who said to me eight years ago, "Never forget that you're superior to every native in India except the Rajas, and they're on an equality," is now a silent, if not extinct species' (*PT*, p. 245) reappears as a remark Mrs Turton makes to Mrs Moore and Adela (*PI*, p. 61).

Forster registered a great difference in India between his two trips. In a 1921 letter home he wrote: 'English manners out here have improved wonderfully in the last eight years. Some people are frightened, others seem really to have undergone a change of heart. But it's too late. Indians don't long for social intercourse with Englishmen any longer. They have made a life of their own' (*HD*, pp. 98–9). He reworked the same sentiment in an article in 1922:

> perhaps in the immediate future the chief issue will not be racial, after all. But isolating the question, one must say this: firstly, responsible Englishmen are far politer to Indians now than they were ten years ago, but it is too late because Indians no longer require their social support; and, secondly, that never in history did ill-breeding contribute so much towards the dissolution of an Empire. (*PT*, p. 246)

The shift Forster perceived is partly reflected in *A Passage to India* by the differences between the second and third sections of the novel, though 'Temple' takes place only two years later than 'Caves', not eight.

When Forster began the book in 1913 it was as a further exploration of sympathy and goodwill – a novel about connection between East and West – but it became much bleaker in the writing as the war and Forster's own periodic depressions intervened. Instead of representing liberalism's power for consensus and compromise, the finished manuscript came 'to signify liberal impotence'.[2] After his second trip to India, Forster was both more pessimistic and quicker to impute cynicism, claiming that his experiences at Dewas left him unable to make the emotional appeal that he felt was necessary for him to connect with an Indian, either in person or in imagination. He finally completed the novel with the aid of the letters of his friend J. R. Ackerley, the new rhythmic style of Proust, and the passion for Arabia of T. E. Lawrence's *Seven Pillars of Wisdom*, which he greatly admired. Forster declared that Lawrence's book moved him deeply, and all the more because of the 'romantic passion for the East which chance or temperament has allotted me'.[3]

A Passage to India was both a critical and a commercial success. Reviews were the best Forster had received with critics in Britain, America, and India praising the new book highly. However, reviewers in the British-Indian press were deeply critical, finding their reflection in the book both unpleasant and inaccurate.[4] Such hostility had in fact been directed at metropolitan novels about India for some time, and it was not mere indignation at the portrayal of the British in India but at the mistakes over practices and history.[5] Forster accepted criticisms that his presentation of Aziz's arrest and trial were inaccurate, in that they contained technical errors, but maintained to one correspondent that he felt 'the reading' of English psychology was true.[6] His own source for this portrayal was the reactions of the British-Indians to the bombing of the vice-regal procession before Christmas in Delhi in 1912.

Indian commentators welcomed the novel in 1924 as one of the fairest British renditions of the country to date. However, a backlash began thirty years later when, in his 1954 article 'Passage to and from India', Nirad Chaudhuri criticised the book for its apolitical liberalism and for having a Muslim protagonist who was necessarily unrepresentative of a predominantly Hindu country or of the 'India question' the novel putatively sought to address. Since Chaudhuri's intervention much debate over the novel has focused on its representation of Indo-British relationships.[7] The key text in this discussion has been Edward Said's 1978 survey *Orientalism*, the perspective of which was first applied at length to *A Passage to India* by Benita Parry.[8] Parry's reading of the novel asserts the context of the colonial 'historical situation' as important to both the study of Forster's story and to the meaning of literary texts: European fiction inherits and informs the Empire's practices of domination over the colonies, through force and representation.

Since the 1980s, a range of feminist and postcolonial approaches have placed different emphases on the ways in which the novel reflects or encodes colonial discursive practices and modes of representation. For example, Sara Suleri argues that, in the use of metaphoric geography, the West's Others most often appear as (dark) holes beyond civilisation, divinity or morality, such that European narrative's most compelling and durable image of the East is a hollow or indeed a cave. This arguably corresponds with other faults, such as muddle and contradiction, which Forster seems to attribute to India whether in the space of Cave, Temple, or Mosque.[9] Where Suleri argues that the centre of the book is the vacancy of the Marabar Caves, Brenda Silver believes that at its heart is the 'unspeakable' colonial trope of rape. Using the work of Frantz Fanon as well as Said, Silver analyses issues of control and resistance throughout the novel in terms of gender, 'race', and sex, such that, while Suleri says that India can only be represented to British-India as a gesture of possible rape, Silver finds considerable ambiguity in the novel, for example arguing that Aziz 'reduced to his sexuality, becomes simultaneously rapist and object of rape'.[10] Another important article has used Said's *Orientalism* to inform a reading of *A Passage to India* in relation to a collection of Indian criticism, offering not only a reading of Forster's novel as one in which colonialism triumphs over liberalism for Adela, Aziz, and Fielding, but also a critique of the shortcomings of Said's approach and of *Orientalism* itself as a 'white text' whose premises are Eurocentric.[11]

The foremost theorist of colonial ambiguity, Homi Bhabha, has read Forster's novel, and others such as Conrad's *Heart of Darkness*, as texts which exhibit their incomprehension of other cultures through their (non-) representations of language and their descent into incoherence.[12] Bhabha's reading is thus linked to a subject I mentioned at the start of this chapter: the text's radical indeterminacy. For most critics, this is exemplified by and encased in Forster's use of the Marabar Caves, and Adela's experience within one of them. The latter has intrigued critics because it remains a lacuna or aporia that the novel itself refuses to explain, despite the presence of an omniscient narrator. The reader is left with the alternatives put forward by Fielding, that either an individual is physically responsible – Aziz, the guide, or someone else – or the explanation lies in features of the mind, such as hallucination (*PI*, p. 230).

Bhabha's approach is one of the most recent to suggest that Forster's spiritual preoccupations in the novel are the correlative of his experience of cultural difference. Forster himself argued that his book was about the human race's attempt to find a 'more-lasting home': that it was at its core about metaphysics. The first and third sections of the novel foreground religion in their titles, while the second, 'Caves', is a reference to the Jain religion founded in the sixth century BC by the reformer Mahavira.[13] The third section also transcribes into fiction Forster's experience of the Hindu Gokul Ashtami festival, as described in *The Hill of Devi*, while repeatedly teasing the reader with Forster's understanding of India as a spiritual but muddled country, in notions such as telepathy, transcendence, and the transposed 'God si love'.[14]

Metaphysical and physical

The metaphysical aspects to *A Passage to India* can be considered from many perspectives, including the postcolonial, but two have come to the fore in critical commentaries. One concerns Forster's own spiritual and personal beliefs, and another the mythological references that have been divined in the text, which I will touch on first. Critics have concluded that ou-boum is a variant on Om (in Hinduism and Tibetan Buddhism, a mystic syllable regarded as the most sacred mantra); that Mrs Moore encounters an unresponsive Brahman in the first cave; that the Marabar is indebted to the shadow-play of Plato's Cave; and that the novel draws upon early fertility rites, with Mrs Moore as a kind of sacrificial god.[15] This last reading has seemed to connect Forster's novel with Eliot's near contemporaneous *The Waste Land*, which also uses such mythological reference points, from the cruelties of April to vegetation rites and rituals of (spiritual) rebirth through water, and some of the same scriptural allusions, such as 'the Peace that passeth Understanding' (*PI*, p. 239) and 'the shadow of a great rock' (*PI*, p. 217).[16] Charting a connection between these two texts also suggests Mrs Moore's role as a prophetic Madame Sosostris figure, a modern Sibyl who lays out the fate of the characters in her cards.[17] Yet, some critics also seek to find a final spiritual meaning in the novel that Forster never intended, and which therefore has to be ascribed to the effects of the (universal) unconscious, cultural or political factors, or language.

With regard to religion, humour also plays a larger part in the novel than many commentators allow. In some ways it appears that existence is comically meaningless, and that God's absent presence renders all religion absurd, not just Godbole's performance at the start of 'Temple'. Forster wrote in one essay that, 'It may seem absurd to turn from Christ to Krishna, that vulgar blue-faced boy with his romps and butter-pats: Krishna is usually a trivial figure. But he does admit pleasure and fun and jokes and their connection with love' (*PT*, p. 317). In at least one critic's view, the novel's 'God of doubtful existence' emerges as 'an inveterate practical joker'.[18]

In many ways more immediately profitable for readers of the novel is Forster's own well-known belief system, which can be briefly summarised in his own words as 'personal relations mean everything to me' (*PT*, p. 318). At the time of *A Passage to India*'s publication, Forster commented in a letter to Malcolm Darling on 15 September 1924 that personal relationships 'still seem to me the most real things on the surface of the earth'.[19] Yet, as Rose Macaulay observed at the time, 'He has quite lost the touch of preciousness, of exaggerated care for nature and the relationships of human beings'.[20] *A Passage to India* retains little of the qualified optimism that shines through Forster's earlier fiction (*A Room with a View*, for example), and I will return later to the question of whether the novel has the same conviction about personal relations as his previous books, or whether the accent should be placed on the word 'still' in his comment to Darling.

What remains strong for most of *A Passage to India* is a belief in 'goodwill' as the best expression of religion and love in personal relations. The goodwill that is so important to Forster signals the difference between impressions and between people in the novel. In opposition to her son, for whom Aziz is simply 'unreliable, inquisitive, vain', Mrs Moore is sufficiently new to British-Indian society to decide, 'Yes, it was all true, but how false as a summary of the man; the essential life of him had been slain' (*PI*, p. 29). Ronny's estimation of Aziz thus fails to describe him, despite its factual accuracy, because it values him at his faults and not his virtues. This marks the gulf between Mrs Moore and her son, and points up the deficiency of the British-Indian community to which Ronny has quickly acclimatised: 'One touch of regret – not the canny substitute but the true regret from the heart – would have made him a different man, and the British Empire a different institution' (*PI*, pp. 44–5). By contrast, Mrs Moore emphasises the importance of goodwill as a desire that is blessed: 'The desire to behave pleasantly satisfies God . . . The sincere if impotent desire wins His blessing. I think everyone fails, but there are so many kinds of failure. Goodwill and more goodwill and more goodwill' (*PI*, p. 45). The atheist Fielding also feels this: 'The world, he believed, is a globe of men who are trying to reach one another and can best do so by the help of goodwill' (*PI*, p. 55). Apart from their affection for Aziz, the connection between Mrs Moore and Fielding, who do not actually like each other, is their belief in goodwill, though hers is a religious, universal conviction and his a secular, personal one. Mrs Moore's feeling for people marks her as an Oriental for Aziz (*PI*, pp. 17, 241), whereas Fielding importantly observes of Adela: 'you have no real affection for Aziz, or Indians generally . . . Indians know whether they are liked or not – they cannot be fooled here. Justice never satisfies them, and that is why the British Empire rests on sand' (*PI*, p. 248).

Aziz's affection for Mrs Moore culminates in his assertion that she was his 'best friend in all the world' (*PI*, p. 302), and he has earlier explained to Fielding that 'The Friend' is 'a Persian expression for God' (*PI*, p. 265), though Forster would also have understood it to have homosexual overtones. Thus, religion and friendship are connected, as Aziz has suggested: 'There is no harm in deceiving society . . . she is not like a friend or God, who are injured by the mere existence of unfaithfulness' (*PI*, p. 94).[21] Given that, as Mrs Moore says, 'everyone fails', a failure at the heart of the novel is Adela's inability to live up to her liberal principles in the face of the prejudice against Indians in which she has been immersed, just as it is Fielding's failure, in the same circumstances, to succeed in being Aziz's friend.

One of the many ways in which Forster signals the British-Indians' failed pretensions and also the absence of their goodwill is through their conceited self-image. Thus, they are repeatedly portrayed *posing* as gods, as when Mrs Moore accuses Ronny of just this (*PI*, p. 43) or when the Collector 'was now revealed like a god in a shrine' (*PI*, p. 154) and 'the Turtons were little gods' (*PI*, p. 23). By contrast, Mrs Moore's benign presence makes her both Aziz's friend and the 'Hindu goddess' (*PI*, p. 214) Esmiss Esmoor, which is an example of the practice at the Festival later of 'inverting the names of deities' (*PI*, p. 301). However it is Godbole, whose name itself suggests the omnipresence of divinity in the pantheism of God joined with nature (bole/tree), who provides the most powerful explanation of the universe and of the Marabar.[22] Godbole's conviction is that all 'performed' the action at the caves: 'When evil occurs, it expresses the whole of the universe. Similarly when good occurs' (*PI*, p. 169).[23] Evil is figured as an expression of the universe as part of an all-pervasive ill-will which covers the world, as though enshrined by the gods of colonialism, under whose over-arching rule 'the spirit of evil again strode abroad' (*PI*, p. 224).

Here we also approach the vision Mrs Moore has in the Marabar: 'that state where the horror of the universe and its smallness are both visible at the same time . . . in the twilight of the double vision' (*PI*, p. 198). It is a vision in which the inconsequentiality of human life is envisaged, as well as its contingency: 'Everything exists, nothing has value' (*PI*, p. 140). Mrs Moore's quest for God's blessing before her death is met in the Marabar by a seeming indifference, as everything is reduced to the same sound of ou-boum. In this regard Forster once wrote on Hinduism: 'The divine is so confounded with the earthly that anyone or anything is part of God. In this chaos, where shall a man find guidance? What promise does he receive?' (*PT*, p. 223). While such comments seem to express bafflement before Hinduism they also suggest the failure of the raj gods, whose indifference to their charges has resulted in smallness amid a vast chaos.

What Mrs Moore has sought in the cave is some intimation of salvation, which has been a subject several times earlier in the novel, when the question of who is to be included in and excluded from heaven has been conjectured upon (e.g., *PI*, pp. 22, 32). Forster said that salvation features in all his work, but decreases in importance to the point that it has almost disappeared from *A Passage to India* (*PT*, pp. 318–19). On the subject of salvation, P. N. Furbank comments about Forster's retreat from novel writing:

> he received his whole inspiration – a vision, a kind of plot, a message – all at once, in early manhood. He became an artist because of that early experience, an experience of salvation, and his inspiration as a novelist always harked back to that moment of enlightenment. For this reason he was content to use and re-use many of the same plot-materials: for instance the jaded traveller unable (for what reason he cannot tell) to respond to the scenes he or she has come to visit; or the picnic party of pleasure invaded by panic forces.[24]

Though the sense of salvation is severely attenuated, those plot-materials remain in Forster's final novel, where the panic forces in the Marabar have different effects on Mrs Moore and Adela. For Mrs Moore, the experience reinforces a feeling of humanity's lack of importance to the universe or to nature, just as the British lack importance for the majority of Indians: 'It matters so little to the majority of living beings what the minority, *that calls itself human*, desires or decides' (*PI*, p. 105; my emphasis). The caves thus function as a metonym, implicitly for colonial alienation and explicitly for the anti-sublime infinite:[25] like the Kawa Dol mirroring 'its own darkness in every direction infinitely' (*PI*, p. 118), they are presented as a claustrophobic microcosm of that which the human mind cannot encompass. The spiritual weight of the novel, that which rests on the Mrs Moore–Godbole axis, therefore, appears to pivot on the message and meanings of the cave, but for Adela it is the physical aspect to her experience that seems most important. While Mrs Moore finds a devastating echo of her own fears over her mortality and significance, Adela is met by reflections of her corporeal and marital fears. Forster's description of the caves runs thus:

> There is little to see, and no eye to see it, until the visitor arrives for his five minutes, and strikes a match. Immediately another flame rises in the depths of the rock and moves towards the surface like an imprisoned spirit; the walls of the circular chamber have been most marvellously polished. The two flames approach and strive to unite, but cannot, because one of them breathes air, the other stone. A mirror inlaid with lovely colours divides the lovers.
>
> (*PI*, pp. 117–18)

A tale of two lovers, the story of the caves echoes not only the inability of Aziz and Fielding to join together at the end of the novel, but also the frustrated union of Ronny and Adela. Almost immediately after this description, Adela remarks how she should like to visit the caves, which seem now to be 'romantic' (*PI*, p. 119). Her journey to them is thus associated from the start with overtones of love's place in her proposed marriage to Ronny.

I will consider the way marriage is presented in the novel in the next section of this chapter, but as prelude it is necessary here to touch on two related aspects that provide its context: gender and sexuality. The novel has been read in terms of sexual symbolism and patriarchal discourse on numerous occasions,[26] but a first point to note can be that the women and the men are largely separate. Mrs Moore and Adela appear to be closer to each other than either is to anyone else. Stella is never described and never speaks: she is as silent and little remarked upon as Aziz's wife, such that women in the novel arguably feature as the means to unite or separate the men. Critics also cannot avoid the fact that the novel's plot turns on an alleged sexual assault on a British woman by an Indian man, and thus its narrative centre cannot easily serve as a metaphor for colonial appropriation. Instead, the allegation echoes stories of assaults that circulated at the time of the insurrection or 'Mutiny' of 1857, mentioned or alluded to several times in the novel, and the 1919 Amritsar massacre.[27]

As critics have suggested, there is arguably an importance to the comment that Adela, 'like Aziz, was always referred to by a periphrasis' (*PI*, p. 173). In the narrative only Mahmoud Ali says 'rape' (*PI*, p. 213) in relation to Adela's experience in the caves, but the fear of miscegenation lies behind the hysterical reaction to the incident. The periphrasis that replaces the incident in the novel (unlike the draft, in which Aziz is Adela's attacker) can also be explained by Forster's reluctance to address the matter of a heterosexual encounter at all. Indeed it has been suggested that Forster gave up writing novels after *A Passage to India* because of his frustration with having to write about sexual relationships in which he had little interest.

To many critics, the book's (absent) centre is therefore the (homosexual) relationship between Fielding and Aziz – whose name means 'beloved' in Arabic and Urdu – which is an image of the friendship between Forster and the book's dedicatee, Syed Ross Masood, whom Forster taught.[28] While there are other occasional moments of eroticism in the book, such as the description of the 'beautiful naked god' (*PI*, p. 219) that is the courtroom punkah-wallah, the relationship between Aziz and Fielding is presented throughout with sexual imagery, from the phallic collar stud swapped at their first meeting to the moment of half-kissing at their last.[29] As significant to some recent critics is the portrayal of homosocial environments, particularly that of the male protagonists, who, as I have said, largely mix with other men. Fielding, who is disliked by the British-Indian women, teaches at a boys' college with Godbole and mixes with Indians rather than Englishwomen. He 'found it convenient and pleasant to associate with Indians and he must pay the price. As a rule no Englishwoman entered the College' (*PI*, p. 57). Aziz, who is seen repeatedly with male friends, as when he is ill in bed, even treats Adela and Mrs Moore like men (*PI*, p. 61). This can be read in terms of purdah, or the divisions that the memsahibs were said to have brought to British-Indian society after they arrived in the mid-nineteenth century, but it also reflects the interest that Forster had in depicting same-sex interaction. For example, an important cross-textual encounter that can be read in both colonial and sexual terms occurs between Aziz and a British officer early in the novel, just before Aziz visits Fielding for the first time. On horseback, Aziz meets a 'stray subaltern' on the maidan and they build up a friendship practising polo, in a scene that anticipates Aziz and Fielding's final moments together. They cultivate 'the fire of good fellowship' and both think, 'If only they were all like that' (*PI*, pp. 51–2). The subaltern reappears at the club much later and simultaneously but unknowingly praises Aziz as the Indian who played with him while condemning him as one of 'these educated classes' (*PI*, pp. 174–5). The scene helps to suggest the importance of Forster's belief in the values of personal relationships to both intimacy and understanding across social boundaries.

From several perspectives, it is also striking how common the word 'queer' appears in the text. Etymologically, 'queer' means 'across' and derives from the Indo-Latin root 'torquere' (to twist), or in English 'athwart'; however, its first slang use to mean 'homosexual' is recorded as 1922.[30] The term thus has several layers of meaning, including its dictionary one of 'odd' or 'strange', and the novel makes its polysemy, including its suggestion of the extraordinary, significant to both events and characters. For example, Adela says to Ronny at the trial that it is 'all queer' (*PI*, p. 215), while afterwards Fielding 'felt restless and thwarted . . . It was a victory, but such a queer one' (*PI*, p. 222). All the main figures in the book are associated with being 'queer' at some stage. Aziz thinks Fielding is a 'queer chap' (*PI*, p. 113), Adela is 'that queer honest girl' (*PI*, p. 237), Mrs Moore 'had turned disagreeable and queer' (*PI*, p. 208), and Fielding has 'a queer vague talk with Professor Godbole' (*PI*, p. 166). More broadly, Fielding thinks of India as a 'queer nation' (*PI*, p. 109), while McBryde argues that 'when an Indian goes bad, he goes not only very bad, but very queer' (*PI*, p. 160). 'Queer' then comes to describe the people in *A Passage to India* in the same way that the word 'extraordinary' attaches itself to the Marabar, suggesting that personal dynamics are as remarkable, and possibly even as ineffable, as the caves.

Which is to say that these words, 'queer' and 'extraordinary', tap into a certain register in the novel that escapes articulation, from the negatives that strew the opening description of Chandrapore, through the narrator's 'uncanny' (*PI*, p. 117, p. 293) and Fielding's talk of Adela having been 'exorcised' (*PI*, p. 229), to the caves' 'ou-boum'. Thus Adela's unresolved experience in the cave is not alone in being inexplicable but stands as a central 'mystery, not a muddle' (*PI*, p. 251) that echoes through much of the rest of the book.[31] For example, similarly indeterminate is the road accident in the Nawab Bahadur's car, about which little can be concluded except 'certainly some external force had impinged' (*PI*, p. 81).

Possible explanations for these undecidable elements are speculated upon in the novel, including hallucination (*PI*, p. 229), telepathy (*PI*, p. 251), or the presence of ghosts.[32] However, as I have mentioned, one of the key words in the book is 'extraordinary'. Not only are the Marabar Caves described as extraordinary in the first and last sentences of the opening chapter, but later Adela also refers to her 'mistake' within them as extraordinary (*PI*, p. 231). Neither of these things – the Marabar Caves nor Adela's 'mistake' – is considered by the novel to be definable, not least because Forster's book is itself concerned with more than just spiritual uncertainty, such as misinterpretation and the problematic negotiation of cultural difference. *A Passage to India* is littered with misunderstandings and misreadings: over the invitation from Mrs Bhattacharya, the reason for Aziz's missing collar stud, the purpose of the bridge party, the 'snake' seen from the train, and the person Fielding has married. The novel repeatedly uses words such as 'muddle' and 'mystery' to characterise what is happening in the narrative, but it is also a matter of interpretation how far this is a reflection of Forster's pessimism, or of British–Indian relations, or of an Orientalist view of India.[33] All that is left behind by such confusions, textually and psychically, is a puzzling echo.

Connection and rhythm

This central image of Forster's method in *A Passage to India* can be understood in many ways, but the Marabar echo is textually linked to the discussion of good(will) and evil in the novel. Adela, for example, decides that Aziz 'never actually touched me once'; instead, she heard the echo and was frightened into hitting out at a shadow (*PI*, p. 184). While Adela's echo is concerned with her own experience, Fielding dimly apprehends a set of all-pervasive repercussions: '"Everything echoes now; there's no stopping the echo. The original sound may be harmless, but the echo is always evil."' This reflection about an echo lay at the verge of Fielding's mind. He could never develop it. It belonged to the universe that he had missed or rejected' (*PI*, p. 264).

The echo seems not to be understood by Fielding because of what he 'missed or rejected' in his own experience of the caves. Where Mrs Moore and Adela both heard the echo – Adela remembered 'scratching the wall with my fingernail, to start the usual echo' (*PI*, p. 184), while Mrs Moore found the echo 'terrifying' (*PI*, p. 138) – Fielding merely 'ran up to see one cave' and 'wasn't impressed' (*PI*, p. 149), just as 'Godbole had never mentioned an echo; it never impressed him, perhaps' (*PI*, p. 138). For Adela, however, the reverberation fluctuates with her accusation of Aziz, such that 'she would hear the echo again . . . and hope her assailant would get the maximum penalty' (*PI*, p. 185). Initially, the echo resounds up and down in her hearing as it did in the cave, but at the moment she decides that she may have made a mistake, 'her' echo goes (*PI*, p. 193). When she revises her story with McBryde, and decides again Aziz is guilty, Adela discovers, 'My echo has come back again badly' (*PI*, p. 203). Only after her capitulation at the trial does she find again that her 'echo has gone' (*PI*, p. 227).

The phenomenon of the echo can be linked to a story told earlier. The Marabar party camps at the Tank of the Dagger (*PI*, p. 212), about which Godbole has already recounted a legend that intimates why, when she has feelings of goodwill towards Aziz, Adela's echo subsides:

> It concerned a Hindu rajah who had slain his own sister's son, and the dagger with which he performed the deed remained clamped to his hand until in the course of years he came to the Marabar Hills, where he was thirsty and wanted to drink but saw a thirsty cow and ordered the water to be offered to her first, which, when done, 'dagger fell from his hand, and to commemorate miracle he built Tank'.
>
> (*PI*, p. 170)

The tank is thus linked to the water imagery in the novel, suggesting a bene-diction as it suggests spiritual renewal in *The Waste Land*. In opposition to the echo, which remains with Adela as the dagger adhered to the rajah, the water tank is an image of blessing, as in 'Temple', or friendship, as in 'Mosque' when Mrs Moore, after meeting Aziz, is described thus: 'A sudden sense of unity, of kinship with the heavenly bodies, passed into the old woman and out, like water through a tank, leaving a strange freshness behind' (*PI*, p. 24). The water is present throughout the narrative except in 'Caves', when the hot weather brings disorder: 'The annual helter-skelter of April, when irritability and lust spread like a canker, is one of [India's] comments on the orderly hopes of humanity. Fish manage better: fish, as the tanks dry, wriggle into the mud and wait for the rains to uncake them' (*PI*, p. 201). Even here Mrs Moore is reminded in the double vision of how 'good' the universe seemed when she first 'saw the water flowing through the mosque-tank' (*PI*, p. 198). The imagery of the tank culminates in the final scene of climactic immersion in 'the great Mau tank' (*PI*, p. 296), which figures once more in the novel's final sentence as one of the many voices of India that will not yet allow Aziz and Fielding to be friends.

The healing power of goodwill lacking in the British-Indian community can be linked to the benediction of water in opposition to the echo that spreads outwards like the net that England has thrown over India (*PI*, p. 11). But, there is something else at work in the production of Adela's experience of the cave and the echo that has a more intimate significance. This is an aspect to the narrative that, as I mentioned earlier, appears to place a question mark over Forster's abiding belief in personal relations in general, but over marriage in particular. For example, before she reaches the Marabar, Mrs Moore 'felt increasingly (vision or nightmare?) that, though people are important, the relations between them are not, and that in particular too much fuss has been made over marriage; centuries of carnal embracement, yet man is no nearer to understanding man' (*PI*, p. 127). Both Adela and Ronny break off their engagement, and at one point Adela says, 'We ought never to have thought of marriage' (*PI*, p. 250). Also, the theory of Oriental pathology developed and expounded by McBryde is explained in terms of a failure of his own personal relations: 'owing to a somewhat unhappy marriage, [he] had evolved a complete philosophy of life' (*PI*, p. 158). His marriage eventually ends in divorce when it is discovered that he is having an affair with the ubiquitous Miss Derek (*PI*, p. 260). Oddly, the only new marriage that features in the novel is Fielding's, though he is the one who has declared: 'About marriage I am cynical' (*PI*, p. 251).[34]

A Passage to India is 'marriage fiction', in Elaine Showalter's terms, at least inasmuch as the purpose of Adela's visit to Chandrapore is precisely to decide whether she and Ronny will marry, and this is a question that is entwined with her experience in India.[35] She believes that if she were to marry him, 'She would see India always as a frieze' (*PI*, p. 41), and after she breaks off the engagement, she notices 'her desire to see India had suddenly decreased' (*PI*, p. 79). Significantly, Adela's thoughts are 'mainly with her marriage' as she goes up to the higher caves with Aziz. In her mind she concludes that she and Ronny have an 'abundance of common sense and good will', but then the rock on which she ascends 'somehow' prompts her to realise they do not love each other: 'The discovery had come so suddenly that she felt like a mountaineer whose rope has broken' (*PI*, p. 143). Adela asks Aziz how many wives he has and enters a cave thinking with one half of her mind about sightseeing 'and wondering with the other half about marriage' (*PI*, p. 144). Adela later compares her real or imagined assault in the cave to a false belief in a marriage proposal: 'the sort of thing – though in an awful form – that makes some women think they've had an offer of marriage when none was made' (*PI*, p. 228).

The alleged sexual attack on Adela might then be considered to be a matter of marriage, and her fears concerning it: 'her disaster in the cave was connected, though by a thread, with another part of her life, her engagement to Ronny. She had thought of love just before she went in, and had innocently asked Aziz what marriage was like, and she supposed that her question had roused evil in him' (*PI*, p. 215). According to Godbole's theory, the evil is assumed by everyone, not Aziz, suggesting that the question of marriage in general is a source of the Marabar incident, just as its hegemony over personal intimacy and sexual relations was a source of unhappiness for Forster – and indeed marriage may be considered to be what stands in the way of Fielding and Aziz's friendship, and so keeps them apart, at the end of the novel (a shared moment at Aziz's house acknowledging the absence of wives marks the beginning of their intimacy). The exclusiveness of marriage stands against the inclusiveness of friendship, in its several meanings.

In the promotion of friendship, connections between people throughout the novel are set out in terms of the theme of invitation and arrival, which denotes a quality of Indian inclusiveness in distinction from British colonial compartmentalising.[36] This is especially evident in the many repeated instances of entreaty and acceptance, which stretch from the invitation for Adela to come to India, to the Bhattacharyas' offer of hospitality, to Fielding's party, and Aziz's subsequent expedition. Significantly, the first spoken words in the novel, said by Aziz to Hamidullah, are 'Am I late?' (*PI*, p. 5). The scene on which Aziz breaks in, the first in the novel after the panoramic descriptive opening, is one in which Hamidullah and Mahmoud Ali are discussing whether 'it is possible to be friends with an Englishman' (*PI*, p. 5).

The British, the British-Indians, and the Indians in the novel understand invitation very differently. When Aziz suggests the Marabar trip at Fielding's party, he is appalled that Adela has taken him at his word and expects arrangements to be made forthwith (*PI*, p. 63). One of the British-Indians whose hollow invitations to Indians are represented by the bridge party, Ronny better understands Aziz's gesture as the articulation of a desire rather than a promise, but also undervalues its emotional significance: 'He meant nothing by the invitation, I could tell by his voice; it's just their way of being pleasant' (*PI*, p. 75). By contrast, at the same party, Godbole says of his raga that the Lord of the Universe will not accept his invitation, and instead 'refuses to come' (*PI*, p. 72), underlining the importance of the invitation, not of the act of coming. God's absence thus means something very different to Godbole from what it means to Mrs Moore in the twilight of the double vision/nightmare: 'absence implies presence, absence is not non-existence, and we are therefore entitled to repeat, "Come, come, come, come"' (*PI*, p. 169). The English are perplexed by this philosophy, such that Mrs Moore asks whether Krishna comes in another song (*PI*, p. 72); and this expectation of a reply from heaven is linked to her crisis in the echoing caves that send back even God's name as ou-boum.

The inclusiveness of India's invitation and the diversity of the country are both signalled by the 'hundred voices' of the final page (*PI*, p. 312). Like most of the other terms in the novel's concluding sentence, the expression completes a cycle of rhythmic references in the text. This particular leitmotif begins with Godbole's song above asking for a hundred Krishnas (*PI*, p. 72), while later '[India] calls "Come" through her hundred mouths, through objects ridiculous and august. But come to what? She has never defined. She is not a promise, only an appeal' (*PI*, p. 128). The effect on the British of this multiplicity – 'the hundred Indias that passed each other in [Bombay's] streets' (*PI*, p. 200) – is to make them feel small like 'dwarfs' (*PI*, p. 252), or insignificant: 'the countryside was too vast to admit of excellence. In vain did each item in it call out, "Come, come." There was not enough god to go round. The two young people conversed feebly and felt unimportant' (*PI*, p. 79). This is also one way of considering how art, and therefore *A Passage to India* itself, is presented in the novel, as when Aziz reads Ghalib's poem, which overwhelms with pathos and touches the hearer with 'a sense of his own weakness' (*PI*, p. 96): 'Less explicit than the call to Krishna, it voiced our loneliness nevertheless, our isolation, our need for the Friend who never comes yet is not entirely disproved' (*PI*, p. 97). In the context of the novel overall, such a sentence manages simultaneously to express a viewpoint on art, friendship, religion, and even the promise of an Indian Independence that never comes.

Having outlined some of the connections and repetitions within the book (and there are very many more), I need to add that Forster's symbols do not add up to a coherent system or argument. They create a musical rhythm within the text, but they are not there to refer to an ultimate reality. Forster considered Proust's *À la Recherche du Temps Perdu* to be a chaotic work redeemed by its use of rhythmic effects, its internal stitching: 'There are times when the little phrase . . . means everything to the readers. There are times when it means nothing and is forgotten, and this seems to me the function of rhythm in fiction: not to be there all the time like a pattern, but by its lovely waxing and waning to fill us with surprise and freshness and hope'.[37] Thus, Forster uses motifs (the wasp, the snake, or the echo) and repeated phrases of speech or thought as one kind of rhythm (he thought rhythm to be the third most important element in a novel after character and story[38]). This is a principal reason for placing Forster as a modernist writer in his later work, when, in Fredric Jameson's terms, his 'style' rests on creating uncertainty as to which is the tenor and which the vehicle in a figure that uses a concrete physical object to stand in for a nebulous metaphysical concept. Thus, Forster offers 'the merest promise of expressivity without having to affirm it as some official "symbol" of the conventionally mendacious kind. Modernism is itself this very hesitation; it emerges in this spatial gap within Forster's figure; it is at one with the contradiction between the contingency of physical objects and the demand for an impossible meaning.'[39]

Another kind of rhythm is only appreciated at the close of the narrative when all of the novel can be surveyed – when the text is amenable to a spatial reading.[40] So, although Forster believed over-structuring to be 'castrating', and debilitatingly in excess of the flexible repetition-with-variation style of 'easy' rhythm, *A Passage to India* is a deeply organised novel, from its over-arching cyclical shape – Aziz wonders at the end 'Was the cycle beginning again?' (*PI*, p. 302) – to its three architecturally arranged sections, which follow triads of the weather (cool weather, hot weather, rains), of religious architecture (Mosque, Caves, Temple), and of human relationship (friendship, enmity, ambivalent reconciliation).[41] For Forster, art could give shape to the chaos of life's muddles, creating through form an 'internal stability, a vital harmony', whereas 'in the social and political category [order] has never existed except for the convenience of historians'.[42]

Personal and political

The ruling society in *A Passage to India* is the group least sympathetically presented by the narrator, as when it is said after the trial that 'British officialism remained, as all-pervading and as unpleasant as the sun' (*PI*, p. 248). To one correspondent, E. A. Horne, who objected in the *New Statesman* on 16 August 1924 to Forster's portrayal of British-Indians, Forster replied: 'you have hit the nail on the head. I don't like Anglo-Indians as a class. I tried to suppress this and be fair to them, but my lack of sympathy came through.'[43] Forster thus shares the views of many of his Indian characters. For example, when Adela says that by marrying Ronny she will become an 'Anglo-Indian', Aziz replies that she should 'Take back such a terrible remark' (*PI*, p. 137).

Under colonialism in India, Forster shows the failure of the personal values that Adela would have discussed at the Schlegels' lunch table.[44] Thus, though Ronny believes in 'the sanctity of personal relationships' (*PI*, p. 76), we have already learned that 'the only link he could be conscious of with an Indian was the official . . . As private individuals he forgot them' (*PI*, p. 69). Again, after he has decided to pass on to Major Callendar what he has gleaned from his mother about her meeting with Aziz, Ronny says to her: 'Nothing's private in India' (*PI*, p. 27), and this is reinforced by the narrator later: 'Accustomed to the privacy of London, she could not realize that India, seemingly so mysterious, contains none' (*PI*, p. 43). Under such conditions, with such little respect for the privacy of others, personal relations seemed doomed.

Following on from his presentation of the 'rainbow bridge' in *Howards End*, Forster at first saw his new Indian novel as a 'bridge of sympathy between East and West',[45] but he made the bridge party a cynical example of British insincerity, arranged only because the Collector wishes to 'amuse' Adela. The seeming gesture of invitation is instead one of exclusion, which has become a habit of mind: 'We must exclude someone from our gathering, or we shall be left with nothing' (*PI*, p. 32). Forster contrasts this Club-mentality with the inclusion he associates with Indians. 'I invite you all' is a representative phrase for Forster to give to Aziz (*PI*, p. 62), and can contextualise the differences that continue to separate Fielding and Aziz: 'Aziz . . . wanted Fielding to "give in to the East". . . When they argued about it something racial intruded – not bitterly, but inevitably, like the colour of their skins: coffee-colour versus pinko-gray' (*PI*, p. 249).

The book's most trenchant attack on Empire is played out in the damage, to life and temperament, done to Aziz, who concludes that under the unequal relations of Empire, 'this pose of "seeing India" which had seduced him to Miss Quested at Chandrapore was only a form of ruling India' (*PI*, pp. 296–7). To underline the link between seeing and ruling, it is also worth remembering that Aziz, who has been surrounded by spies at Chandrapore, remains under observation (*PI*, pp. 284–5) for the rest of his life after the trial.

What happens to Aziz as a consequence, and also answers the question posed in the discussion that he intrudes on at the start of the novel, is something hinted at early on: 'The complexion of his mind turned from human to political. He thought no longer, "Can I get on with people?" but "Are they stronger than I?"' (*PI*, p. 53). The lesson of the Marabar Caves for Aziz is that British–Indian relations are always founded on an inequality of power. Thus Aziz thinks India 'must imitate Japan. Not until she is a nation will her sons be treated with respect. He grew harder and less approachable. The English, whom he had laughed at or ignored, persecuted him everywhere; they had even thrown nets over his dreams' (*PI*, p. 257). Hamidullah's response to this is to chide Aziz for not joining him and Mahmoud Ali in their 'intrigues', alluding to organised political bodies attempting to oppose the British: 'Hamidullah had called in on his way to a worrying Committee of Notables, nationalist in tendency, where Hindus, Moslems, two Sikhs, two Parsees, a Jain, and a Native Christian tried to like one another more than came natural to them. As long as someone abused the English, all went well' (*PI*, p. 97).

The decade in which Forster's final novel gestated in his mind created an unbridgeable divide between Britain and India, not least because of the false promise of Indian independence after the war, which was instead followed in 1919 by the horror of the Amritsar massacre, exacted in retribution for an attack on an Englishwoman, Miss Sherwood. The years 1913–23 also spanned the Rowlatt Acts (extending wartime repressive measures, including imprisonment without trial, to postwar India), Gandhi's return from South Africa, an upsurge in Nationalist feeling, the Treaty of Sèvres which effectively dissolved the Ottoman empire and prompted the Khilafat agitation in India (1919–24) led by Maulana Abul Kalam Azad, the inauguration of Gandhi's non-cooperation policy in September 1920, and a visit to India by the Prince of Wales in 1922.[46] Such events form a backdrop to the novel and several of them are alluded to, but Forster's narrative places a greater stress on the attitudes of mind that animate colonial discourse and anti-colonial struggle.

A Passage to India presents politics as a barrier to friendship, and thus recognises that politics provides a major context for the failure of friendship at the end of the book; yet Forster also hoped goodwill could ameliorate the effects of larger power inequalities in people's day-to-day interactions. Later, when he travelled to India for a third time, shortly after his mother's death in 1945, he concluded: 'The big change I noticed was the increased interest in politics' (*TCD*, p. 315). Writing on the eve of Independence he again hoped for friendship: 'I do pray that young English people who like Indians and want to be with them will be encouraged to go to their country', which is precisely the decision Forster made for himself when his liking for Masood took him there in 1912. But, he continues, 'Goodwill is not enough. Of that I am too sadly convinced. In fact, at the present moment goodwill out there is no use at all. The reactions to it are instantly cynical. The only thing that cuts a little ice is affection' (*TCD*, pp. 322–3). Affection is also important but far from common in *A Passage to India*. Adela is said to have too little for Indians, and Aziz says he has too little for the country itself; yet, he has speculated as to whether all that India needs is 'kindness' (*PI*, p. 108), and when he gains his freedom at the courtroom 'all that existed' for him 'was affection' (*PI*, p. 223).

As is also recognised in the wider problems of the liberal dilemma, Forster's aim in *A Passage to India* was in part to present a belief in the efficacy of personal relations and, for reasons to do with sexuality, religion, and colonialism, simultaneously to question it.

Notes

1. Chhatarpur was where Forster's friend J. R.Ackerley was Private Secretary to the Maharajah in 1923. Ackerley's experience fed into his journal *Hindoo Holiday* (1932).
2. David Medalie, *E. M. Forster's Modernism* (Basingstoke and New York: Palgrave, 2002), p. 27. For an alternative view of the role *A Passage to India* has played in the aesthetic construction of modernism, see Quentin Bailey, 'Heroes and Homosexuals: Education and Empire in E. M. Forster', *Twentieth-Century Literature*, 48:3 (Fall 2002), 324–47.
3. See P. N. Furbank, *E. M. Forster: A Life* (London: Cardinal, 1988), vol. II, pp. 119–20.
4. For reviews in articles and correspondence of *A Passage to India*, including those by D. H. Lawrence, Rebecca West, and L. P. Hartley, see Philip Gardner (ed.), *E. M. Forster: The Critical Heritage* (London: Routledge and Kegan Paul, 1973), pp. 196–297.
5. See B. J. Moore-Gilbert, *Kipling and 'Orientalism'* (Kent: Croom Helm, 1986), pp. 10–11.
6. Furbank, *E. M. Forster: A Life*, vol. II, p. 127.
7. For example, see G. K. Das, '*A Passage to India*: a Socio-Historical Study', in *A Passage to India: Essays in Interpretation*, ed. John Beer (London: Macmillan, 1985), pp. 1–15.
8. See Benita Parry, 'The Politics of Representation in *A Passage to India*' in Beer, *A Passage to India*, pp. 27–43.
9. Sara Suleri, *The Rhetoric of English India* (Chicago: University of Chicago Press, 1992), pp. 132–48.
10. Brenda R. Silver, 'Periphrasis, Power, and Rape in *A Passage to India*' *Novel*, 22 (Fall 1988), 94.
11. Zakia Pathak *et al.*, 'The Prisonhouse of Orientalism', *Textual Practice*, 5:2 (1991), 195–218.
12. Homi Bhabha, 'Articulating the Archaic', in *Literary Theory Today* ed. Peter Collier and Helga Geyer-Ryan (Ithaca: Cornell University Press, 1990), pp. 203–18.
13. See Benita Parry, *Delusions and Discoveries: Studies on India in the British Imagination 1880–1930* (Macmillan: London, 1972).
14. See for example Harish Trivedi, *Colonial Transactions: English Literature and India* (Manchester: Manchester University Press, 1995).
15. For further discussion and references see Robert L. Selig, '"God si Love": On an Unpublished Forster Letter and the Ironic Use of Myth in *A Passage to India*', *Journal of Modern Literature*, 7 (1979), 471–87, repr. in *E. M. Forster: Critical Assessments, Volume III: The Modern Critical Response*, ed. J. H. Stape (Sussex: Helm, no date), pp. 331–45.
16. In Forster's 1937 article, 'London is a Muddle', he ends with a seven-line quotation from Eliot's poem (*TCD*, pp. 351–2).

17. Mrs Moore plays patience at various times in the novel and the phrases she mutters seem a commentary on the narrative: 'black knave on a red queen' (*PI*, p. 89), 'Red ten on a black knave' (*PI*, p. 90), 'Red nine on black ten' (*PI*, p. 195). The narrator also suggests a connection: 'To be one with the universe! So dignified and simple. But there was always some little duty to be performed first, some new card to be turned up from the diminishing pack and placed, and, while she was pottering about, the Marabar struck its gong' (*PI*, p. 198).

18. Selig, "God si Love", p. 337.

19. Furbank, *E. M. Forster: A Life*, vol. II, p. 124.

20. Rose Macaulay, 'Women in the East', *Daily News*, 4 June 1924, p. 196.

21. On 'The Politics of Friendship in *A Passage to India*' see the essay of that name in David Ayers, *English Literature of the 1920s* (Edinburgh: Edinburgh University Press, 1999), pp. 210–23.

22. Which indeed might be considered the same thing when 'the whole universe was a hill' (*PI*, p. 181).

23. The best guide in Forster's work to Godbole's pronouncements comes in his discussion of, and attraction to, Neo-Platonism, as when he says in *Alexandria: A History and a Guide*: 'We are all parts of God, even the stones, though we cannot realise it; and man's goal is to become actually, as he is potentially, divine. Therefore rebirth is permitted, in order that we may realise God better in a future existence that we can in this; and therefore the Mystic Vision is permitted, in order that, even in this existence we may have a glimpse of God.' The divinity of stones is a question throughout *A Passage to India*. Forster appears to be comparing the Neo-Platonic and Hindu Gods as disparately unified, all-embracing, and unattainable.

24. Furbank, *E. M. Forster: A Life*, vol. II, p. 133.

25. The identification of imperialism with infinity in *Howards End* is noted by Fredric Jameson in his essay 'Modernism and Imperialism', in *Nationalism, Colonialism, and Literature*, ed. Seamus Deane (Minneapolis: University of Minnesota Press, 1990), p. 57.

26. See, for example, Bonnie Blumenthal Finkelstein, *Forster's Women: Eternal Differences* (Ithaca: Columbia University Press, 1975), and Jenny Sharpe, 'The Unspeakable Limits of Rape: Colonial Violence and Counter-Insurgency', *Genders*, 10 (1991), 25–46.

27. After the alleged assault, the Club develops the air of the 'Residency of Lucknow' and it is said to be time to 'Call in the troops and clear the bazaars.' As Mrs Moore remarks, 'the machinery has started', which is to say not just that the trial must take place but that the animus (the 'evil') has started. The narrator comments that some Anglo-Indians 'kept up their spirits by demanding a holocaust of natives' while it later emerges that Aziz's grandfather fought the British in the 'Mutiny' (*PI*, p. 265).

28. See, for example, Bette London, 'Of Mimicry and English Men: E. M. Forster and the Performance of Masculinity', in *A Passage to India: Theory into Practice*, ed. Tony Davies and Nigel Wood (Buckingham: Open University Press, 1994), pp. 90–115.

29. For example, see Joseph Bristow, *Effeminate England: Homoerotic Writing after 1885* (Buckingham: Open University Press, 1995), Joseph Bristow (ed.), *Sexual Sameness: Textual Differences in Lesbian and Gay Writing* (London and New

York: Routledge, 1992), and Robert K. Martin and George Piggford (eds.), *Queer Forster* (Chicago: University Of Chicago Press, 1997).

30. *Chambers Dictionary of Etymology*, ed. Robert K. Barnhart (New York: Chambers, 1988), p. 874.

31. I have argued elsewhere that 'muddle' can be reconsidered in terms of the post-colonial concept of hybridity, especially as advanced by Homi Bhabha. See Peter Childs (ed.), *E. M. Forster's A Passage to India* (London: Routledge, 2002), pp. 46–8.

32. Of the English, it is Mrs Moore who believes in ghosts. On 'Telepathy' see Nicholas Royle's chapter of that name on *A Passage to India* in his *E. M. Forster* (Plymouth: Northcote, 1999).

33. See, for example, Paul B. Armstrong, 'Reading India: E. M. Forster and the Politics of Interpretation', *Twentieth Century Literature* 38:4 (Winter 1992), 365–85.

34. Husbands and especially fathers are generally absent from Forster's novels.

35. Showalter questions the success of even Fielding's marriage in her essay, 'A Passage to India as "Marriage Fiction": Forster's Sexual Politics', *Women and Literature*, 5:2 (1977), 3–16.

36. Because the principle of 'only connect' from *Howards End* is so important to Forster, it is significant that when Mrs Moore passes Asigrah at sunset and identifies it on the map, the narrator comments: 'what could she connect with it except its own name? Nothing . . . But it had looked at her twice and seemed to say: "I do not vanish"' (p. 199). In Bombay: '"you took the Marabar Caves as final?" they laughed. "What have we in common with them, or they with Asigarh?"' The Anglo-Oriental College at Aligarh was where Theodore Morison was Principal when he asked Forster to become Latin tutor to his ward, Syed Ross Masood. Forster began his first Indian visit with Masood in Aligarh, within a stronghold of Muslim nationalism.

37. Forster, *Aspects of the Novel*, p. 115.

38. 'Extracts from Forster's Commonplace Book', in *Aspects of the Novel*, p. 125.

39. Fredric Jameson, 'Modernism and Imperialism', p. 55.

40. The idea of spatial reading largely derives from cubist theory, which argues that a three-dimensional object or event needs to be analysed from all angles and not just one. See Joseph Frank, 'Spatial form in Modern Literature', in *The Widening Gyre: Crisis and Mastery in Modern Literature* (New Brunswick, NJ: Prentice-Hall, 1963).

41. This gives the novel the symphonic three-part rhythm Forster discusses in relation to Beethoven's Fifth Symphony in *Aspects of the Novel*, pp. 115–16, and to Woolf's *To the Lighthouse* in 'Virginia Woolf' (*TCD*, p. 243).

42. Forster, 'Art for Art's Sake' (*TCD*, p. 88).

43. Furbank, *E. M. Forster: A Life*, vol. II, p. 129.

44. A 'Miss Quested' appears as one of the Schlegels' friends in *Howards End*.

45. Furbank, *E. M. Forster: A Life*, vol. II, p. 106.

46. For a discussion of this context see Frances B. Singh, 'A Passage to India, the National Movement, and Independence', *Twentieth Century Literature*, 31:2–3 (Summer–Fall 1985), 265–78.

13

RANDALL STEVENSON

Forster and modernism

Discussion of E. M. Forster and modernism might well be brief. Forster was scarcely a modernist. His career followed a path distinct from those of the major modernist writers, coming close only in *A Passage to India* to the innovative forms distinguishing their writing. Forster can nevertheless be usefully considered – as a novelist and a critic – alongside modernists such as Marcel Proust, James Joyce, Virginia Woolf, and D. H. Lawrence. Gaps between his writing and theirs open worthwhile lines of enquiry about the nature of each – in particular, about the pace and enthusiasm with which different authors altered their strategies in response to the challenges of modernity experienced early in the twentieth century.

Forster summarised these challenges in a lecture delivered in 1944. Assessing 'English Prose between 1918 and 1939', he emphasised the influence of 'a huge economic movement which has been taking the whole world, Great Britain included, from agriculture towards industrialism' – a process, he explains, which 'began about a hundred and fifty years ago'. '[P]ersonally, I hate it', he adds. 'So I imagine do most writers' (*TCD*, p. 267). Other critics were offering similar historical perspectives around the same time. Forster's 'huge economic movement' corresponds closely with the 'project of modernity' – based on faiths in reason, technology, progress, and industry – which Theodor Adorno and Max Horkheimer influentially defined in *Dialectic of Enlightenment* (1944), retracing its origins to Enlightenment thinking and the Industrial Revolution in the later eighteenth century.

Inevitably, modernity's threats and pressures were especially evident towards the end of the Second World War. But technological advances and an increasingly commercial age ensured they also seemed particularly threatening at the beginning of the twentieth century, concentrating the concern – even 'hate' – of much of Forster's own fiction before the First World War. Barely apparent in some of his earliest novels, this concern intensified as the Edwardian years went on. *Where Angels Fear to Tread* (1905) and *A Room with a View* (1908) are not directly focused on the wider problems or economic movements of their age. Instead, each adopts patterns Forster might have found in his 'favourite author', Jane Austen (*AH*, p. 24), following the moral and spiritual education of central figures towards – in the latter novel, anyway – the conventional comedic conclusion of marriage. Satire in each novel is broadly directed on constraints in the English character, contrasted with relaxed Latin counterparts encountered in the civilised, liberating atmosphere of Italy. If this criticism has a specific target, rather than the unfeeling English character generally, it is the suburban Sawston society depicted in *Where Angels Fear to Tread* and carried over into *The Longest Journey* (1907) – a society representative of English constraint, probity, and propriety at their narrowest and most damaging.

In *The Longest Journey* and *Howards End*, on the other hand, Forster moves further from Jane Austen and closer to Edwardian contemporaries such as Arnold Bennett and H. G. Wells, often critics of the growing industrialisation or commercialism of their age. Deficiencies of spirit and imagination in *Howards End* figure not as a general problem with the English character, but rather as the consequence of specific pressures at work within contemporary society. These pressures are personified in the Wilcox family, representatives of 'the business mind', of the 'darkness in high places that comes with a commercial age', and of the 'great outer life . . . a life in which telegrams and anger count' (*HE*, pp. 178, 329, 25). Primarily a comic novelist, Forster nevertheless views this 'darkness' with an optimism differing from anything in Bennett or Wells: a faith that the enlightenment achieved by individuals in his earlier fiction may be extended over contemporary society as a whole. Even the Wilcoxes – Henry Wilcox at any rate – may be redeemable through the 'personal relations . . . private life . . . personal intercourse' which Margaret Schlegel considers 'supreme values' (*HE*, pp. 79, 25). Not necessarily hostile to 'the business mind', but ready to acknowledge 'all that [it] has done for England', Margaret stresses that English life may be re-equilibrated through the interconnection of Wilcox values with her own. 'Only connect! That was the whole of her sermon. Only connect the prose and the passion, and both will be exalted, and human love will be seen at its highest. Live in fragments no longer. Only connect . . .' (*HE*, pp. 178, 183–4). By the end of the novel, with Margaret and Henry married and settled in rural retreat at Howards End, much of this connection seems achieved, fragmentation resisted, and the commercial and industrial forces threatening English life for the moment successfully contained.

These connections within the social sphere are consolidated by others extending outwards through landscape and nature. Throughout the novel, 'starting from Howards End' and its rural setting, Margaret has 'attempted to realize England' as a whole (*HE*, p. 202). Her attempt is matched by a 'love of the island' [sic] shown in much of the narrative – one based around faith in nature and the 'binding force' it can exercise on individual character and on human affairs generally (*HE*, p. 258). This is an influence strongly affirmed throughout Forster's pre-First World War fiction, in his short stories often more directly even than in his first novels. A return from Italian to English landscapes in *The Longest Journey* and *Howards End* contributes to a still more immediate role for nature, at the core of affirmative visions established at the end of each novel. Margaret's fated but long-deferred inheritance of Howards End allows the Wilcox world of telegrams and anger to recede 'like the ebb of a dying sea', Margaret to reassure her new husband that 'nothing has been done wrong', and her sister Helen to anticipate 'such a crop of hay as never!' (*HE*, p. 340). In *The Longest Journey*, despite Sawston and the novel's many encounters with death, a vision of 'the fields of his earlier youth' likewise allows Stephen Wonham the hopeful conclusion that 'he guided the future of our race, and that, century after century, his thoughts and his passions would triumph in England' (*LJ*, p. 289).

Forster, in other words, developed a late version of the Romantic vision which initially resisted pressures of modernity and industrialisation in the late eighteenth and early nineteenth centuries. Like the Romantics, his early fiction emphasises inner qualities of spirit, imagination, or intuition and their affirmative resonances with an unsullied, non-urban world. Yet such affirmations invariably contain notes of uncertainty or precariousness. The end of *The Longest Journey* observes that 'a lurid spot passed over the land' (*LJ*, p. 289), though the passing train responsible interrupts only briefly Stephen's idyllic night on the downs. The concluding idyll of *Howards End* – or at any rate its future survival – is more firmly threatened by the rust-coloured suburban sprawl spreading across the meadows from London; evidence that 'life's going to be melted down, all over the world' (*HE*, p. 337). This dissolution – the threat of having to 'live in fragments' after all, without 'binding force' – continued to concern Forster in the novel he began three years later and completed in 1914: *Maurice*. It still finds some promise of refuge in 'the greenwood' but only for individual characters, fortunate but solitary fugitives within an 'England . . . built over and patrolled' (*M*, pp. 219–20). Forster later confirmed that *Maurice* marked the last moment in history when such refuge was available, even for fortunate individuals, remarking in a 1960 note on the novel that the 'greenwood' disappeared in 'the transformed England of the First World War' (*M*, p. 219). Looking back in a 1960 introduction to *The Longest Journey*, he likewise recorded that 'the England that Stephen thought so good and seemed destined to inherit is done for. The growth of the population and the applications of science have destroyed her between them' (*LJ*, pp. lxix–lxx).

Forster's pre-First World War fiction thus sought compensations for advancing modernity and materialism at a time when nature's capacity to provide them seemed threatened with rapid, even terminal decline. With the greenwood apparently gone by 1914 – confirming fears in *Howards End* that 'the earth as an artistic cult has had its day' (*HE*, p. 106) – Forster's fiction faced a possible impasse, or at any rate a considerable imaginative challenge. Comparable challenges inevitably extended over contemporary writing more generally: their urgency helps account for the growing pace of stylistic and formal innovation, characteristic of modernism, shaping fiction by Forster's contemporaries during and just after the First World War. Developments in D. H. Lawrence's work at the time both illustrate these innovations and relate significantly to some of Forster's fiction: Forster admired Lawrence, and the two writers are often comparable, sometimes surprisingly closely. Lawrence's *The Rainbow* (1915) traces a long process of industrial encroachment on nature: in the sequel, *Women in Love* – especially in Chapter 17, 'The Industrial Magnate' – Gerald Crich emerges as an updated version of Henry Wilcox in *Howards End*. Forces of modernity and industrialisation which Gerald represents appear in *Women in Love* a still graver source of ills throughout contemporary society. Yet just as Wilcox is rescued from his world of 'telegrams and anger' by one of the Schlegel sisters, so even Gerald's rational, chilly nature might have proved redeemable through relations with Birkin, as a friend, or – less promisingly – with Gudrun Brangwen, as a lover. These possibilities remain tragically unrealised, though through Birkin's affair with the other Brangwen sister, Ursula, Lawrence does establish more affirmative potentials for relationship – ones further explored throughout the novel. Alongside anxieties about modernity and industrialisation, *Women in Love* thus extends faiths expressed in *A Room with a View* in 'the holiness of direct desire' (*RV*, p. 204), or, in *Howards End*, that 'personal relations are the important thing for ever and ever, and not this outer life of telegrams and anger' (*HE*, p. 170).

Yet the intensity of Lawrence's concentration on personal relationships shapes a fiction significantly different from Forster's – particularly in its readiness to shift attention further from 'outer life'. 'Direct desire', in Lawrence's work, is not only presented more directly – often in stronger sexual detail – but with more intimate, expansive attention to the effect of powerful emotions on individuals and their psyches. Determination to register relationships' seismic effects within the self adds to Lawrence's need for what he called 'a deeper sense'[1] than fiction usually offered – one which he developed throughout *The Rainbow* and *Women in Love*. In each, even single lines of conversation are often separated by whole paragraphs describing the complexities of conversants' unspoken inner feelings. These are also presented extensively, and more immediately, through Lawrence's frequent use of free indirect style, allowing characters' inner thoughts to be expressed largely in their own voice, albeit mediated through the controlling tones of the author.

In expanding and deepening representations of inner consciousness in this way, Lawrence's work was typical both of general developments in modernist writing during early decades of the twentieth century, and of particular forms this had begun to follow by the start of the 1920s. Such developments were already apparent by the turn of the century, in Joseph Conrad's use of narrators whose cognitive idiosyncrasies ensure that individual psychology and thought-processes are bound into storytelling with new intimacy. New concentration on individual minds and thoughts also figured in Henry James's use of 'intense perceivers' or 'polished mirrors', as he called them – focalising characters, each functioning as 'a definite responsible intervening first person singular' through whose perceptions the world of the fiction is presented.[2] Inner focalisation was further facilitated by techniques developing during and after the First World War: not only Lawrence's free indirect discourse, but Dorothy Richardson's more immediate transcription of inner thought as stream of consciousness – a tactic subsequently extended with celebrated stylishness throughout James Joyce's *Ulysses* (1922). Even by 1919, these and other writers were already confirming views Virginia Woolf expressed in an essay first published in that year, 'Modern Fiction'. 'The proper stuff of fiction', Woolf remarked, 'is a little other than custom would have us believe it', and best provided if novelists chose to record the mind's 'myriad impressions', and to explore 'the dark places of psychology'.[3]

Extended indirect and free indirect discourse in novels such as *Mrs Dalloway* (1925) and *To the Lighthouse* (1927) show Woolf acting on this conclusion herself. *To the Lighthouse* also suggests why it had come to be shared so widely. 'Did nature supplement what man advanced? Did she complete what he began?' Woolf asks in the middle section of the novel, set mainly in the war years. Affirmative answers are made impossible by 'the silent apparition of an ashen coloured ship . . . a purplish stain upon the bland surface of the sea as if something had boiled and bled, invisibly, beneath'. War and its destructive machinery leave little hope that 'beauty outside mirrored beauty within', or that the natural world could 'reflect the compass of the soul'. Instead, the novel records of nature that its 'contemplation was unendurable', and that 'the mirror was broken'. In place of beauty and order lost in the natural, outer world, *To the Lighthouse* discusses – and develops through its own styles – 'the vision within'. 'In those mirrors, the minds of men', the novel remarks, 'dreams persisted . . . good triumphs, happiness prevails, order rules'.[4] *To the Lighthouse* suggests in this way that novelists early in the twentieth century may have chosen to look within and concentrate on the mind because there seemed nowhere else to look – no prospect of the order and affirmation a natural world had once seemed able to provide. Advancing pressures of modernity, and the dwindling potential of nature to resist them – progressively clarified in Forster's early writing – help to account for a direction increasingly followed by modernist fiction during and after the war.

Another such direction – another opportunity offered by 'the vision within' – figures in Woolf's fiction, and is emphasised in her other writing. 'Life is not a series . . . symmetrically arranged', Woolf comments in 'Modern Fiction' (p. 160), complaining in her diary about the 'appalling narrative business of the realist: getting on from lunch to dinner' and resolving to 'read Proust' and 'go backwards and forwards' instead. Increasingly focused within individual consciousnesses, modernist narrative relied more and more on what Woolf called in *Orlando* (1928) 'time in the mind' rather than 'time on the clock'.[5] In novels such as *Mrs Dalloway* or *To the Lighthouse*, Woolf does go back as well as forwards, using characters' memories – like Joyce in *Ulysses* – to stitch past events into single days of present consciousness.

These new fictional tactics and new emphases on 'time in the mind' represent a further phase of modernist resistance to the pressures of modernity – in particular, to a temporality increasingly rationalised and commodified in the early decades of the century. 'Clocking-in' for factory work, principles of scientific management or assembly-line production, or Daylight Saving Time – first imposed to boost industrial production during the war – each subjected life to more and more rigorous control by 'time on the clock'. Resulting stresses are inescapably apparent in *Women in Love*. Gudrun's hatred of 'the mechanical succession of day following day, day following day . . . the terrible bondage of this tick-tack of time'[6] even extends into a nightmare figuration of Gerald as clockwork mechanism – just the kind of machinery on which his soulless work processes so comprehensively relied. Similar stresses and imaginative involutes are widely apparent throughout modernist writing: in the anarchist attack on Greenwich, symbol and centre of temporal ordering, described in Conrad's *The Secret Agent* (1907), for example. Another instance appears in Stephen Dedalus's much-quoted conclusion in *Ulysses*: that history itself is a 'nightmare' from which he is 'trying to awake'.[7] Industrialised temporality and contemporary historical crises – the First World War, above all – challenged conventional convictions of orderly progress through time, compromising structural principles on which much Victorian and Edwardian fiction had been based. Modernist fiction, as a result, had to explore new forms and structures: ones able to recover through memory, like Proust, a lost human time.

By the beginning of the 1920s, in other words, fiction had developed several forms and strategies resistant to the kind of pressures troubling E. M. Forster's fiction before 1914. In his critical writing, Forster was naturally ready to recognise the merits of these developments, albeit less enthusiastically than Virginia Woolf. Forster was less 'appalled' than Woolf by the conventional narrative business of 'getting on from lunch to dinner', emphasising in *Aspects of the Novel* that, unavoidably, '[y]es – oh dear yes – the novel tells a story', and that 'a story is a narrative of events arranged in time-sequence' (*AN*, pp. 17, 20). Attempts by modernist writers, such as Gertrude Stein, 'to emancipate fiction from the tyranny of time' he therefore considered 'instructive' in their failure (*AN*, p. 28). Yet Forster sought a comparable 'emancipation' in his own critical practice in *Aspects of the Novel*: resolved, he repeatedly explains, to 'exorcise that demon of chronology', to 'refuse to have anything to do with chronology', and to provide an analysis of fiction thoroughly independent of history (*AN*, pp. 8, 15). Some of this analysis develops Forster's view that 'there seems something else in life besides time . . . something which is measured not by minutes or hours, but by intensity' (*AN*, p. 19) – an idea already apparent in his early fiction. *Where Angels Fear to Tread*, *A Room with a View*, and the aptly named short story 'The Eternal Moment', all show brief yet intense experiences dominating entire subsequent lives. In *Aspects of the Novel*, views of this kind extend into a distinction between 'the life in time and the life by values' (*AN*, p. 19) apparently quite consistent with Woolf's division of 'time on the clock' from 'time in the mind'.

Forster was more explicitly sympathetic to modernism's wider interests in psychology. His 1944 lecture acknowledged that 'a great enrichment to fiction' had resulted from 'the psychological movement' (*TCD*, p. 268) shaping the work of Proust, Gertrude Stein, Dorothy Richardson, Joyce, Woolf, Lawrence, and others (*TCD*, p. 269). He also recognised this movement as an attempt to resist or evade the social and commercial pressures of modernity which his lecture described. 'Writers are intimidated by the economic changes but stimulated by the psychological', he remarked, adding that the modernist authors he named 'look outside them and find their material . . . [b]ut they arrange it and re-create it within, temporarily sheltered from the pitiless blasts and the fog' (*TCD*, pp. 276, 272). Sympathetic to this urge to work within, intriguingly ambivalent about modernist temporality, and in need of shelter from the blasts of modernity himself, Forster might well have re-emerged – in his only post-war novel, *A Passage to India* (1924) – as a modernist writer himself.

There are critics who consider that this is exactly what happened. Malcolm Bradbury describes Forster as 'an Edwardian and Georgian writer who wrote nearly all his fiction before the First World War and then became a Modernist'.[8] Certainly, as Bradbury suggests, differences from Forster's pre-war fiction are inescapably apparent from the first page of *A Passage to India* to its last. A distant, inhospitable setting obviously invalidates any form of the late-Romantic English pastoral so significant for earlier novels, and with it much of the faith in relationship and connection central to *Howards End*. Instead, *A Passage to India* begins with description of the meaner, unsavoury aspects of Chandrapore, and of the Marabar Hills, sinisterly personified, lying beyond the town. At the novel's end, far from supporting human values and connections, the natural world seems – still with sinister animacy – almost deliberately to force characters apart. Of Fielding's tentative friendship with Aziz, Forster concludes, 'the horses didn't want it – they swerved apart; the earth didn't want it, sending up rocks through which riders must pass single file' (*PI*, p. 312). If not actively hostile, the Indian landscape is presented throughout the novel as at least so ineffably indifferent – so immeasurably vast and formless – that it disrupts not only cohesive human relations, but coherence itself, overwhelming possibilities of order, morality, or understanding.

A Passage to India thus moves decisively beyond the habitual concern with 'muddle', emotional or interpersonal, which dominates Forster's early fiction, and towards more wide-ranging concerns with 'mystery' – with perplexities pervasive both within the human sphere, and in its relation with what lies beyond. These focus on the Marabar Caves, a context both for immediate mystery, in Adela Quested's unexplained encounter, and for Forster's wider vision of a universe of ultimate nullity: one existing outwith consciousness and its powers of assimilation; outside human orders of language, logic, and reason. This is in many ways a modernist vision, widely shared by authors discussed above. As their fiction focused further within the mind, it inevitably became more concerned with the reliability of consciousness's connections with the outer world – with how trustworthy 'those mirrors, the minds of men' could be. Contemporary history, meanwhile, made that outer world seem more than ever resistive to reason and order. That empty 'ou-boum' – the only resonance of all human enterprise in the Marabar Caves – may be in part a distant, desolate echo of the nightmare experience of the First World War, likewise reflected in Woolf's vision of a newly hostile external reality in the middle section of *To the Lighthouse*.

A Passage to India, in other words, is closely aligned with modernism's new awareness of epistemological complexities, showing Forster responding in cognate terms to historical factors underlying each. Yet there are significant differences of style and strategy. In particular, the novel's narrative voice sustains a good deal of confidence even in exploring the limits of the knowable and the horizons of its own omniscience. The Marabar Caves may lie beyond human understanding, art, or reason, but Forster is memorably eloquent in saying so, providing descriptions of detailed declarative clarity. This may be mildly anomalous in itself: it contrasts sharply, at any rate, with some of the practices of modernist fiction. Conrad's *Heart of Darkness*, for example, envisages another set of horrors supposedly beyond civilisation or understanding; another kind of utter hollowness at the heart of life. Yet Conrad communicates incertitude and incomprehension differently and more immediately, dramatising the limits and relativity of cognition through a narrator, Marlow, repeatedly concerned with the inadequacies of his own version of events. 'Do you see the story? Do you see anything?' Marlow asks, concluding with confidence – scarcely shared by his listeners – only that 'you see me, whom you know'.[9] His conclusion extends beyond his immediate audience, within the novel, to its readers generally – also to readers of modernist literature more widely. By habitually interpolating some 'first person singular' – whether narrator or transcribed inner consciousness – between reader and events represented, modernist writers ensure that the relativity of all truth, and the uncertain nature of its construction within individual minds, remain issues inescapably apparent throughout their fiction.

Forster, of course, does at times enter the consciousness of characters in *A Passage to India*. Sections of free indirect style record Adela's thoughts, for example, just before her disastrous experience in the Marabar Caves, necessarily preparing readers for the possibility that her encounter was merely fantasy or hallucination. The caves also offer a kind of black hole – another 'eternal moment', though a bleak one – around which the narrative continues to gravitate. In repeatedly returning to it, later accounts – individual, or official in the enquiries of the court – follow paths rather more recursive than in Forster's earlier fiction, and more challengingly plural in their conflicting versions of events. Yet movements into mind, memory, or unconventional chronology in *A Passage to India* remain fairly limited and local, matching modernism's formal and structural innovation neither in scale nor effect. Critics who claim *A Passage to India* as a modernist text inevitably concentrate less on its overall form and style than on more particular tactics and tropes. Malcolm Bradbury, or Peter Childs in *Modernism* (2000), for example, each consider Forster's use of symbol and rhythm central to the modernist status they claim for *A Passage to India*. Yet each device is regularly present in conventional narrative. Defined by Childs as 'the repeated use of expressions, incidents, or characters' to 'accumulate resonances and meanings',[10] rhythm might be a fundamental component of all narratives, not only modernist ones.

Symbolism might be thought more specific to modernist fiction, offering a convenient means of retaining and expanding significances for an external, object world within the subjective consciousnesses presented. Yet its use is scarcely exclusive to modernist fiction, nor a defining characteristic of it, as some of Forster's early novels confirm. *A Room with a View*, for example, describes Lucy Honeychurch's formative meeting with George occurring as if at the 'entrance of a cave', and close to 'the tower of the palace, which rose out of the lower darkness like a pillar of roughened gold . . . throbbing in the tranquil sky' (*RV*, pp. 40–1). This description is as suggestive as any symbol in *A Passage to India*, and as significant for the text in which it appears. So is the later description of a book, settled in lucent stillness on the Honeychurch lawn. Yet neither instance moves *A Room with a View* beyond conventional social comedy – not, at any rate, in the direction of modernism.

Even in *A Passage to India*, then, Forster appears a writer approaching modernism in theme and outlook, but without much adopting related innovations in form and style. Yet only the harshest of critics would consider that a poorer novel results. Those mentioned above may be doing *A Passage to India* a disservice in their eagerness to claim it as modernist, obscuring the particular powers of Forster's examination of postwar uncertainty, and of a declining British empire, largely through different and more conventional means. Their eagerness may nevertheless indicate a problem with the category of modernism itself. Through long critical use, a term once essentially taxonomic may have become too readily honorific – used too widely to define the *best* of early twentieth-century writing, rather than only one set of forms and styles, next to which Forster's talents, or other more conventional ones, might still find their admirers.

This may be why some of the best recent critics of Forster, such as David Medalie, continue to devote so much effort to associating his work with the modernists. In *E. M. Forster's Modernism* (2002), Medalie amply clarifies Forster's views of 'modernity as a crisis and even as an apocalypse; something which must be opposed'.[11] In tracing Forster's opposition, too, Medalie reaches the sensible conclusion that 'in relation to some of the major currents which have been identified in modernism, Forster's modernism may indeed occupy a marginal position' (p. 194), leaving only a 'reluctant modernism' evident in his work (p. 1). But *E. M. Forster's Modernism* is less persuasive in suggesting that Forster 'directs us towards a broader conceptualisation and understanding of modernism itself' (p. 1), or that by finding a space for him 'within a sufficiently flexible account of modernism . . . our understanding of modernism itself is extended and enriched' (p. 193). A sufficiently broad and flexible conceptualisation of zebras, as a species, might allow the odd intriguing horse to be included within it, but how far would zoology be advanced as a result? As one of Forster's characters might have remarked, 'No, no, this is going too far. We must exclude someone from our gathering, or we shall be left with nothing.'

Of course, as that remark suggests – puzzling over the subcontinent's infinite range of creatures in *A Passage to India* (*PI*, p. 32) – arguments about boundaries, in literature or life, may inevitably be inconclusive. Modernism has never been an exact category, and might perhaps be extended as Medalie suggests to include any early twentieth-century writer responding critically to contemporary 'conditions of modernity' (p. 195). Yet it would be difficult to think of many writers who could be *ex*cluded from such categorisation, especially given Forster's own description, quoted earlier, of comprehensive suspicion of modernity among his contemporaries. Any literary category is worthwhile only insofar as it clarifies specific characteristics genuinely shared among authors, pointing to historical forces collectively shaping their work. Rather than enriching, 'broader conceptualisation' may simply be vaguer, impoverishing understanding of modernist writers and of the real significance of Forster's relation to 'conditions of modernity'.

Much of this significance is to be found in the clear evidence Forster offers of modernity's pressures on an author *not* readily disposed to believe 'the proper stuff of fiction' other than convention had established. For in making these pressures clear, Forster's early fiction shows equally clearly how unlikely he was to follow modernist methods of dealing with them. It also highlights reasons for this reluctance, personal and social as well as artistic. As critics have often pointed out, those modernist authors who were involved at all in English society usually encountered it as outsiders: Conrad and James as foreign nationals, for example, and D. H Lawrence on account of working-class origins. Though an arch-Bloomsburyite, at the centre of London intellectual life, even Virginia Woolf talked of finding herself, as a woman, 'outside' established society, and 'alien and critical' towards it[12] – an internal exile also discussed by Dorothy Richardson in *Pilgrimage* (1915–67). Homosexuality might have contributed to comparable feelings for Forster, though ones impossible to discuss openly. At any rate, though a sharp critic of English society in his early fiction, Forster remains complicit with many of its values. *Where Angels Fear to Tread* suggests that the English may have much to learn from Italy, yet readily stereotypes the 'morality . . . of the average Latin', contrasting it with 'the Englishman, whose standard is higher' (*WAFT*, pp. 46–7). *Howards End* highlights disastrous disconnections inherent in the English class system, but treats patronisingly or implausibly characters from outside the middle class, excluding anyone from further down the social scale, barely ironically, by remarking that '[w]e are not concerned with the very poor. They are unthinkable' (*HE*, p. 43).

The Longest Journey is bitterly critical of Sawston, but Forster admits in an introduction that it offers an image of 'the great world in miniature' based partly on his own public school (*LJ*, p. lxviii). No author viewing the great world through memories of his public school is altogether an outsider to England or its class system. However critical Forster may have been of class, it remained in any case crucial to him as a central subject of his fiction. Even in *A Passage to India*, English biases and hierarchies remain a principal concern, with Aziz taking over the role of disadvantaged outsider occupied in *Howards End* by Leonard Bast.

Concerns with class and social interconnection – long-established interests of English fiction – offered Forster much less incentive than the modernists to depart from conventional styles. Even when he did employ tactics modernism developed, it was often in ways more familiar from the nineteenth century than the twentieth. Early novels regularly employ free indirect style, one of D. H. Lawrence's principal devices for transcribing characters' inner consciousness in *The Rainbow* and in *Women in Love*. But free indirect style can be a double-edged tool: able either to extend contacts with inner thought, or, on the other hand, to accentuate authors' control over its presentation. Far from a modernist invention, free indirect style flourishes in the work of the nineteenth-century writer Forster most admired, Jane Austen, but employed mostly as a satiric tool, transcribing characters' thoughts and outlooks in ironic contrast with implied authorial norms. It is this satiric method which Forster mostly follows in his early fiction, rather than wholeheartedly seeking Lawrence's 'deeper sense' of character and consciousness.

Commitment to social interconnections, personal relations, and their comedic resolution of course offered Forster little reason to do otherwise. Too deep or sympathetic a sense of characters' inner natures risks diminishing their satiric potential and unduly complicating the social patterning comic vision requires. Except in the sketchily developed figure of Leonard Bast, or at moments in *Maurice* and *The Longest Journey*, Forster naturally excludes figures too resistive to such patterning – characters too thoroughly alone or alienated from the fabric and values of their society. By contrast, in *The Rainbow* Lawrence not only traces nineteenth-century industrialisation at length, but shows its effects in unravelling coherent social community and organic connections with the earth, leaving the individual thoroughly isolated as a result. Ursula emerges at the end of the novel as one of the first of modernism's many lonely, alienated characters, with 'no father nor mother nor lover . . . no allocated place in the world of things'.[13] Such radical disconnection contributes to a conclusion, also typical of modernism, not at the level of social community, characters' experiences, or the 'world of things' the novel depicts, but at a meta-level of vision largely beyond them. For Forster, this view of radically isolated individuals and an irresolvable world apparently became available only after his own experience of exile and the alien – not in the comfortable landscapes of Italy, but in India and elsewhere, around the time of the First World War. Though a more challenging outlook results in *A Passage to India*, it is only through the denials of personal interrelation and social community, at the novel's end, that its implications come fully into view. Forster's subsequent silence is significant, and disappointing. The moment at which he was most fully aligned with modernist vision, and perhaps readiest to adopt its tactics, also proved his last as a novelist.

This silence could be construed simply as a failure of nerve: as Forster's recognition of artistic imperatives which he felt unwilling or unequipped to realise in his own writing. Forster might in this way be taken at his own estimate: as a novelist of moderate talents, unable to develop as decisively as his contemporaries even those radical conclusions his fiction eventually managed to reach. Michael Levenson suggests this verdict in assigning Forster to 'an ambiguous position in the history of modern fiction' on the grounds that 'he could never muster the conviction for a programmatic assault on traditional forms', demonstrating instead only 'an evolutionary rather than a revolutionary change'.[14] A more positive view might acknowledge that – even in reaching the verge of modernist modes – Forster had to undertake the longest journey of any of his contemporaries. A novelist initially so rooted in the manners of English society and its comic fiction – so mired in the legacies of Jane Austen and the Romantics – might perhaps be admired for managing to travel as far as he did. That journey, and its conclusion in *A Passage to India*, offer at any rate an exemplary evolution. Few authors demonstrate as clearly as Forster the reshaping of an inherently nineteenth-century imagination by the demands of the twentieth. Without much sharing the revolutionary initiative of modernism, his work thoroughly illumines the expanding modern pressures which made it so necessary. This is reason enough to continue considering Forster alongside modernist writing, perhaps even to discuss 'E. M. Forster's Modernism', providing its revealing limitations are fully and firmly recognised.

Notes

1. D. H. Lawrence, letter of 5 June 1914, *The Collected Letters of D. H. Lawrence*, ed. Harry T. Moore (London: Heinemann, 1962), vol. I, p. 282.
2. Henry James, *The Art of the Novel: Critical Prefaces*, ed. R. P. Blackmur (London: Charles Scribner's Sons, 1962), pp. 70–1; *Notes on Novelists: with Some Other Notes* (London: J. M. Dent & Sons, 1914), p. 275.

3. Virginia Woolf, 'Modern Fiction' (1919; revised 1925), in *The Essays of Virginia Woolf*, ed. Andrew McNeillie, vol. IV (London: Hogarth Press, 1994), pp. 161, 160, 162. Subsequent references are to this edition.

4. Virginia Woolf, *To the Lighthouse* (1927; repr. Harmondsworth: Penguin, 1973), pp. 146, 152, 153.

5. Virginia Woolf, *A Writer's Diary*, ed. Leonard Woolf (1953; repr. London: Triad, 1985), p. 185; *Orlando* (1928; repr. Harmondsworth: Penguin, 1975), p. 69.

6. D. H. Lawrence, *Women in Love* (1920; repr. Harmondsworth: Penguin, 1971), p. 522.

7. James Joyce, *Ulysses* (1922; repr. Harmondsworth: Penguin, 1992), p. 42.

8. Malcolm Bradbury, *The Modern British Novel* (London: Secker and Warburg, 1993), p. 176.

9. Joseph Conrad, *Heart of Darkness* (1899; repr. Harmondsworth: Penguin, 1995), p. 50.

10. Peter Childs, *Modernism* (London: Routledge, 2000), p. 191.

11. David Medalie, *E. M. Forster's Modernism* (Basingstoke and New York: Palgrave, 2002), p. 7. Subsequent references are to this edition.

12. Virginia Woolf, *A Room of One's Own* (1928; repr. Harmondsworth: Penguin, 1975), p. 96.

13. D. H. Lawrence, *The Rainbow* (1915; repr. Harmondsworth: Penguin, 1971), p. 493.

14. Michael H. Levenson, *Modernism and the Fate of Individuality* (Cambridge: Cambridge University Press, 1991), pp. 78–9.

14

GARY DAY

Forster as literary critic

It used to be the case that anyone studying English literature had at least heard of Forster's *Aspects of the Novel*[1] and its famous distinctions between story and plot, flat and round characters. We can make no such assumptions today when literary study, dominated by theory, disdains such old-fashioned terms. But Forster's short book has much to tell us, not just about the elements of fiction, but also about the nature of criticism which is too often seen, rather simplistically, as a critique not so much of literature, a term it barely recognises, as of the social order. There is no reason why criticism should not look at wider issues but if it takes so little heed of the complexities of art, how can it hope to enlighten us about the much greater complexities of society?

Forster formulates his views about the novel in reaction to Aristotle's *Poetics*, a conception of history, and a sense of Englishness. In a perhaps typically English, self-deprecating sort of way, he regards the novel as a lower form of art. But that is simply a ruse to boost its status. Aristotle, Forster tells us, was wrong to think that human happiness and misery took the form of action; we must seek for that in the secret life which is the novelist's special territory. Plot, therefore, is not as important to the novel as it is to drama. Forster wants to bracket history out of his discussion of the novel mainly because it tempts us to think in terms of periods, which then prompts us to read novels as mere reflections of their time and so lose what is distinctive about them. In addition, the historian, like the dramatist, is concerned with action which, as we have said, is not the novelist's primary interest. We should think of novelists not in chronological order but as contemporaries and, when we do, we will notice that they have a lot more in common than we might think, given that they may be separated by a couple hundred years. Forster believes that human nature changes very little over time. He is prepared to concede that it may change over four, or fourteen thousand years, but four hundred years is insufficient to produce any real change. If human nature is to change, he muses, it will be because we look at ourselves in a new way and all vested interests are against our doing so. Should we succeed, it may mean the end of imaginative literature. Forster's picture of novelists writing side by side owes something to T. S. Eliot's conception of tradition as having a 'simultaneous existence' and 'a simultaneous order'[2] and it signals his problematic relationship with modernism.

Forster's Englishness comes out in three ways; first in his emphasis on affection, second in his refusal to define the novel or to adopt a particular method in his approach to it, and third in his subdued but definite sense of class. In 'Notes on the English Character' (1926) he tells us that one of the qualities of the English is their 'undeveloped heart.'[3] Art is an attempt to develop that heart. Accordingly, Forster's test of whether a novel is good or bad 'will be our affection for it, as it is the test of our friends and anything else we cannot define' (*Aspects*, p. 38). And, true to the tradition of English empiricism, he avoids theory and proceeds by examples. But lest we think that Forster is provincial we should note his comment that: 'No English novelist is as great as Tolstoy . . . No English novelist has explored man's soul as deeply as Dostoyevsky. And no novelist anywhere has analysed the modern consciousness as successfully as Proust' (*Aspects*, p. 26). As for Forster's class sense, we will come to that in due course, but it is worth mentioning here his remark that 'the character of the English is essentially middle class' ('Notes', p. 11).

Forster's criticism of the novel, then, is shaped by his opinion of drama, history, and Englishness. This should help us have a broader view of *Aspects* than merely the source of handy, but perhaps outmoded distinctions. Forster's view of criticism itself is partly conditioned by how it was being professionalised by such people as F. R. Leavis at Cambridge. Forster regards critics more as the enemy than the friend of art. Their first crime was to classify books without having properly read them and their second was to relate them to some 'tendency' (*Aspects*, p. 31). Critics then compound this offence by adopting a provincial outlook which exaggerates the value of domestic novels compared to the great European ones. Not that Forster is unaware of the inherent difficulties of practising criticism; for instance, how hard it is to focus on the work without being drawn into wider discussions. Another more serious problem is the loss inevitably incurred whenever we try to translate the experience of one medium into another; something is always lost.

Forster does not object to criticism *per se*, only to those particular versions which either impose their principles on the created work or else insert it into some larger system. The core of Forster's disagreement with professional critics is that they ignore what he considers to be the most important aspect of the novel: its human dimension. Forster's insistence on the human element of art is, in part, a reaction to the modernist novel which, in broad terms, was more concerned with form than content. He acknowledges the achievements of modernist writers and pays tribute to their experiments but, in the end, he cannot endorse their work. Henry James 'shuts the doors on life' (*Aspects*, p. 145) in his pursuit of beautiful patterns and, while the mythology of James Joyce's *Ulysses* may be 'fascinating', it is ultimately a 'simplification' that leads us 'away from truth' (*Aspects*, p. 113). Virginia Woolf could not understand Forster's attachment to the 'humane as opposed to the aesthetic view of fiction'. 'Why', she asked in her review of *Aspects*, 'is the pleasure that we get from the pattern in *The Golden Bowl* less valuable than the emotion which Trollope gives us when he describes a lady drinking tea in a parsonage?'[4]

Part of the answer may lie outside the province of art. Since the late nineteenth century Britain had seen the growth of state bureaucracy which sought to regulate all aspects of behaviour. In 'The Ivory Tower' (1938) Forster complains that modern society seeks to control the individual in 'birth, death, work and play' making it almost impossible to either 'escape' or to 'express' a personal vision of life.[5] The prominence that Forster gives to the 'human' in his account of the novel can therefore be seen as a way of reasserting the claims of the personal life in a society organised along increasingly impersonal lines. And here we may be able to answer Woolf's question. Forster finds more pleasure in a lady drinking tea than in the pattern of *The Golden Bowl* because it is a sign of Trollope's distance from the formal character of the modern world in a way that James' attention to shape and structure is not. T. S. Eliot's observation that poetry was 'not the expression of personality but the escape from personality' ('Tradition', p. 21) is another example of how the abstract nature of some modernist poetics complements the anonymity of the state and mass culture. It is not the novel's job to endorse the institutions of society but to expose their shortcomings, to show other possibilities for life in the face of official pressure to conform. The artist's 'duty to humanity', Forster says, is 'not to fit in'. Instead, he or she should 'feel things and express things that haven't yet been felt and expressed' and by these means 'develop human sensitiveness in directions away from the average citizen'.[6] He or she can only do this if they are free to experiment, a sentiment that brings Forster closer to modernism as much as his commitment to the human distances him from it.

'There are', he wrote, 'two forces' in the novel, 'human beings and a bundle of various things not human beings, and it is the novelist's business to adjust these two forces and conciliate their claims' (*Aspects*, p. 101). The distinction is convenient but artificial. The human element is 'people' and an example of the 'non human' is 'pattern' which is of course designed by the human author. The idea that the novel is divided against itself invites comparisons with Freud whose ideas were well known in English intellectual circles by the time Forster was writing *Aspects* and, while they may not have directly influenced him, it is quite possible that Forster could have absorbed them indirectly. It would not be hard to interpret his image of the novel as a 'swamp' (*Aspects*, p. 25) or his claim that story has a 'primitive appeal' (*Aspects*, p. 52) in terms of Freud's account of the unconscious. The novelist's attempt to balance conflicting claims also suggests an analogy with parliamentary democracy, which ideally seeks to balance different demands. While we may be tempted to dismiss this as a rather fanciful comparison we shouldn't forget that *Aspects* was published in 1927, one year after the General Strike when British society briefly but alarmingly divided along class lines. Class is not a strong presence in *Aspects* but neither is it entirely absent with the result that it qualifies Forster's use of the word 'human'. Class conditions our understanding of that term as it does our understanding of 'English'. Forster begins his discussion of the novel proper by imagining how three types of men would answer the question 'what does the novel do?' (*Aspects*, p. 40). These types, among whom is a middle-class golfer, roughly correspond to the traditional divisions in English society between the upper, the middle, and the working class. Forster shows a heightened awareness of class in 'The Ivory Tower' where he defends the need of the 'bourgeois' to escape in order to create works of art, and his unusual use of such terms can be attributed to the heightened class consciousness of that decade. But even in 1926 Forster had wondered about what effect the literate working class would have on English society ('Notes', p. 24). His view of the lower orders is made plain when he asserts that 'the movie-public' are the 'modern descendants' of 'cave men' (*Aspects*, p. 87).

In the end, however, Forster was less concerned with class than with the depredations of commercialism which have led to England being 'gashed with roads and spattered with adverts' ('Ivory', p. 123). Of course these developments cannot be divorced from considerations of class, but that is not really how Forster sees the matter. Business has led to a decline in public taste, it has destroyed the countryside and vulgarised the towns. But though Forster may deplore these changes, and though he may want to put the claims of culture above the demands of economics, he knows this is impossible. Regrettably, 'learning is connected with earning' and likely to remain so (*Aspects*, p. 29). Even the psychological adjustment we make in reading fantasy is seen in terms of 'pay[ing] something extra'. The mingling of culture and commerce does not mean that they are the same thing, only that they are connected, so it is important to distinguish between them. Briefly, we are transformed by art but deformed by the demands of business. Of course that is an exaggeration, but what the novelist requires from the reader, 'human feelings and a sense of value for the characters, [and] intelligence and memory for the plot' (*Aspects*, p. 103), are not the sort of qualities normally required in the corporate world where finance must always take precedence over feeling. Still, novels must be sold if they are to be successful.

It is time to move from some of the contexts of *Aspects* to the components of the novel itself. These are story, plot, people, fantasy, prophecy, pattern, and rhythm. 'Yes – oh dear yes – the novel tells a story' (*Aspects*, p. 40). Forster is apologetic about this aspect of the novel because, going back to pre-historic times, it caters for the lowest part of our nature. At its most basic, story respects the fact that things happen in sequence, at its best it makes us want to know what happens next. Sir Walter Scott is Forster's example of a novelist who only tells a story. His characters are 'passionless', his dialogue 'perfunctory', and his scenery 'cardboard', yet he had 'the primitive power of keeping the reader in suspense' (*Aspects*, pp. 45, 47). If the other elements of the novel such as 'plot', 'people', and 'pattern' are 'noble', this one is base. The 'noble' elements are what give the novel 'value', which is measured by 'intensity' (*Aspects*, p. 42), while the story, which pertains to time, is measured by the clock. This distinction between value and time is a reminder of the novel's divided nature.

Forster expresses the basic distinction between story and plot as follows: 'If it is a story, we say: "And then?" If it is a plot we ask: "Why?"'. His example couldn't be clearer. 'The king dies and then the queen died is a story; the king dies and then the queen died of grief is a plot' (*Aspects*, p. 87). Story only excites our curiosity, but plot requires our intelligence and memory. We need intelligence to be able to recognise a new fact and to relate it to others already encountered, and memory, because unless we can remember what has happened, we won't be able to make sense of what will happen. As Forster notes, sticking with his example: 'If by the time the queen dies, we have forgotten the existence of the king, we shall never make out what killed her' (*Aspects*, p. 87). There is always an element of mystery to plot because we have to wait to find out why events occurred in the way they did. We are constantly revising our opinion of them in the light of new information but it is not until the end of the novel that we can see how everything fits into place. The complete sequence of events, the overall design, has an aesthetic quality which means we have to see plot in relation to pattern as well as story.

We mentioned earlier that the novel was an unstable entity and nowhere more so than in the tension between plot and character. Plot is about action, character is about thought. In the drama a character is revealed by what they do, in the novel by what they think. Of course characters in a novel express themselves through their behaviour, but not completely. And it is the novelist's rendering of the secret life that marks the difference between drama and the novel. Forster's interest in the inner life, incidentally, aligns him with modernism but his portrayal of it, from the standpoint of an omniscient narrator, is thoroughly traditional. Although we can question Forster's distinction – isn't psychology more important than plot in *Hamlet*? – it doesn't invalidate his point that the novelist has to struggle with the conflicting demands of characters and events. Forster's imagery of the plot 'as a sort of higher government official' is at odds with his earlier claim that it is one of the 'noble' qualities of the novel (*Aspects*, p. 86). This 'official' wants 'individuals' to show more 'public spirit' to, as it were, subordinate their own interests to those of the wider community (*Aspects*, pp. 86–7). Forster's use of these terms is highly reminiscent of those he used to describe the relationship between art and society, a relationship which we now find is internal to art itself. The plot controls the characters in much the same way as the state controls individuals. This is most in evidence as the novel nears its end where events have to be 'wound up', usually by death or marriage, and the pervasiveness of these conventions mean our 'final impression' of character is one of 'deadness' (*Aspects*, p. 94).

Forster is saddened by the fact that novels have to conclude. He is tempted to throw himself into the work to see where it will lead (*Aspects*, p. 95). Here again we can detect Forster's attraction to the experimental fictions of modernism where plot figures less prominently than it does in traditional narratives. His wish to abandon himself to his art is paralleled by characters like Lucy Honeychurch in *A Room with a View*, who long to escape convention but dare not risk censure. Similarly, Forster applauds André Gide's attempt, in *Les Faux-Monnayeurs* (1927), to replace plot with a discussion on the art of the novel, in particular whether it is possible to combine 'truth in life with truth in art' (*Aspects*, p. 98). But, in the end, these speculations are not as satisfying as the subtly worked intricacies of a good plot. Whatever its shortcomings, plot offers more security than the dizzying self-reflections of modernism.

Forster's view of character was old fashioned even at the time. The idea that novelists stood outside their characters and knew everything about them had already been rejected by modernist writers like Joyce and Woolf. They experimented with point of view and while Forster agrees that the 'power to expand and contract perception is one of the great advantages of the novel form' he does not think it as important 'as a proper mix of characters' (*Aspects*, p. 82). He begins his discussion of character by making the point that, 'since the novelist is a human being there is an affinity between him and his subject matter which is absent in many other forms of art' (*Aspects*, p. 54).

Neither the painter nor the sculptor *need* represent human beings while the musician cannot represent them even if she or he wanted to. Later Forster comments that 'the more the arts develop, the more they depend on each other for definition' and one of his favourite metaphors for the novel is music, which is 'the nearest parallel' (*Aspects*, p. 149) to fiction that he can find. Having placed music furthest from fiction he now claims it is the art that comes most close to it. Forster distinguishes between characters in life and characters in novels. He claims that the main facts of human life are: 'birth, food, sleep, love and death' (*Aspects*, p. 57) but the main fact for fictional characters is their 'tireless pre-occupation with human relationships' (*Aspects*, p. 63). The most important difference between real and fictional characters is that we can know more about the latter than the former. The novelist makes visible 'the hidden life' of his or her characters while the hidden life of 'real people' remains largely invisible (*Aspects*, p. 55). This hidden life is composed of 'the pure passions, the dreams, joys, sorrows and self-communings which politeness or shame prevent [us] from mentioning' (*Aspects*, p. 56). It is here that we start to get a more precise sense of the relation between the novel and society, for fiction's focus on the inner life not only legitimises our own internal musings, perhaps even holding out the promise that we too can be known, it also reminds us of the innate complexity of human beings and thus it challenges the generally reductive representations of ourselves that we encounter in politics, popular culture, the media, and the workplace.

Which leads nicely to perhaps Forster's most famous distinction: that between 'flat' and 'round' characters. While Forster is happy to define what he means by the former, he is more reticent about the latter, preferring to define them 'by implication' (*Aspects*, p. 80). Flat characters embody a single idea or trait. An example is Mrs Micawber in Dickens' *David Copperfield* (1849–50) whose constant cry of 'I will never desert Mr Micawber' encapsulates her essence. Forster does not dismiss flat characters, partly because their constancy answers our need for permanence in art, but mostly because a good novel requires their presence as much as it does round ones. The fact that flat characters are generally comic suggests that round characters, if not tragic, are likely to be more serious. A definition of a round character emerges from Forster's discussion of Lady Bertram in Jane Austen's *Mansfield Park* (1814), which is that they respond to change. In the case of Lady Bertram this involves accepting her part in the scandalous behaviour of her daughters. So, in addition to 'being ready for an extended life' (*Aspects*, p. 79), round characters also exhibit a capacity for self-knowledge. The true test of a round character, however, is if they are 'capable of surprising in a convincing way' (*Aspects*, p. 81), which means that they offer new pleasures in contrast to the repetitive ones of the flat characters. As a final point on this matter we can say that the difference between flat and round characters is partly a class one. The humour of flat characters places them in a tradition of comic working-class types and their failure to develop also associates them with the cinema-going public whom, we remember, Forster described as the modern descendants of 'cavemen'.

Forster's distaste for criticism takes on a new intensity as he approaches the topics of fantasy and prophecy, implying that to analyse them is worse than 'peep[ing] and botanis[ing] upon our mothers' graves' (*Aspects*, p. 100) – an image that would surely intrigue a Freudian. Fantasy and prophecy are associated with the subconscious which is the crucial factor in distinguishing between the creative and the critical state. In the former 'a man is taken out of himself. He lets down as it were a bucket into his subconscious and draws up something which is normally beyond his reach. He mixes this thing with his normal experiences, and out of the mixture he makes a work of art'.[7] No such thing happens with criticism whose emphasis on conscious knowledge makes it altogether different from the art on which it comments. Summing up the difference between the two states Forster writes: 'Think before you speak is criticism's motto; speak before you think is creation's' ('Raison', p. 405).

It is perhaps because fantasy and prophecy are so closely associated with creativity that Forster's language is here even less analytic than in the rest of *Aspects*. His fear may be that to examine these topics in detail risks losing the benefits they confer. Consequently it is hard to know exactly what he means by either of them. They both have 'gods' and while they imply the supernatural, they 'need not express it' (*Aspects*, p. 106). A surprising instance of fantasy is *Ulysses* because of the use Joyce makes of 'the world of the *Odyssey*' (*Aspects*, p. 113). Forster does not particularly like Joyce because, in reaction to his Victorian predecessors, he delights in depicting filth and squalor. Once again we encounter Forster's unease with modernist works. He much prefers the classics which give us a 'restful feeling' (*Aspects*, p. 107).

Forster is as vague about prophecy as he is about fantasy. He tries to refine the distinction between them by saying that prophecy refers to 'any of the faiths that have haunted humanity' or 'a particular view of the universe' with the implication that fantasy has a more local view of the world. Prophecy itself is concerned not with predicting the future but with 'a tone of voice' (*Aspects*, p. 116). Forster's claim is that because the prophetic novelist's particular view of the universe creates his unique tone of voice, it reveals the novelist's style more than any other aspect of the novel. The serious nature of prophetic fiction requires the reader to adopt an attitude of humility and suspend their sense of humour. We shall not hear what the prophet says if we are proud nor if we laugh. This underlines a vital element of criticism, that without adapting ourselves to the character of the work, we are unlikely to appreciate what it has to offer. An example of a prophetic novel is Dostoyevsky's *The Brothers Karamazov* (1880) 'where the characters and situations stand for more than themselves' in particular they 'reach back' (*Aspects*, p. 123), though to what is not quite clear. Forster uses the words 'melting' and 'unity' to convey this experience which, he says, parallels Saint Catherine of Siena's description of the soul's relationship to God: 'God is in the soul and the soul is in God as the sea is in the fish and the fish is in the sea' (*Aspects*, p. 122). Coincidentally, Freud uses a similar image when talking about a sense of oneness with the world; he says it is an 'oceanic feeling', but instead of attributing it to religion, he locates its source in the infant's relationship with the mother.[8]

The last 'aspects' are pattern and rhythm. As we noted earlier, pattern is closely connected with plot and appeals to our aesthetic sense making us see the work as a whole. As when he was discussing Henry James, Forster's fear is that the beauty of pattern is too often achieved at the expense of life. Forster also looks for beauty in rhythm. We are back with the metaphor of music. There are two kinds of rhythm. The first is one 'we can all hear and tap to' but the second is more subtle. It arises from the relation between the movements and, while some people can certainly hear it, no one can tap to it (*Aspects*, p. 146). While it is relatively easy to find an example of the first kind of rhythm, for example the recurrence of a musical phrase in *À la recherche du temps perdu* (1913–27), Forster is unable to offer us an example of the second merely asking us to assent to the proposition that, as we read a work like Tolstoy's *War and Peace* (1865–9) 'great chords begin to sound behind us, and when we have finished every item – even the catalogue of strategies – lead a larger existence than was possible at the time' (*Aspects*, p. 150).

Opening with a commitment to the dense humanity of fiction, Forster closes *Aspects* groping for words to describe its aesthetic effect. His claim that it is the various 'items' of the novel which 'lead a larger existence' suggests he has moved from a conception of literature as life to a conception of life as literature. In doing so, it looks as if Forster has sided with the modernists after all. But we shouldn't forget that, in Forster's view of the novel, modernist elements co-exist with traditional ones. He may proclaim the virtues of character and plot but he also promotes artistic experiment and the primacy of the inner life. One problem for students of Forster's criticism, then, is to try and determine the balance between these two components of his thought. Another, is to understand the relation between Forster's casual judgements on novelists, scattered throughout the book, and his more general comments about criticism. If the human heart is our only guide to what is a good or bad novel, then what weight do we give to Forster's dismissal of Scott? On what grounds could Forster defend his opinion if it is simply a matter of whether or not he likes Scott? Without some clearly stated principles such arguments remain unresolved though, of course, the danger with a set of rules is that works are then judged according to how well they conform to them.

Forster's later critical writings differ little in kind from *Aspects*. 'The Ivory Tower' is slightly unusual because we find him looking at the political role of the writer. Forster is responding to the charge that the writer should not set himself apart from the rest of society because he or she has a duty to the community and his argument is that unless writers can 'escape' for a short time they are unlikely to produce anything that will benefit the rest of society. He refers to Marcus Aurelius, Machiavelli, and Milton to show that it is perfectly possible to reconcile an active political life with the solitude necessary for writing. The mention of these names suggests that Forster now acknowledges that we cannot view writers as if they stand outside history which he did in *Aspects*. However, he was talking about novelists there and, in any case, what still comes across most strongly in 'The Ivory Tower' is that history teaches us about human nature. We learn that man possesses both 'the herd instinct' and the 'instinct for solitude' ('Ivory', p. 119) and that both must be respected.

'The Raison d'Être of Criticism', first published in 1947 and reprinted in *Horizon* magazine the following year, is Forster's most definitive late statement on the subject, though music rather than literature is his focus. However, since we know that Forster equates the novel's effect with that of music, what he says about one applies to the other. Affection was Forster's guide to the novel and he begins this essay with the suggestion that love is the start of criticism. This may strike us as embarrassing but it contains an element of truth. Is it so unreasonable to consider love as a motive for why people are drawn to art, literature, and music? Or that it contributes to them spending their lives trying to understand and explain these things? The job of criticism is to give love full value by clarifying and controlling it. It can do this by constructing theories about particular art forms, by discussing particular works, and by stimulating us to examine them for ourselves. Nevertheless, Forster is not altogether happy with these activities for he wants to 'establish the raison d'être of criticism on a higher basis than that of public utility' ('Raison', p. 403). In particular, he would like 'to establish some spiritual parity between it and the object it criticizes' ('Raison' p. 403) but this is not possible because, as we saw earlier, the critical state does not, like the creative one, 'let buckets down into the subconscious' ('Raison', p. 405). It is this that gives art its power to transform us 'toward the condition of the person who created it' ('Raison', p. 406), an effect quite different to the restful feeling he says we get from the classics.

Criticism, then, has only a limited role in our experience of art. At best, it sharpens our senses and keeps our minds alert and, at worst, it threatens to dissipate the power of art. Its aim is always to keep emotion and imagination under control and, in this respect, it behaves rather like that official Forster used to personify plot who demanded that 'character' obey its orders. But, using the terms of Forster's argument, we can put a more positive spin on his idea of criticism. The analogy between criticism and those non-human forces of the novel, such as plot, suggests that criticism is a part of art's internal harmony as much as it is a collection of criteria brought to bear on the work from the outside. The internal harmony of art distinguishes it from everything else in human culture and is the source of its value. Everything else, Forster argues in 'Art for Art's Sake', has order imposed on it from without, but art's order comes from within.[9] This crucial distinction protects Forster from the charge that he contradicts himself. Earlier, he opposed the creation of art to the conformism of society and therefore it appeared that art was not on the side of order, but now he is saying that it is. We need to appreciate that the order of art is quite different to the order of society: one is a condition of freedom, the other is a means of curtailing it.

We have seen that criticism can belong to the order of art. But what exactly is this order? According to Forster's account of the novel, it is the relationship between repetition and variation. Flat characters are an example of repetition and round characters are an example of variation. We can also see criticism itself in terms of repetition and variation. It is a form of repetition because it reproduces at least part of the work in commenting upon it, and it is a form of variation because it reproduces the chosen part of the work in a different medium and in a different context. By varying the work even as it repeats it criticism can startle us into a new perception of the poem, painting, or piece of music that may well provoke us to love it. Criticism, in short, has the capacity to be creative and as such, it can have 'spiritual parity' with its object. Forster admits as much when he writes, in 'Does Culture Matter?', that 'the appreciator of an aesthetic achievement becomes, in his minor way, an artist'.[10]

And if criticism cannot finally be separated from creation, neither can history from art. Forster tells us that history 'develops' while art 'stands still', a distinction that is very similar to that between repetition and variation. He says that the novel needs both repetition and variation but treats art and society as if they were antithetical. What is more, he reverses his priorities.

He prefers variation to repetition in the novel while preferring the stationary nature of art to the ongoing process of history. More could be said about these reversals and shifts of valuation but the real question is this: Forster's account of the novel shows that repetition and variation are indissociable so why shouldn't the same logic apply to art and history? Wasn't it Forster himself who advised 'only connect'? For that is one of the fundamental tasks of criticism, to concentrate on the work, to make links between its different parts and thus to know it better than it can know itself. Ideally it is a process of recognition and enrichment; recognition of the work's value and enrichment of our experience of it. It is true, as Forster says, that criticism can make the work of art almost disappear, but it is equally true, as Forster doesn't quite say but *Aspects of the Novel* implies, that criticism can bring it into clearer view. And by improving our view of the work, we improve our view of the society in which it lives.

Notes

I would like to acknowledge the help of Kaye Towlson, the English librarian at De Montfort University, for her help in tracking down Forster's articles.

1. E. M. Forster, *Aspects of the Novel* (1927; Harmondsworth: Penguin, 2000). All further page references are incorporated in the text, preceded by an *Aspects* cue.
2. T. S. Eliot, 'Tradition and the Individual Talent', in *Selected Essays* (London: Faber and Faber, 1979), p. 14. Hereafter referred to as 'Tradition and the Individual Talent' with page references given in the text.
3. E. M. Forster, 'Notes on the English Character', in *Abinger Harvest* (London: Edward Arnold, 1965), pp. 11–24, p. 13. Hereafter referred to as 'Notes' with page references given in the text.
4. Virginia Woolf quoted in P. N. Furbank, *E. M. Forster: A Life* (London: Sphere Books, 1988), p. 146.
5. E. M. Forster, 'The Ivory Tower', in *London Mercury*, 39 (1938), 119–30, pp. 123, 125. Hereafter referred to as 'Ivory' with page references given in the text.
6. E. M. Forster, 'The Duty of Society to the Artist', *Listener*, 27: 694 (1942), 565–6. Hereafter referred to as 'Duty' with page references given in the text.
7. E. M. Forster, 'The Raison d'Être of Criticism', *Horizon*, 28 (1948), 37–411; quote from p. 403. Hereafter referred to as 'Raison'.
8. Sigmund Freud, *Civilisation and its Discontents*, trans. David McLintock (Harmondsworth: Penguin, 2002), p. 4.
9. E. M. Forster, 'Art for Art's Sake', in *Two Cheers for Democracy* (Harmondsworth: Penguin, 1972), pp. 96–103.
10. E. M. Forster, 'Does Culture Matter?' in *Two Cheers for Democracy*, pp. 108–14; quote from p. 113.

15

MARCIA LANDY

Filmed Forster

Five novels by Forster were adapted for the cinema in the 1980s and 1990s –
A Passage to India (1984), *A Room With A View* (1986), *Maurice* (1987),
Where Angels Fear to Tread (1991), and *Howards End* (1992). They have
all generated debate about their style and politics. These adaptations are
implicated in contemporary disagreements about the means and ends of
historicising through film, particularly about the exploitation of 'heritage'
culture. The appropriation for film of canonical literary texts from an earlier
era has been identified with the commercial values of the heritage industry
and its often retrograde or nostalgic view of British culture and politics.
Through discussion of the styles of the Forster adaptations, my chapter tests
the adequacy of this assessment.

Traditionally, discussions of literary adaptation focused on a film's fidelity
to its 'original', on the 'notion of a text as having and rendering up to
the (intelligent) reader a single, "correct" meaning which the filmmaker has
either adhered to or in some sense violated or tampered with'.[1] More recently,
this view of adaptation has altered. 'The most successful adaptations of
literature . . . aim for the spirit of the original rather than the literal letter;
they use the camera to interpret and not simply illustrate the tale; and they
exploit a particular affinity between the artistic temperament and preoccupations of the novelist and filmmaker'.[2] Filmmakers are free to alter aspects
of the source and make changes to suit their artistic and ideological predilections, and critics are free to explore 'the complex interchange among eras,
styles, nations, and subjects'.[3] Adaptation is now 'neither translation nor
interpretation, neither incarnation nor deconstruction; rather it is a mutual
and reciprocal transverse transformation that nevertheless restores neither to
its original place'.[4] In other words, the traditional hierarchy between canonical novel and commercial film, words and images, is being undermined,
and the door left open for reflection on the cultural character and effects of
adaptation.

Forster's novels are set during the Edwardian period and dramatise cleavages and contradictions in courtship, marriage, the family, and property arising from the mobile character of modernity. Forster's novelistic world is largely but not exclusively that of the upper-middle classes, and its dimensions are intimate rather than epic and monumental. Barbara Rosecrance has written of *Howards End*, 'the scale of the novel's world is small, its architecture domestic'.[5] Forster's social and cultural milieu is connected to micro-history, and this history is conveyed through character studies and through their connections to geography and landscape – houses, railway stations, places of business, universities, hotels, pensions, flowers, and gardens. The novels involve numerous allusions to art, literature, painting, and music. These references are not mere embellishment and the display of erudition: they distinguish characters within the narratives, identifying their ethical, psychological, sexual, and gendered conflicts. They are reflexive, providing insight into the novel's conception of its role as artefact, a key to the visual and auditory character of Forster's style.

Forster's novels complicate the boundaries between prevailing and countervailing images of modernity and femininity. His novelistic world, whether involving travel to Italy or, to a lesser degree, India, is English: the English characters carry their cultural baggage with them – in their physical appearance, gestures, uses of language, their intellectual (or anti-intellectual) and moral confrontations with each other. The reader is invited to contemplate the limits and possibilities of the characters' development in their confrontations with alien landscapes. In its uses of melodrama with its affective scenarios of desire, betrayal, abandonment, and fulfilment, and particularly its nuanced allusions to sight and sound, Forster's style lends itself to cinematic treatment. Sense perception is critical to the novels' exploration of the possibilities and limits of communication across national, transnational, gendered, sexual, and linguistic barriers.

That Forster's novels were not adapted to the screen during his lifetime had much to do with his resistance to their being filmed, though he did grant the rights for a television production of *A Passage to India* in 1965. His novels were finally adapted for film over a decade after his death and during the Reagan and Thatcher era, a time associated with the transition to Conservative policies of privatisation, economism, assault on the welfare state, fierce nationalism, and imperial aspirations. In Britain, the Thatcher years had the effect of polarising responses to British culture and politics: on the one hand, witnessing the production of a number of modernist films in which the cinematic image becomes a weapon, a force, to unmask the ceremonial trappings of British heritage, as exemplified by the films of Derek Jarman and Peter Greenaway;[6] on the other, the generation of a much larger number of costume dramas that reverted in more celebratory fashion to earlier moments of the national past as exemplified by *Chariots of Fire* (1981), *The Return of the Soldier* (1982), *Another Country* (1984), and the Forster adaptations set in the Edwardian era. These re-creations of Edwardian life 'occurred within a context of financial difficulty for British film and television', involving 'decline in cinema attendance, loss of American funding, inflationary constraints, and increased costs of production'.[7] From the late 1970s onward, British television found a market in American public television with *Masterpiece Theatre* and *Upstairs Downstairs* followed by a plethora of films based on classic novels.

Consonant with the production of 'quality' films was the growth of museums and the commercial development of historic sites, country houses, and gardens. British heritage had become a transnational commodity. Tourism, particularly from the USA but from other areas of the globe as well, helped to make history 'a profitable commodity in post-imperial Britain'. Specifically, the appeal of the Edwardian era may be attributable to the productions' engagement with questions of social class, gender, sexuality, and nation.[8] Andrew Higson's study, *English Heritage, English Cinema: Costume Drama Since 1980* (2003), as the title suggests, equates historical films and costume dramas, period films that include both fictional as well as historical personages.

Heritage films share certain common themes – Englishness, femininity and masculinity, heterosexuality and homosexuality. They focus on social class, particularly on the upper class, either in its decline or its ascendancy. Their retrospective look at history often involves a preoccupation with the national past, moving steadily backward from the Edwardian and Victorian eras to the Renaissance (as evidenced by several Elizabethan films and by *Shakespeare in Love* (1998)). These films share a predilection for literary sources or remakes of earlier films – among the authors selected for adaptation are Jane Austen, Henry James, Thomas Hardy, Daniel Defoe, and Forster.

Stylistically, romance is central to the narratives' dramatisation of the social, sexual, and gendered obstacles that frustrate the characters' realisation of their desires. The romantic scenarios are enhanced by the films' emphasis on costume, jewellery, décor, and *mise en scène*, a visual construction of milieu analogous to painting, particularly landscape painting, an emphasis on architecture, and a scrupulous evocation of interiors of houses with their overabundance of furniture, vases, paintings, and sculpture. The method of acting is of paramount importance. Associated with such actors as Anthony Hopkins, Helena Bonham Carter, James Wilby, Judi Dench, Rupert Graves, Prunella Scales, and Hugh Grant, among others, the heritage films align themselves with professional and theatrical intertextuality, a reflexive concern with the cinematic medium, and an authorial signature while at the same time offering a visual and auditory spectacle for the viewer.

A Passage to India

A Passage to India was the first of Forster's novels to be filmed. It had been adapted for the stage during Forster's lifetime by Santha Rama Rau and was modified for television in 1965, but Forster did not release the rights to film the novel. In 1981, John Brabourne and Richard Goodwin bought the film rights and selected David Lean as director. In his long career in British cinema, Lean worked in a variety of film genres – war films such as *In Which We Serve* (1942); adaptations of classics such as *Great Expectations* (1946) and *Oliver Twist* (1948); popular novels such as *The Bridge on the River Kwai* (1957); the woman's film exemplified by *Brief Encounter* (1945); and historical epics such as *Doctor Zhivago* (1965) and *Ryan's Daughter* (1970). Lean's final film, *A Passage to India*, is a mixture of modes – literary adaptation, melodrama, courtroom drama, mystery, and costume film.

Lean's decision to make the Marabar Caves episode central to the narrative and to give Adela Quested (Judy Davis) greater prominence in the narrative guides his adaptation of the novel. The film viewer is presented with a tidier, more focused, narrative trajectory than that found in the novel. *Passage* begins as Adela purchases tickets for her 'passage to India'. The viewer is presented with posters of India and with Adela's lingering gaze on one of the Marabar Caves. Her character is further developed through the shipboard journey she shares with Mrs Moore (Peggy Ashcroft). Their arrival in India is accompanied by spectacular scenes of the Viceroy and his wife being greeted by orderly images of Indian troops, crowds on balconies, and a procession. These scenes visually establish the former glory of the British on a scale missing in the novel and situate Adela as voyeur within the imperial landscape.

While characters such as Aziz, Fielding, and Mrs Moore are transferred to the film intact and while episodes such as Mrs Moore's encounter with Aziz in the mosque, the 'bridge party', the tea party at Fielding's, the Marabar Caves, the trial and its aftermath, and the reunion of Fielding and Aziz are included in the cinematic narrative, the film establishes its own conceptions of character and landscape. In his portraits of India, Forster attempted to 'internalize the symbolic landscape of India to make it more human'.[9] The film veers in another direction: it identifies the 'human' more specifically with Adela's femininity and, further, links femininity to colonialism. Thus, the viewer is given a depiction suited to cultural politics since the 1980s particularly in relation to critical controversies concerning feminism, identity politics, and social power. The viewer is also treated to the stylistic signature of Lean's filmmaking, its uses of history and romance. In its adaptation of the novel, Lean's *A Passage to India* is a revisionist reflection on postcoloniality. Coming after the independence of India – only a future prospect in the novel – the film's historical treatment can be seen through the lens of popular cinema and through Lean's melodramatic and epic predilections.

Arthur Lindley has discussed the film as a work that 'straightens' Forster out in heterosexual and narrative terms.[10] In Lindley's view, Forster's novel sets out to subvert melodramatic conventions that involve an admirable female protagonist and an affective treatment of her buried desires, her pain and suffering, and vulnerability to social pressures. In the Lean film, Adela, rather than being priggish and ordinary, is attractive. Her character is 'softer, dreamier, more emotional, and more sexually responsive than her original'.[11] If Forster's novel works against the grain of the sentimental romantic novel, the Lean film, according to Lindley, repositions the protagonist in this genre and the other characters correspondingly. For example, the Fielding character is repositioned as heroic (James Fox), while Aziz (Victor Banerjee) is reduced to a minor role as agent of the melodrama, thus subordinating, if not eliminating, the important homosexual aspects of their relationship.

Although Lean certainly did not want to portray rape explicitly (a bizarre idea suggested to him by a Hollywood producer), he did want to make the fantasy of rape central to the film's melodrama. While the novel only makes reference to Adela's illness on the day of her visit to the caves, the film diagnoses her experience as sexual hysteria. Adela's bike ride through the countryside to the temple at Khajuraho is pivotal in characterising her sexual fantasies. There she views statues of men and women in various sexual embraces, culminating in her being chased away by the licentious temple monkeys. The eroticism of this episode is reinforced by a night-time scene of her in bed, intercut with images of her dancing with Ronny, of windblown curtains, and a flashback to the sculptures, ending with a loud clap of thunder as she rolls over.

Forster laid the groundwork for merging the white woman's fantasies about the 'Orient' with fear and desire about miscegenation. Adela's position is complicated by her desire for adventure, by her ambivalence toward Ronny Heaslop (Nigel Havers), and by her lack of insight about India. Adela is the novel's instrument for prising open prevailing racist fantasies, exposing how representations of the 'other' are central to the management of a colonised culture. The Marabar Caves are the crucial element in the novel's investigation of difference and its consequences, revealing the limits of both verbal and visual language, and the difficulties of translating one culture to another. Lean's film, by recasting the Marabar incident (by eliminating the role of a guide who disappears after Adela flees), links imperialism to the hysterical fantasies of a young woman with limited sexual experience, who becomes aroused by India, and who finds no outlet for her sexuality in her relationship with her fiancé. Thus, the figure of woman becomes a sign of abnormality: 'The ideological point is . . . to disavow the moral culpability for a tainted history and to sanitize that history by re-enacting colonialism as a female disease and thus confer responsibility onto the female'.[12]

A Passage to India seems compatible with the properties assigned by critics to heritage cinema. The film is legitimised by canonical authorial literary and cinematic signatures – both Forster's and Lean's – and with 'quality' production. Both novel and film address British imperialism. In the treatment of natural landscape, architecture, and ritual, the film highlights the spectacle of former imperial power. The film does not suppress but reinterprets political conflict in sexual terms, offering a 'fantasy of extravagance, decadence, promiscuity, and passion'.[13] The portrait of female sexuality is the hinge on which the film turns for rendering the past comprehensible to its contemporary audience. The film's adaptation of the novel is not a case of infidelity to the literary text or of an inevitable disparity between literature and film, a distinction between words and images – but, in its adaptation of the Forster source, a case of providing an interpretation of the past tailored to the cultural politics of the 1980s.

Where Angels Fear to Tread

Charles Sturridge's film adaptation of Where Angels Fear to Tread (1991) is tightly tied to the chronology, events, and dialogue of the Forster novel. The director was not new to adaptations of canonical literary works, having collaborated with Derek Granger on a celebrated television production of Evelyn Waugh's Brideshead Revisited (1981). His adaptation of Waugh's A Handful of Dust appeared in 1988. Forster's satiric comedy of Edwardian life is indeed (as is A Room with a View) cinematic with its carefully delineated descriptions of the Italian countryside, the town of Monteriano, and character portraits that are transferable to the cinema screen. Tourism is the dominant trope of both novel and film. Conversations between Harriet (Judy Davis) and Philip (Rupert Graves), and Philip and Caroline (Helena Bonham Carter) take place during carriage rides as does the death of the infant kidnapped by Harriet. The journeys through the Italian landscape become the measure of the stages of the characters' spiritual transformations, for better or worse, as they move farther away from the constraints of English life typified by the town of Sawston and by the matriarchal Mrs Herriton (Barbara Jefford).

Widowed Lilia Herriton's (Helen Mirren) trip to Italy, leaving her young daughter Irma in the care of the Herritons, her impulsive marriage to Gino Carella (Giovanni Guidelli), her disillusionment with Italy and her new spouse, her subsequent death in childbirth, and her sister-in-law Harriet's implacable determination to kidnap the baby, Lilia and Gino's heir, that results in the infant's death, are reminiscent of the Gothic horror tale. But both the novel and film have different, more philosophic, and comically satiric designs on the characters as manifested in the juxtaposition of Philip and Caroline to Mrs Herriton and Harriet and their differing perceptions of inheritance, art, and ethics. In the case of Harriet and her mother, the world can be reduced to property and propriety, in the case of the unfortunate Lilia to a nostalgic and excessive sense of romance and rebellion. The threatening but enigmatic and physically attractive character of Gino animates Philip's and Caroline's different spiritual journeys.

The film provides expansive views of the Tuscan landscape in contrast to tightly framed and constraining shots of English interiors, albeit equipped with maps, letters, postcards, and Baedeker guidebooks. The décor of the hotel and of Lilia and Gino's house are presented economically, uncluttered by objects. Lilia's defiant walk in the countryside, after being ordered by Gino not to leave the house unaccompanied, dramatises her isolation from the Italian milieu and her growing sense of entrapment. In her escape from the severe restrictions of Sawston and her fantasy of a new life in Italy through marriage to Gino, Lilia has opted for escape into pleasure and romance, but she fails to achieve gratification and awareness of the choice she has made. Tragically, she only dimly sees beyond the physical world into the social and cultural intricacies of the life she has adopted.

Harriet's role is the focal point of the film's satiric treatment of melodrama. Her journey to Italy casts her as avenging angel, a role earlier adopted but then abandoned by Philip and Caroline. The treatment of the 'night at the opera' scene can be viewed as exemplary of the novel's exploration of differences between Harriet, on the one hand, and Philip and Caroline on the other. Harriet's responses to *Lucia di Lammermoor* are highly affective. She is agitated by the audience, the singer, and by the bouquet and billet-doux that drops in her lap, culminating in her statement, 'Call this classical? . . . It's not even respectable!' (*WAFT*, p. 96). Harriet is neither an unsympathetic nor a negligible character. Despite her judgemental attitude toward Gino, her impatience to get hold of the baby and return to Sawston, her blindness to the landscape, her contempt for the local opera performance, and her kidnapping of the baby that leads to catastrophe, she is the instrument for altering Philip and Caroline. In the role of Harriet, Judy Davis was described by one critic as a 'pinched xenophobe . . . with an array of mannerisms that make rather more meat out of Harriet than is provided for by Forster'.[14] Yet, in appearance, gesture, and action, Harriet's antagonistic character is as necessary to the novel and the film as are Mrs Herriton, Philip, Caroline, and Gino.

By contrast, Caroline and Philip are forced to confront passion, desire, and different, if impure, social and ethical imperatives, and the necessity of taking sides on the moral and psychic consequences of their decisions. The portraits of Caroline and Philip reveal a journey away from conventional moral and aesthetic norms, a quest for a more expansive vision of life. The Dante-esque 'selva oscura' of their own dark night in the woods converts Philip and Caroline to a more generous, less judgemental view of life. However, the film, like the novel, does not provide a happy ending in the romantic union of Philip and Caroline, though they are allied by their earned greater ability to reflect on life, love, desire, and death.

Where Angels Fear to Tread was neither a major success at the box office nor was it critically acclaimed. The onus of the criticism fell on the film's direction and on the acting. One critic described how the actors 'merely bellow their lines or otherwise strut and fret through their parts in one-note characterisations. Here, the mores and pieties of Britain's upper classes are reduced to banalities'. Similarly, Sturridge's direction was described as 'heavy handed'.[15] If *A Passage to India* charts its own cultural and political course in adapting the novel, *Where Angels Fear to Tread* adheres to a form of adaptation that capitalises on and relies heavily on its source. Reviewer Terence Rafferty complained that the film is a 'textbook example of bad literary adaptation. It marches us through the book's events with a grim literal-mindedness that makes the story seem foolish – naïve, old-fashioned, clumsily symbolic'.[16] This dismissive judgement does not, however, examine the character and effects of the 'grim literal-mindedness' of the Sturridge adaptation. The film appears to endorse a notion of 'fidelity' in adaptation as homage to the timeless character of the novel, presenting the novel as a cinematic object to be consumed unchanged in its entirety. That the film largely failed to engage its audiences points to its failure to meet contemporary audience expectations. For example, the film's treatment of milieu, character, and décor does not offer images of an Edwardian past that capitalises on the visual pleasures of heritage filmmaking. More problematic is the failure of the adaptation to interrogate that past. The adaptation is not critically self-reflexive about its historical distance from its source: 'instead we are placed back in a world whose evasions and silences are accepted as natural'.[17]

A Room with a View

The most commercially and critically successful adaptations of Forster novels have been those made by producer Ismail Merchant and director James Ivory, particularly *A Room with a View* and *Howards End*. *A Room with a View* followed Merchant Ivory's adaptations of *The Europeans* (1979) and *The Bostonians* (1984), films that are scrupulously researched and fastidious in their creation of period settings. Similar to *Where Angels Fear to Tread*, *A Room with a View* focuses on English tourism abroad and links it to portraits of life in England, remaining close to the narrative events, characters, thematic material, and dialogue from the novel. While *A Room with a View* is similarly faithful to the Forster novel, its style is self-conscious about its status as an adaptation and an historical text, even adopting ornate mock-Victorian chapter titles from the novel to structure its own 'chapters'.

Novel and film trace Lucy Honeychurch's (Helena Bonham Carter) journey from Italy to England and her return to the Italian pension at the end. The scenes at the Pension Bertolini introduce the reader to the diverse cast of characters and into the complexities of Edwardian social life through the trope of travel. The perspectives of the characters are centred on social distinctions and questions of life and art. The film, like the novel, employs a wide range of references to painting, sculpture, architecture, and music to explore the ways in which each of the English characters confronts (or resists) choices about his or her life. At the centre of the film's treatment of different cultural and social perspectives, the Reverend Beebe (Simon Callow) tells Lucy – after hearing her play the piano – 'If Miss Honeychurch ever takes to life as she plays, it will be very exciting – both for us and for her' (*RV*, p. 31). His comment is proleptic.

Free-spirited George Emerson (Julian Sands) and his outspoken father (Denholm Elliott) are at one extreme of the film's exploration of the conflict between passion for life and art as sexual sublimation. Lucy's initial response to George is flight. Her decision to avoid him is reinforced after his rescue of her when she faints in the Piazza Signoria on seeing the stabbing of a young man and after George's impulsive kissing of her that follows his rescue. Lucy is unable to evade him and on the day of the English group's outing to the Tuscan countryside he kisses her again. Her simultaneously troubled attraction to him and her repulsion from him is temporarily resolved by her decision to leave Italy, a decision abetted by her cousin Charlotte (Maggie Smith) and by her impulsive engagement to Cecil Vyse (Daniel Day Lewis) upon her return home to England.

Lucy's ambivalence toward her fiancé is symptomatic of her larger conflict over passion, more explicitly over sexual desire. While she ultimately breaks her engagement to Cecil, she refuses, at first, to contemplate a future with George. Her mother admonishes her, 'How you do remind me of Charlotte' – her spinster cousin and Lucy's companion in Italy. In the context of both novel and film, celibacy appears problematic, a violation of the desired union of aesthetics, passion, and life articulated by Mr Beebe and by the narrator. Lucy's embarrassed attempts at escape after her broken engagement, her plan for undertaking another journey, this time to Greece with the Misses Alan, are scorned by Lucy's mother as well as by Mr Beebe and Mr Emerson as a sign of her becoming a spinster like Charlotte and the Misses Alan. No possibility of passion can be envisioned in such a life, and the suggestion of lesbianism is muted by George's frequent, and to her troublesome, reappearances.

The film does not exclude homosexual passion. The nude men – Freddy Honeychurch, George, and Mr Beebe – jumping and splashing in the Sacred Lake are referred to by the narrator as being 'after the fashion of the nymphs in *Götterdämmerung*' (RV, p. 130) and as a foreshadowing of the Garden of Eden 'when we no longer despise our bodies' (RV, p. 126). Cecil is excluded from the group, treated in mocking fashion. In the film, as played by Daniel Day Lewis, Cecil is set apart from the other men. He is not part of the ritual bathing at the Sacred Lake. He is barred as well from Lucy and George's marital world of bliss. He is not malevolent but a caricature, an extreme instance of aestheticism. He regards Lucy as a 'Leonardo Da Vinci woman', disdains sports, and lives only through his books and music. In the novel, the narrator describes Cecil thus: 'For all his culture, Cecil was an ascetic at heart, and nothing in his love became him like the leaving of it' (RV, p. 173). Mr Beebe's character bears resemblance to Fielding and to Philip Herriton.

A Room with a View creates a pictographic sense of the Italian and English landscapes through selection of prominent historical sites, shot in long and medium distance. The landscapes resemble paintings, but the scenes are not static. A moving camera captures different views of the Pension Bertolini, the Piazza Signoria, Santa Croce, and the landscapes near Fiesole, Summer Street, and Windy Corner. Similarly, a moving camera situates the characters in relation to the interior landscapes, giving the scenes the quality of a painting tableau, grouping characters in various poses. The objects in the rooms – paintings, sculptures, vases, books, photographs, postcards, mirrors – are indicative of the film's reflexivity about its own status as an aesthetic artefact, as are references to Miss Lavish's (Judi Dench) novel and her comments on novelising.

Processed for highly saturated colour, the film calls attention to landscape, clothing, and décor. The highly nuanced acting reinforces the tableau quality of the characters' posing in their milieu. The delivery of their lines is dramatic but not melodramatically excessive, measured and never hasty in delivery, attentive to received diction and especially to the behavioural constraints of their roles. The actors' use of facial expression and gesture are carefully calculated to convey their sense of social status and their personal idiosyncrasies. For example, in contrast to Julian Sands's George Emerson, whose movements are loose and who speaks in wild, erratic phrases, Daniel Day Lewis's characterisation of the aesthete Cecil is highly choreographed: his gestures are mechanical, and his words delivered less as casual conversation and more as if he were reading a novel. Similarly, Maggie Smith's gestures and speech are stylised, choreographed to convey her abjections, obsequiousness, and veiled aggressiveness. The acting is enhanced by the costuming – its texture and colours – as well as by association with architecture and natural landscape. If, for Forster, ethics and aesthetics are, ideally, united, the film makes every effort to call attention to aesthetic artefacts, and to the role of cinema as the instrument of art appreciation.

The enthusiastic critical and commercial success of the film both gratified and surprised its creators, 'grossing $34 million in the US and Canada alone, and over $60 million worldwide'.[18] The film also received numerous nominations for awards in Britain, Italy, and America, and the consensus was that 'Everything about this film is delightful, the sets, costumes, photography, and James Ivory's subtle direction'.[19] It was also praised for the excellence of the actors and for its use of music, particularly Kiri Te Kanawa's arias from *Gianni Schicchi* and *La Rondine*. Reviewers applauded the film's formal excellence without discussion of its address of contemporary culture and its treatment of the past. In short, the adaptation produced a visual feast for audiences hungry for history and spectacle, providing different modes of critical engagement for sectors of the audience. Its reconstruction of the Edwardian world affords the pleasures of an escape into the past similar to the experience of visiting a museum or concert hall. Or it may be conceived in terms of romantic fantasies identified with popular entertainment or with advertisements for travel and tourism. Or it may generate favourable responses from certain viewers for its investigation of familial, gendered, or sexual conflicts.

Maurice

The Merchant Ivory production of *Maurice* is constructed around episodes that highlight the diverse transformations in the characters of Maurice (Hugh Grant) and Clive (James Wilby). The film maintains the novel's exploration of homosexuality. It also follows episodes from the novel, including Mr Ducie's (Simon Callow) lecture on the mysteries of the male and female bodies, the love affair between Clive and Maurice at Cambridge, Clive's conversion and marriage, the pressures of Maurice's attempts at seeking normality, the machinations of Mr Borenius (Peter Eyre) to eradicate fornication, and Maurice's sexual relationship with Scudder (Rupert Graves).

Maurice the novel is character-driven, focusing on Maurice Hall and Clive Durham's differing responses to their homoerotic desires. For many critics, the novel is, if not a failed enterprise, a pallid attempt at writing. Barbara Rosecrance writes that this is a novel 'whose interest lies not in its artistic claim, which is slight, but rather in its expression of an inner conflict whose psychological and social implications reflect their historical context and reveal heretofore hidden aspects of the man [Forster]'.[20] The complex interrelations between the characters and the social milieu characteristic of the novel *A Room with a View* are channelled into the protagonist's quest for male companionship. Maurice's journey entails his exploration of physical passion. His quest for experiencing '"the unspeakable vice of the Greeks"' (*M*, p. 38) involves a painful exploration of the pleasures of the body until Maurice confirms 'his spirit in its perversion' by cutting 'himself off from the congregation of normal man' (*M*, p. 185). The novelistic portrait of Maurice appears to be an attempt at deepening, if not repudiating, chaste male figures such as Philip Herriton in *Where Angels Fear to Tread*, and Cecil Vyse and Mr Beebe in *A Room with a View*.

The film appears to have other designs on its audiences. In his love for Clive, nourished in the atmosphere of university life at Cambridge, Maurice experiences a form of bliss heretofore denied him, unaware, as yet, that this involves a suppression of the body. Clive's Platonism and his conversion to a 'normal' life after his illness and journey to Greece threaten to destroy Maurice who is left to pick up the pieces of his life without his lover. Clive's conversion leads Maurice first to explore his 'malady'. He consults with Dr Barry only to learn that what he experiences sexually is to remain unspeakable 'rubbish'. Maurice's trip to Mr Lasker-Jones also ends in failure.

One of the major departures of the film from the novel is the insertion of scenes of Risley's (Mark Tandy) arrest for solicitation of a guardsman, his appeal to Clive for aid, and his trial. While the film calls attention to the illegality of homosexuality at the time, it also provides a stronger motive than provided in the novel for Clive's conversion to 'normality'. In general, as critics have noted, the film distances the viewer from Clive and Maurice's internal dilemmas, shifting the focus to the social and political world against which Maurice rebels and to which Clive succumbs.[21]

As described by film critics Mark Finch and Richard Kwietniowski, *Maurice* is exemplary of art house movies: it is a costume drama with a 'fastidious *mise en scène* and suitable star image'; it is an adaptation from a 'hallowed' literary source; and a treatment of homosexuality that 'offers a respectable combination of sexuality and titillation'.[22] In their view, the film can be profitably regarded as a melodrama, a weepie, that features 'tears and queers', ending with the inevitable melodramatic 'if only things had been different' between Clive and Maurice.[23] The 'happy ending' to Maurice's dilemma is provided through the sexual encounter with the game-keeper, Alec Scudder, enabling Maurice to reject his family, his economic position, and social intercourse with members of his own class. However, both novel and film leave the reader with a series of questions concerning Maurice's never-repudiated love for Clive and his physical desire for a lower-class man.

The happy ending, like all happy endings, is ambivalent. Actually, the film has two endings, one being Maurice's unrequited love for Clive, the other, Maurice and Alec's amorous reunion. In the order of events, the viewer is first presented with Maurice's rebellious confrontation with Clive where he confesses his relationship with Alec. Following this encounter, there is the amorous reunion of Maurice and Alec. The men kiss as Scudder utters the romantic formula that 'they need never be parted'. But the last scenes are of Clive, framed by a window, with a brief flashback to an image of Maurice at Cambridge waving at Clive as Anne (Phoebe Wilcox) comes to him and rests her head on his shoulder. The ending leaves in suspension the conflicts portrayed throughout the narrative, involving physical desire and social con-formity. The spectator is left with two views of relationships – one of the two embracing men, Alec and Maurice, and the other of the immobile Clive and Anne framed by the window – that can serve to elicit different inter-pretations on the part of viewers – a happy ending of romantic realisation or an unhappy ending conveyed in the image of the frozen heterosexual couple.

Similarly to *A Room with a View*, *Maurice* places great emphasis on vision, on architecture, décor, rooms with a view, and social gatherings that frame the milieu of the middle and upper classes. The film relies on strategies of distantiation. Often assigned to household servants, spectatorship serves to underscore, even create suspense, about illicit encounters between men. The growing relationship of Clive and Maurice is intercut with the many views of Cambridge's cloistered walks, stately chapels, and dining rooms. The episodes at the university are intercut with images of Maurice's family home, later of Clive's at Pendersleigh. The houses are first photographed in medium long shot, so that they are set within a gracious landscape; the inte-riors are carefully photographed to call attention to the décor replete with stained glass windows, stairways, period furniture, and elaborately set tables for the ritualised meals. The homosexual relationships are rendered visually acceptable, since they are identified with an earlier moment in history and integrated into an upper-class social milieu that is presented as respectable and visually appealing.

Despite its dependence on the characters, events, and dialogue from the novel, *Maurice* can be accused neither of literalism nor of infidelity to its source. With the exception of the insertion of Risley's arrest and trial and the reversal of the order of Maurice's encounters with Alec and Clive at the end, the film adheres to the novel, even to its indistinct struggle to portray homosexuality. In its style, its tableau rendering of social encounters, and its elaborately constructed exteriors and interiors, *Maurice* can be likened to a moving image museum, permitting its curious viewers to visually roam a landscape often restricted to the privileged. Nonetheless, the narrative is not seamless: the style also reveals the presence of another heritage, involving the transgression of sexual and social class identity and conformity.

Howards End

Arguably, the most deftly orchestrated of the Merchant Ivory adaptations of Forster is *Howards End* (1992). As in their other Forster adaptations, the sense of place is tightly linked to character. The inheritance of property in *Howards End* is allegorically entwined with issues of social class, family, national identity, and modernity. Family is at the basis of the struggle over inheritance. The film focuses on three families, the Schlegels, the Wilcoxes, and the Basts. The Schlegels, of mixed German and English ancestry, include the rational, pragmatic, but empathetic Margaret (Emma Thompson), the impulsive Helen (Helena Bonham Carter) who battles in the name of social-ism, economic justice, and social responsibility, their effeminate brother Tibby (Adrian Ross Magenty), and their Aunt Juley (Prunella Scales). Helen is the fulcrum of the film's melodrama and its gendered politics, although Margaret is the weightier character.

The Wilcoxes are represented by the first Mrs Wilcox, Ruth (Vanessa Redgrave), a spectre from the past, and the patriarchal Henry (Anthony Hopkins), who, according to Helen, is a man who can 'reconcile science with religion . . . talk of the survival of the fittest, and cut down the salaries of their clerks and stunt the independence of all who may menace their comfort' (*HE*, p. 189). The entire family – Wilcox's daughter Evie (Jemma Redgrave), the sons Paul (Joseph Bennett) and Charles (James Wilby), and Charles' abject wife, Dolly (Susie Lindeman) – is portrayed as unimaginative, snob-bish, and obsessed with property and class propriety. The lives of the Wilcoxes and Schlegels become intertwined through Ruth Wilcox, who, bonding in friendship with Margaret, leaves Howards End to Margaret in a hastily scrawled bequest. Margaret marries Henry and ultimately inherits Howards End.

The third family, the Basts, is comprised of Leonard (Samuel West), an insurance company clerk with a desire to better his social and intellectual status, and his wife, Jacky (Nicola Duffett), a one-time (possibly continuing) prostitute and demanding wife, whose lives become tied to the Schlegels', thanks to Helen's mistaken appropriation of Leonard's umbrella after a Beethoven concert. Leonard and Jacky are brought into the Wilcox orbit through Henry's mistaken advice to Helen and Margaret about the solvency of the insurance company for which Leonard works. Leonard quits the firm and thereafter becomes unemployable. In championing the Basts and seeking to make restitution for Henry's error, Helen recklessly brings the Basts to Evie's wedding to confront Henry with his moral obligation to Leonard and inadvertently exposes Henry's sexual infidelity to his first wife in his liaison with Jacky. Thus, the fate of the three families becomes further intertwined and altered in the narrative's undermining of social propriety and traditional lines of inheritance.

Helen's sexual encounter with Leonard ends in her becoming pregnant with his child, producing the violence at Howards End that results in Leonard's inadvertent death at Charles's hands. The arrest of his son humbles Henry, thereby leaving the way open for Margaret to finally become the acknowledged master of Howards End with Helen and her child as guests. As an 'intruder', she inherits the property not by virtue of biological ancestry but by her love of the land (like Henry's first wife) and her ability to affirm ethical and properly humane behaviour. The film ends on a tenuous vision of reconciliation of the Wilcox family with Margaret and of Margaret's reconciliation with Henry. The final image of the film with Helen and children (the local farmer's son is also present) is set in a large open field, the pastoral view disturbed by sights and sounds of a mowing machine. As the image recedes, the viewer is left with uncertainty about the future of the house and its inhabitants but with a vivid visual memory of the English landscape.

The Merchant Ivory film has been acknowledged as one of the finest examples of adaptation from a canonical literary work. The film earned numerous awards in both the US and UK for best actress, screen adaptation, directing, art direction, and best picture.[24] Reviews of the film were largely, though not uniformly, positive.[25] *Howards End* is regarded as a work that best exemplifies the qualities of heritage filmmaking in its treatment of character, natural landscape, architecture, and décor. The casting of the characters is typical of Merchant Ivory's use of actors who are identified with their own or other directors' costume dramas. The actors are not glamorous; their successful acting (the case also in *A Room with a View*) is dependent on the restraint and delicacy of their delivery. From the earliest scene of Mrs Wilcox wandering in the garden at Howards End with her dress trailing gracefully behind her as she surveys the house, to the final scenes at Howards End where the tragedy of Leonard Bast climaxes, the film orchestrates the relationship of character, landscape, and inheritance. The film's self-conscious and detailed re-creation of the Edwardian milieu is visible in the frequent framing of the various architectural sites – Wickham Place, the Wilcox town flat in the same street, Oniton, the Porphyrion Insurance Company, the department store, the concert hall, Oxford, and Howards End.

The architectural landscape of the country and the city as described in the novel is symptomatic of deep-seated transformations in the national landscape and in English culture and society. As the novel's narrator contemplates: 'The Age of Property holds bitter moments even for a proprietor' (*HE*, p. 146). Furthermore, 'The feudal ownership of land did bring dignity, whereas the modern ownership of movables is reducing us again to a nomadic horde' (*HE*, p. 146). In the film, the contrast between the traditional countryside and the modernity of the city is conveyed through images of the telegraph, the railway station, the sound of trains in the Basts' cramped lodgings, automobiles, and the movement of people on the street. The film's uses of colour and lighting are instrumental in developing the contrast between country and city. The Basts' lodgings are dark and claustrophobic, while Leonard's fantasies of escape, nourished by his readings of such writers as George Meredith, are identified with an expansive natural landscape conveyed through bright colours – greens, yellows, lavenders, and blues. The wedding party to which Helen brings the uninvited Basts poignantly highlights their being out of place in the upper-middle-class environment, and Leonard's elimination from the narrative by death, buried under the fallen bookcase, serves as commentary on his being destroyed by the culture to which he had aspired – even if his son will inherit Howards End.

While reviewers have praised the consummate artistry of Merchant Ivory's adaptation of *Howards End*, responses to the film's treatment of national history and identity are mixed. For some critics, the film is 'a conservative, nostalgic representation of a traditional, elite English identity'.[26] The film is 'the most accomplished of the breed' that 'offers escape into an imaginary paradise'.[27] The reviewer for the *New York Review of Books* registered reservations: '[T]he war between the Schlegels and the Wilcoxes and Forster's anger may have sunk beneath the waves of the film's visual beauty'.[28] And according to Mary Katherine Hall, 'the novel recognises and problematises culture's relationship to capitalism, the film reifies and sacralises culture'.[29] Her comments suggest a profound uneasiness about heritage filmmaking. Other critics regard *Howards End* and other 'heritage' films in a less totalising fashion, as refusing 'the essentialism of pure, authentic identities', and dramatising rather 'the unfixity and instability of identity'.[30]

Epilogue

Critical responses to the five Forster adaptations reveal that adaptation can never be innocent or value free. Strict fidelity of film to novel, if even possible given the differences between the two forms of expression, is no longer the prime criterion in evaluations of adaptation. Conversely, cinematic liberties taken with a novel are not necessarily a wanton sign of disrespect for or a violation of the literary source. The current critical literature has complicated adaptation by connecting it to a re-examination of the meaning of authorship, canonicity, the text's position in different historical, national, and cultural moments, and the differing modes of production and reception for the works. The Forster adaptations reveal significant conceptual differences from each other. Lean's *A Passage to India* in its epic and melodramatic address of British history is revisionist, offering a gender-inflected view of history. The film is not merely nostalgic for the earlier glory of empire: it isolates femininity as a means of reinterpreting failures of the past.

In contrast to Lean's treatment of a Forster novel, Sturridge's *Where Angels Fear to Tread* is an adaptation that adheres tightly to the source. Intentionality aside, in its apparent fidelity to the Forster novel the film offers an implicit interpretation of the uses of the past as inherited from the novel, constituting a commentary on adaptation. This form of adaptation is antiquarian in its respect for the literary text and its historical moment. It implies that the landscape and its characters are transparent, can speak for themselves without the filmmaker's interference. The film uses the technology of cinema to do justice to the literature. Unlike the Lean and Merchant Ivory films, the Sturridge adaptation is not self-critical or reflexive about its relation to its source. It is also not inclined to monumentality or to the opulence of spectacle.

The three Merchant Ivory films bear markings identified with heritage filmmaking in their attention to landscape, architecture, *mise en scène*, costuming, intertextuality, acting styles, editing, camera work, uses of colour, and music. In each of the three films, romance plays a central role, though sensuality (even in the love scenes in *Maurice*) is attached less to the bodies of the male and female characters and more to their appearance as works of art in a highly ornate milieu. Each of the adaptations, to a greater or lesser degree, situates conflicts over femininity and sexuality at its centre, and each alludes to homoeroticism, although only *Maurice* takes up the theme overtly. In the Lean version of *A Passage to India* the figure of woman serves to account for the undoing of empire. In *A Room with a View* and *Howards End* femininity is central to a utopian vision of a benevolent society perhaps as a concession to contemporary post-feminist audiences. The Merchant Ivory adaptations are connected to both the novelist's and filmmakers' pervasive struggles with aestheticism and life, theatricality and 'reality'. In the case of Forster's novels, this struggle was identified with cultural and political questions concerning ethical values and the role of art. The contemporary return to the past with Forster's novels – as embodied in Merchant Ivory's cinema – takes place within a cultural and political landscape different from both the novel and its adaptation. Both are now faced with the prospect of being assimilated into the moving image museum identified with television and the Internet, and, hence, with disturbing questions about the meaning and role of both the literary and cinematic 'heritage'.

Notes

1. Brian McFarlane, *Novel to Film: An Introduction to the Theory of Adaptation* (Oxford: Clarendon Press, 1996), p. 8.
2. Neil Sinyard, '"Lids Tend to Come Off": David Lean's Film of *A Passage to India*', in *The Classic Novel: From Page to Screen*, ed. Robert Giddings and Erica Sheen (Manchester: Manchester University Press, 2000), pp. 147–63. Quote from p. 147.
3. Dudley Andrew, 'The Well-Worn Muse: Adaptation in Film History and Theory', in *Narrative Strategies: Original Essays in Film and Prose Fiction* (Macomb: Western Illinois Press, 1980), pp. 9–19. Quote from p. 16.
4. Kamilla Elliott, *Rethinking the Novel/Film Debate* (Cambridge: Cambridge University Press, 2003), p. 229.
5. Barbara Rosecrance, *Forster's Narrative Vision* (Ithaca, NY and London: Cornell University Press, 1982), p. 105.
6. Peter Wollen, 'The Last Wave: Modernism in the British Films of the Thatcher Era', in *Fires Were Started: British Cinema and Thatcherism*, ed. Lester Friedman (Minnesota: Minnesota University Press, 1993), pp. 35–52.
7. D. L. LeMahieu, 'Imagined Contemporaries: Cinematic and Televised Dramas about the Edwardians in Great Britain and the United States, 1967–1985', *Historical Journal of Film, Radio, Television*, 10:3 (1990), 243–57. Quote from p. 245.
8. LeMahieu, 'Imagined Contemporaries', pp. 245–7.
9. Sara Suleri, 'The Geography of *A Passage to India*', in *E. M. Forster*, ed. Harold Bloom (New York: Chelsea House, 1987), pp. 169–77. Quote from p. 170.
10. Arthur Lindley, 'Raj as Romance/Raj as Parody: Lean's and Forster's Passages to India', *Literature/Film Quarterly*, 20:1 (1992), 61–8. Quote from p. 62.
11. Lindley, 'Raj as Romance/Raj as Parody', p. 62.
12. Laura Kipnis, '"The Phantom Twitchings of an Amputated Limb": Sexual Spectacle in the Post-Colonial Epic', *Wide Angle*, 11:4 (1989), 42–51. Quote from p. 50.
13. Andrew Higson, *English Heritage, English Cinema: Costume Drama Since 1980* (Oxford: Oxford University Press, 2003), p. 84.

14. Jonathan Romney, 'Where Angels Fear to Tread', Sight and Sound, 1:3 (1991), p. 57.
15. Barbara Cramer, 'Where Angels Fear to Tread', Films in Review, 43:5–6 (May–June 1992), 184–6. Both quotes from p. 185.
16. Terrence Rafferty, 'Yes, But', in 'The Current Cinema', New Yorker (4 May 1992), pp. 74–8. Quote from p. 74.
17. Cairns Craig, 'Rooms without a View', Sight and Sound, 1:2 (July, 1991), 10–14. Quote from p. 12.
18. Robert Emmet Long, The Films of Merchant Ivory (New York: Harry N. Abrams, Publishers, 1997), p. 145.
19. Pat Anderson, 'A Room with a View', Films in Review, 36:6–7 (June–July 1986), pp. 361–2. Quote from p. 362.
20. Rosecrance, Forster's Narrative Vision, p. 155.
21. Margaret Goscilo, 'Ivory-Merchant's Maurice', Literature/Film Quarterly, 17:2 (1989), 99–108. Quote from pp. 102–3.
22. Mark Finch and Richard Kwietniowski, 'Melodrama and "Maurice": Homo Is Where the Het Is', Screen, 29:3 (Summer 1988), 72–80. Quote from p. 72.
23. Ibid., p. 79.
24. Frank Magill (ed.), Magill's Cinema Annual: A Survey of the Films of 1992 (Pasadena: Salem Press, 1993), pp. 486–9.
25. Higson, English Heritage, English Cinema, pp. 174–9.
26. Higson, English Heritage, English Cinema, p. 155.
27. Geoff Brown, 'Paradise Found and Paradise Lost: The Course of British Realism', in The British Cinema Book, ed. Robert Murphy (London: BFI Publishing, 1997), pp. 187–97. Quote from p. 196.
28. Noel Annan, 'Oh, What a Lovely War', New York Review of Books, 39:9 (May 14, 1992), 3–4. Quote from p. 4.
29. Mary Katherine Hall, 'The Reification of High Culture in Merchant Ivory's Howards End', Literature/Film Quarterly, 31:3 (2003), 221–5. Quote from p. 225.
30. Higson, English Heritage, English Cinema, p. 154.

16

PETER MOREY

Postcolonial Forster

Following his third and final visit to India during the last three months of 1945, Forster reflected on the increasing politicisation he had found among the educated class of a country which was on the brink of winning independence from Britain. This change appears to be behind an undercurrent of regret that runs through his essay, 'India Again', subsequently incorporated into *Two Cheers for Democracy*. Yet although the Indians he met on this trip were more interested in discussing politics than art for its own sake as Forster would have preferred, nevertheless he comments that beneath this educated crust:

> externally India has not changed. And this changelessness in her is called by some observers 'the real India'. I don't myself like the phrase 'the real India'. I suspect it. It always makes me prick up my ears. But you can use it if you want to, either for the changes in her or the unchanged. 'Real' is at the service of all schools of thought.[1]

In this statement Forster acknowledges that notions of what makes for the 'authentic' India (and authentic Indians) are sites of political controversy. He also demonstrates his own acute consciousness of the pitfalls of the tradition of writing and thinking about India of which his most famous novel, *A Passage to India*, is a part. If *Passage* is the great anti-colonial statement in English fiction of the first half of the twentieth century, and Forster the great debunker of imperial pomposity, then we can gain a stronger sense of his unfolding relationship with India, of which the novel records only a fragment, by paying attention to some of his other utterances on India. These include *The Hill of Devi* – recording his two trips to the subcontinent in 1912 and 1921 as the guest of the eccentric Maharajah of Dewas Senior, a tiny, nominally independent princely state at the heart of India – and the Indian essays collected in *Abinger Harvest* and *Two Cheers for Democracy*. In his previous novel, *Howards End*, Forster had famously remarked that the

English lacked a mythology. It might be suggested that imperialism in general, and the writing of empire – such as that of Rudyard Kipling – in particular, sought to provide such a mythology. This urge to self-dramatisation among the British in India is something Forster is always aware of and constantly holds up to scrutiny. The success or otherwise of his critique has, in recent years, been a matter of considerable debate and contention among critics in the burgeoning field of postcolonial studies.

Postcolonial criticism is one of the most recent offshoots of that process of cultural and political self-assertion that followed the post-Second World War wave of decolonisation. Although there was a concomitant increase in scholarly interest in literature from and about the former colonies in the mid-twentieth century, it might be fair to say that the publication in 1978 of *Orientalism* by the exiled Palestinian critic Edward W. Said marked a defining moment in the development of the field.[2] It set out to trace the history of western attitudes to non-western peoples, and was immediately and massively influential. Not only did the book explain the origins of many historical attitudes leading to cultural and racial prejudices, it also provided a new critical framework for understanding colonial literature. According to Said, the Orient is 'the place of Europe's richest and oldest colonies . . . and one of the deepest and most recurring images of the Other'.[3] Orientalists, for Said, are western travellers, writers, soldiers, traders, and administrators: in short, any European who produces a text in any medium about those parts of the world Europe colonised in the eighteenth and nineteenth centuries. The basic distinctions that were set in place by the Orientalists – between west and east, self and other, us and them – subsequently dominated relations between the colonisers and those they colonised. In turn, the representations that they produced fed in to a body of knowledge about the colonised regions and peoples that was used to perfect systems of political control. Said draws in part on Michel Foucault's understanding of the symbiotic relationship of knowledge and power; they mutually reinforce one another. Essentially, Orientalism is a discourse, a tradition of speaking and thinking, what Said calls a set of 'enunciative possibilities' about the non-west which facilitated colonisation by setting up the colonies and their inhabitants as everything post-Enlightenment Europe was not – irrational, backward, bestial, untrustworthy, licentious – and thus *in need of colonisation and correction*. As outsiders to the cultures they describe, Orientalists offer an act of representation that always focuses on certain already acknowledged attributes of their subjects. In short, they give edited and subjective 'highlights' of those characteristics deemed recognisable and 'authentic'. Such representation is never neutral. Drawing on post-structuralist ideas, Said asserts that language can only ever re-present experience, never give access to unmediated reality. Thus, he says: 'The things to look for are style, figures of speech, setting, narrative devices . . . not the correctness of the representation nor its fidelity to some great original'.[4] While this relationship of representation and power was, arguably, fairly solid at the height of the imperial age, by the early twentieth century, and particularly after the First World War, confidence in that binary divide between coloniser and colonised came increasingly under threat. This is the moment of Forster and his passages to and from India.

I have dwelt on Said's ideas because they marked a decisive shift away from a tradition of criticism that basically shared the same liberal humanist individualist perspective as Forster himself.[5] In place of the confident idea of literature and culture as an adjunct of moral education, postcolonialism's concern with representation and history has given us a more dispassionate critical perspective on the writings of empire, known as colonial discourse analysis, which seeks to trace the connection between individual texts and this wider corpus of colonialist values. Most postcolonial criticism of Forster attempts some form of colonial discourse analysis, and usually centres on *A Passage to India*.

However, it should be noted that critics dealing with Forster have, from the very beginning, been concerned with the issues of representation and authority the novel throws up. Indian critics have long been exercised by Forster's representation of their pre-independence countrymen in *A Passage to India*; indeed, in a review which appeared just a few months after the novel was published in 1924, Nital Singh lamented the fact that, in his view, Forster had painted his Indian characters as either 'full of religious prejudice', or 'footling meddlers'.[6] The most famous of these early Indian attacks on Forster's novel comes from the irascible and long-lived intellectual Nirad C. Chaudhuri who notes the influence it had in contemporary politics, creating a climate where the British could eventually, 'leave India with an almost Pilate-like gesture of washing their hands of a disagreeable affair'.[7] For Chaudhuri, the characters in *Passage* are 'insignificant and despicable', the Indians being 'malodorous' and the British 'absurd'. The wily old Brahmin Professor Godbole comes in for particular criticism; he 'is not an exponent of Hinduism, he is a clown'.[8] Forster errs in making the Muslim Aziz his central Indian character because of the ambiguous relationship between the Muslim community and the British, and merely succeeds in making the imperial system seem 'drab and asinine'. 'Passage to and from India' is a characteristically trenchant yet elegant piece. However, although it makes the valid point that the failure of the British in India was in not extending the rights of citizenship to their subjects, rather than, as Forster's individualist diagnosis insists, to do with 'bad manners', it appears in the end to be at least partly about retrospectively justifying the British Raj. Chaudhuri has sometimes been attacked as an apologist for empire and his criticisms of Aziz and his ilk – he 'would not have been allowed across my threshold, not to speak of being taken as an equal'[9] – are frankly snobbish. In the essay, as elsewhere in his writing, Chaudhuri takes those westernised Indians like himself to be the apogee of Indian society and the proudest product of the imperial connection. Other critics have agreed with aspects of Chaudhuri's argument, without endorsing some of his cruder polemicism: Avtar Singh Bhullar agrees that Godbole cannot be taken seriously as a supposedly enigmatic sage, and D. C. R. A. Goonetilleke attacks the simplistic outsider's view which imagines that mass conflicts like the anti-colonial struggle are the product of individual thoughtlessness.[10]

Indeed, the presence or otherwise of references to the political background of the time portrayed in *Passage* has stimulated debate among critics over the years. Some, like M. K. Naik, have been baffled by the lack of any direct reference to contemporary upheavals such as the Civil Disobedience movement of 1920 led by Mahatma Gandhi.[11] Others, including G. K. Das, have suggested that the novel does subtly allude to its context; the aftermath of the 1919 Amritsar massacre – when British troops fired on unarmed Indian protesters – finds echoes in briefly mentioned acts of resistance and protest in the run up to Aziz's trial.[12] One of the most sustained but at the same time quirky attempts to situate Forster's novel in its political context is Frances B. Singh's essay '*A Passage to India*, the National Movement and Independence'. Singh suggests a link between the novel and contemporary Muslim politics with its emphasis on the Islamic heritage also invoked from time to time by Aziz. Yet, having set up this intriguing line of enquiry, she instead suggests that ultimately Aziz shows greater affinity with the Hindu-inflected nationalism of Gandhi. Hinduism's allegedly greater inclusiveness when compared to Islam or Christianity means that Aziz can be read as a 'political Hindu' despite his proud Muslim heritage: surely something of an exaggeration![13] Singh draws some insightful parallels between Godbole's dance at the Gokul Ashtami festival and the Gandhian sense of salvation on a national level but, in the end, the essay is perhaps hampered by a slightly naïve correlation between the text, the wider political landscape, and the author's beliefs. Phrases such as, 'Forster's commitment to love and "connection" would make him think along the same lines as Gandhi', not only ignore the vast gulf between Forster's liberal individualism and Gandhi's highly radical brand of collectivist action, they also suggest that one can 'read off' Forster's relation to the wider ideologies of the time directly and unproblematically from the words on the page.[14] This is the kind of reflective model of literary understanding most postcolonial criticism would reject.

In fact, one can gain a sense of how the shift to a recognisably post-colonial form of criticism takes place by examining the work of one of the most fascinating and shrewd of contemporary critics, Benita Parry. Parry has written extensively on Forster over a number of years, drawing on his essays and diary entries to provide several informed and sensitive readings of *Passage*. For example, her seminal work on British fictions of India, *Delusions and Discoveries*, contains a lengthy, sustained interpretation of the novel which, among other things, reads the Hinduism of the 'Temple' section as a meaningful political intervention in its own right.[15] Since then, Parry's work has been increasingly influenced by the preoccupations of postcolonial theory. A shift in tone and a refocusing on the politics of narrative is detectable around the early 1980s, and becomes fully visible if one compares Parry's essays in Das and Beer's collection *E. M. Forster: A Human Exploration* (1979) and in Beer's *E. M. Forster: Essays in Interpretation* which appeared six years later. In the earlier piece, entitled '*A Passage to India*: Epitaph or Manifesto' we are treated to an incisive and accurate analysis of *Passage*'s political contradictions. One can agree with Parry when she says that the novel attempts to articulate:

> dissent from the conventions and aspirations of the late bourgeois world . . . [but that it] omits to make the critical connection between these and the social and political structures they accompanied and sustained. Because of this there is a vacuum at the core of the political fiction . . . Just as liberalism was unable to produce a fundamental critique of western colonialism, so is a consciousness of imperialism's historical dimensions absent from *Passage*.[16]

This is astute in itself. However, the opening of the later essay – prefaced by an epigraph quotation from *Orientalism* – is even more decisively shaped by that concern with narrative and power characteristic of postcolonialism: something indicated in the essay's highly significant title 'The Politics of Representation in *A Passage to India*'. The consciousness of a longer discursive history, of which the novel is merely one instance, is foregrounded from the outset: '*Passage* can be seen as at once inheriting and interrogating the discourses of the Raj.' It is 'the limit text of the Raj discourse, existing on its edges, sharing aspects of its idiom while disputing the language of colonial authority'.[17]

This interest in the structures of thought applied by the coloniser to the colonised is also present in the work of Abdul JanMohamed. For him, colonialist thinking is characterised by binarisms – those 'us-and-them' structures Said sees in Orientalism – producing what he calls a 'Manichean Allegory', where differences of skin colour, physical features, and so on are interpreted also as signs of moral and metaphysical difference. JanMohamed suggests that *Passage* represents an attempt to find a syncretic solution to the Manichean opposition characteristic of colonialism and its literature. For a liberal writer like Forster this effort takes the form of a bracketing of the 'values and bases of his culture'.[18] However, the characters' failed attempts at communication seem to suggest their author's 'recoil' from the chaos of cross-cultural encounters. In the end, 'the narrative decision to turn India into a metaphysical protagonist inherently antithetical to western liberal-humanism',[19] means that, for all its efforts to 'connect', it is still working through the binary structures of Manichean allegory.

This is, however, only one view of the matter. Since the 1980s, an increasing number of critics have come to question the straightforward dualities colonialism would seem to invest in. Perhaps the most famous of them is Homi K. Bhabha. Bhabha argues that the operation of colonial power is far more ambivalent than the Manichean view would allow. Drawing on the work of the deconstructionist philosopher Jacques Derrida and the Freudian revisionist Jacques Lacan, he claims that power in the colonial scenario is never simply a one-way street. Instead, colonial ideas carry inherent contradictions that surface when applied to an Other. For Bhabha this is illustrated in the moments of doubt scattered across *Passage* and symbolised by the Marabar Caves, where the confident programme of imperial power and knowledge is disturbed by what he calls, 'the uncanny forces of race, sexuality, violence, cultural and even climatic differences', a threat which 'breaks down the symmetry and duality of self/Other, inside/outside'.[20] Along with the complication of power comes a problematisation of identity that Bhabha terms 'hybridity'. Not only is colonial identity the result of the interaction of coloniser and colonised – they mutually shape one another – but the attempt by the coloniser to turn the colonised into a mini version of himself results in a threat to a sealed off idea of 'us and them'. For example, the gap between the coloniser's own culturally produced language and the different meaning systems of the indigenous population means that whatever concepts are forced on the colonised they will inevitably reinterpret them in ways they find comprehensible or useful. In short, meaning spirals away from the coloniser's control; we might take as an example the way the Indians take up, alter and chant the name of Mrs Moore – 'Esmiss Esmoor' – during the trial. Here the English word, or name, is misappropriated by the Indian crowd and Mrs Moore is transformed into a rallying cry and, we learn, even a minor deity. If this is the fate of the coloniser's language when it meets the uneducated Indian mass, then those Indians who are westernised create another kind of dilemma. According to Bhabha, they pose a threat to the idea

that English and Indian identities are complete opposites as the more successfully they 'mimic' the coloniser the harder it becomes to insist upon an
essential difference which justifies withholding certain rights, such as the
right to liberty from imperial rule. Colonial fiction is full of mimic men and
Bhabha sees Dr Aziz as one of them. He insists that the mimic man is not
to be viewed as a slavish follower of the colonial master, but as a menacing
parody whose very existence challenges his authority. Against this loss of
authority, the coloniser constructs stereotypes of his colonial subjects: lazy,
childlike, ignorant, licentious, and so on. Yet even this, according to Bhabha,
is a self-betraying tactic. From a psychoanalytic perspective, stereotyping
others betrays not simply fear and loathing but also desire. Bhabha rarely
offers full-scale textual readings, but Peter Childs and Patrick Williams,
in their *Introduction to Postcolonial Theory* offer the useful example of
District Superintendent McBryde's belief in an 'oriental pathology' in which
Aziz, precisely because he *is* an Indian male, is bound to be licentious – he
visits brothels and keeps a stash of pornography in his room – and, expanding the stereotype further that, as McBryde insists at the trial, 'the darker
races are physically attracted to the fairer'.[21] Psychoanalysis would see this
as a very revealing comment, suggesting not simply narcissistic self-regard
but a covert longing actually to *be* the object of the colonised's desire.[22]

If Bhabha is not given to detailed textual analysis – dealing rather in theoretical models – the founding father of postcolonial study in its present
form, Edward Said, is, conversely, more concerned with literature's relation
to material history. For him, despite the 'intermittent crossings' back and
forth over the British/Indian divide, India ultimately serves in *Passage* as a
signifier of 'massive incomprehensibility'.[23] Owing to the novel's metaphysical focus, and despite those undercutting ironies, the 'sense that India and
Britain are opposed nations . . . is played down, muffled, frittered away'.[24]
Forster's apparent refusal to take sides in a context where compromise was
no longer possible is compounded by the illusions produced by his individualist outlook: 'Forster's presumption is that he can get past the puerile
nationalist put-ons to the essential India; when it comes to ruling India . . .
the English had better go on doing it, despite their mistakes: "they" are
not yet ready for self-rule.'[25] This rather stark conclusion is perhaps a little
unfair and not fully borne out by the subtleties of the novel. Having said
this, it is possible to concur with the assertion that in *Passage* Forster has
'found a way to use the mechanism of the novel to elaborate on the already
existing structure of attitude and reference' which marks British fictions on
India without actually changing it.[26]

One of the results of the rise of postcolonial criticism is an increased
attention to questions of language, its deployment, ellipses, and relation to

power, among critics offering close readings of *Passage*. The titles of three such works – '*Periphrasis*, Power and Rape', 'The *Unspeakable* Limits of Rape', and *The Rhetoric of English India* (emphases added) – illustrate such concerns. In the first of them, Brenda R. Silver examines how both Adela and Aziz come to be spoken of in indirect terms after the charge of rape has been made against the doctor. The Anglo-Indians avoid naming them, instead resorting to depersonalised abstractions such as 'the victim', and 'the accused'. These acts of periphrasis, of 'speaking around' rather than naming, work to 'split' and objectify those to whom they refer. Silver claims that the result in *Passage* is that the colonial subject – here Aziz – is placed in the same position of disempowerment traditionally occupied by women under a patriarchal system. She reads this feminisation of the colonised as a key strategy of subordination in the colonial context and, in this particular instance, as a metaphorical act of rape. Recalling McBryde's theories of Indian sexual promiscuity, Silver notes: 'In this construction the Indian man, reduced to his sexuality, becomes simultaneously rapist and object of rape.'[27]

This position is not without its critics, however. Jenny Sharpe, in 'The Unspeakable Limits of Rape', argues that Adela's experience 'is framed by racial tensions that cannot be understood as simply another form of patriarchal violence'.[28] Sharpe attacks Silver for discussing racial codes too generally and for eliding the very real differences between race and gender to come up with her figurative reading of rape. The result of this is a highly 'problematical reading of third world men as occupying the space of first world women that permits the latter to serve as a model for all oppressed peoples'.[29] In short, too many differences in the experience of power are overlooked in Silver's model. Instead, Sharpe suggests a much more historically specific model for *Passage*'s wary standoff. When the British of Chandrapore discuss the alleged rape they do so in terms that recall an earlier experience of women coming under threat: the 1857 Indian Mutiny or Sepoy Rebellion. Rather than assert a trans-historical idea that the colonised = the feminised, Sharpe traces 'the signification of rape . . . to the historical production of a colonial discourse on the native assault of English women in India' stemming from 1857.[30] The Mutiny marks the beginning of the racial discourse wherein white women are sexually threatened by brown men. The sensational British newspaper accounts of the time emphasised the sexual violations perpetrated by the mutineers. 'Our women' were under attack and even though the details were 'unspeakable' they operated powerfully on the imagination and were enough not merely to justify the brutal reprisals by which the British eventually restored order, but also to inaugurate a tradition of racial-sexual stereotyping we can still see operating in the minds of the panicked British of Forster's novel.

Sara Suleri reads *Passage* as shaped by thwarted invitations and misreadings. From Fielding's innocent request to Aziz to make himself at home on their first meeting, through the trip to the caves, hastily arranged as a substitute for a visit to Aziz's house, to Godbole's song where the invitation to Krishna to come to the lover remains unanswered, the text is pocked by disappointments and misunderstandings. Ultimately what is frustrated is that intimacy between Englishman and Indian represented in the Fielding/Aziz relationship. Moreover, Suleri revises the conventionally understood race and gender dynamics of imperialism to suggest that the novel offers us an alternative model to that of the male coloniser penetrating the female space of the colonised: 'the most urgent cross-cultural invitations occur between male and male with racial difference serving as a substitute for gender'.[31] There are several homoerotic images that support such an interpretation, including the image of the half-naked punkah puller at the trial: 'untouchable' both in the sense of being a social outcaste and because he represents a homosexual union that can never be attained.

This attention to language, culture, and power finds its most sustained articulation in the two chapters Bette London devotes to Forster in her book, *The Appropriated Voice: Narrative Authority in Conrad, Forster and Woolf*. London's work displays a creditable attention to the dynamics of the narrative technique in *Passage* which at times borders on the forensic. Advocating what she calls 'an interested reading', London is concerned to trace the relationship of the orchestrating narrative voice presiding over the novel to some of the more controversial utterances made by the characters. She reads *Passage* against the background of Forster's Indian letters, journal entries, and essays, 'to suggest the complexities of his position as a cultured subject, bound up with historically available discourses on race, class and nationality'.[32] Clearly, Forster sets out to distance himself from the more intolerant utterances of his Anglo-Indian characters. However, London claims that their very deployment provides evidence of the text's infiltration by the voices it sets out to reject or suppress. One might wish to ask whether the text is 'infiltrated' in the manner London suggests, the phrase carrying with it the implication of inadvertency, or whether Forster is deliberately 'expressing' them, in both senses of the term: to articulate but at the same time to squeeze out or expel. In any case, London has a keen eye for the way that theatricality and what might be called textual apprehension work to structure the text and impel characters' behaviour. The British are always playing a part, acting up for those who are observing them: something that, as George Orwell famously noted, is intrinsic to the authority position the imperial sahib has constructed for himself. But this is a reciprocal process too, with 'the British writing an identity based upon the reading of an India they invent, while the Indians read this British "writing" and reconstruct themselves'.[33] In this model of the colonial relationship as theatrical performance, India's part is designated by the British who keep all the desirable roles – 'hero, victim, martyr, loyal friend' – for themselves. London claims that this stereotypical casting can be frustrated by improvisation, by departing from the agreed script, but apparently this is only possible through British improvisation: for example, in Adela's deviation from the agreed script when she backs down and withdraws her charge against Aziz. (This is an unusual and perhaps rather restrictive interpretation of the British–Indian relationship as depicted in the novel, and one that certainly goes against the idea of mimicry as a subversive tool that can be used by Indians to undermine colonial power.)

In the second Forster chapter, 'The Politics of Voice', London rightly asserts that a 'crisis of voice' is at the heart of *Passage*. She goes on to underscore the proximity of Forster's own narrative tones to those of the colonial oppressors about whom he is otherwise so scathing, and the slippage that sometimes occurs between them. She cites as examples those moments where the Orientalist tones that occasionally appear in Forster's Indian diaries and letters, as collected in *The Hill of Devi*, find their way into *Passage*, placed in the mouths of the less attractive British figures but also absorbed at times into the judgemental interjections of the omniscient voice.[34] This, then, is evidence of how Forster offers 'a pre-eminent example of the ways we are all implicated in and by the conditions of our discourse'.[35]

London's reading is focused and impressive. Yet it tends to negate the possibility of any Indian agency being presented in the novel and, in the end, while Forster's text may well be 'implicated' in a dominating Eurocentric discourse, this need not necessarily mean it simply reproduces it. Likewise, it might be objected that in treating the personal correspondence in *The Hill of Devi* as qualitatively the same as, and therefore interchangeable with, the novelistic tones of *Passage*, London treats language as a flat surface where letters, for example, with their different dynamic of address and reception are forced to occupy the same discursive space as fiction. Attention to textual ambiguities and those spaces that are either crammed full of contending voices, or where the narrative stands back and disavows the panoptic invasion of omniscience, might suggest a different relationship of narrative and power. Thus, while it is not difficult to find examples of classic Orientalist commonplaces – one might even cite as an instance Forster's famous assertion that the mystery of the Marabar Caves was a 'trick' he felt justified in using 'because my subject matter is India' – nevertheless, such attitudes are constantly undermined not least by being set against evidence that directly contradicts them. At the same time, the imperialist voice is mercilessly lampooned at various points, especially during the racial panic attack at the Club on the evening of Aziz's arrest, when the siege mentality is expressed by characters whose self-dramatisation as heroes of an outpost of empire is rendered with caustic irony: the Collector treats his listeners to an 'august colloquy'; Mrs Turton towers 'like Pallas Athene'; and Ronny Heaslop is hyperbolically described as a 'martyr'.[36] In fact, as I have argued elsewhere, it could be claimed that it is here, in what Mikhail Bakhtin would call the novel's polyphony – the many voices circulating in the text's dialogic structure – that we might actually see the ambiguities of Forster's liberalism made manifest.[37] The variety of tones – British imperialist, liberal humanist, Hindu, Muslim, Indian nationalist, mock-heroic and so on – could be seen to establish 'a resistance . . . to the dominance of any one discourse'.[38] Through this use of many voices, often in the form of parody and pastiche, Forster is able to present the appearance of being non-committed, of seeing both sides (a classic liberal position) at a time of acute political struggle, a struggle that only finds its way into the text at a tangent to the main action. The liberal master narrative is marked by tolerance. Effectively, 'Forster effaces himself as narrator among other voices – like the God Krishna obscured by bric-a-brac in the Gokul Ashtami festival.'[39] He refuses the centrality and power that normally come with omniscience, while the multitude of voices provide a spectrum of difference which holds in abeyance the contest for power, a contest which was becoming particularly bitter in the historical moment of 1924. The same can be said of Forster's frequent use of free indirect speech in *Passage*. Along with irony and polyphony, moments where the attribution of an utterance is uncertain – as in the central encomium to the Mediterranean as 'the human norm' during Fielding's voyage home – allow the narrative to distance itself from any one perspective.

Ultimately, the view of Forster's relationship to Orientalist tropes depends on whether one reads his writing as simply a carrier of colonial discourse, or as actively shaping, modifying, and sometimes rejecting that discourse in ways that anticipate the disruptive ambiguities favoured in postcolonialism. In the latter case, it might also be possible to see a politically destabilising quality in Forster's use of symbols in *Passage*. In *Aspects of the Novel*, Forster describes how a book can be given shape through pattern and rhythm created by the deployment of recurring images. Such images form a kind of *leitmotif* but, importantly, they should not be tethered to a single meaning. Forster argues that this flexibility distinguishes them from mere symbols, where there is usually a one-to-one correlation between an image and the character or idea it stands for. Despite this it is hard not to conclude that Forster is indeed talking about symbolism, albeit of a fluid and flexible kind. The rhythm of a novel is created by the 'repetition plus variation' of these images or symbols.[40] They take on different meanings in different contexts. (Thus, the meaning of the Marabar Caves changes according to who views them, at what time of day, and in what proximity. Similarly, the sky takes on different connotations as the day, and the year, rolls around.)

On the face of it, symbolism and symbolic structures typify the British in India and their outlook. This applies not simply to those great imperial displays of power – such as the *Durbars* or gatherings of Indian princes at which British might was displayed and policy announced – but also in daily life. This is perhaps inevitable in a society that invests so much in the attempt to create England and Englishness abroad. In British Indian society everything stands in for something else, something more recognisable and controllable, more English. (One example of this symbolic surrogacy in *Passage* occurs when the Club members sit down to a meal made up of things standing in for their absent British equivalents – 'Julienne soup full of bullety bottled peas, pseudo-cottage bread' – prepared by native cooks who do not understand this stodgy fare.[41]) In other words, the Raj is freighted with symbols and the need for them is heightened at times of crisis; they help to galvanise a sense of identity. This is why the whole Club quivers to attention when the National Anthem is played – it is a clarion call, a symbol of Englishness abroad: 'though they perceived neither Royalty nor Deity they did perceive something, they were strengthened to resist another day'.[42] In the same way, the word 'white' connotes far more than skin colour, which explains why Fielding offends the 'herd' by suggesting that the white races are actually 'pinko-grey'. Similarly, Adela becomes a symbol of violated English womanhood after the supposed assault. But in her retraction of the charge she renounces this role, shakes off her symbolic meaning. In short she lets the side down. Human symbols, like the King of 'God save the King', or Adela, or young Mrs Blakiston – who, 'with her abundant figure and masses of corngold hair . . . symbolised all that is worth fighting and dying for; more permanent a symbol perhaps than poor Adela'[43] – these human symbols have culturally fixed value projected on to them by the besieged community. So the British construct their sense of self partly on the basis of these fixed, connotative symbols. However, those recurring symbols which shift and change in significance, which in E. K. Brown's phrase 'expand' or 'accrete meaning'[44] – like the sun, the moon, the sky, landscape, nature and animals, gods and ghosts – always slip beyond the colonising culture's paranoid control. Beyond the mental horizon of British India, things are always taking on and shaking off meaning seemingly at random. In that sense they can never be brought under Britain's discursive control: the most obvious example of a symbol of indeterminate meaning is the 'echo' or reverberation set in train by the incident at the Marabar Caves – English power-knowledge never gets the better of it or comes to terms with it.

Yet, perhaps there are also human subjects in *Passage* who lie beyond the ken of Britain's panoptic attentions, and even those of the omniscient narrating voice. The most celebrated example of such a one is the punkah puller who catches Adela's attention during the trial. He is one of Jenny Sharpe's eponymous 'figures of resistance' who were to go on to be active participants in the decolonisation struggle of subsequent years. Sharpe reminds us that although history records the doings of those educated Indians who formed the nationalist vanguard, independence would not have been possible without the participation of the lower castes and untouchables like the punkah wallah. Recalling a phrase from Gayatri C. Spivak, Sharpe says: 'Exorbitant to the story . . . [the punkah puller] marks the place of that other that can be neither excluded nor recuperated' by the dominant ideology.[45] Taking this idea a stage further, Teresa Hubel has argued for the punkah wallah as one of those 'subaltern subjects' who have recently become the objects of historical scrutiny as Indian historiography has shifted focus from the deeds of national elites to the struggles of the disempowered. For Hubel, the radicalism of the punkah wallah lies in the very fact that, in contrast to the educated Indians who take up most of Forster's attention in *Passage*, he stands outside the elite dialogue and is 'never subsumed by the western writing mind'.[46] Working the fan, and thereby exercising control over the courtroom environment, the punkah wallah may appear to stand for a timeless, unchanging India, but actually he can be read as representing a perspective the text seeks to endorse but cannot, in its own terms, articulate; he, and figures like him form 'vortexes of unintentional meaning'[47] which allow the subaltern perspective into Forster's book.

Thus, postcolonial approaches, while they may question Forster's ability to transcend the intellectual conditions of his time, often emphasise his highly conscious arrangement of devices and awareness of the pitfalls of representing India. The impression is reinforced by attention to the numerous Indian-related writings; alongside the quotation about the 'Real India' used to open this essay, one can place Forster's distrust of 'the faked East . . . which exists to be the background of some European adultery'.[48] This aversion to easy generalisation marks Forster's outlook. One can see it as an adjunct of that individualism he was to champion most famously when, in the face of a hostile European situation in the 1930s, he remarked: 'I hate the idea of causes, and if I had to choose between betraying my country and betraying my friend, I hope I should have the guts to betray my country.'[49] Transposed to the east, a similar sentiment finds expression near the end of his 'Salute to the Orient' when, remarking how '*an* Oriental' always hates the European *nation* which governs him (emphasis added), he concludes that, 'The individual in the East must succeed as an individual or he has failed', and prays 'that the East may be delivered from Europe the known, and from Russia the unknown and may remain the East'.[50] Forster is all for independence in this and other essays, but it is that cultural independence which accompanies the goodwill and intelligence of individuals he desires: political autonomy seldom enters the equation.

However, while one can trace the same advocacy of individualism and of art as the supreme mode of human communication and order as drives Forster's essays on culture in general, there is nevertheless a detectable shift in the context wherein he attempts to erect these enduring principles; one might almost call it a tremor that radiates outward not just from the alien terrain of India, but from the times themselves. In other words, just as critics have noted the slight sense of anachronism caused by the lengthy gestation period of *Passage* – straddling the First World War – so too, I would suggest, one can detect a slow shift in the tone and preoccupations of Forster's essays on India. Although he revisited the topic of India throughout his career, chronologically there are three main blocks of essays: those pre-First World War pieces which display a freshness and an openness to an unfamiliar culture, and a concern that it be better understood in the west; those set around the time of the sea-change in Indian politics circa 1920 lamenting that which is passing in the ferment; and, lastly, the batch intersected by the Second World War, from the memorial essay on Syed Ross Masood to 'India Again' with its rueful recognition of the redundancy of political liberalism and the lack of interest in the cultural values he has always espoused.

The first period is fairly represented by several of the essays in the section of *Abinger Harvest* entitled 'The East'. This batch is notable partly for the insight it gives us into some of the raw materials for *Passage* – in 'The Nine Gems of Ujjain' and 'The Mosque' for example – and partly because, as in the entries in *The Hill of Devi* that date from this time, one is treated to the new sensations and rearrangement of priorities that come with initiation into India: as evidenced in 'Pan' and 'The Suppliant' where the difference between east and west is identified in attitudes to hospitality. The archly entitled 'Advance, India!' records Forster's ambivalent reaction to the enforced compromises of an 'advanced' Muslim wedding ceremony. He seems faintly appalled by the aesthetic clumsiness of the event – especially when the prayers of the orthodox are interrupted by a gramophone blaring out a western popular song – but he recognises the courage it has taken the two families to break free of the shackles of convention. The awkward, controversial 'advance' seems to represent that of India as a whole, resulting in what Forster calls 'the unlovely chaos between obedience and freedom'.[51]

'Advance, India!' was written on the eve of war in 1914. Forster spent some of the war years in Alexandria, working for the Red Cross and accumulating the material which would find its way into his *Alexandria: A History and a Guide* (1922) and *Pharos and Pharillon* (1923). When he returned to India in 1919, albeit vicariously via a review of 'Two Books by Tagore', a change of tone seems to bespeak the change of context:

> When a writer of Tagore's genius produces such a sentence as 'Passion is beautiful and pure – pure as the lily that comes out of the slimy soil; it rises superior to its defilement and needs no Pears' soap to wash it clean' – he raises some interesting questions. The sentence is not attractive – in fact, it is a Babu sentence – and what does Tagore, generally so attractive, intend by it? Is he being dramatic . . . satirical . . . or is it an experiment that has not quite come off? Probably an experiment, for throughout the book one is puzzled by bad tastes that verge upon bad taste.[52]

For all his expansive sympathies, Forster here, as elsewhere, exalts a notion of taste that is distinctly conservative not to say Eurocentric: an idea of the aesthetically appropriate which balks at Indian writing that moves beyond conventional preoccupations and uses a western image. Although extending a tepid welcome to the spirit of experiment he detects among Bengali writers, the phantasm of 'taste' ensures that the review remains faintly patronising. Likewise, the deployment of the epithet 'Babu' – a derogatory Anglo-Indian term for an English-educated Indian – is uncharacteristic. In order to make his point about 'taste', Forster conveniently forgets what Babus are and who made them.

I have chosen this review to stand for a broader change detectable in Forster's Indian pieces around this time. Though they are seldom as tetchy as the Tagore appraisal, nevertheless I would suggest that a reorientation can be seen taking place: an accommodation to contemporary events such as the Muslim *Khliafat* agitation over Britain's policy in Turkey, the Non-Cooperation Movement of 1920–2, and the appearance of Gandhi on the Indian political scene. Forster realises that things are no longer the same, indeed, that they *can* never be the same again, and that the old India embodied by princely states such as Dewas Senior, is passing forever. This impression is strongest in his 1922 essay on 'The Mind of the Indian Native State'. Here, Forster is fully cognisant of the new political realities bearing down on the princely fiefdoms, and acknowledges that they are useful to the British as a counterweight to metropolitan Indian nationalism. Absolute autocracy sits awkwardly in the radicalised landscape of postwar India, proclaiming its validity through pomp, circumstance, and gestures of power which have less and less to do with reality. Forster suggests that the Maharajahs who benefit from the feudal system preserved in the native states are baffled by British constitutionalism – particularly as the British themselves are ruled over by a King-Emperor. Despite the seismic upheavals going on all around them, 'they do not regard anything but Royalty as permanent, or the movements against it more than domestic mutinies. They cannot understand, because they cannot experience, the modern world.'[53] This sounds like, and is, Orientalism at work. Forster claims here to understand the hearts and minds of the princes, despite the fact that in *Aspects of the Novel* he has claimed that fiction differs from life precisely because in life you cannot know people perfectly.[54] Forster's sympathetic account of these states is based on his view of them as a last bastion of the individual touch in statecraft, set adrift in an age of democracy and mass movements. While recognising their idiosyncrasies and anachronism he values them as rural models ruled over by distinctive (and often odd) personalities, something to set against the centralising tendencies of both the British and the nationalists. Similarly, educational advances of the kind which have stirred nationalism across India, and which Forster advocates elsewhere, would be anathema to the princely ruler: 'So long as his are uneducated peasants, a Prince is in a strong position from every point of view. They revere him with the old Indian loyalty, and a glimpse of his semi-divine figure brings poetry into their lives. And he understands them even when he is being indifferent or unjust, because like them he is rooted in the soil.'[55] Once more an ideological slippage takes place and we are able to spy the lineaments of Orientalism here. Unwittingly Forster is here employing the rhetorical tropes of the British Raj to describe an ideal of individualism and the personal touch. He valorises 'the old Indian loyalty', and 'uneducated peasants', both staple elements of colonial discourse used to discredit urban nationalists; prefers the 'half-divine' figure of the Prince to extremist politicos (significantly, all nationalists are referred to as 'extremists' in this essay); and, as I have argued elsewhere: 'the final sentence, proclaiming empathy between ruler and ruled through mutual rootedness is at once a panegyric on "natural law" and a possible mechanism for despotic power. And it does not seem to matter that it is despotic. Forster's libertarian principles are immediately suspended when the Grail of individual contact, of personal relations, is in sight.'[56]

Thus, while Forster concedes that the underpinning principles of Victorian liberalism to which he finds himself still wedded were based on economic exploitation – in the essay 'The Challenge of our Time', for example[57] – and that this exploitation impacted most directly on the colonised peoples, he is finally unable to identify wholeheartedly with those anti-colonial forces that were setting about to rectify matters. Too much that he values must be sacrificed along the way. It is for these reasons that one feels such a strong sense of regret percolating through 'India Again'. Indians now have little time for anything which does not address their pressing political problems.

This emphasis on the civilised individual led Forster to posit, as a counter-weight to the mass politics of the interwar years, his famous 'aristocracy of the sensitive'.[58] Perhaps its leading Indian member was Forster's close friend the reformer and educationalist Syed Ross Masood, whom the novelist cred-ited with awakening his interest in India and Indians: so much so that he dedicated *Passage* to him on its completion. Masood is essentially an artist with a highly developed – if not unerring – aesthetic sense, whose tolerant and at times pitying attitude to the British Forster celebrates in his memorial essay. (He attributes these characteristics in part to the time Masood spent in his youth with the liberal imperialists Sir Theodore and Lady Morison, and one is tempted to read this posthumous celebration of urbanity over dogmatism as a case of Forster lauding those qualities in his friend that most resonate with his own ideals.[59])

What is one to make of this ambivalent attitude to the conflicting realities presented by India in the first half of the twentieth century and the problem of how to represent them in art? One might, perhaps, say that Forster certainly recognises Orientalist tropes such as the 'exotic fallacy' and the serviceable myth of the 'Real India'. However, he is not above using them himself to satirise those he disagrees with and to bolster a way of life he finds conducive. Ultimately, Forster may not believe in the 'Real India', but he does have an enormous emotional investment in the idea that there are 'real Indians': not the metropolitan, cosmopolitan voices leading the Nationalist movement, but a landed nobility personified on the one hand by the impulsive, warm-hearted Maharajah of Dewas Senior, whose antics he celebrates in *The Hill of Devi*, and the cultivated, suave Syed Ross Masood. This stress on the individual and on aesthetics might remind us of Raymond Williams' perspi-cacious comments on the politics of the Bloomsbury group more generally; they exhibit 'sympathy' rather than 'solidarity' with the lower class. Like-wise, for Forster, although there is sympathy for the colonised there is no real sense of solidarity with them in their struggle.[60] While this may be disabling if we come to Forster seeking answers to international questions that, far from being resolved in 1947, have spilled over into our own day in the tensions between India and Pakistan, in neo-colonialism, and in the strategic intru-sions of global power politics, nevertheless, Forster's thoughtful probing of the faultlines of cultural identity, especially in *Passage*, offers a rich reading experience which promises to keep critical interpretation of the writer and his work alive for years to come.

Notes

1. E. M. Forster, *Two Cheers for Democracy* (London: Edward Arnold, 1951), p. 328.
2. Edward W. Said, *Orientalism: Western Conceptions of the Orient* (Harmondsworth: Penguin [1978] 1985).
3. Ibid., p. 1.
4. Ibid., p. 21.
5. For example, G. K. Das and John Beer's 1979 centenary volume of essays on Forster bears the full title *E. M. Forster: A Human Exploration* (London and Basingstoke: Macmillan, 1979).
6. Nital Singh, 'Indians and Anglo-Indians as portrayed to Britons' in the *Modern Review* (Calcutta), cited in *E. M. Forster: The Critical Heritage*, ed. Philip Gardner (London: Routledge and Kegan Paul, 1973), p. 266.
7. Nirad C. Chaudhuri, 'Passage to and from India', *Encounter* 2:6 (1954), 19.
8. Ibid., p. 21.
9. Ibid., p. 21.
10. Avtar Singh Bhullar, *India: Myth and Reality* (New Delhi: Ajanta Publications, 1985), p. 63; D. C. R. A. Goonetilleke, *Images of the Raj: South Asia in the Literature of Empire* (London: Macmillan, 1988), p. 98.
11. M. K. Naik, 'Passage to Less than India', in *Focus on Forster's A Passage to India*, ed. V. A. Shahane (Bombay: Orient Longman, 1975).
12. G. K. Das, '*A Passage to India*: A Socio-Historical Study', in *A Passage to India: Essays in Interpretation*, ed. John Beer (London and Basingstoke: Macmillan, 1985). Das offers an extended contextual reading of *Passage* in his book *E. M. Forster's India* (London and Basingstoke: Macmillan, 1977).
13. Frances B. Singh, '*A Passage to India*, the National Movement and Independence', *Twentieth Century Literature*, 31:2–3 (1985), 265–78.
14. Ibid., p. 272.
15. Benita Parry, *Delusions and Discoveries: Studies on India in the British Imagination 1880–1930* (Harmondsworth: Penguin, 1972). The magisterial original edition is preferable to Verso's 1998 re-issue which has been rather over-zealously edited by Michael Sprinker.
16. Benita Parry, '*A Passage to India*: Epitaph or Manifesto', in Das and Beer, *E. M. Forster*, p. 131.
17. Benita Parry, 'The Politics of Representation in *A Passage to India*', in Beer, *A Passage to India*, pp. 28, 30.
18. Abdul R. JanMohamed, 'The Economy of Manichean Allegory: The Function of Racial Difference in Colonialist Literature', *Critical Inquiry*, 12 (1985–6), 74.
19. Ibid., p. 77.
20. Homi K. Bhabha, 'Signs Taken for Wonders: Questions of Ambivalence and Authority under a Tree Outside Delhi, May 1817', *Critical Inquiry* 12 (1985), 155.

21. E. M. Forster, *A Passage to India* (Harmondsworth: Penguin, 1989), p. 222.
22. Peter Childs and Patrick Williams, *An Introduction to Postcolonial Theory* (Hemel Hempstead: Harvester Wheatsheaf, 1997), p. 128.
23. Edward W. Said, *Culture and Imperialism* (London: Chatto and Windus, 1993), pp. 242, 244.
24. Ibid., p. 246.
25. Ibid., p. 247.
26. Ibid., p. 248.
27. Brenda R. Silver, 'Periphrasis, Power and Rape in *A Passage to India*', *Novel*, 22 (1988), 94.
28. Jenny Sharpe, 'The Unspeakable Limits of Rape: Colonial Violence and Counter-Insurgency', in *Colonial Discourse and Post-Colonial Theory: A Reader*, ed. Patrick Williams and Laura Chrisman (Hemel Hempstead: Harvester Wheatsheaf, 1993), p. 224.
29. Ibid., p. 226.
30. Ibid., p, 222.
31. Sara Suleri, *The Rhetoric of English India* (Chicago: University of Chicago Press, 1992), p. 133.
32. Bette London, *The Appropriated Voice: Narrative Authority in Conrad, Forster and Woolf* (Ann Arbor: University of Michigan Press, 1990), p. 8.
33. Ibid., p. 63.
34. Ibid., p. 90.
35. Ibid., p. 89.
36. E. M. Forster, *A Passage to India* (Harmondsworth: Penguin, 1985) pp. 188, 189, 190.
37. Peter Morey, *Fictions of India: Narrative and Power* (Edinburgh: Edinburgh University Press, 2000). For more on polyphony, see Mikhail Bakhtin, *Problems of Dostoevsky's Poetics* [ed. and trans. Caryl Emerson] (Minneapolis: University of Minnesota Press, 1984).
38. David Lodge, *After Bakhtin: Essays on Fiction and Criticism* (London: Routledge, 1990), p. 22.
39. Morey, *Fictions of India*, p. 70.
40. E. M. Forster, *Aspects of the Novel* (Harmondsworth: Penguin, 1990), p. 149.
41. Forster, *Passage to India*, p. 67.
42. Ibid., p. 47.
43. Ibid., p. 188.
44. E. K. Brown, *Rhythm in the Novel* (Toronto: University of Toronto Press, 1950), pp. 9, 44–59.
45. Gayatri C. Spivak, quoted in Jenny Sharpe, 'Figures of Colonial Resistance', *Modern Fiction Studies*, 35:1 (1989), 152.
46. Teresa Hubel, *Whose India? The Independence Struggle in British and Indian Fiction and History* (Leicester: Leicester University Press, 1996), p. 104.
47. Ibid., p. 85.
48. E. M. Forster, *Abinger Harvest* (London: Edward Arnold, 1936), p. 290.
49. Forster, *Two Cheers*, p. 78.
50. Forster, *Abinger Harvest*, p. 300.
51. Ibid., p. 344.
52. Ibid., p. 365.

53. Ibid., p. 370.
54. E. M. Forster, *Aspects of the Novel* (Harmondsworth: Penguin, 1990), p. 69.
55. Forster, *Abinger Harvest*, p. 378.
56. Morey, *Fictions of India*, p. 76.
57. Forster, *Two Cheers*, p. 68.
58. Ibid., p. 82.
59. Ibid., pp. 299–300.
60. Raymond Williams, *Problems in Materialism and Culture* (London: Verso and NLB, 1980), p. 155.

Ackerley, J. R., *E. M. Forster: A Portrait* (London: Ian McKelvie, 1970)

Adams, David, *Colonial Odysses: Empire and Epic in the Modernist Novel* (Ithaca, NY: Cornell University Press, 2003)

Advani, Rukun, *E. M. Forster as Critic* (London: Croom Helm, 1984)

Armstrong, Paul B., 'E. M. Forster's *Howards End*: The Existential Crisis of the Liberal Imagination', *Mosaic*, 8 (Fall 1974), 183–99

   'Reading India: E. M. Forster and the Politics of Interpretation', *Twentieth Century Literature*, 38:4 (Winter 1992), 365–85

Bailey, Quentin, 'Heroes and Homosexuals: Education and Empire in E. M. Forster', *Twentieth-Century Literature*, 48:3 (Fall 2002), 324–47

Bakshi, Parminder Kaur, *Distant Desire: Homoerotic Codes and the Subversion of the English Novel in E. M. Forster's Fiction*, Sexuality and Literature 5 (New York: Peter Lang, 1996)

Beauman, Nicola, *Morgan: A Biography of E. M. Forster* (London: Hodder and Stoughton, 1993)

Beer, Gillian, 'Negation in *A Passage to India*', in *A Passage to India: Essays in Interpretation*, ed. John Beer (1985), pp. 44–58

Beer, J. B., *The Achievement of E. M. Forster* (London: Chatto and Windus, 1962)

Beer, John, "*A Passage to India* and the Versatility of the Novel" in *A Passage to India: Essays in Interpretation*, ed. John Beer (1985), pp. 132–52

Beer, John, ed., *A Passage to India: Essays in Interpretation* (Basingstoke and London: Macmillan, 1985)

Bentley, Michael, *The Liberal Mind: 1914–1929* (Cambridge: Cambridge University Press, 1977)

Bernstein, George L., *Liberalism and Liberal Politics in Edwardian England* (Boston and London: Allen and Unwin, 1986)

Bhabha, Homi K., *The Location of Culture* (London and New York: Routledge, 1994)

Bloom, Harold, ed., *E. M. Forster* (New York: Chelsea House, 1987)

Boehmer, Elleke, *Colonial and Postcolonial Literature: Migrant Metaphors*, 2nd edn (Oxford: Oxford University Press, 2005)

   Empire, the National and the Postcolonial, 1890–1920: Resistance in Interaction (Oxford: Oxford University Press, 2002)

Born, Daniel, 'Private Gardens, Public Swamps: *Howards End* and the Revaluation of Liberal Guilt', *Novel*, 25 (1992), 141–59

Bradbury, Malcolm, ed., *Forster: A Collection of Critical Essays* (Englewood Cliffs, NJ: Prentice-Hall, 1966)

Bradshaw, David, and Kevin J. H. Dettmar, *A Companion to Modernist Literature and Culture* (Oxford: Blackwell, 2006)

Bradshaw, David, ed., *A Concise Companion to Modernism* (Oxford: Blackwell, 2003)

Bristow, Joseph, 'Against "Effeminacy": The Sexual Predicament of E. M. Forster's Fiction', in *Effeminate England: Homoerotic Writing after 1885* ed. Joseph Bristow (Buckingham: Open University Press, 1995), pp. 55–99

  '*Fratum Societati*: Forster's Apostolic Dedications', in *Queer Forster*, ed. Robert K. Martin and George Piggford (1997), pp. 113–36

Butler, Christopher, *Early Modernism: Literature, Music and Painting in Europe, 1900–1916* (Oxford: Clarendon Press, 1994)

Buzard, James, *The Beaten Track: European Tourism, Literature, and the Ways to Culture, 1800–1918* (Oxford: Clarendon Press, 1993)

  'Forster's Trespasses: Tourism and Cultural Politics' (1988), reprinted in *E. M. Forster*, ed. Jeremy Tambling (1995), pp. 14–29

Carey, John, *The Intellectuals and the Masses: Pride and Prejudice Among the Literary Intelligentsia, 1880–1939* (London: Faber and Faber, 1992)

Cavaliero, Glen, *A Reading of E. M. Forster* (Basingstoke and London: Macmillan, 1979)

Childs, Peter, ed., *A Routledge Sourcebook on E. M. Forster's 'A Passage to India'* (London and New York: Routledge, 2002)

Colmer, John, *E. M. Forster: The Personal Voice* (London and Boston: Routledge and Kegan Paul, 1975)

Crews, Frederick C., *E. M. Forster: The Perils of Humanism* (Princeton: Princeton University Press, 1962)

Cucullu, Lois, *Expert Modernists: Matricide and Modern Culture: Woolf, Forster, Joyce* (Basingstoke and New York, Palgrave, 2004)

  '"Only Cathect": Queer Heirs and Narrative Desires in *Howards End*', in *Imperial Desire: Dissident Sexualities and Colonial Literatures*, ed. Richard Ruppel and Philip Holden (Minneapolis: University of Minnesota Press, 2003), pp. 195–222

  'Shepherds in the Parlor: Forster's Apostles, Pagans, and Native Sons', *Novel*, 32:1 (1998), 19–50

Das, G. K., *E. M. Forster's India* (London and Basingstoke: Macmillan, 1977)

Das, G. K., and John Beer, eds., *E. M. Forster: A Human Exploration: Centenary Essays* (London and Basingstoke: Macmillan, 1979)

Davies, Tony, and Nigel Wood, eds., *E. M. Forster* (Buckingham: Open University Press, 1994)

Delaney, Paul, '"Islands of Money": Rentier Culture in E. M. Forster's *Howards End*', (1988), reprinted in *E. M. Forster*, ed. Jeremy Tambling (1995), pp. 67–80

Dowling, David, *Bloomsbury Aesthetics and the Novels of Forster and Woolf* (Basingstoke and London: Macmillan, 1985)

Duckworth, Alistair M., ed., *Howards End: E. M. Forster's House of Fiction* (New York and Oxford: Twayne/Maxwell Macmillan International, 1992)

Ebbatson, Roger, *The Evolutionary Self: Hardy, Forster, Lawrence* (Brighton: Harvester, 1982)

Edwards, Mike, *E. M. Forster: The Novels* (Basingstoke and New York: Palgrave, 2002)

Elert, Kerstin, *Portraits of Women in Selected Novels by Virginia Woolf and E. M. Forster* (Ume: Acta Universitatis Umensis, 1979)

Finkelstein, Bonnie Blumenthal, *Forster's Women: Eternal Differences* (New York and London: Columbia University Press, 1975)

Fletcher, John, 'Forster's Self-erasure: *Maurice* and the Scene of Masculine Love', in *Sexual Sameness: Textual Differences in Lesbian and Gay Writing*, ed. Joseph Bristow (London and New York: Routledge, 1992), pp. 64–90

Fordonski, Krzysztof, *The Shaping of the Double Vision: The Symbolist Systems of the Italian Novels of E. M. Forster* (Frankfurt am Main and Oxford: Peter Lang, 2005)

Friedman, Alan Warren, 'E. M. Forster', in *Fictional Death and the Modernist Enterprise* (Cambridge: Cambridge University Press, 1995), pp. 186–206

Furbank, P. N., *E. M. Forster: A Life* (2 vols., London: Secker and Warburg, 1977–8)

Gardner, Philip, ed., *Commonplace Book* (London: Scolar Press, 1985)

ed., *E. M. Forster: The Critical Heritage* (London: Routledge and Kegan Paul, 1973; reprinted 1997)

Gibson, Mary Ellis, 'Illegitimate Order: Cosmopolitanism and Liberalism in Forster's *Howards End*', *English Literature in Transition*, 28 (1985), 106–23

Gillie, Christopher, *A Preface to Forster* (Harlow: Longman, 1983)

Goodyear, Sara Suleri, 'Forster's Imperial Erotic', (1992), reprinted in *E. M. Forster*, ed. Jeremy Tambling (1995), pp. 151–70

Goscilo, Margaret, 'Forster's Italian Comedies: Que(e)rying Heterosexuality Abroad', in (eds.), *Seeing Double: Revisioning Edwardian and Modernist Literature*, ed. Carola M. Kaplan and Anne B. Simpson (Basingstoke and London: Macmillan, 1996), pp. 193–214

Graham, Kenneth, *Indirections of the Novel: James, Conrad, and Forster*, (Cambridge: Cambridge University Press, 1988)

Greenslade, William, *Degeneration, Culture and the Novel, 1880–1940* (Cambridge: Cambridge University Press, 1994)

Haralson, Eric, '"Thinking about Homosex" in Forster and James', in *Queer Forster*, ed. Robert K. Martin and George Piggford (1997), pp. 59–73

Henley, Ann, '"But We Argued About Novel-Writing": Virginia Woolf, E. M. Forster and the Art of Fiction', *Ariel*, 20:3 (July 1989), 73–83

Herz, Judith Scherer, 'The Double Nature of Forster's Fiction: *A Room with a View* and *The Longest Journey*', *English Literature in Transition*, 21 (1978), 254–65

Passage to India: Nation and Narration (New York: Twayne, 1993)

The Short Narratives of E. M. Forster (Basingstoke and London: Macmillan, 1988)

Herz, Judith Scherer, and Robert K. Martin, eds., *E. M. Forster: Centenary Revaluations* (Basingstoke and London: Macmillan, 1982)

Hoffman, Michael J., and Ann Ter Haar, '"Whose Books Once Influenced Mine": The Relationship between E. M. Forster's *Howards End* and Virginia Woolf's *The Waves*', *Twentieth Century Literature*, 45:1 (Spring 1999), 46–64

Hoy II, Pat C., 'The Narrow, Rich Staircase in Forster's *Howards End*', *Twentieth Century Literature*, 31:2–3 (Summer–Fall 1985), 221–35

Hutchings, Peter J., 'A Disconnected View: Forster, Modernity and Film', *E. M. Forster*, ed. Jeremy Tambling (1995), pp. 213–28

Jameson, Fredric, 'Modernism and Imperialism', in *Nationalism, Colonialism, and Literature*, ed. Seamus Deane (Minneapolis: University of Minnesota Press, 1990), pp. 43–66

Jay, Betty, ed., *E. M. Forster: 'A Passage to India'* (Basingstoke and London: Palgrave, 2003)

Jeffreys, Peter, 'Cavafy, Forster, and the Eastern Question', *Journal of Modern Greek Studies*, 19 (2001), 61–87

   Eastern Questions: Hellenism and Orientalism in the Writings of E. M. Forster and C. P. Cavafy (Greensboro, NC: ELT Press, 2005)

Kaplan, Carola M., 'Absent Father: Passive Son: The Dilemma of Rickie Elliot in *The Longest Journey*', (1987) reprinted in *E. M. Forster*, ed. Jeremy Tambling (1995), pp. 51–66

Keating, Peter, *The Haunted Study: A Social History of the English Novel, 1875–1914* (London: Secker and Warburg, 1989)

Keeling, Bret L., '"No Trace of Presence": Tchaikovsky and the Sixth in Forster's *Maurice*', *Mosaic*, 26:1 (March 2003), 85–101

King, Francis, *E. M. Forster and his World* (London: Thames & Hudson, 1978)

Kirkpatrick, B. J., *A Bibliography of E. M. Forster*, 2nd edn (Oxford: Clarendon Press, 1985)

Lago, Mary, *E. M. Forster: A Literary Life* (Basingstoke and London: Macmillan, 1995)

   comp., *Calendar of the Letters of E. M. Forster* (London and New York: Mansell, 1985)

   ed., 'E. M. Forster Special Double Issue', *Twentieth Century Literature*, 31:2–3 (Summer–Fall 1985), 137–341

Lago, Mary, and Furbank, P. N., eds., *Selected Letters of E. M. Forster*, vol. I (London: Collins, 1983)

   Selected Letters of E. M. Forster, vol. II (London: Collins, 1985)

Lane, Christopher, 'Betrayal and its Consolations in *Maurice*, "Arthur Snatchfold", and "What Does it Matter? A Morality"' in *Queer Forster*, ed. Robert K. Martin and George Piggford, pp. 167–91

   The Burdens of Intimacy: Psychoanalysis and Victorian Masculinity (Chicago and London: University of Chicago Press, 1999)

Langland, Elizabeth, 'Gesturing Towards an Open Space: Gender, Form, and Language in E. M. Forster's *Howards End*', in *Out of Bounds: Male Writers and Gender(ed) Criticism*, ed. Laura Claridge and Elizabeth Langland (Amherst: University of Massachusetts Press, 1990), 252–67. Reprinted in *E. M. Forster*, ed. Jeremy Tambling (1995), pp. 81–99

Levenson, Michael, *Modernism and the Fate of Individuality: Character and Novelistic Form from Conrad to Woolf* (Cambridge: Cambridge University Press, 1991)

Levine, June Perry, 'Two Rooms with a View: An Inquiry into Film Adaptation', *Mosaic*, 22:3 (Summer 1989), 67–84

Lewis, Robin Jared, *E. M. Forster's Passages to India* (New York: Columbia University Press, 1979)

London, Bette, *The Appropriated Voice: Narrative Authority in Conrad, Forster and Woolf* (Ann Arbor: University of Michigan Press, 1990)

Markley, A. A., 'E. M. Forster's Reconfigured Gaze and the Creation of a Homoerotic Subjectivity', *Twentieth Century Literature*, 47:2 (Summer 2001), 268–92

Martin, John Sayre, *E. M. Forster: The Endless Journey* (Cambridge: Cambridge University Press, 1976)

Martin, Robert K., 'Edward Carpenter and the Double Structure of *Maurice*', *Journal of Homosexuality*, 8 (1983), 35–46; reprinted in *E. M. Forster*, ed. Jeremy Tambling (1995), pp. 100–14

'"It Must have been the Umbrella": Forster's Queer Begetting', in *Queer Forster*, ed. Robert K. Martin and George Piggford (1977), pp. 255–73

Martin, Robert K. and George Piggford, eds., *Queer Forster* (Chicago and London: University of Chicago Press, 1997)

Martland, Arthur, *E. M. Forster: Passion and Prose* (Swaffman: The Gay Men's Press, 1999)

Masterman, C. F. G., *The Condition of England* (London: Methuen, 1911)

Matz, Jesse, '"You Must Join My Dead": E. M. Forster and the Death of the Novel', *Modernism/Modernity*, 9:2 (April 2002), 303–17

May, Brian, *The Modernist as Pragmatist: E. M. Forster and the Fate of Liberalism* (Columbia and London: University of Missouri Press, 1997)

McConkey, James, *The Novels of E. M. Forster* (Ithaca, NY: Cornell University Press, 1957)

McDowell, Frederick P. W., *E. M. Forster*, rev. edn (Boston: Twayne Publishers, 1982)

Medalie, David, *E. M. Forster's Modernism* (Basingstoke and New York: Palgrave, 2002)

Meisel, Perry, *The Myth of the Modern: A Study in British Literature and Criticism after 1850* (New Haven: Yale University Press, 1987)

Miracky, James J., *Regenerating the Novel: Gender and Genre in Woolf, Forster, Sinclair and Lawrence* (London and New York: Routledge, 2003)

Page, Malcolm, *Howards End* (Basingstoke and London: Macmillan, 1993)

Page, Norman, *E. M. Forster* (Basingstoke and London: Macmillan, 1987)

Parry, Benita, 'The Politics of Representation in *A Passage to India*' (1985), reprinted *E. M. Forster*, ed. Jeremy Tambling (1995), pp. 133–50

Rahman, Tariq, 'The Double-Plot in E. M. Forster's *A Room with a View*', *Cahiers victoriens et édouardiens*, 33 (1992), 43–62

Rapport, Nigel, *The Prose and the Passion: Anthropology, Literature, and the Writing of E. M. Forster* (Manchester: Manchester University Press, 1994)

Raschke, Debrah, 'Breaking the Engagement with Philosophy: Re-envisioning Hetero/Homo Relations in *Maurice*', in Martin and Piggford, eds., *Queer Forster*, ed. Robert K. Martin and George Piggford (1997), pp. 151–66

Raskin, Jonah, *The Mythology of Imperialism: Rudyard Kipling, Joseph Conrad, E. M. Forster, D. H. Lawrence and Joyce Cary* (New York: Random House, 1971)

Reed, Christopher, 'The Mouse that Roared: Creating a Queer Forster', in Martin and Piggford, eds., *Queer Forster*, ed. Robert K. Martin and George Piggford (1997), pp. 75–88

Robbins, Ruth, *Pater to Forster, 1873–1924* (Basingstoke and New York: Palgrave Macmillan, 2003)

Roessel, David, 'Live Orientals and Dead Greeks: Forster's Response to the Chanak Crisis', *Twentieth Century Literature*, 36:1 (Spring 1990), 43–60

Rose, Jonathan, *The Edwardian Temperament, 1895–1919* (Athens, Ohio and London: Ohio University Press, 1986)

  The Intellectual Life of the British Working Classes (New Haven and London: Yale University Press, 2001)

Rosecrance, Barbara, *Forster's Narrative Vision* (Ithaca, NY, and London: Cornell University Press, 1982)

Rosenbaum, S. P., *Edwardian Bloomsbury: The Early Literary History of the Bloomsbury Group* (Basingstoke and London: Macmillan, 1994)

Royle, Nicholas, *E. M. Forster* (Plymouth: Northcote House in Association with the British Council, 1999)

Rusticcia, Frances L., '"A Cave of My Own": E. M. Forster and Sexual Politics', *Raritan*, 9:2 (1989), 110–28

Said, Edward W., *Orientalism: Western Conceptions of the Orient* (New York: Pantheon Books, 1978)

  Culture and Imperialism (New York: Knopf, 1993)

Schwarz, Daniel R., 'The Originality of E. M. Forster', *Modern Fiction Studies*, 19 (1983), 623–41

Scott, P. J. M, *E. M. Forster: Our Permanent Contemporary* (London: Vision Press, 1984)

Shahane, Vasant A., ed, *Approaches to E. M. Forster. A Centenary Volume* (New Delhi: Arnold Heinemann, 1981)

Shaheen, Mohammad, *E. M. Forster and the Politics of Imperialism* (Basingstoke and New York: Palgrave Macmillan, 2004)

Showalter, Elaine, '*A Passage to India* as "Marriage Fiction": Forster's Sexual Politics', *Women and Literature*, 5:2 (1977), 3–16

Shusterman, David, *Quest for Certitude in E. M. Forster's Fiction* (Bloomington: Indiana University Press, 1965)

Sillars, Stuart, '*Howards End* and the Dislocation of Narrative', in *Structure and Dissolution in English Writing, 1910–1920* (Basingstoke and London: Macmillan, 1999), pp. 31–61

Silver, Brenda R., 'Periphrasis, Power, and Rape in *A Passage to India*', *Novel*, 22 (Fall 1988); reprinted in *E. M. Forster*, ed. Jeremy Tambling (1995), pp. 171–94

Singh, Frances B., '*A Passage to India*, the National Movement, and Independence', *Twentieth Century Literature*, 31:2–3 (Summer–Fall, 1983), 265–78

Stallybrass, Oliver (ed.), *Aspects of E. M. Forster: Essays and Recollections Written for His Ninetieth Birthday 18th January 1969* (London: Edward Arnold, 1969)

Stape, J. H., 'Comparing Mythologies: Forster's *Maurice* and Pater's *Marius*', *English Literature in Transition, 1880–1920*, 33:2 (1990), 141–53

  An E. M. Forster Chronology (Basingstoke and London: Macmillan, 1993)

  E. M. Forster: Critical Assessments (4 vols., Mountfield: Helm Information, 1998)

  'Leonard's "Fatal Forgotten Umbrella": Sex and the Manuscript Revisions to *Howards End*', *Journal of Modern Literature*, 9:1 (1981–2), 123–32.

Stape, J. H., ed., *E. M. Forster: Interviews and Recollections* (Basingstoke and London: Macmillan, 1993)

Stevenson, Randall, *Modernist Fiction*, rev. edn (London: Prentice Hall, 1997)

Stoll, Rae H., '"Aphrodite wth a Janus Face": Language, Desire, and History in *The Longest Journey*' (1986–7), reprinted in *E. M. Forster*, ed. Jeremy Tambling (1995), pp. 30–50

Stone, Wilfred H., *The Cave and the Mountain: A Study of E. M. Forster* (Stanford: Stanford University Press, 1966)

  'Forster, the Environmentalist', in *Seeing Double: Revisioning Edwardian and Modernist Literature*, ed. Carola M. Kaplan and Anne B. Simpson (Basingstoke and London: Macmillan, 1996), pp. 171–92

Suleri, Sara, *The Rhetoric of English India* (Chicago: University of Chicago Press 1992)

Summers, Claude J., *E. M. Forster* (New York: Ungar, 1983)

  E. M. Forster: A Guide to Research (New York and London: Garland, 1991)

Tambling, Jeremy, ed., *E. M. Forster* (New Casebooks series) (Basingstoke and New York: Palgrave, 1995)

Trilling, Lionel, *E. M. Forster* (New York: New Directions, 1943; London: Hogarth Press, 1944)

Trotter, David, *The English Novel in History, 1885–1920* (London and New York: Routledge, 1993)

Wagner, Philip, 'Phaethon, Persephone, and *A Room with a View*', *Comparative Literature Studies*, 27 (1990), 275–84

Weatherhead, Andrea K., '*Howards End*: Beethoven's *Fifth*', *Twentieth Century Literature*, 31:2–3 (Summer–Fall 1985), 247–64

Widdowson, Peter, *E. M. Forster's 'Howards End': Fiction as History* (London: Chatto and Windus for Sussex University Press, 1977)

Woolf, Virginia, 'The Novels of E. M. Forster' (1927), reprinted in *The Essays of Virginia Woolf*, ed. Andrew McNeillie, vol. IV (London: Hogarth Press, 1994), pp. 491–502

INDEX

Cambridge Companions to...

AUTHORS

Shakespeare's History Plays edited by Michael Hattaway

Shakespearean Tragedy edited by Claire McEachern

Shakespeare's Poetry edited by Patrick Cheney

George Bernard Shaw edited by Christopher Innes

Shelley edited by Timothy Morton

Mary Shelley edited by Esther Schor

Sam Shepard edited by Matthew C. Roudané

Spenser edited by Andrew Hadfield

Wallace Stevens edited by John N. Serio

Tom Stoppard edited by Katherine E. Kelly

Harriet Beecher Stowe edited by Cindy Weinstein

Jonathan Swift edited by Christopher Fox

Henry David Thoreau edited by Joel Myerson

Tolstoy edited by Donna Tussing Orwin

Mark Twain edited by Forrest G. Robinson

Virgil edited by Charles Martindale

Edith Wharton edited by Millicent Bell

Walt Whitman edited by Ezra Greenspan

Oscar Wilde edited by Peter Raby

Tennessee Williams edited by Matthew C. Roudané

Mary Wollstonecraft edited by Claudia L. Johnson

Virginia Woolf edited by Sue Roe and Susan Sellers

Wordsworth edited by Stephen Gill

W. B. Yeats edited by Marjorie Howes and John Kelly

TOPICS

The Actress edited by Maggie B. Gale and John Stokes

The African American Novel edited by Maryemma Graham

The African American Slave Narrative edited by Audrey A. Fisch

American Modernism edited by Walter Kalaidjian

American Realism and Naturalism edited by Donald Pizer

American Women Playwrights edited by Brenda Murphy

Australian Literature edited by Elizabeth Webby

British Romanticism edited by Stuart Curran

Canadian Literature edited by Eva-Marie Kröller

The Classic Russian Novel edited by Malcolm V. Jones and Robin Feuer Miller

Contemporary Irish Poetry edited by Matthew Campbell

Crime Fiction edited by Martin Priestman

The Eighteenth-Century Novel edited by John Richetti

Eighteenth-Century Poetry edited by John Sitter

English Literature, 1500–1600 edited by Arthur F. Kinney

English Literature, 1650–1740 edited by Steven N. Zwicker

English Literature, 1740–1830 edited by Thomas Keymer and Jon Mee

English Poetry, Donne to Marvell edited by Thomas N. Corns

English Renaissance Drama edited by A. R. Braunmuller and Michael Hattaway (second edition)

English Restoration Theatre edited by Deborah C. Payne Fisk

Feminist Literary Theory edited by Ellen Rooney

The French Novel: from 1800 to the Present edited by Timothy Unwin

Gothic Fiction edited by Jerrold E. Hogle

Greek and Roman Theatre edited by Marianne McDonald and J. Michael Walton

Greek Tragedy edited by P. E. Easterling

The Irish Novel edited by John Wilson Foster

The Italian Novel edited by Peter Bondanella and Andrea Ciccarelli

Jewish American Literature edited by Hana Wirth-Nesher and Michael P. Kramer

The Latin American Novel edited by Efraín Kristal

Literature of the First World War edited by Vincent Sherry

Medieval English Theatre edited by Richard Beadle

Medieval Romance edited by Roberta L. Krueger

Medieval Women's Writing edited by Carolyn Dinshaw and David Wallace

Modern American Culture edited by Christopher Bigsby